D. W. Hamlyn

A HISTORY OF
WESTERN PHILOSOPHY

VIKING

VIKING

Penguin Books Ltd, Harmondsworth, Middlesex, England
Viking Penguin Inc., 40 West 23rd Street, New York, New York 10010, U.S.A.
Penguin Books Australia Ltd, Ringwood, Victoria, Australia
Penguin Books Canada Limited, 2801 John Street, Markham, Ontario, Canada L3R 1B4
Penguin Books (N.Z.) Ltd, 182–190 Wairau Road, Auckland 10, New Zealand

First published 1987

Filmset in Linotron 202 Times
Typeset, printed and bound in Great Britain by
Hazell Watson & Viney Limited,
Member of the BPCC Group,
Aylesbury, Bucks

British Library Cataloguing in Publication Data
Hamlyn, D. W.
  A history of Western philosophy. —
  (Viking philosophy)
  1. Philosophy — History
  I. Title
  190'.9   B72

  ISBN 0-670-80243-3

Library of Congress Catalog Card No.: 86–51116.

Contents

Preface

I am grateful to Professor Ted Honderich for suggesting that I write this book. My undertaking it required some pressure on his part, but its execution has proved interesting and rewarding to me, and I hope that the same will be true of others.

There are many to whom I owe a debt with respect to particular parts of my discussion. I owe a special debt, however, to my wife, Eileen, who read the whole of the draft of the book, and made many suggestions with regard to it. I asked her to read it as an educated member of the public would; but she is not totally ignorant of philosophy either, and her comments have been invaluable. I must finally acknowledge, with many thanks, the contribution to the writing of the book made by Maureen Cartwright, who not only typed the book but also made countless suggestions about style. Not only would the book not have been completed in a reasonable time without her assistance; it would have been much the poorer also. I am extremely grateful.

[1]
Introduction

A history of philosophy should not be a history of ideas alone. Nor should it be simply a branch of history. History of philosophy should also be philosophy. From the standpoint of the history of ideas, it is important to try to think oneself into the position from which those ideas emerge, and it is not enough merely to chart their influences on others. To do that exclusively may, however, be inimical to an understanding of the contribution of those ideas to philosophy as a whole. A balance is therefore required. If one is to think oneself into the mind of a past philosopher one needs, for this ultimately impossible task, knowledge not only of his biography, but of his setting, both social and intellectual. It is not evident that one needs all this in order to understand his thought as a contribution to philosophy.

Some may say that it is not insignificant that I use the word 'his' in what I have just said. For historical and social reasons philosophy has been an almost exclusively male-dominated discipline. I shall mention only one female philosopher in the following and she is not entirely typical; I could perhaps have mentioned one or two more in modern times, but that would not really have affected the fact that philosophy has been a male preserve. This is a fact which one would have to take account of if one were interested in the historical background of philosophy. It forms part of the social setting, and a history of thought and culture would have to take note of it. But, although feminists may not like my saying so, it is a point of no importance for the *history of philosophy*.

From time to time certain historians of philosophy protest at this kind of judgement, maintaining that we risk serious misunderstandings of the thought of the past unless we take a full account of the historical circumstances in which it was produced, and of the ideas behind its expression. For such commentators the historian of philosophy must be like the anthropologist and soak himself in the thought of the period with which he is concerned. The trouble with this is that if the attempt to get oneself into the mind of a past philosopher were really achieved, one would lose the historical perspective which makes the assessment of that thought possible. On the other hand, if one were to go to the other extreme and concentrate only on what a past philosopher may say to *us*, one might have to write off much, although not all, of past philosophy as of no consequence. One has to keep a balance, and that runs the risk of criticism from both extremes.

In any case, the history of philosophy cannot be concerned merely with ideas. Philosophy centres on problems, even if only the problems of understanding something or other. The solution to problems requires justification, and justification requires argument. A history of philos-ophy – even one concerned, as this one is, with philosophy over a large scale – would be nothing if it conveyed no flavour of the arguments which philosophers have used, and provided no assessment of them. There are histories of philosophy which are splendid in providing facts – facts about the philosophers concerned and about what they said – but which give little sense of whether the philosophers concerned are philosophically important and why. There are equally histories of philosophy which are splendid for fitting philosophers into the history and culture of their period, but which equally give no sense of what is philosophically import-ant and why.

I shall give the dates of the philosophers I consider, and in most cases a few biographical details, but only to the extent that this seems relevant for an understanding of the philosophy. I shall say next to nothing about their historical background, except where it seems essential for that same understanding. I shall equally say next to nothing about the social back-ground. I shall concentrate, wherever possible, on the argument, and that means a concentration on what philosophers have written. Philo-sophical style varies, however, and philosophers have not always accepted the same models for argument. Sometimes – and this *is* a point of historical importance – they have looked for their models to disciplines which have been particularly successful in their time; for example, some philosophical Rationalists of the eighteenth century looked to geometry. Such moves have nearly always been mistaken. In one way or another, philosophical argument remains dialectical as Plato or Socrates saw it; it is a matter of discussion, argument and counter-argument. Where, however, the counter-argument depends, as it did not in Socrates' time, on publications, it is of some importance for the progress of the subject that justification of a philosophical position should involve explanation of how one comes to it. That means that the best philosophical argument is discursive.

When a past philosopher has provided such discursive argument I shall do my best to go through it. That occupies more space than a mere summary of thought and conclusions. If, therefore, I give more space to some philosophers than to others, that is not always because the for-mer have written more; it is sometimes because they have argued more discursively. In that sense, given what I have said about the value of discursive argument, the space that I have given to a philosopher is some indication, though not an overriding one, of that philosopher's importance. For if the argument is clear, whatever the background of ideas, it is there for us today to assess and to decide how far we can accept it, even if we require some changes in the terms of reference.

For somewhat the same reasons, or at any rate for connected ones, I shall be selective in my choice of philosophers to discuss. It should be emphasized that there have been many more philosophers than those mentioned in this book, and when one comes to contemporaries one may lack a proper historical sense and be somewhat embarrassed in one's choice. Historical perspectives change, and philosophers who in the past seemed important no longer seem so today. No doubt the same will be the fate of many who seem important at the present time. It would be a mistake, however, to represent philosophical importance as something quite relative. The scope of philosophy is fairly broad, although the popular view of philosophy as concerned with the philosophy of life, with recommendations as to how we should live, is one based upon a rather narrow view of the subject, one that has much to do with romanticism. Yet, although the scope of philosophy is broad, it is still possible to see a continuity of interests and problems from the Greeks, who began it all, to the present day. That continuity may not always be clear, and may be overridden by other things, but I believe that it is there.

It may be there too in eastern philosophy, with which this book has no concern. There are, I believe, many misconceptions about eastern philosophy, not all of which is mystical and religious in its orientation. Experts in oriental philosophy sometimes point out parallels between it and western philosophy, and it would be surprising if such parallels did not exist. There has been little contact, however, between the two traditions, and for that reason there is no real continuity between them, except that which the general nature of philosophy and its problems inevitably produces. That is in itself a good reason for considering the history of western philosophy by itself. For in that there is a true continuity, although one that is sometimes tortuous in its course.

It is commonly said that philosophy makes no progress, and it may be suggested that what I have said about continuity merely confirms that. It is a mistake even to raise that question. For it presumes that philosophers are like scientists; they can settle one issue and then move on to the next. If a history of philosophy ought to make anything clear it is that it is not like that. That is not to say that some philosophical perspectives are not better than others. It is possible to argue, for example, that, whatever the merits of his philosophy in other ways,

Descartes brought about a revolution in thinking, by concentrating on the point of view of the individual, which was a fundamental mistake; it is one which has not entirely been put right even now, despite Wittgenstein. If it were to be put right, philosophers would have thereby eliminated a perspective which has led to problems being seen in a certain way, and a way that may be an obstacle to their solution. They would not thereby have solved the problems themselves. That, however, is not to say that there are no such solutions and that none has been arrived at. A history of philosophy should show otherwise.

Moreover, the solution to a philosophical problem may consist in a certain way of putting things, one that abolishes misunderstandings. One may thereby be given a map for finding one's way around intellectually, as Wittgenstein once suggested. As any cartographer knows, one does not always need the same map for the same purposes. So if a particular map ceases to be of use, that is no reason for speaking of a lack of progress or the reverse. Are we in any better position than Plato was to answer some of the questions that he raised? The answer is undoubtedly 'Yes', although he himself might not have seen our answers as what he wanted. The same may be true of the next generation relative to us.

What, then, is the point of a history of philosophy? Apart from the strictly historical sense that it ought to provide for philosophers, it ought to provide a due sense of the complexity and many-sidedness of philosophical issues. That may be to the benefit of philosophy, since no individual can work out for himself all the aspects of an issue to which he ought to pay attention. In that way a history of philosophy, if it concentrates on the argument, ought to be a source-book of philosophical considerations. That means that it ought to be, not just a source-book of philosophical fallacies, a record of human error, but a source of wider understanding also.

[2]
The Presocratics

The Milesians

Western philosophy, it is customary to say, began with the Greeks. So it did, but it did not begin in Greece. The first philosophers whose names have come down to us lived, towards the end of the seventh century B.C., in Miletus, a sea-port on the western coast of Asia Minor. It was, it is true, a Greek colony, but situated where it was it was bound to be subject to influences from people of other nationalities who lived in the hinterland – in Lydia, Persia, and Babylon itself. Not that that helps us to see why philosophy began when and where it did, since there is no evidence of philosophy as we have come to know it in those cultures. India was too far away and communications with it too precarious for us to find it plausible to see influences from that source. Egypt, the other great power, apart from Persia, represented a technological civilization, and there is no evidence of anything philosophical there. In the ancient world Egypt was seen as the source of mathematics, as Babylon was of astronomy (the apparent movements of the heavenly bodies being recorded there on clay tablets). The employment of mathematics by the Egyptians was seen as so important that the Greeks tended to think that any Greek showing evidence of mathematical ability and innovation must have gone there. So it is recorded that Thales, the first of the so-called Milesian philosophers, went to Egypt. On the whole it is most unlikely that he did. But these influences combined with the religious and mythological ideas that were endemic to the Greeks somehow produced philosophy.

But what was it that they produced? Aristotle said that philosophy begins with wonder, and there is certainly evidence of that in the thinking of the earliest Greek philosophers. Thales, who lived round about 600 B.C., is reported as saying that all things are full of gods, and there are many references to certain things as divine in subsequent philosophers, without that implying a specific religious attitude. Nature is simply thought of as something godlike. At the same time, Aristotle's claim that Thales said that the 'first principle' of all things is water, and the subsequent thesis put forward by Anaximenes, Thales' next successor but one, that different stuffs are formed from air by the reciprocal processes of condensation and rarefaction look like early science – an early attempt to identify the basic nature of physical reality, and to explain how the observable facts of physical things are derivable from it. Yet the longest of the three fragments that we have of Anaximenes' writings (if writings they were) says that air encloses the whole world in the way that our soul 'being air' holds us together and controls us. Whatever else it was, the soul was for the Greeks the principle of life. Air or breath are the clearest indications of life; hence the connection between the soul and air. But the implication is that the world at large is similarly alive and has a soul. If that is right, Anaximenes' selection of air as the basic stuff is not dictated by purely physical considerations. The thought is a mixture of different elements.

I have spoken in the above of fragments. That is all that we have of the writings of the so-called presocratic philosophers, the philosophers who preceded Socrates. Those fragments have been preserved for us by later Greek writers, not all of whom had a definite interest in the history of thought. It was Aristotle who first showed a systematic concern for the history of his subject, and this concern was taken further by Theophrastus, his main disciple. Later Greek commentaries on Aristotle, by, for example, Simplicius in the sixth century A.D., sometimes quote passages from earlier philosophers; but the extent of a quotation is often uncertain (the situation not being improved by the lack of quotation marks in Greek). There are variant readings, and testimonia of varying reliability, sometimes derived from philosophers of other persuasions who referred to earlier philosophers, sometimes with approval, sometimes in criticism, but often enough for their own purposes. All this has made the study of early philosophy contingent on the work of scholars, particularly that of the great German scholar Herman Diels, who at the turn of this century produced the first edition of *Die Fragmente der Vorsokratiker*, on which all subsequent collections of fragments of, and remarks about, the early Greek philosophers have been based. On the other hand it means that more or less any statement about those philosophers must be subject to the qualification 'if our sources are correct'. That qualification must always be remembered in reading what I shall go on to say.

Given these facts about the thought of Thales and Anaximenes (and it has to be confessed that there are other things reported of them, including speculations about the nature of the heavenly bodies, the earth and certain natural phenomena) it might be wondered what makes them specifically philosophical. With Anaximander, the immediate successor of Thales in Miletus, there is perhaps more to go on. What struck Aristotle and others about Anaximander is that he refused to identify the underlying stuff with any of the four traditional elements – earth, fire, air and water – preferring to invoke what he called the *apeiron* (indefinite or boundless) in this respect. This was presumably on the grounds that it was impossible to generate these elements from any one of their members. The authors who report Anaximander's views, however, speak of the heavens and worlds coming to be from the *apeiron*, saying that it is the source of coming-to-be for existing things and that they are destroyed back into it. The words suggest less a stuff that could be transmuted into other stuffs, as it seems to be with Anaximenes' air, than a reservoir of being of an indeterminate kind from which the state of things at any one time comes into existence and then passes back into it. Moreover, Simplicius, our main source in this respect, goes on to quote what is generally taken to be the one surviving fragment from Anaximander – 'according to necessity; for they pay penalty and retribution to each other for their injustice according to the assessment of time'.

What this means one can perhaps only guess. We may suppose, however, that Anaximander was impressed by the inevitability of the changes that go on in the world – hot/cold, summer/winter, youth/age – changes that can be represented, as they were by the Greeks generally, as shifts from one state to its opposite. Anaximander wants to make sense of this inevitability and suggests that we construe it on the model of human justice. In summer, for example, the world is taken over by the hot; but this is a kind of usurpation for which the penalty must be paid. But the penalty – the taking over by the cold – involves another act of injustice, a further penalty, and so on. Underlying this is something like the modern notion of natural law, but construed in moral/political terms. If there is in this point of view wonder at the state of things, there is puzzlement too. If people express that puzzlement, asking why it should always be like that, Anaximander says 'Look at it like this . . .'. There seems something genuinely philosophical in this conception, even if it is difficult to say clearly why it is philosophical, and even if from other, more scientific points of view, Anaximander's account may seem anthropomorphic and even crude. There are other aspects of his thought – about cosmology, about the world and about animals – which reveal that he was an abstract and ingenious thinker. Abstraction and ingenuity do not add up to being philosophical, but the questions that Anaximander seems to have been concerned with, implicitly if not explicitly, are of a character which is different from those of others of his time, and it is not unreasonable to suggest that here philosophy is born.

The Pythagoreans

Philosophy may have continued at Miletus, but we know nothing of it until, at the end of the presocratic period, Miletus produced Leucippus, the founder of Atomism. In the interval the centre of interest moved elsewhere. The next two main figures to appear are Pythagoras and Heraclitus. The latter lived at Ephesus – again on the coast of Asia Minor; the former came from Samos, an island in the Aegean Sea off Asia Minor, but migrated to Croton in southern Italy, there setting up a cult and a school. Heraclitus mentions Pythagoras – somewhat abusively, as was his wont with other major thinkers. In fact we know little about Pythagoras, and not much about his school, because it was bound by rules of secrecy. It was in part a religious cult, of which Pythagoras was the leader and prophet, bound by rules, some of which have much in common with taboos in other societies. There was a general regard for the sanctity of life and an acceptance of the doctrine of the transmigration of the soul. But it was also a school concerned with doctrines and inquiries of genuine intellectual interest. The main emphasis was on mathematics – arithmetic construed as an investigation into the patterns of numbers, geometry construed as an investigation into the metrical patterning of shapes, and harmony construed as an investigation into the patterning of musical intervals. Numbers were thought of as derived from units, which could themselves be identified with dots or pebbles used in counting; so that there is an easy transition from arithmetic into geometry, which could itself be construed as concerned with the ratios between lengths. Harmony likewise – a concern with the properties of musical intervals, not harmony in the modern sense – could be related to the other two disciplines because the relations between various musical intervals could be discovered by comparison of the lengths of strings which, when plucked, produced the different tones.

It appears that some Pythagoreans at least let this go to their heads, seeing similarities between mathematical properties and all sorts of other and quite different properties of things – even abstract things such as justice, which was likened to four, as a square number, justice being, so to speak, all square. There resulted a sort of number mysticism. Aristotle says that they thought that the principles of numbers were the properties of all things, implying that the Pythagoreans saw the world as governed by the same structural consideratons as govern mathematics. At some stage, however, the Pythagoreans discovered the existence of incommensurables – numbers such as root two, which cannot be expressed in terms of a rational fraction. We know that at some time between this period and that of Aristotle a proof of the incommensurability of root two was produced. (Interestingly enough, perhaps, in the light of the use of such arguments by Zeno the Eleatic, a little later, the proof is of a *reductio ad absurdum* form.) A proof is not of course a method of discovery, and we can only guess at what brought them to recognize the existence of incommensurables and thus of irrational numbers. (It is likely to involve some technique of approximation.) But the discovery must have been a shattering one; for if things are like numbers and if there are numbers which are not rational, because not expressible in terms of a rational fraction, the inference to draw is that the world is not a totally rational place. There is even a story of one, Hippasus of Tarentum, being drowned at sea for revealing the Pythagorean secrets; another story attributes the discovery of incommensurability to the same person. Perhaps the Pythagoreans thought that the discovery should be hushed up, although it has to be said that the whole of this account of the discovery of incommensurables has been disputed.

However that may be, Aristotle reports that some Pythagoreans set out their fundamental ideas in parallel columns of opposites, beginning with 'limited/unlimited' and moving downwards through 'odd/even', 'one/many', 'right/left', 'male/female', 'resting/moving', 'straight/crooked', 'light/dark', 'good/bad' to 'square/oblong'. The implications are that we have a good, rational set of concepts, and a bad, irrational one, that somehow the concepts at the top of the columns explain what is lower, and that if the world is to be explained in terms of these ideas we need both of each pair of opposites. Although the Pythagoreans are clearly interested in the structural properties of the world, and less or not at all in the dynamic properties that reveal themselves in change, it is also clear that they came to the realization that simple, rational structures were not enough. The world is not all good, all rational, all perfect.

Heraclitus

The notion of opposites plays a significant part in Heraclitus' thought too, but in a quite different way. Heraclitus was an aristocrat who despised his fellow citizens in Ephesus and his fellow men generally. He lived towards the end of the sixth century B.C. and perhaps into the fifth century. He had one disciple that we know of, Cratylus, who seems to have adopted a more extreme version of his master's views. There survives a fairly large number (something over 100) of fragments in the form of epigrams, which may or may not have been part of a book. In the ancient world he was known as the 'riddler' and 'the obscure', and rival interpretations of Heraclitus' views have been rife. There has been Heraclitus the sceptic, the Hegelian, the Nietzschean, the Marxist and so on. The key notion in what he has to say, however, is that of the *logos*, which is a principle according to which things are organized and which manifests itself in various forms – as war, strife, fire, God and so on.

Heraclitus prides himself on having discovered this, which he thinks is perceptible by means of the senses provided that men have souls that understand their language. It is a fair guess that the point of the epigrams is to direct your gaze in such a way that you see what Heraclitus, but no one else, has seen.

One of the fragments (Fr.50) says 'Listening not to me but to the *logos* it is wise to agree that all things are one'. The unity of things seems therefore to be the central thought, but in what sense? That is an arguable matter, but it seems that Heraclitus did not mean, as Parmenides was to mean, that there is no real plurality, no difference between things. Rather he thought that most men were content to regard what happens in the world as one damned thing after another, but that he, as Anaximander did, knew better. While, however, it is a corollary of Anaximander's views that the ideal state of things would be one of balance and rest, Heraclitus thought that this would mean the end of the world; the nature of things depends upon a strife between the opposites. Balance depends upon conflict, unity upon plurality, sameness on difference, and *vice versa*. Men see the obvious things, the differences, the change, the plurality; he, Heraclitus, sees that there is an underlying unity, constancy and so on, and sees that the one set of things and the others are mutually dependent.

So, if there is a train of thought, it goes as follows: All things are one. Why? Because differences are summed up in opposites; but opposites are always to be found in one thing. So wherever there is difference, there are opposites, and wherever there are opposites there is something that unifies them. But unity itself is opposed to plurality; so they too must be unified in something. So there must be a mutual dependence between them. And the same applies to other opposites, rest and motion, balance and strife. Hence we must see unity in diversity, rest in motion, balance in strife, and *vice versa*. But the key notion in all this is what has been called the unity of opposites – the fact that opposites are always to be found in one thing. And a large number of fragments have this as their message, many but not all of them fastening on to the idea that opposites are often relative, so that the same thing can manifest both opposites (they are in the logical sense contraries).[1] Thus sea-water is good for fishes but bad for men, so that the same thing can be both good and bad. A road on a hill is both up and down, depending on the point of view from which you regard it. Moreover the same thing is evident, in a sense, in the phenomena of ordinary change. It is the same thing that is young and old, living and dead. 'Living' and 'dead' are not, as 'good' and 'bad', 'up' and 'down' are, relative terms. But change

[1] Whether Heraclitus had an explicit realization of this is another matter.

makes it possible for us to attribute to the same thing opposed terms. It may be that Heraclitus saw no difference between this phenomenon and that in which, as we should see it, there is a change in the point of view, as is the case with the road up and down the hill. He may have thought of all of them as forms of change; but it is to be noted that in each case the change presupposes an identity in the thing that undergoes it.

Plato and Aristotle emphasized the place that change had in Heraclitus' thought, claiming that according to Heraclitus things are like a river in which there are always different waters flowing, and that you cannot for that reason step twice into the same river. (Cratylus seems to have gone further and said that you could not even do it once, since during the step the waters must change.) Hence they also attribute to Heraclitus the view that everything is in flux. So it is, of course; but if the doctrine of the unity of opposites has validity, flux equally implies its opposite. So the model on which to see things is something in which change and constancy are coincident. The notion of a river in a sense fulfils those criteria, since a river's identity as a river depends upon change in its waters; without that it would be not a river, but a lake. The other notion that Heraclitus invokes in this respect is that of fire, which remains the same fire, while subject to constant changes in its flickering and burning. So he likens the world to a fire in a way that has caused some to see him as a successor to the Milesians, putting fire in place of water or air. But he is not that exactly; fire is what for him best represents the nature of things. The same principles – the *logos* – that govern the world at large in this way also govern the individual soul, and in one fragment Heraclitus perhaps implies that he saw the message that he wanted to convey in himself.

Many of the other fragments have a certain cryptic fascination, and it is perhaps impossible to provide a sytematic account of them all. In his own way Heraclitus is trying to convey a message which he thinks we can all see if we use our senses rightly. It is no wonder that different people have seen different messages there; it is the nature of the prophet to be taken in different ways. There is nevertheless discernible in Heraclitus' remarks a train of thought, and one plausible account of that is the one that I have outlined. There is, however, strictly speaking, no *argument* for whatever conclusions Heraclitus wants to come to. Heraclitus is again saying 'See it like this . . .'. And the impatience with which he regards the fact that most people refuse to see it in this way at all, or cannot be bothered to ask how it should be seen at all, is notable.

Parmenides and the Eleatics

With Parmenides the situation is different. Although he wrote in Homeric-style poetry, there is discoverable in it a strict, deductive argument, albeit for a conclusion which many would find absurd. Thus, if strict argument provides the life-blood of philosophy, with Parmenides philosophy truly comes to life. He lived in Elea in Italy, probably in the first half of the fifth century B.C. Elea is not far from Croton, and it is possible that he was influenced by the Pythagoreans. Some have seen evidence for that in the poem, but there are no positive grounds for that view. It looks as if, both in the style of his argument and in the considerations with which he was concerned, Parmenides introduced something radically new, and there is little in the background which does anything to explain how he came to do so.

The poem, a good deal of which has been preserved by Simplicius, has three parts: an introduction, which tells an allegorical story of a revelation undergone by Parmenides in the form of a message from the goddess Dikē (Justice or Right); a section called the 'Way of Truth', which argues that the right account of 'what is' is utterly different from what men generally suppose; and a section entitled the 'Way of Opinion' or 'Way of Seeming', in which Parmenides sets out what he thinks the best account of the world which accords with the 'beliefs of mortals' so that 'no thought of mortal men shall ever outstrip thee'. The relation between these parts of the poem has been the subject of much dispute, and in any case much less of the last part survives than of the other two parts. The account that that last part puts forward is based again on opposites, such as light/dark, dense/rare, same/different. Exactly what is being said is not clear, but it must be what Parmenides thinks is the best account, in cosmological form, of the world as the senses represent it to us. It is not, however, as the second part of the poem demonstrates, good enough; but there is no better account, so that the only conclusion to draw is that what the senses tell us should be rejected in favour of reason.

The second part of the poem, the 'Way of Truth', gives us what Parmenides thinks reason tells us. It is in fact a piece of deductive metaphysics, starting from premises that are supposed to be necessarily true and leading deductively to conclusions which must equally therefore be accepted as necessarily true. Parmenides represents an opposition between 'two ways of inquiry' of which only one is acceptable. They are expressible in the form of 'It is' and 'It is not'. There has been much argument both about the reference of 'it' and about the sense to be attached to 'is'. The most plausible answer to the question of the reference of 'it' (which is not explicit in Greek, since the verb 'is' need not have, and does not have in this context, an expressed subject) is anything you like. Whatever you select to discuss, it will be shown to come to the same in the end. As far as concerns the meaning of 'is' the most convenient account is that it means 'exists', though Parmenides himself would no doubt not have recognized any distinctions between senses of 'is'. The crucial initial argument is contained in fragments 2, 3 and 6. That it is an argument is evident from Parmenides' frequent use of the word 'for', by which he indicates that he is giving reasons for what he is saying. There are perhaps alternative ways of reconstructing the argument, but one plausible way is as follows:

(1) Either X exists or X does not exist (where 'X' can refer to anything you like) (= the two ways of inquiry in fragment 2)
(2) If X can be thought, X can exist (= fragment 3 on one plausible interpretation; also fragment 6, line 2)
(3) Nothing cannot exist (= fragment 6, line 2)
(4) Hence, if X can be thought it is not nothing
(5) Hence, if X can be thought it must be something
(6) Hence, if X can be thought, X must exist (= fragment 6, line 1).

Steps 4 and 5 in this argument have to be supplied; the others are to be found in the text. Step 1 is a version of the Law of Excluded Middle and thus has a claim to be necessarily true. So does step 2 on the more arguable basis that thinkability is a sufficient condition for logical possibility. Step 3 is unacceptable on any ordinary interpretation of what it says. To make it acceptable one would have to construe 'Nothing' as a proper name and as the name of something that cannot exist. It may be possible to suggest reasons why Parmenides thought the proposition more plausible than it is, but it is impossible to enter into such complexities here. The falsity of 3 leaves the whole argument deductively valid but such that it has a false conclusion – which is just as well, as will appear.

Fragment 8, a passage of some length, starts from the position reached in the initial argument: 'One way only is left to be spoken of, that it is.' To think or say 'It is not' is impossible, for it in effect contradicts itself. From this Parmenides draws the conclusion that 'what is' must be uncreated and imperishable – 'So coming into being is extinguished and perishing unimaginable.' That is the point that seems to have captured the imaginations of his predecessors, who tried to show that, despite what he said, coming into being and destruction are somehow possible. It is not the only conclusion which Parmenides draws, however; and in fact, if the position reached in the initial argument is accepted, there is no way of avoiding either that conclusion or the others which Parmenides comes to. For the argument, or one major strand in it (for Parmenides offers more than one reason for his conclusion), is deductively valid and the conclusion cannot be avoided once the premises are accepted. That is why I said that it was fortunate that the conclusion of the initial argument is false.

The major strand of the argument is to argue that, in effect, there is no time as we understand it. To distinguish past and future from the present involves the possibility of saying 'it is not' – for to say that it was or will be is to imply a contrast with 'it is'. So, if it is, 'it *was* not in the past, nor *shall* it be'. Hence the only thing that can be said is that it *is*; it is, he says, 'all at once, one, continuous'. There is only an eternal now, a *simul nunc* as other philosophers have put it, and thus no time proper. It follows from this that there can be no phenomenon which involves time, and past, present and future. The immediate conclusion drawn is the impossibility of coming into being and passing away. But later in fragment 8 he generalizes the conclusion, saying that 'all these are names (*sc.* mere words) that mortals laid down believing them to be true – coming into being and perishing, being and not being, change of place and variation of bright colour'. So with the elimination of time all possibility of being at one time and not at another, and all possibility of change of any kind, is eliminated also.

Following this, Parmenides seems to have turned to spatial considerations, arguing similarly that there cannot be spatial distinctions any more than there can be temporal distinctions. He expresses this point by means of an analogy that has given rise to much misinterpretation on the part of both his immediate successors and later commentators. For he says that 'what is' is 'bounded on every side, like the bulk of a well-rounded sphere, from the centre equally balanced in every direction'. Empedocles certainly seems to have taken him as saying that reality is a sphere, and many other commentators have spoken of Parmenides' belief in a spherical universe. In fact, however, he says only that it is *like* a sphere. The simile is meant to illustrate the completeness of 'what is', the impossibility of its being opposed to anything, and the impossibility of spatial differentiation. In fact the only thing that you can say about 'what is' is 'It is'. It is an austere and, one might think, barren conclusion, but it *does* follow from the premises of the initial argument, and what makes Parmenides a giant among the Presocratics is his willingness to follow through the deductive conclusions of his austere argument from its premises. It is, as I have said, fortunate that there is a false proposition among those premises.

The third part of the poem, the 'Way of Opinion', follows. But Parmenides makes clear that it is in his view all false – it is the 'deceitful ordering of [his] words'. It is however the best account of the world as mortals see it, and no better can be produced. So, if it will not do – and the 'Way of Truth' indicates, or would if it were completely valid, that it will not do – there is no better to be had. What makes Parmenides so remarkable is his willingness to rely on strictly deductive argument and to hold fast to its conclusion however implausible that is. Some might see in this a kind of paranoia, but it also marks the birth of true philosophy or of one aspect of it – the appeal to argument that is as rigid as it can be. Deductive metaphysics of this kind will appear again in this history. It is always a failure, not simply because of the implausibility of its conclusions, but because reason alone cannot provide us with sound premises from which to deduce the nature of reality. All the same, it is remarkable that the enterprise begins so early and with so little in the background to explain its incidence.

There is little indication, either, that any of Parmenides' successors, apart perhaps from some of his disciples, really understood what he was doing. The remaining Presocratics were obviously impressed by him but thought that their task was simply to get round his conclusions. Much the same is true of Plato and Aristotle. Both of these, especially Plato, speak almost in tones of reverence of Parmenides, but they show little sensitivity to his actual argument. The two known disciples of Parmenides are Melissus and Zeno. The former did not receive a good press in the ancient world and has not received much attention since; Zeno's paradoxes, on the other hand, especially those which argue for the impossibility of motion, are still hotly discussed.

Although Melissus of Samos is generally thought of as a disciple of Parmenides he seems to have been in one respect at least critical of him. He seems to have disliked Parmenides' argument against temporal and spatial distinctions, either because he thought that the very statement that there are no such distinctions implied their possibility, or because he thought that the assertion that 'what is' is complete and bounded might suggest the existence of something else to do the bounding. He wanted, above everything else, the thesis that 'what is' is one (something that Parmenides never explicitly says in the passages that we have, but is certainly implied by them and is certainly attributed to him by later thinkers). In consequence he said that 'what is' is unlimited or infinite both temporally and spatially, and he tried to rule out what might therefore seem to be a possibility – the division of 'what is' – by saying that it is not corporeal. Since extension does not necessarily imply corporeality, that is not a very encouraging move and tends to confirm the low opinion of Melissus that was held by some others, including Aristotle.

In one fragment (fragment 8), however, Melissus used an argument of the type that Zeno was renowned for – the *reductio*. In this case he used his opponents' beliefs, trying to show that they were inconsistent. They in effect criticized the Eleatics for flying in the face of common sense, but Melissus thought that he could show that they themselves were prepared to desert common sense at certain points, to go beyond what the senses immediately reveal, in order to defend common sense at other points. For example, they believed that things changed imperceptibly, or were composed of things that they were not obviously composed of, such as water, according to Thales. Melissus argued that they were not entitled to such beliefs if they thought that common sense and ordinary observation were to be defended at all costs. He concluded that if his opponents thought that there were many things they ought to hold only that they were all just the same as Parmenides' 'one' was. (And there was the implication, in all probability, that in that event there was nothing to be said for the thesis that there actually were many 'ones'.)

All Zeno's arguments have something of this nature, being aimed at demonstrating that Parmenides' opponents were not entitled on their own showing to beliefs in plurality, change and distinction – the things that Parmenides explicitly ruled out. The arguments that we have fall into three main groups, concerned with these three things, although the third is in the dress of arguments against the notion of place (presumably because being at different places is crucially something that distinguishes objects). It is impossible to go into detail here.[1] The arguments against the notion of place are infinite regress arguments and probably depend on the conception of place that seems to have been endemic among the Greeks and is expressed formally in Aristotle – that the place of a thing is the immediate but unchanging container of that thing. Thus a table may be in the air that surrounds it, that in a room, that in a house, and so on. Reference to each of these in turn gives the place of a thing, as long as they themselves do not move, that is change their place. But, Zeno argues, in that case there is no such thing as *the* place of a thing, since the possible reference to further and further containers can go on *ad infinitum*. If there is no place of a thing one cannot distinguish things by reference to their places – or so Zeno probably meant to say, since the conclusion is not explicitly drawn. There is much to discuss in the argument but I shall leave matters there.

The arguments against plurality or pluralism are complex, and one of them, which argues that if there are many things they must be both finite and infinite in number, is scarcely intelligible as it has been handed down to us. The main argument, given in fragment 1, seems to start from the

[1] Anyone who wishes to read a thorough discussion of the arguments should read the article on 'Zeno of Elea' by Gregory Vlastos in the *Encyclopaedia of Philosophy* (ed. P. Edwards, New York, London: Collier-Macmillan, 1967).

consideration that if you try to produce a plurality of things by division you must eventually come down to things that are one or units in some absolute sense. (It is not clear that that must be so, but it may be that some of Zeno's opponents thought that it must be.) Zeno then argues that in that case the units in question cannot have size (since anything having size must be capable in principle of being divided and cannot therefore be a unit in an absolute sense). If they do not have size they make no difference to things when added to or taken away from them; they are therefore as good as non-existent. On the other hand, if they have size they must be capable in principle of being divided *ad infinitum*. They must therefore be conceivable as an infinite collection of parts having size. So they must be infinitely big. Zeno sums this up by saying that if there are many things they must be so small as to have no size at all and so big as to be infinitely big.

The first part of that follows only if it is true that in division we have to get to units in an absolute sense; the second follows only if division *ad infinitum* can be thought of as completed in parts which have finite size, so that they can be summed up again *ad infinitum*, producing something of infinite size, despite first impressions. Neither of these arguments is valid, however, and the second involves serious misunderstandings of what is involved in saying that something is infinitely divisible. One cannot think of the division as completed, and certainly not so as to result in parts of finite size rather than infinite smallness. Still, the argument is sophisticated and is the first use of considerations concerning the notion of infinity.

The arguments for which Zeno is best known are those against the possibility of motion. We have preserved for us four such arguments, but we are told by Proclus, the late Neo-Platonic philosopher, that there were at least forty. That fact, if it is one, ought to induce scepticism about any attempt to fit the arguments into any neat system. I say that because it has become quite common to arrange the four arguments into two pairs. The first pair, the Dichotomy and the Achilles, is concerned with the possibility of motion on the assumption that things are divisible *ad infinitum*; the first of them postulates one moving body, and the second postulates two. The second pair of arguments, the Arrow and the Moving Rows, is concerned with the possibility of motion on the assumption that things are divisible only *ad finitum*, with the same arrangement between the members of the pair. Our sources, however, do not necessarily imply such an arrangement; the interpretation entails going beyond the text of Aristotle, the main source, in the case of the Arrow, and perhaps positively distorting it in the case of the Moving

Rows. The Dichotomy and the more famous Achilles and the Tortoise do, however, seem to have that kind of relationship.

The Dichotomy argues simply that in order to move from point *A* to point *B* one has first to move to a point *C* half-way between, then to a point *D* half-way between *C* and *B* (or possibly between *A* and *C*), then to a point *E* half-way between *D* and *B*, and so on *ad infinitum*. But one cannot complete the infinite sequence of moves which that entails (Zeno appears to have added 'in a finite time', but Aristotle admits that it is not necessary to add that – the question is whether an infinite sequence can be completed at all). The Achilles argues similarly, positing a race between Achilles and a tortoise, with the tortoise being given a start proportional to his slowness relative to Achilles. If, then, Achilles is to get from *A* to *B* he must first get to *C*, the starting point of the tortoise. But the tortoise will then have moved to *D*, and when Achilles gets to *D* the tortoise will have moved to *E*, and so on *ad infinitum*. Hence the tortoise will always be just a little ahead of Achilles and the latter cannot catch him. In fact, of course, we know that Achilles *can* catch the tortoise; if the latter's start is proportional to the relative speeds, Achilles will catch up the tortoise at the finishing post, just as in the Dichotomy the runner, if that is what he is, will actually get to *B*.

Discussion of these two arguments seems never ending, and there have been very conflicting reactions to them, from accusations of triviality to recognitions of profound insights into the notion of infinity. The arguments evidently depend on the assumption that any finite distance can in fact, and not merely in principle, be divided *ad infinitum*, which seems to be a point about physics. It is equally evident that any physical distance can be construed mathematically in the sort of terms that Zeno presupposes. So the problem is how the one is to be matched to the other. What does *not* follow is that motion is impossible. I leave further details to the reader's ingenuity. As an Eleatic, Zeno himself would not have been opposed to the conclusion of these arguments. But his opponents would have been; so the probable tenor of the arguments is to show that even a pluralist must accept Eleatic conclusions about the impossibility of motion.

The other two arguments are less sophisticated, at any rate as they have been handed down to us. I shall not discuss the Moving Rows, which seems on the face of it to depend on a failure to recognize certain aspects of relative motion, although a gloss on it by some interpreters makes it an argument for the impossibility of motion if there are things or spaces which are indivisible in principle. For on that account motion could not be continuous; to be so the moving body would have to fall across an in principle indivisible space, which is *ex hypothesi* impossible.

A similar moral might be abstracted from the Arrow, but as Aristotle reports it (and the text is uncertain) Zeno argued that anything that occupies a space equal to its own dimensions must be at rest. He then argued that at any moment of an arrow's flight it must occupy a space equal to its own dimensions. If it is then at rest at any moment of its flight, it must be at rest at every moment of its flight. It cannot therefore be in motion and cannot hit its target. Once again, of course, we know that arrows do actually move and sometimes hit their targets. But apart from issues about the relation between 'any' and 'every', the premise of the argument seems quite false. Objects always occupy spaces equal to their own dimensions; they could not do otherwise. It does not follow that they are at rest.

The later Presocratics
The ingenuity of Zeno's arguments is remarkable, and it must have been upsetting to the more dogmatic philosophers to have such arguments directed at them. As with Parmenides, however, there is little evidence that there was much understanding of them, or – at least until Aristotle – much of an attempt to deal with them on their own merits. The other philosophers of the presocratic period either ignored such arguments or thought that they could get round them in some way. Empedocles of Acragas in Sicily, a picturesque thinker and many-sided character, writing again in Homeric verse, thought it enough to postulate the existence of four unchanging elements, earth, fire, air and water, and two other things (we should say *forces*, but Empedocles does not have that notion) love and strife. The elements themselves are neither created nor destroyed, and so conform to Parmenidean principles as far as that goes. But they can be mixed together by love, which Empedocles thinks of as a kind of substance or stuff mingling with them, so that new compounds can be formed. Similarly, strife acts in the opposite way, splitting up compounds into elements. It seems that Empedocles thought of this as some kind of response to Parmenides, in that no new elements come into existence and none is destroyed. It is in fact, however, a quite inadequate response, since Parmenides' argument is quite general and applies as much to compounds as it does to elements. *Nothing* new can come into existence and *nothing* can be destroyed.

Empedocles seems to have thought that the processes which he had in mind held good on the cosmic scale. He speaks of an initial sphere, which gets split up by strife until there is a complete separation out of the elements, which are then brought together again by love until the cycle is completed. (It has to be said that this account of the cosmic cycle is disputed.) He goes into picturesque details of the effects of this process at various stages with respect to living creatures (at one stage there can be separate limbs unattached to bodies!).

Empedocles also wrote a second poem, entitled *Purifications*, in which he goes into the kind of rituals and practices that are necessary to attain salvation and escape the 'wheel of birth'. Some interpreters have seen an incompatibility between this and the poem on nature, but here again it is likely that love and strife have a role to play and have a significance that approaches the ethical. It is clear that Empedocles believes that men can become gods in another incarnation, just as they can become animals and other forms of life. Empedocles said that he himself had been 'a boy and a girl, a bush and a bird and a dumb sea fish'. The question is whether that is to be taken literally. The theory may be, as one interpreter, M. R. Wright, has argued, that if love has the upper hand in our lives, then when death and the dissolution of the body comes our elements may be reconstituted into higher forms, and we may even become gods. If strife has the upper hand then the tendency is in the opposite direction.

Philosophically Empedocles is not very interesting. Anaxagoras – who came from Clazomenae in Asia Minor but lived for some time in Athens, and who was a friend of Pericles, the great Athenian general, in the mid fifth century B.C. – is more interesting, if only because considerations about infinity return. Anaxagoras may have realized that Empedocles' theory was not subtle enough to deal with Parmenides, but he too thought that the answer lay in mixture and separation, although in a much more complicated way. It is probable that he was impressed by the facts of nutrition – that men and animals take in food and something of a quite different kind may result; you eat wheat but you put on flesh and acquire blood, bone etc. This looks like the coming into being of something new, which is forbidden by Parmenidean principles. Anaxagoras thought that this problem could be dealt with by supposing that there are portions of flesh, blood, bone etc. in the wheat, which are taken into the body, the irrelevant substances being presumably excreted. Anaxagoras seems to have shared the earlier philosophers' propensity for generalization. He seems to have supposed that anything could result in this way from anything. The only way to deal with that was to suppose that there is a portion of everything in everything, and this is a central doctrine in his theory.

If however that doctrine is taken literally there is a problem. For how can everything have a portion of *everything*? Some commentators have suggested that he really meant something less than that. But Anaxagoras seems also to have supposed that everything is infinitely divisible, and

[1] M. R. Wright: *Empedocles: The Extant Fragments* (Yale U.P., 1981).

the fragment which is the opening sentence of his book (which, incidentally, was on sale in Athens for a drachma – a day's wage for a workman
on the Acropolis) speaks for an initial state of things in which there is a
mixture of an infinite number of infinitely small things. If that is taken
seriously (as surely it should be), Anaxagoras was committed to belief
in an actual (and not merely potential) infinity of things. But that belief
provides a possible way of interpreting the claim that everything has a
portion of everything. For a grain of wheat has in it portions of flesh,
bone etc. as well as portions of wheat. But it contains a preponderance
of wheat, because, as Anaxagoras said, everything is what it has most
of. But all these portions have themselves portions of the same and other
things, each portion being at that level what it has most of. And this
goes on *ad infinitum*. One never comes to pure wheat or pure anything
else; at any stage of division what there is has a portion of everything.
So the doctrines that everything has a portion of everything and that
things are divisible *ad infinitum* are complementary, and the latter
doctrine saves the former.

Unfortunately, Anaxagoras did speak as if there were elements out of
which things are composed, calling them 'seeds'. But his real view must
be that such elements comprise merely the kinds of thing that turn up in
the process of analysis; nevertheless they never exist in a pure state. To
isolate an element or seed is merely to specify a kind of thing that turns
up at any given level in the analysis of what we perceive. But, as he said,
'from the weakness of our senses we fail to perceive the truth'; a piece
of apparently pure gold is nothing of the kind. Everything is a mixture,
and substantial changes are, once again, a matter of mixture and separation. That is no more a satisfactory reply to Parmenides' claim that
coming to be and passing away are impossible than was Empedocles'
similar claim; but Anaxagoras at least realizes that one cannot suppose
in the face of Eleaticism that the great variety of things arises from a
small number of unchanging elements. Nevertheless the supposition that
what there is comes from the mixture and separation of an actual infinity
of infinitely small things brings with it its own obvious problems. For one
thing, it surely runs foul of Zeno's arguments against infinite division –
the Dichotomy and the Achilles; and if those arguments are answerable,
or conceivably so, there is no indication that Anaxagoras saw how to
answer them. He was either oblivious to them or thought he could just
ignore them, possibly failing to see their significance.

Anaxagoras does see, however, that it is necessary to postulate some
agency to bring about the mixture and separation, and invokes *nous*
(intellect, reason or mind). It is, he says, the one pure thing, the one
exception to the principle that everything contains a portion of every-

thing, and controls what happens to everything else. In Plato's *Phaedo*, Socrates is made to say that he was interested in this view of Anaxagoras' because the reference to *nous* seemed to suggest a kind of rationality in the world and a possible answer to the question whether things were for the best. But when he examined Anaxagoras' views he was disappointed, because it seemed that *nous* operated merely as a mechanical cause despite the promises in its name. The implied criticism is perhaps justified, but it is clear that Anaxagoras was a great deal more sophisticated than Empedocles, and that is evident in other views of his, including his views on sense-perception, which I have not space to discuss. However, Anaxagoras represents a relatively subtle attempt to deal with some of the problems thrown up by the Eleatics. It is a failure all the same; no such attempt can be a success unless it grapples with the arguments of the Eleatics, and no Presocratic did that.

The final presocratic school, the Atomists, represented by Leucippus of Miletus and Democritus of Abdera (who is technically not a *presocratic*, being a contemporary of Socrates), were once again less sophisticated, although both as anticipators of the later Epicurus and as possible forerunners of modern atomism they have received some attention. It is however dangerous to see merit in ancient thought simply because the ideas put forward have a similarity to ideas used in different and later contexts: it all depends on what the ideas are used to do. The ancient Atomists of the presocratic period said that all that really existed were atoms and the void (the latter being the empty spaces between atoms). Atoms constituted what-is, the void what-is-not. That looks like an explicit reaction against Parmenides, and amounts to a flat and flagrant rejection of his views about the impossibility of what-is-not. There is however no sensitivity to his arguments. Atoms move in the void, perhaps as a result of an initial vortex; they collide with each other and form compounds, partly because they become hooked on to each other and partly perhaps because they form vibrating systems in which atoms cannot easily escape from the complex. Atoms vary in size, although all are invisible; otherwise they vary only in shape and arrangement. They do not, as such, have weight, this being merely an apparent property of bodies, because larger atoms tend to sink to the bottom or centre of any system, the finer and smaller atoms having a chance to escape. *Qua* atoms they are indivisible, but scholars dispute whether they are so merely as a matter of fact or such that they are indivisible in principle. There are ways on either count in which they could be taken as trying to evade Zeno's arguments, but it is just as likely that they did not see the relevance of those arguments; if so their general theory remains one merely about the nature of the physical world.

It may well appear that such a theory can account for only some properties of things in the world – basically size, shape and, derivatively, weight. It will not deal with colour, smell, taste etc. On this point Democritus, at all events, showed the influence of the Sophists, to whom we shall come in the next chapter. Suffice it to say now that the Sophists emphasized the contrast between nature and convention (*nomos*), between what exists as a fact of nature and what is, so to speak, manmade. Democritus said that colour etc. exist only by convention (*nomos*); in reality there exist simply atoms and the void. It is not strictly true that colour etc. are a product of convention in any literal sense. What might be thought to be true is that such properties are anthropocentric, in the sense that it is only because human beings are what they are and have the kind of senses that they have that they come to attribute colour etc. to objects at all. That is presumably what Democritus meant to say, although it is another step to assert that in that case colour etc. do not amout to being objective properties of things – and Democritus seems to want to say that as well. The truth is that on his view impressions of colour etc. arise from interactions between atoms from bodies and the atoms that make up the sense-organs, and indeed the atoms that make up the soul (for the Atomists were materialists through and through).

With the Atomists, apart from some individual eclectics, the period of presocratic philosophy comes to an end – not because it could go no further along the lines with which it was concerned, but because there were new developments in philosophy, one of which was due to the Sophists, as already mentioned.

[3]
The Sophists and Socrates

The Sophists

In the period with which we have so far been concerned there has been little concern with human beings except as part of nature. There is of course the Pythagorean emphasis upon the transmigration of souls and the practices supposed to facilitate this, so that the next life may be superior to the present one; there are similar concerns in Empedocles' poem on 'Purifications'. Heraclitus too passes judgements on various practices in his society. But there is nothing that really deserves the name of ethics. The Atomists, like the later Epicurus, emphasize the role of pleasure as a guide to conduct; but since it is Democritus who expresses this view and he is not strictly a Presocratic, this may reflect the concerns of a slightly later period – the influences of the Sophists, and perhaps Socrates.

It is with Socrates that ethics properly begins, but an important stimulus to it is provided by the Sophists, despite the fact that Socrates, to judge by the Platonic evidence, is so opposed to them. To contemporaries, in any case, they probably seemed closer to him than they do to us today. The Sophists were itinerant teachers who provided courses or individual lectures on various things, and charged money for the privilege. Some of them at least seem to have done very well out of it. It is tempting to attribute current disapproval of them to that fact, but it is doubtful whether charging fees for services rendered would have been a cause for disapproval with the average Athenian of the mid fifth century B.C. Socrates objected to them because he thought that they claimed to provide more than they actually did. In particular, he took them to say that they could teach men virtue, and he thought that they did nothing of the kind.

It is from the term 'sophist' that we derive our term 'sophistry', and it is clear that to their contemporaries they seemed clever-clever, even tricksters, in that they engaged in specious arguments. Once again, however, if we go by Plato's dialogues, Socrates' own arguments, considered purely as arguments, are often little better than those of his Sophist opponents. There can be little doubt that Socrates' contemporaries would have found him just as annoying in this respect as they found the Sophists; on the other hand, many extended to them all a similar cautious admiration. Socrates, however, had a fascination all of his own, as Alcibiades is made to bear witness in Plato's *Symposium*; it is the character of the man and the depth of his moral consciousness that make him unique.

The period in which the Sophists came into prominence was one of considerable social change, and one in which the Greeks became more conscious of the customs and practices of other people in the world. The historian Herodotus travelled around the Mediterranean and reported, among other things, on the variety of customs followed by non-Greeks. All this drew attention to how much in the world is, so to speak, manmade and not simply part of nature. There arose in consequence an emphasis on the contrast between what is in this sense a human product and what is natural and non-human, between *nomos* (convention) and *phusis* (nature). It is not clear that the Sophists spoke with one voice about that contrast, but there was certainly a tendency on their part to lay weight on *nomos* against *phusis*, whether by 'nature' was meant nature in general or human nature. I make that distinction because, although some Sophists were concerned simply to depreciate the extent to which what we know about the world is a fact of nature, others, such as perhaps Antiphon, were concerned with the contrast between what men are in themselves as a fact of nature, what they naturally desire and aim for, and what is imposed upon them by society. In this latter aspect they were the first sociologists, and certainly the first social relativists. But those whom we have come to believe to be most important among the Sophists, Protagoras and Gorgias for example, seem more concerned with the distinction between nature and convention in a general way. For that reason one of their main aims was to depreciate the study of nature, and thus the whole line of philosophy that existed up to this time.

Protagoras is reported as claiming that man is the measure of all things, both of the things that are that they are and of the things that are not that they are not. To judge by Plato's *Theaetetus*, where this report is given, this meant that everything is as it seems to a man – not just men in general but each individual man. This leads to a complete relativism, with no possibility of absolute truth. We also learn of Protagoras' scepticism about the gods and his tendency to emphasize the possibility of producing arguments on each side of any given issue. (This is a tendency that receives an almost canonical statement in the anonymous *Dissoi Logoi* – the two-fold or double arguments – which seems to have been produced a little later, at the beginning of the fourth century.) Despite all this, Protagoras was not a political or social iconoclast. In his view, although there is no absolute truth, it is still possible to make the better *logos* or argument the stronger. All men have a sense of justice even if their talents in other respects are not equal, and it is the task of the Sophist to bring this out and to provide by teaching the means to its realization.

Gorgias was, if anything, even more radically opposed to nature and its study. He wrote a book in which he made a three-fold claim: (1) there is nothing; (2) even if there were anything we could not know of it; and (3) even if we could know of it we could not communicate it to others. This might be described as an argument by 'strategic withdrawal'; if the more radical position is not found convincing one falls back to a somewhat less radical one. But even the least radical position rules out the possibility of a study of nature. From what we can gather of Gorgias' arguments from later reports, they were, unsurprisingly, not very good, and he tended to use whatever points of argument he could lay his hands on. But the sweeping character of his objective is clear, as are the drastic means that he used to reach it.

There remains the possibility of concentrating on what is man-made and on what is necessary to further men's aims in society. That was in large part the point of the Sophists' teaching. The teaching could take various forms, and we hear of longer and shorter courses. (Socrates is made to say in Plato's *Cratylus* 384b that he could not afford the fifty-drachma course given by Prodicus on language, only the single-drachma course or lecture!) Plato's *Protagoras* 315–16 gives a marvellous pen-picture of various Sophists at work in different ways – discussion while walking up and down, the *ex cathedra* lecture, and the use of question and answer. Some of the subjects of study, astronomy, for instance, seem to have been scientific, and Socrates himself was associated with such matters in the public mind. Gorgias taught rhetoric, Prodicus language and grammar in general, and Hippias memory training. These were all useful acquisitions for a society where so much depended on being able to influence public opinion in the assembly. So the teaching was aimed in particular at the acquisition of various skills (*technai*) of this kind and the production in the pupil of that which would make him 'good' (*agathos*). This sort of goodness need not be interpreted in the moral sense, since it is predominantly a goodness at various things which would make the individual dominant in whatever sphere he found himself. Indeed the ideal for the Greek, or at any rate the Athenian, was to be *kalagathos* – not only good in that sense, but also *kalos* (noble). The aim was to be not only excellent at whatever was valued at the time, but recognized by all as being so.

It may be that some at least of the Sophists were so carried away in the statement of their aims as to represent what they were concerned with as the most important of human concerns. Socrates is made by Plato so to characterize them. But in that respect they may have had a bad press. Socrates clearly thought that there were much more important things than the aims pursued by the Sophists. He may indeed have seen them as corrupting, although *Republic* 492–3 represents them as inculcating 'nothing else than the opinions of the multitude'. At all events they failed, in his opinion, to teach moral excellence or virtue. Their claim to teach *aretē* (excellence) was to him not only misleading, but also corrupting, because it suggested that they could bring about *moral* excellence, whereas they did nothing of the kind.

Socrates

Whatever the truth of this matter, it is clear that Socrates himself was a man of a quite different character from the average Sophist. He wrote nothing. The only piece of strictly contemporary evidence is a scene in Aristophanes' comedy *The Clouds*, in which he is represented as a Sophist concerned with such matters as the length of the jump of a flea, while hanging in a basket from the ceiling because the air is thinner there. The characterization is of course meant to be funny, and for that reason cannot be taken as accurate (although a joke must surely have some basis in reality if it is to be telling). For the rest, Socrates lives, and lives indeed, in the pages of Plato, who was a young man when he knew him. There are also some accounts of Socrates in Aristotle and others, but none of these, with the possible exception of Xenophon, the historian, is a first-hand witness. In consequence, the actual Socrates is lost to us, and we have merely the Platonic Socrates. Plato did not write the dialogues in which Socrates appears as the main character as historical documents, although in the second Platonic letter – if it is genuine, which it may well not be – there is a graceful compliment to Socrates, his master, in which the works of Plato are said to be really 'the work of Socrates restored to youth and beauty'. My belief is that Plato put into the mouths of historical characters the views which he took himself to have derived from them, directly or otherwise. Socrates was certainly Plato's main source in that respect, although the influences on Plato were manifold. It is impossible to believe, however, that everything put into Socrates' mouth in the dialogues could have been said or held by Socrates, although it is likely that in the earlier dialogues there is a closer relation to Socrates' actual views than in the later, very Platonic, dialogues.

We know comparatively little of Socrates the man. He was born in 470 B.C. and was executed in 399 B.C., when Athens had lost the Peloponnesian war against Sparta and just after the restoration of democracy from the oligarchy which had been set up at the end of that war. He was prosecuted for impiety in 399, although in the course of the trial the charge was changed to corruption of the young. The death penalty was demanded by the prosecution, and the judges, perhaps angered by Socrates' suggestion that a suitable penalty would be free maintenance by the state (a suggestion later altered to a fine), granted it. Socrates' defence is ostensibly given in Plato's *Apology*. There was a delay in the execution because a ship had been sent on a sacred mission to Delos and no executions could take place until it returned. Plato's *Crito* purports to tell of a discussion between Socrates and Crito while Socrates was in prison, during which Crito urges him to escape and Socrates refuses. Plato's *Phaedo* allegedly tells the story of Socrates' last day, during which there is a discussion between him and various friends and fellow-philosophers, mainly Pythagorean, about the immortality of the soul. (Plato was not there; he was said to be ill.) At the end of the discussion the executioner brings in the hemlock, which naturally had to be self-administered. Socrates drinks it and eventually dies, his last words being 'Crito, we owe a cock to Asclepius. See to it and don't forget.' Asclepius was the god of healing, and the exact significance of the words has been the subject of considerable debate.

Socrates did not come from the higher strata of Athenian society. He was a citizen, but his mother was a midwife, and his wife, represented as a shrew, was a vegetable-seller. He laid claim to an inner voice; we are told that during military service at the siege of Potidaea he remained in thought – possibly a trance – for twenty-four hours. He had a strange fascination for numbers of people, including Alcibiades, the contro-versial Athenian general at the end of the Peloponnesian war, whom Athens could neither do without nor tolerate because of his reprobate character. But he also described himself as the gadfly of Athens, and this too must have been how he struck large numbers of people – as a constant source of irritation. At all events, for one reason or another, he came to be thought of as the source of those features of Athenian society which led to Athens' downfall in the war – a questioner of accepted mores, ways of behaviour and beliefs whom conservatives, at all events, could not stomach. For one thing, he employed irony or mock-modesty, claiming that although others thought that they knew things, he himself knew nothing. That was the implication of the story told in the *Apology* that the Delphic oracle had declared that Socrates was the wisest man in Greece. Socrates, puzzled by this assessment of him, finally came to the conclusion that the god had said this because, while he, Socrates, knew that he knew nothing, others thought that they knew things and did not.

One of Socrates' central doctrines was that virtue is knowledge. It is not altogether clear, however, what he meant by that doctrine. Many of the things said in Plato's dialogues suggest that he may have thought of virtue as an excellence at life, and that he construed that in terms of skill, on the analogy of various specific crafts (*technai*). Skill, however, is to be differentiated sharply from mere knack, and Socrates is made to make that point strongly against Gorgias' claims on behalf of rhetoric in the dialogue of that name. Plato often associates knowledge and skill with the notion of a *logos*. That much-used and highly ambiguous Greek word means in this context something like 'principle', so that the implication is that skill proper presupposes knowledge of the principles underlying its subject matter. The main point that Socrates is made to make against Gorgias, however, is that rhetoric is concerned with issues which are at the level of cosmetics. It is concerned only with gratification and has no more serious end; hence the main criticism of the claim of rhetoric to be a fundamental art is that it is not concerned with the serious things of life; and knowledge, Socrates says, does have that concern.

There seems to be an element of 'persuasive definition' in Socrates' claim; he wants to restrict knowledge to matters of serious concern, and to define it so. Another related factor is the connection that emerges in Plato's presentation of Socrates' thinking between knowledge and self-knowledge. Socrates professes a deep concern with the saying that was written above the temple at Delphi – 'Know thyself'. It seems clear that Socrates would probably not have counted something as knowledge unless it had that connection with self-knowledge. Hence, in so far as virtue is knowledge, and knowledge implies self-knowledge, virtue must involve both a knowledge of and a care for oneself, for one's soul. That may indeed be Socrates' central message, and the view fits in with what Kierkegaard was later to see as so important in Socrates. It makes Socrates a prophet of inwardness and of a concern for one's real self.

That, however, is not entirely what Plato seems to have seen in him. One other interpretation of the Delphic oracle story is that to acquire virtue one should get rid of prejudices and presumptions about what one knows; that was what ordinary men so evidently failed to achieve. Another Socratic doctrine is that all the virtues form a unity; one cannot have one of them without the rest. Socrates is made to argue for this by reference to the dependence of all the virtues on knowledge, but on any ordinary interpretation it is a severe doctrine. Did Socrates think that if one had knowledge proper one would have all the virtues, and that one could not have them, nor *a fortiori* any one of them, without the knowledge that he had in mind? If so, what form was that knowledge to take? The dialogues present Socrates as looking for definitions of the various virtues, as if the achievement of that would be an important step on the road to complete virtue. But they equally present Socrates as failing to arrive at those definitions, so that the only substantial outcome of the discussion is the realization on the part of the interlocutors that they did not know what they thought they knew. Aristotle presents Socrates as looking for such definitions because they were to function as the first principles of moral reasoning – the premises from which he could reach conclusions on moral issues. If one knew the appropriate definitions one could use them in order to argue and decide upon what one should do in particular cases. This presents a severely intellectual view of moral thought – and is indeed a wild-goose chase.

It is a wild-goose chase because no general principles can tell you what to do in particular cases. In the Platonic dialogues the person whom Socrates interrogates is often led to offer a definition of a virtue which constitutes a general principle of this sort. Courage consists in keeping your place in the ranks in war; justice consists in paying your debts; piety consists in prosecuting those guilty of offences against the gods. There is often a dramatic setting which leads up to and elicits such a definition. It is often said that Socrates then points out that such an answer is too specific and does not do justice to the nature of the virtue in question. Subsequent discussion elicits other such definitions and in the course of it all Socrates introduces some of his characteristic doctrines. But the outcome is generally negative, and the parties to the discussion go away no wiser, apart from the realization that they did not after all know what they thought they did. Up to a point this is a correct account of what happens. But Socrates also indicates that the answers given to his request for a definition are also inadequate as a guide to conduct. If you go by the rule that you should repay your debts you may, as the first book of the *Republic* indicates, give back a sword to someone who has since gone mad and is likely to run amok with it. That cannot be right.

It is a possible view that Socrates did not think that complete definitions of moral virtues, and thus definite rules to guide conduct, were possible; hence the negative conclusion of the dialogues. That view fits in with the Kierkegaardian view of Socrates that I referred to above. It is no good looking for rules or principles to guide conduct. It is of more importance, and of greater efficacy, to look into oneself, with the aim of acquiring a good character, of producing a good soul. However this may be, it is not what Plato or Aristotle saw in Socrates, and Plato's aim in ethics might be characterized as that of developing a form of moral knowledge which could be applied to particular situations and in social and political contexts. If Socrates appears to be sceptical about the possibility of virtue being taught in his discussions with Sophists as portrayed in the *Protag-*

oras and *Gorgias*, Plato in the *Republic* clearly thinks that, given appropriate social and political conditions, a form of education will give to suitable persons moral and political insight which can then be applied practically. At other times Plato reveals a certain pessimism about the actual possibility of this happening, but he does not suggest doubt about the coherence of the aim. I suspect that in these respects, as in others, Plato was a very different sort of man and a very different sort of philosopher from Socrates.

One other Socratic doctrine which is brought out by Plato, in the *Protagoras* and *Gorgias* in particular, is the doctrine that weakness of will (*akrasia*) is impossible; if a man is led by passion to do that which he apparently knows he should not do, he cannot really have had that knowledge in the first place. Knowledge cannot be dragged around, like a slave, by passion. Hence people cannot do what they know they should not do. That doctrine fits in with the pre-eminence given to knowledge in relation to virtue. If virtue is knowledge, then if you really know, you cannot fail in virtue, whatever your passions. On any ordinary interpretation of 'knowing what you should do' it seems manifestly false, however, that one cannot both know what one should do and act otherwise. Hence the Socratic doctrine was a source of puzzlement to other philosophers, including Aristotle, who in the end sought to retain the doctrine but reinterpret it. I suspect however that if the real, as opposed to the Platonic, Socrates held to this doctrine it was because he meant by knowledge all that is involved in the 'know thyself' and the part that that plays in goodness of soul.

By and large the Platonic Socrates also takes an austere view of the place of pleasure in the moral life – except in the *Protagoras*, where, at least in the course of the argument, he is made to embrace a form of hedonism. This has seemed surprising to commentators, both ancient and modern, and the fact that Socrates is made to take an opposite attitude in the *Gorgias* may be responsible for the fact that subsequent schools of moral philosophy, particularly the Cyrenaics under Aristippus and the Cynics under Diogenes or possibly Antisthenes, took opposing positions towards pleasure while thinking of themselves as Socratics. For the Cyrenaics advocated the pursuit of pleasure as the end of the good life, while the Cynics advocated the opposite, preaching an austere view of the conduct of life. All in all it is difficult to get a sure view of what Socrates was like. The Platonic Socrates is all we have – and he is barely consistent.

However all that may be, the picture that emerges from the Platonic dialogues is of a strange, ugly man, bearding people whom he meets and getting them into a position in which they make claims about virtues of one kind or another. The Socratic method of challenging those claims is a form of cross-questioning, in which, as a rule, Socrates makes the running while his interlocutors are confined to saying 'Yes' and 'No'. Sometimes the interlocutors, like Protagoras in the dialogue of that name, protest at not being allowed to say anything at length. But Socrates' aim is to put their claims to the test, and in the *Theaetetus* he is made to describe his profession on the analogy of his mother's – the midwife's. His aim is to bring thoughts to birth and then to examine them to see whether they are good thoughts, or, as he puts it, mere windbags. (It has to be remembered that in Greek practice a weak or sickly child was usually not allowed to survive.) That description of his method makes it essentially negative.

Aristotle says that two things may fairly be attributed to Socrates – general definitions and inductive arguments. We have already tried to get a view of Socrates' attitude to general definitions. An inductive argument in this context, and in Aristotelian usage, is an argument which uses particular cases or examples to give point to some general moral or principle. Socrates continually appeals to examples in order to get his interlocutor to accept some general principle explicitly or implicitly. But the general tendency of the argument seems negative; for what tends to emerge is some inconsistency between the principle invoked and the position initially embraced by the interlocutor.

In some of his dialogues, notably the *Meno* and *Phaedo*, Plato elevates that practice into a method of hypothesis-formation and testing. In the *Phaedo* in particular, Socrates is made to describe a method by which a hypothesis is put forward and tested for coherence. If it survives that test the procedure is to try to derive the hypothesis from one which is 'higher', and then again from a 'higher' one still, until one comes to 'something adequate'. Probably what is being described here is a method for producing conviction on some matter; it is not necessarily a method of arriving at truth. If the interlocutor can be prevailed upon to put forward a hypothesis, perhaps on what a given virtue is, that hypothesis has first to be tested to see whether it fits together both in itself and in relation to other beliefs that the interlocutor holds. But suppose that the interlocutor is sceptical about accepting any such hypothesis; then it must be derived from some belief that he does have, so that Socrates can say 'If you accept p you must accept q, and if q then r . . . and if that then h, which is the hypothesis under consideration; so you must accept h'. In fact one meets such forms of argument only incidentally in the earlier dialogues. That is because the only point of conviction arrived at in those dialogues is that the interlocutor does not after all know what he thought he did. One does not arrive at a positive conclusion.

I suspect that the general tendency of Socratic argument was indeed negative in this way. That might be explained in different ways, but it is very possible that it was because Socrates thought that the real aim of the exercise was to produce a moral sense that could come only from self-knowledge. For this to be possible, illusions and prejudices had to be removed. But merely producing conviction concerning the nature of morality was not enough. One had to have a proper sense of what that morality consisted in, of what goodness of character amounted to. And it was the Sophists' failure to grasp that and what he saw as their extravagant claims to teach virtue that Socrates thought so objectionable. However that may be, people came eventually to see him as a disturbing influence on society, and the charge of corrupting the young followed. Philosophers, Plato in particular, took a quite different view of him, and there were many who clearly saw Socrates as their 'guru'. But Plato tried to abstract from what Socrates had to say more positive doctrines, and although he tried to put them into the mouth of Socrates, their ascription to Socrates became gradually more and more implausible. One cannot get to Socrates except through Plato, but I suspect that Plato was as wrong about him as anyone else. Certainly they were different sorts of philosopher.

[4]

Plato

Whether or not Plato was a different sort of philosopher from Socrates, he was a different man socially. He was born in about 427 B.C. of a wealthy family. In all probability he had no intention of becoming a philosopher until he came under the influence of Socrates. At Socrates' death, when Plato was about twenty-eight, he left Athens (perhaps for political reasons) and went to Megara, where he probably came under the influence of Eucleides, the head of the Megarian school of philosophy, a sort of off-shoot of the Eleatics. He eventually went to Sicily on the invitation of Dion, the brother-in-law of Dionysius I, the tyrant of Syracuse, to undertake the education of Dionysius' son, who was to become Dionysius II. It is tempting to see in this an attempt to follow out the recommendation of the *Republic* to produce a philosopher-king. However that may be, he ran into trouble with Dionysius I and had to return to Athens. A story current in the ancient world claimed that he was sold as a slave by Dionysius and that his friends had to rescue him; it was even said that money collected for the ransom was eventually put towards the founding of his philosophical school, the Academy. Whether or not that is true, Plato did set up the school on his return to Athens, in a grove to the north-west of the city which went by the name of the Academy. When Dionysius I died and his son became tyrant, Plato was persuaded by Dion to return to Syracuse on two occasions. There was civil war there and Dion managed for a time to oust Dionysius, only to be killed himself. There was no doubt a close relationship between Plato and Dion, and thirteen Platonic letters, the authenticity of most of which has been questioned from time to time, have to do with affairs of Sicily.

The longest, the seventh letter, which may well be genuine, speaks rather disparagingly of Dionysius II's talents as a philosopher and of a lecture that Dionysius gave on philosophical issues. Plato indeed generally disparages didactic works on philosophy, and philosophy in a written form. The seventh letter speaks of philosophy being best pursued by philosophers living together so that a flame kindled in the soul of one can pass to others. Was that how the Academy itself was conducted? We do not know. A philosophical school at this time was in all probability little more than a guild, an assembly of dedicated people centred on a few buildings with, perhaps, a temple to the Muses. It is said that over the door of the Academy was written 'Let no one enter here who has not studied geometry'. There were distinguished mathematicians associated with the Academy, particularly Eudoxus; and it has been claimed that it was mathematics that was mainly studied there, rather than philosophy. This seems incredible, but Plato's own position in the Academy and his relationship with others remain a little obscure. Aristotle was a member of the Academy for twenty years. But when Plato died the property passed to his nephew Speusippus, then to Xenocrates, and so on as long as the Academy lasted – which it did, in one way or other, for centuries.

In between his travels and whatever went on in the Academy, Plato wrote dialogues. A few of those which have come down to us are probably spurious, but the great bulk are his. Despite his suspicion of written philosophy, Plato may have begun writing them as an attempt to preserve something of the spirit of Socrates' philosophizing, although it is very doubtful whether they were meant as historical documents. As Plato's views developed and changed, Socrates became more and more implausible as a protagonist in the discussions and as a proponent of the views presented. In some of the late dialogues Socrates ceases to be such a protagonist – for instance the *Sophist* and the *Statesman* (the first two, it has been said, of a trilogy to be completed by the *Philosopher*, which was for some reason never written); and the *Laws*. This last work, which is also the longest and least read, was said to be still on the wax (that is, written on wax tablets with a stylus, but not yet transcribed on to papyrus) when Plato died, and is thus presumably the last work to be written. The later dialogues also pay less attention to literary style and dramatic setting than the earlier ones.

We have already glanced at some of the earlier dialogues in considering Socrates. The smaller Socratic dialogues discuss various virtues, or in the case of the *Ion* the nature of art. The *Protagoras* and *Gorgias* are bigger in scale and are concerned with Socrates' relation to the Sophists and the teaching of virtue. The *Protagoras* in particular contains marvellous pen-portraits of Socrates and certain Sophists. All these dialogues might be thought to be more or less Socratic. But gradually views that are essentially Plato's own begin to appear. In my opinion, the first emergence of something distinctively Platonic comes in the *Meno*, to which we shall return below. After that comes the *Phaedo*, ostensibly the report of Socrates' last day, but a dialogue in which Socrates is made to hold views which are more plausibly taken as Platonic. At around the same date comes the *Symposium*, the story of a feast at which the participants, ending with Socrates, speak of love; once again it contains marvellous portraits of the participants, and a wonderful final speech by

Socrates, who eventually succeeds in drinking the others under the table. The *Republic* is generally and rightly thought of as the centre-piece of the mature Plato. After that comes a group of critical dialogues in which Plato seems to look back and perhaps seriously criticize his earlier views – the *Parmenides*, *Theaetetus*, *Sophist*, *Statesman* and *Philebus* (in the last of which there are hints, put in the mouth of Socrates, of obscure metaphysical views which Aristotle also ascribes to Plato). The position of one or two other dialogues is disputed, particularly that of the *Timaeus*, which contains Plato's cosmology and which was thought in the early Middle Ages to be 'Plato's philosophy' and therefore late. Its dramatic date is immediately after the *Republic*, and there is much in favour of dating its composition then.

The Meno *and* Phaedo

The *Meno* begins as if it is to be a continuation of the discussion in the *Protagoras* and *Gorgias* on whether virtue can be taught. But after a few 'Socratic' moves Meno mentions a dilemma (labelled as 'sophistic' by Socrates but treated seriously all the same) concerned with how one can carry on such an inquiry at all. For either one knows the answer already, in which case learning is not in question, or one does not, in which case one does not know what to look for. The dilemma depends on the acceptance of the proposition that with regard to anything one either knows or does not know, and this is reinvoked in a different context and to a different end in the *Theaetetus*. It is a dilemma which seems plausible, but fails to take account of the fact that one can know some things and to some degree about something, but not know other things or not know them fully. It is arguable that its acceptance depends on a certain view of knowledge – that knowledge entails having an object before the mind – but that is a matter of dispute. In any case, Socrates does not so respond to it. Instead he refers to a doctrine held by priests and poets that the soul is immortal, has lived innumerable lives and has come to know everything. But when it is reborn it forgets and needs to be reminded of what it once knew. This is the first of certain great Platonic doctrines – the doctrine of recollection, that knowledge is a matter of recollecting what one once knew, and that learning is really such recollection.

It is in fact an incoherent doctrine, since it gives rise to an infinite regress – if *all* knowledge is recollection there can be no first knowledge. That however is not something that Plato gives any indication of realizing. As a solution of the dilemma the doctrine has certain oddities too, since in effect it says that we do not really ever learn anything, we merely recollect what we already know implicitly. The doctrine appears only twice more in an explicit form – in the *Phaedo*, where it is said that we recollect what Plato calls 'Forms', a notion to which we shall return, and in the *Phaedrus*, where it is made the explanation of the effects of artistic awareness. In the *Meno* Socrates is made to give a sort of demonstration of the doctrine by getting a boy to arrive at the solution of a geometrical problem: what is the length of the side of a square twice the area of a given square? He does this by the technique of question and answer, and by, at a certain stage, reference to a construction added to a diagram drawn in the dust. This leads the boy to the realization that the length required is the diagonal of the original square. Socrates claims, though this has been greeted with scepticism by a whole host of commentators, that he has not been teaching the boy, merely drawing out of him what he already knows. At the end, the boy is said to have true belief only, because he is like someone just woken up from sleep; but the true belief could be turned into knowledge by repetition of the same procedure.

The example is in fact very favourable to Socrates' case, since with a certain knowledge of things mathematical (which it is clear the boy has) someone could conceivably work out the answer, perhaps with a little assistance. That is what mathematical knowledge is like; it is what a later generation of philosophers called '*a priori*'. Because of that, some commentators have said that Plato is putting forward a view of such *a priori* knowledge – claiming indeed that it involves some form of innate knowledge or at all events a substitute for that. As Socrates initially presents the doctrine, however, we are told that the soul has come to know *everything*, and that if someone recollects one piece of knowledge he can, with determination, work out the rest. Hence there is a certain conflict between two aspects of Plato's presentation of the issue. At the end of the geometrical example the discussion returns to what is ostensibly the subject of the dialogue – the teachability of virtue. Socrates invokes for the first time the notion of *hypothesis*, saying that on the hypothesis that virtue is knowledge it must be teachable. He then argues that it is knowledge because it depends on practical wisdom. At the end of that, however, he casts doubt on the hypothesis, on the empirical grounds that people do not seem able to teach it.

Socrates then says that there is in fact a substitute for knowledge – true belief. If you want to go to Larisa you will get there if you have a true belief about the right road, whether or not you have knowledge. The trouble with true beliefs is that they do not stick in people's minds and need to be tied down by 'calculation of reason' so that they become knowledge – and that is what recollection amounts to. It is such true beliefs, not knowledge, that are possessed by priests, poets and statesmen. As things are, therefore, virtue comes not by teaching but by something more like inspiration. There are many things about this that have been the subject of controversy, particularly what is meant by 'calculation of reason'. Elsewhere Plato associates knowledge with a *logos*, with understanding the reason why, and it may be that this is what he has in mind here. It is less than clear that Socrates himself would ever have suggested that true belief was a substitute for knowledge, and the general epistemological framework of the dialogue is dubiously Socratic. One thing is clear, however – here Plato suggests that true beliefs can be turned into knowledge. By the time of the *Republic* he had come to a different view.

The *Phaedo* is in this respect a bridging dialogue and it introduces for the first time a doctrine which is completely absent from the *Meno* – the theory of Forms or Ideas, which has generally been thought to be the essential Plato. The dialogue, as we have already seen, purports to describe a discussion between Socrates and two Pythagoreans during his last day, ending with his death. It is reported by Phaedo, Plato not being present, because, it is said, of an illness. Socrates claims that he is not afraid to die, because death is the release of the soul from the body and the limitations that the body causes. The *Phaedo* is a marvellous literary piece, and Socrates' discussion of death is on a very elevated plane. Cebes and Simmias express a certain scepticism about the soul's survival of death (a philosophical scepticism, no doubt, since as good Pythagoreans they must have accepted the doctrine willingly enough), and Socrates goes on to offer certain arguments for the indestructibility of the soul, directed to the conclusion, as he puts it, that our souls exist in Hades. The arguments are of very unequal worth, and it is likely that Plato recognized that fact. The dialogue ends, however, with a 'myth' about what happens to the soul after death – one that elaborates with some changes a parallel myth that ended the *Gorgias*. Myths in Plato are what the *Timaeus* calls a 'likely story' – the presentation of what Plato believes where philosophical argument comes to an end.

The first argument takes as its premise the doctrine that everything comes from its opposite and leads to the conclusion that, just as the dead come from the living, so the living come from the dead, and that the dead must exist as souls in Hades. It is not a good argument, to say the least; it depends upon a confusion between different kinds of opposite, and by no means sustains the conclusion that the living and the dead come from each other reciprocally, let alone that our souls exist in Hades. It may be that Plato was sensitive to the muddles in the argument, for he goes straight on to another argument. Cebes invokes the doctrine of recollection which is now associated with the theory of Forms. That doctrine – which is never really argued for in the dialogues but presented as something agreed about – is to the effect that, distinct from particular things, particular beautiful things, or particular equals, to give the example given here, there is something which is beautiful itself or equal itself and this is to be identified with absolute beauty or equality. Plato gives us no idea of how he came to believe in the existence of such things, but most of the examples that he initially gives involve 'relative terms' – terms such as 'beautiful' or 'good', which are relative in the sense that whether or not some particular thing is to be called beautiful or good is a relative matter, depending on the standard invoked or the basis of comparison. 'Equal' is not so much relative as relational: relative terms presuppose an implicit relation to, or comparison with, something, whereas relational terms make that relation explicit. It is probable that Plato ran these two together.

We can only guess at the source of this doctrine. It is notable that most relative terms fall into pairs of opposites – good/bad, beautiful/ugly, and so on – and it may well be that Heraclitus' use of such pairs of opposites influenced Plato. The main source of the doctrine must, however, have been Socrates. This is not to say that Socrates himself believed in such absolutes. But Plato may well have thought that Socrates' questions about the nature of various virtues could be answered only by postulating an absolute standard to which one can appeal in making particular decisions. Indeed in the *Euthyphro*, Socrates demands of Euthyphro a standard or paradigm to which we can appeal in deciding which things are pious or holy and which are not. Yet if such standards are demanded by Socrates' 'What is it?' questions, considered as requests for moral guidance, the form of the question seems to suggest that the answer must be in the nature of a universal or abstract essence. Hence a Form is in Plato's view something that must provide a standard and also be an abstract essence or universal – something that is in fact reflected in different locutions that Plato uses to refer to a Form. For example, he speaks sometimes of Beauty, and sometimes of 'the beautiful itself', locutions which in Greek can be understood as closer to each other than they seem in English. There is in fact no such thing as something which is both the nature of beauty and that which can provide the standard by which to judge putative instances of beauty. There is indeed a logical inconsistency between the two roles that a Form has to play, and there is some reason to think that by the time he came to write the *Parmenides* Plato may have come to see that. The doctrine is however presented as a received view in the dialogues up to the *Republic* and *Timaeus*.

As far as concerns the argument in the *Phaedo*, Plato argues that since things such as sticks and stones can be seen as equal in some respects and not in others, they are by the standard of the Form defectively equal and are seen as such (a very questionable claim). If that is so, whenever we see something as defectively equal in this way we presuppose a knowledge of absolute equality, which we cannot have got from experience; we are simply reminded of it by the example. We must then have had that knowledge before we were born, and we must have existed in consequence before being born. There is much that is questionable in both the epistemology and the use that is made of it, but, as is pointed out by Simmias and Cebes, the argument proves at best the pre-existence of the soul and does not rule out the possibility that on death it is dispersed like smoke. So the discussion goes on to another argument.

This one turns on an analogy between souls and Forms on the one hand and bodies and particular things on the other. The Forms are presented as unities and as constant in certain respects (the Form *equal* is always equal). Hence, if by analogy the soul is similarly one and constant, it cannot be split up in such a way as to be dissipated like smoke. But the argument depends on the strength of the analogy, and Cebes and Simmias produce rival analogies pointing in other directions. Simmias suggests that the soul may be related to the body as the attunement of the strings of a musical instrument to that instrument; but when the instrument is destroyed, so is the attunement. Cebes suggests that the analogy might be with a person and the garments that he wears. Just as a person, after wearing out various garments, may wear out himself, so may the soul, after wearing out various bodies, wear out itself.

Socrates' reply to Simmias is complicated, being concerned in the main to find fault with the analogy. To answer Cebes, Socrates offers an 'autobiography' explaining how he came to be interested in Forms and invoking the hypothetical method that was mentioned in the last chapter. Socrates represents the inquiry into Forms as a 'second way of voyaging', by comparison with a direct inquiry into things to see why they are as they are. The question 'why' that he wanted answered had to do with the purpose of things, and this was not provided by the kind of inquiry that the Presocratics engaged in. The theory of Forms provided such an answer, but as a kind of second best. It is generally taken that the 'second way of voyaging' is taking to your oars when the wind drops and you cannot use your sails; you will get to the same destination that way, but with greater expenditure of effort. So the theory of Forms will provide an answer to the purpose of things, but indirectly and with increased effort. It will do that, presumably, because if all things share in Forms (as Plato tends to put it), they share to some extent in perfection while falling short of it. The world, as Plato comes to put it in the *Timaeus*, is a mixture of reason and necessity, a mixture of rationality and brute, blind force. But participation in the Forms ensures that there is *something* rational and purposeful about it.

Given this, Socrates can go on to the final argument of the *Phaedo* and the reply to Cebes. It involves a certain amount of apparatus and a theory of causality which I shall gloss over to some extent. Socrates has so far explained a sense of the question 'Why?' which is answered by reference to a Form. He now indicates that Forms can exist in pairs of contraries, as can things which share in them; and he says that when one of these things is approached by the contrary it can either be destroyed or it can withdraw. No justification is offered for these exclusive alternatives. In the case of snow, when it is approached by heat it is destroyed by melting. Socrates' purpose is to show that when the soul is approached by death it is not destroyed but withdraws from the body. According to the theory of causality another answer to the question 'Why?' is possible apart from simple reference to the Form. This is so when there are things which are essential instances of a Form, as snow is of cold and fire is of heat; they are essential instances of the Form in the sense that snow must be cold and fire must be hot. The second kind of explanation becomes available when something of that kind is in something else. Fire thus of necessity brings heat to anything that it is in. On this model, soul, which is the source of life, is so because it brings life to whatever it is in, by being itself essentially alive. A dead soul makes no sense. On the approach of death it must either be destroyed or withdraw. Which?

At this point Plato fails grievously; for he allows Cebes to say that if that which is undying, being everlasting, cannot avoid destruction, what on earth will? Socrates agrees, simply appealing to other analogies to bolster up the case. But the sense in which the soul has been shown to be undying is that it makes no sense to speak of death in its connection, and that does not entail that it is everlasting. A table cannot be said to die, but that does not make it everlasting. So the argument, perhaps not surprisingly, fails. Elsewhere (*Republic* X and *Phaedrus*) Plato gives other arguments for the indestructibility of the soul which are no more successful. Yet it is something that he clearly could not help believing.

The Republic

I have gone into some detail over these two dialogues because in them the mature Platonic view is set out. I shall go into less detail from here onwards. The *Republic* is in any case a dialogue in which in some ways the general theme is more important than the details. But the middle books (V–VII) contain the epistemological and metaphysical foundations for a theory of education that is supposed to have moral and political importance. They begin at the end of Book V with a distinction between knowledge and belief which has been much discussed. This is followed by three similes – those of the Sun, Line and Cave – which are meant to illustrate a scheme of education for the Guardians of an ideal state which is in turn spelled out in some detail. It is worth noting that the distinction between knowledge and belief seems to reserve knowledge for the Forms, so that we have belief only of sensible things. This means in turn that there is no possibility of turning belief into knowledge as the *Meno* suggested. One must simply replace belief by knowledge, and the scheme of education reflects that fact.

As we shall see that the simile of the Cave illustrates, education is construed as a process of getting progressively new insights, a recognition of a reality that the ordinary man has no knowledge of. The change of mind from the *Meno* comes, I believe, because the metaphysics of the *Phaedo* has infected the epistemology. Plato believes that knowledge is reserved for the Forms because the Form F cannot be other than F; he thinks that in consequence one cannot be mistaken about the Form, and knowledge has the impossibility of error as its precondition. Error is possible in the case of sensible things, so that we cannot have knowledge of them. Both the conception of knowledge as involving impossibility of error, and the belief that the Form's inability to be other than it is makes error in its case impossible, are mistaken; but those mistakes are essential to Plato's conclusion.

The rest of the *Republic* provides the core of his political philosophy, although some of the same ground is covered in a more austere, duller and more pessimistic way in the *Laws*. The *Republic* is ostensibly about justice, and the first book is by itself a fairly typical Socratic dialogue. It is in the main a discussion between Socrates and a Sophist, Thrasymachus, who repudiates conventional conceptions of justice, such as obedience to the laws, on the grounds that laws are made only in the interest of the stronger; it is much better, if one can, to act in one's own interest. The main business of the dialogue begins in the second book when Glaucon and Adeimantus, the main protagonists, demand that Socrates show that justice is a good thing both in itself and for its consequences; and they paint a picture of justice as chosen as a second best only, and such that the reputation of justice counts for more than its reality. By 'in itself' they say that they mean 'in and of itself dwelling in the soul'. Socrates' answer to this part of their request is given in Book IV, where he shows that justice (which turns out to mean something like righteousness or complete virtue) in the soul amounts to harmony of soul, which is obviously better than disharmony. It is not until Book IX that Socrates concerns himself with the effects of justice, now interpreted as the pleasure or pain that it produces.

Socrates' procedure is to invoke an analogy with a situation in which the same thing is written up in small and large letters, so that it is easier to read what is written in the large letters. The analogy is a curious one since Socrates argues that if one wants to get a view of justice in the individual it is better to look at it in the state – the latter being, so to speak, an individual writ large. On this basis he sets out to construct an ideal state. He first describes a minimal but austere state in which everyone performs just one function and there are no luxuries. He then enlarges on this to make it more realistic. Much space is given over to a discussion of the place, if any, of the arts in such a state. In the earlier books Plato seeks to put a severe restriction on the place of such arts, on the grounds that they often turn out to be corrupting in one way or another. In Book X he returns to the issue from a more metaphysical point of view and seeks to exclude the arts altogether, on the grounds that they present a mere copy of a copy of the true reality constituted by the Forms. In the earlier discussion he then goes on to describe the setting-up and education of a class of Guardians to govern the state. He posits that there must be three classes in the state – the Guardians proper; those meant to assist the Guardians, the so-called Auxiliaries, who are responsible for defence; and the Craftsmen, who are all to keep to their own function. Although Plato allows the possibility that there may be movement between the classes, he obviously thinks that this is undesirable, and even contemplates the existence of a 'noble lie' which lays down that the members of the three classes come from distinct gold, silver and iron or brass races.

Despite this, Book V goes into considerable detail about the social institutions which he thinks should exist in order to prevent faction and disorganization of the state. There is to be community of property, women and children, and corporate life in general, with the aim that there shall not be disputes about anything. The state is to be an organic unity, which, he says, will be like a body such that when one member suffers the whole body grieves. Before he gets to this point, however, he completes the parallel between the state and the soul, by arguing from the facts of mental conflict to the thesis that there must be three parts to the soul, parallel to the three classes in the state. Each class in the state has its own virtue – the Guardians wisdom, the Auxiliaries courage, and the Craftsmen prudence. Justice is the virtue of the whole state working together (a conclusion which Plato reaches by process of elimination, given an initial list of four cardinal virtues). Analogously, it is claimed, there is a virtue attached to each part of the soul – wisdom to reason, courage to the spirited part, and prudence to the appetitive part in its relation to the others. Justice in the soul arises when all three parts work together under the guidance of reason. Such single-mindedness is represented as the health of the soul; conflict corresponds to illness. The obvious desirability of health over sickness is taken to be enough to show that justice in the soul is the best state of affairs.

There are problems about how this internal justice of the soul is taken to be related to justice in the more ordinary sense, which is concerned with the activities of one individual in relation to others. Plato has little if anything to say about that. The general implication is that justice in the soul depends on justice in the state, and that depends upon the various aspects of social organization that he specifies. At the end of the discussion of this a certain pessimism is expressed about its possibility, and it is at this point that Plato says that it is only likely to come about if philosophers become kings. That leads him into discussion of the epistemological and metaphysical basis of the education of Guardians, philosophers being distinguished from ordinary men (whom Plato calls 'lovers of sights and sounds') by their acquaintance with the Forms, and thus by their possession of knowledge, as opposed to mere belief. It is important to recognize that the Guardians when educated are supposed to govern the state through that insight in every case. There are to be no laws as such. In later dialogues, the *Statesman* and the *Laws*, the recognition of the place of law returns but only as a second-best.

The simile of the Cave describes in allegorical terms the progressive illumination of people who are originally confined in their experience to shadows only (although they would not recognize that description of the situation). They have to be released from the chains that bind them, and recognize the objects which, through the light of a fire behind them, cast the shadows on the end wall of the cave. They are then to be led up out of the cave into the daylight, to the recognition of objects in the daylight world and finally to an ability to look at the sun itself. That is what education was for Plato – a process of enlightenment. He subsequently describes its nature – years of music and gymnastics, years of mathematics of various forms, and finally in maturity years of dialectic (presumably philosophy, although he says very little about what it consists of – perhaps logical classification and division of things according to the pattern laid down in the later dialogues). Only then, after reaching what Plato calls the Form of the Good, can they be allowed to come down into the Cave, to return to the state to govern it.

After all this, Plato gives an account of the pathology of political institutions – a pathology which he seems to think is bound to be given realization. There will be a deterioration from the ideal state through aristocracy, timocracy, oligarchy, democracy to tyranny. By analogy with these progressively worsening forms of political organization he also describes worsening forms of the organization of the soul, ending up with the tyrannical man, who is not necessarily a tyrant, but one who is totally governed by his passions. This leads Plato into a discussion of the amount of pleasure to be derived from possible lives. There are three arguments for the thesis that the just life is also the most pleasant, one from the diagnosis of the tyrannical man, one from supposed beliefs about the superiority of intellectual and rational pleasures over others, and the third from a thesis about the nature of pleasure itself. This last maintains that bodily pleasures all result from the filling-up of a previous lack and thus have an admixture of pain. Rational pleasures are said to be pure and thus the only real pleasures (although Plato spoils his case by admitting that sensuous pleasures, like those of smell, are pure also). There is a further detailed discussion of pleasure and its place in the good life in the later dialogue, the *Philebus*.

The *Republic* ends, after a further discussion of the arts and another argument for the soul's indestructibility, with another myth, in which rebirth occurs after purification from previous sins. But each soul has to choose its new life, and many choose badly. It is only philosophy that can produce the wisdom necessary to make the right choice. After the choice the souls pass through the river Lethe and forget what has happened; and so a new life begins. We should be warned. The *Republic* is a curious work in many ways, but there is no doubt that it represents Plato's mature thought as well as his most mature skill at dialogue writing. If the *Timaeus* is to be put with it we get a very different work – a work that is in a sense one long myth, a creation story and an account of the physical world. But it is consistent with at least some of the *Republic*. The sensible world is created by a Demiurge or Craftsman as a copy of the world of the Forms, so that there is a Form for everything in this world. But this world falls short; it is subject to constant Heraclitean flux, and rises above chaos only through its possession of a world-soul which gives it the rationality that it has. Here rationality tends to mean regularity and order, and it is the heavenly bodies moving on fixed orbits which provide the best evidence of that. Plato's account of it all, of the cosmology, of the place of mathematics in it, of time and eternity and so on, even of the place of man and other living beings, is fascinating in its detail but too complex to record here.

The later dialogues

From this point onwards, Plato moves into a critical phase, which I shall describe only in a sketchy way. Many of the details are technical and most of the interpretation of it is controversial. The first part of the *Parmenides* portrays a discussion between Socrates as a young man and Parmenides and Zeno. The young Socrates is no doubt the young Plato, and the discussion is a reflection of Plato's looking back on his past self. As one would expect from the characters of the dialogue, there are many Eleatic echoes in the dialogue, and the second part, which is notable in that respect, has proved particularly impervious to interpretation. The first part, however, is clearly a critique of the theory of Forms of the middle dialogues.

The young Socrates is led to expound the theory of Forms in response to a puzzle put by Zeno as to how things can be both like and unlike if they are many. Socrates says that there is no problem about that, since they can share in the relevant Forms. The same applies to their being both one and many – a man can be one man but have many parts. But Socrates says that he would be extremely surprised if Forms could be both one and many, or indeed mixed up and separated from each other. In the *Sophist*, Plato presents a doctrine of the blending of Forms, and it is a fair inference that the young Socrates' claim that he would be surprised about these things is meant to be an indication that the mature Plato thinks otherwise. Similar things hold good of Socrates' response to Parmenides about what there are Forms of. He has no doubt about Forms of one, many, like, beautiful, good and the like; he is doubtful about Forms of man, fire and water (notions which, it may be noted, are non-relative as opposed to the relativeness of the earlier ones); and he thinks it would be absurd to suppose that there are Forms of mud, hair, dirt or anything worthless or foul. Parmenides replies that these restrictions are just a function of Socrates' youth. Once again a fair inference is that the mature Plato thinks that there are no restrictions on the world of Forms.

Parmenides goes on to present Socrates with a dilemma: if things do share in Forms the latter will become split up among the things or reduplicated; if they do not share in Forms there will simply be two unconnected worlds. Either way the theory of Forms will not do the work that it was meant to do. In the course of the argument Parmenides also produces a sub-argument, which has become known, through Aristotle, as the 'third-man argument'. If Socrates, Plato, etc. all share in the Form Man, then since the latter is a man it too will share in a Form, so that there must be another Form Man (a third man, apart from Socrates etc., and the first-order Form). The same again applies to that, so that there is an infinite regress. Discussion of the significance of this argument has been intense in recent times; but it is clear that the argument works only if the Form F is itself F and if anything that is F is so in virtue of a Form different from itself (the so-called self-predication and non-identity assumptions). These two assumptions go with the two roles that Plato has given to Forms up to this point – that of being the standard case and that of being the nature in virtue of which things are what they are. It may be that Plato now saw an incompatibility between these two roles given to Forms, but if so there is no real indication that he dealt with the problem satisfactorily. The second part of the dialogue, which is concerned with complex relations between One, Many and a whole host of other notions, succeeds only in shedding darkness on the subject.

If the *Parmenides* can be viewed as critical of Plato's earlier views on Forms, the *Theaetetus* can be viewed in a similar way with respect to his views on knowledge. In form the dialogue is like the earlier Socratic dialogues, but that is in many ways deceptive. There are also echoes of the *Meno*. The 'hypotheses' about the nature of knowledge that are considered are that it is (1) perception (construed as the simple receipt of sense-impressions, (2) true belief, and (3) true belief together with a *logos*, of which three interpretations are offered. Most of the section concerned with belief is given over to a discussion of the impossibility of false belief if it is held, as it was in the *Meno*, that one either knows something or does not. A good deal of the section concerned with perception is given over to a discussion of Protagorean relativism and Heraclitean flux (a doctrine which Socrates, no doubt quite unhistorically, associates with Protagoras); both these doctrines are refuted. The dialogue ends negatively, however, with no satisfactory account of knowledge being reached. It may well be that Plato was groping his way towards a more sophisticated conception of knowledge than he had presupposed in the earlier dialogues; but if he had reached any conclusion on that, he does not tell us in any direct way what it was.

The *Sophist*, the third of the 'critical' dialogues, involves ostensibly an attempt to define the Sophist by means of the technique of logical division and classification, which is demonstrated in what cannot be an altogether serious way. But its main concern is again with false belief, considered not, as in the *Theaetetus*, in relation to a certain conception of knowledge, but in relation to the intelligibility of believing 'what is not'. As indicated earlier, the possibility of Forms blending with each other is formally introduced, but what blending actually amounts to has been the subject of considerable discussion. We are also told of five 'greatest kinds' – being, sameness, difference, rest and motion – which are 'greatest', it appears, because everything, including these very

Forms, presupposes them. In the end Plato explains false belief, *via* false statement, as saying of 'what is' what is not the case with regard to it. But the main importance of the dialogue lies in the new conception of the world of Forms that is implicit in it. Both the *Statesman* and the *Philebus* add to this the idea that it is order and the proportional relations between Forms that are important. It is a possible view that, whereas in the *Phaedo* Plato had represented mere participation in the Forms as an indication that the world in which we live has some purpose and goodness (a view that is worked out in the *Timaeus*), it is the conformity of the world to the structural relations between Forms that has now come to be seen as the important thing. The movements of the heavenly bodies on fixed orbits in time (the 'moving image of eternity' as the *Timaeus* puts it) were always seen by Plato as evidence of the divine. The world is now seen as a copy of structured eternal relations between Forms. Law, we might say, is the divine order of things.

There are echoes of such a view also in the final book of the *Laws*, where there is laid down the institution in the ideal state of a 'nocturnal council' (so called because they meet only at night) to preserve among other things belief in two truths – the immortality of the soul, and the presence of mind among the heavenly bodies. Plato was always looking for the eternal, by contrast with the changing and relativistic world of the senses. The exact place in which he found it varied, but it was always a function of an eternal, perfect and paradigmatic world of Forms, however that was to be construed. That conception determined his whole conception of philosophy, his ethics, politics and aesthetics, as well as his general metaphysics.

[5]

Aristotle

One cannot treat Aristotle in the way in which I have tried to present Plato. There are arguments in plenty in Aristotle, but they are not generally presented in discursive form. Aristotle did write dialogues, but little of them survives. The vast corpus of philosophical work by Aristotle that we have takes the form of treatises, written in a style the merits of which have been much debated. They may or may not have been lecture notes, but they were in any case much edited in the ancient world, so that what we have now are for the most part compilations of different works, perhaps written at different times. Scholars have attempted to sort out some of the chronological issues associated with their writing, but conclusions on that are inevitably a matter for argument. The works that we have are products of the school – the Lyceum – that Aristotle set up in Athens as a rival to the Academy. It continued in existence along with the Academy for a very long time, though little is known of what went on there for most of its history.

Aristotle was not an Athenian. He was the son of a doctor, and was born in 384 B.C. in Stagira in northern Greece, where his father was court physician to the King of Macedon. When he was about eighteen he came to Athens and he was a member of the Academy for twenty years – a very long time. When Plato died, Aristotle left Athens and spent some time in Asia Minor, where he married. He then went to Lesbos, where evidence from his biological works suggests that he studied zoological phenomena. In 343–2 he was invited by Philip, King of Macedon, to undertake the education of the future Alexander the Great; what that consisted of has always been a matter for speculation. When Philip died and Alexander came to the throne, Aristotle returned to Athens and set up his school, the Lyceum, in a grove of that name, in property that he presumably rented. (He was reputed to be a wealthy man who liked ornament and a certain degree of opulence; but as a foreigner he could not own property in Athens.) On his death the headship of the school passed to his friend and pupil Theophrastus, who was, among other things, the first historian of philosophy; it is probable that, on a change of the Athenian law, he came to own the school. The details of Aristotle's will are preserved for us in Diogenes Laertius' *Lives of the Philosophers*. Aristotle did not die in Athens, for in response to anti-

Macedonian feeling at the death of Alexander, he left Athens, lest, as he is said to have put it, the Athenians sin twice against philosophy. He went to Chalcis in Euboia, where he died in 322 B.C. of a stomach complaint.

Logic

Aristotle is perhaps best known as the founder of formal logic – of, in his case, the theory of the syllogism, although what goes by that name in so-called traditional logic is an elaboration, and often a corruption, of Aristotle's theory by later logicians, particularly the medieval schoolmen. Aristotle investigates what combinations of premises which predicate something of all, none, some, or not all of something else, lead validly to what conclusions, and infers that the arguments in question fall into three figures. In the first figure the premises will in effect be of the form: ' — B is C' and ' — A is B', with the conclusion ' — A is C' (where the gaps can be filled by 'all', 'no', 'some' or 'some — not'). It is clear that one term – the so-called 'middle term' – must be common to both premises. In the second figure the middle term is the predicate in each premise; and in the third figure it is the subject in each. Not all possible combinations of such premises in each figure produce valid syllogisms, and the theory seeks to show which are the valid syllogisms and to give proofs of their validity. The *Prior Analytics* gives a formal exposition of the theory of the categorical syllogism (where the premises and conclusion make categorical assertions) as well as a certain treatment of modal syllogisms (where the premises and conclusion state that something is possibly or necessarily so), of hypothetical syllogisms such as those found in the *reductio ad impossibile* ('if p, then q; but q is impossible; therefore not p'), and some other arguments which do not strictly conform to the pattern of the theory of the syllogism.

Despite what I have said above about hypothetical syllogisms, Aristotle's logic is a logic of *terms*; the arguments are valid or invalid according to the relationships between the terms involved. Later logic, as introduced by the Stoics in particular, was propositional, concerned with relationships between propositions without reference to the terms which they contain. It is a question of some interest, although one which is difficult to answer, why Aristotle approached the matter through terms, and how propositional logic came to be developed later. Not all arguments, after all, are of the pattern of the syllogism as Aristotle expounded it, and it is clear that Aristotle did not think that they were. Aristotle begins the *Prior Analytics* by saying that the subject of his inquiry is demonstration, but not all syllogisms provide demonstration as

Aristotle conceives it. Demonstration involves proceeding validly from premises which hold good universally and necessarily to a conclusion which does the same. If it be added that the premises and conclusion must also be positive, rather than negative, then demonstration is possible only *via* a syllogism in the first figure, as indeed Aristotle proves. That is important for science as Aristotle conceives it and as is set out in the *Posterior Analytics*. These works, together with other 'logical' books, were later called the '*Organon*' (tool, or instrument).

Science

For Aristotle, science proper is an investigation of the forms that nature takes. Natural objects have certain forms and the changes that they may undergo are limited by those forms; not anything can come to be from anything. The word that is here translated 'form' is the same one which Plato used for his Forms, and is the same as the one which is often translated in the Aristotelian context as 'species'. Aristotle would have nothing of Platonic Forms; he argues against them in various places on the grounds of the lack of economy that they presuppose, and on the grounds that they do not achieve what Plato sets out to achieve. Indeed in one place he refers to them as 'mere twitterings'. Plato's theory does not seem to have convinced his pupils and associates in the Academy and some of Aristotle's most forceful criticisms of his theory were formulated while he was still a member of the Academy. Yet there is a sense in which Aristotle's view of things was still embued with Platonism. His theory of species and genera is often presented as if it were simply a theory of classification, so that what count as species and genera are products of human ways of classifying things, and to that extent, so to speak, man-made. That is not Aristotle's view of things at all. For him, as for Plato, nature has form; it contains species. It is indeed species that are the persistent aspects of nature, particular things being to some extent or other transitory.

Preservation of form is the rule, but deviations from the rule are not impossible. This means that the idea of form is still, as with Plato, something of an ideal; but it is one that nature approximates to in itself. Form is not something quite separate from nature; it is Plato's suggestion that it is so separate that Aristotle objects to. It is matter, the stuff of which particular things are made, that is responsible for those deviations from the norm that do occur, although matter also delimits the kinds of form that are possible. Not anything can be composed of anything, just as not anything can come to be from anything. Given all this, the task of the scientist is to discover the form in the variations for which matter is responsible; and to discover that form is to discover what is necessarily so for things of that kind. That is where demonstration becomes pertinent. For if anything that holds good of the genus holds good of one of its species, then if certain properties belong of necessity to the genus they must equally belong as of necessity to the species. The aim of the scientist is therefore to show that things fall into such relationships, and thus why they are as they are. That is what understanding nature comes to.

But it is impossible to think of science as starting off in that way. Hence one must be able to arrive at the principles which serve as the premises for demonstration in some other way than by demonstration. It is, Aristotle says, the mark of the foolish man to think that everything can be proved. The last chapter of the *Posterior Analytics* presents the issue from the point of view of the individual coming to have the knowledge in question. It is a passage in which Aristotle seems to have Plato's doctrine of recollection in mind, and he finds that as absurd as many other things about Plato, even if he recognizes the same problem. To solve it, he presents an account in terms of what in this century has been called 'genetic epistemology' – a theory of how the acquisition of knowledge is possible. It is severely empiricist in its terms of reference. Repetition of sensations produce, if they persist, perception; repetition of these produces experience, and repetition of that knowledge. The account is not satisfactory, since it is not clear that mere repetition would be enough for the purposes in question. But it is against this developmental theory that Aristotle claims that people have the power of seeing the general in the particular by a form of intuition. To use particular cases to point to a general moral which can be so seen is to use induction. Hence it is that many of Aristotle's works in different areas of knowledge start from an appeal to particular cases or even beliefs about such cases. The aim is to get the reader to see the general truths on which the science depends and from which demonstration can proceed.

Aristotle sometimes calls this procedure 'dialectical'. The *Topics*, which is his formal rule-book of dialectic, defines dialectic as involving arguments which start not, as science does, from premises which are universally and necessarily true, but from premises which are true for the most part only, or are held to be true by most people, or by one's opponent. In other words, anything will do as a premise, provided that it is accepted by the parties to a discussion, so that argument can proceed from it. The procedure is indeed very like that which Socrates embraces as a method of hypothesis in the *Phaedo*. Although science proper is concerned ideally with demonstration, it cannot be separated in practice from dialectic. That is why so many of Aristotle's works start with a survey of opinions held by others. History of philosophy with respect to any particular set of issues is engaged in not for its own sake, but because it forms the basis from which dialectic can proceed. It is not a bad conception of the history of philosophy, pragmatic though it is.

It is commonly said that Aristotle's model of science was biology, and it is sometimes claimed that over many issues he generalized from what holds good in biology. This is an exaggeration, although it is true that the biological works constitute a very considerable part of the Aristotelian corpus. His knowledge of biological phenomena was formidable, even if he was often mistaken on points of detail, and even on points of observation. But his conception of what goes on in the field of biology is at one with his conception of nature in general. The study of nature is the study of change in natural bodies and of the concepts that are involved in our understanding of such change – concepts such as those of place, time, the void and the infinite. The work called the *Physics* is a compilation of discussions of such things, and ends with a majestic, though invalid, argument for the existence of a prime mover – something that is responsible for the movement of other things without being moved itself. Aristotle thinks that such a prime mover is called for if change or motion is to exist at all, and the argument for the prime mover's existence has much in common with what was later called the cosmological argument for the existence of God – we need to postulate the existence of God if we are to make any sense of the features that we observe in the world. The prime mover is indeed Aristotle's God and is called that elsewhere in his works.

Aristotle says that change is the actualization of the potential *qua* potential. That formula has often been criticized as empty, but there is more to it than appears at first sight. Aristotle represents his distinction between potentiality and actuality as of crucial importance for understanding the possibility of change. Plato had put forward in the *Sophist* the notion of the *power* of affecting or being affected. Aristotle uses the same word (*dunamis*), but tends to mean by it not power, but possibility or potentiality. Natural bodies have their respective natural potentialities – fire to go upwards, earth to go downwards (for Aristotle had no conception of gravity). If there is a reason why those potentialities should be realized in general, then the natural bodies will move in the relevant directions unless they are prevented by something else from doing so.

This means that, given adequate causality, things will move or change in conformity with their potentiality, which is inbuilt through the matter of which they are composed. They cannot move or change of themselves in any direction whatever. The form of change that they undergo is the actualization of what they have the potentiality to do. Nature, one might say, is organized along certain causal lines determined by the potentialities that go with various kinds of matter. But, it must be emphasized once again, the actualization of any potentiality depends on there being a cause of that actualization; and such a cause must be actual. Thus, as Aristotle frequently says, although potentiality may be prior to actuality in the individual, actuality must be prior to potentiality in nature at large. The same is true of the relationship between form and matter. It is arguable whether Aristotle believed in matter without form, so-called prime matter, but every particular thing is a combination of form with matter, and comes about *via* the imposition of form on matter, which may already have some form, but does not have that particular form. Hence once again form is prior to matter in nature at large in the sense that form needs to be presupposed to explain how things are. Aristotle's God, the prime mover, the ultimate explanation of things, turns out, not perhaps surprisingly, to be pure form, without matter and without potentiality. His activity is pure thought.

In the foregoing I have made reference to causality. What is generally known as Aristotle's doctrine of four causes has come in for much critical comment, particularly with reference to what is usually called 'final causality' – teleology. But the four causes are really four kinds of reason why, four kinds of answer to the question 'For what reason?'. Indeed Aristotle's exposition of the matter in *Physics* II.3 is clearly dialectical in character. He simply sets out the different sorts of thing that are taken to provide explanations, and ends 'This then perhaps exhausts the number of things which are called "cause".' As with many other Aristotelian distinctions, however, although this distinction is initially made in a tentative way, it eventually becomes hardened into firm doctrine.

The four 'causes' are: (1) 'that out of which a thing comes to be and which persists' (the so-called material cause – the matter of which something is composed); (2) 'the form or pattern, the definition of the essence' (the so-called formal cause); (3) 'the primary source of the change or coming to rest' (the so-called efficient cause); (4) the end or that for the sake of which (the so-called final cause). It should be clear on reflection that references to the matter of which a thing is composed, its form, what makes it as it is, and that for the sake of which whatever happens to it does so, can all on suitable occasions provide an answer to the question 'Why?'. There is nothing more than that to the doctrine of the four causes, except that Aristotle comes to separate the material cause from the other three because he generally opposes form to matter. There is, however, a certain ambiguity about the 'final cause'. The examples that he gives on introducing the notion suggest that by 'end' he means purpose, that is, the purpose that someone may have in mind in doing something; when Aristotle considers the place of teleology in nature, however, and says that nature does nothing in vain or without reason, he does not mean to ascribe such purposes to all natural objects. In these cases the end is that to which they tend; it is their function. The heavenly bodies, on the other hand, are moved by the prime mover because it inspires them with love and desire; they have it as their goal or purpose (for something that has no matter could not be their cause in any other way). But this is the big exception to the rule over teleology in nature, apart from human intentions and purposes. Elsewhere reference to teleology is a reference to the function that things may have or to the end-states to which they tend, and this is particularly pertinent in biology.

Metaphysics and ontology

So much for the special sciences, the sciences of particular kinds of phenomena – though what I have said provides only a small taste of what is there. Towards the beginning of his *Metaphysics* (a title given to a collection of Aristotelian works in the ancient library at Alexandria – it means 'the works that come after the Physics'), Aristotle lists, as one of the problems to be dealt with, whether there can be a general science of being-*qua*-being as well as particular sciences concerned with this and that. Can there be a science simply of what is, a general ontology? A view that has had some currency in recent times[1] is that initially Aristotle thought that the answer to that question was 'No', but that he eventually came to think that it was possible to answer the question with a qualified 'Yes'. It was a 'Yes' that made the science of being-*qua*-being identical with theology, despite the fact that theology seems at first sight to be concerned with one kind, even if a supremely important kind, of being. (There is a reference to this point at the end of the first section of Book VI of the *Metaphysics*.)

This became possible through a development in Aristotle's theory of meaning, which has been called the doctrine of 'focal meaning'. Aristotle is clearly impressed by the fact that different things are often referred to by the same word; the doctrine of the four causes is a case in point. Sometimes the definition corresponding to the use of the word is the same in each case, and then we have synonymy; sometimes it is not, and then we have homonymy only. In the latter case there is in effect a

---

[1] Particularly through the work of G. E. L. Owen, in many papers but especially in 'Logic and Metaphysics in Some Early Works of Aristotle', to be read most conveniently in *Articles on Aristotle*, eds. J. Barnes, M. Schofield and R. Sorabji, Vol. 3 (London: Duckworth, 1979).

difference of sense. The doctrine of focal meaning is the doctrine that in some cases of homonymy there is an explanation for the same use of the word, although with different senses, in terms of the focal role performed by one thing or one use in particular. Thus different things, for example climates, people, symptoms, are called 'healthy', although not in the same sense, because they are related to health in differing ways. Health thus provides the focus for the use of 'healthy'. Whatever may be the case of Aristotle, because of local peculiarities of the Greek language, we should not call health 'healthy'. But in the case of another Aristotelian example, 'medical' – where things are called medical because of a relation that they have to the doctor, the medical man – the focal thing, the doctor, is also called by the same name as the things related to it. Thus the use of 'medical' with respect to the doctor provides the focal meaning from which the others are derivative.

Aristotle applied this doctrine to the notion of 'being' in two stages. In the first stage the various things that are said to be are all related to what is called substance, this being the primary kind of thing. Hence Aristotle can say at the end of the first section of Book VII of the *Metaphysics* that the question which was asked of old and is continually raised even now, and is always the subject of doubt, 'What is that which is?', is really the question 'What is substance?'. For while there are various kinds of things that exist, they are all subsidiary to substance. In the second stage, exemplified in the rest of *Metaphysics* VII, Aristotle applies the same treatment to the notion of substance. Various things are called 'substance', and for various reasons, but they must all be related to something that is substance in the primary way. Aristotle seems to suggest that the conditions for being substance in this primary way are satisfied only by God. That is why the study of God (and, Aristotle thinks, of that which approximates to the divine in us, that is, reason) is the study of substance *par excellence*, and the study of substance is the study of 'what is' *par excellence*; so that theology becomes in a certain sense equivalent to the study of being-*qua*-being.

The beginning of this extended treatment of ontology is to be found in the *Categories*, a work which Aristotle may have written while still a member of the Academy and before the theory of focal meaning had been elaborated. It is again a dialectical work, in that it appeals to our intuitions at crucial points. Aristotle starts from a point of view that he shared with Plato, that words mean things (a so-called realist theory of meaning). Words form propositions through combination of names and verbs, as Plato pointed out, and as is repeated by Aristotle in the *De Interpretatione* (which is a companion piece to the *Categories*). If we take the notion of a subject of discourse – that about which we are talking when we say things – Aristotle notes that there are two sorts of relation that things predicated of that subject can have to it: they can be said of it, or they can inhere in it. The latter, Aristotle defines in such a way that to be in a subject a thing must be in it though not as a part, and must depend on it for its existence. (This formal condition has caused some trouble for commentators, but the difficulties can be overcome if strict attention is given to the terms of reference of the discussion.) It is not made clear why these two relations are fastened upon; we have to take it that they are the ones that Aristotle sees as pertinent to the notion of predication, as indeed they may be. He then goes on to indicate that things so predicated of a subject may be said of it but not in it, in it but not said of it, both said of it and in it, or neither, according to the case and the subject in question. It is clear that things which are neither said of nor in a subject are the prime candidates for being subjects themselves, although Aristotle does not draw that conclusion explicitly. They are particular things, particular substances, as he comes to call them, such as a particular man or horse.

Given these, Aristotle goes on to consider what questions can be asked about them (or so it appears from the terms of reference that he uses): 'What is it?', 'How big is it?', 'What sort of thing is it?', 'Where is it?' and so on. The answers to these questions, such as 'A man', 'Six feet tall', 'White', specify substance, quantity, quality, place and so on. These, Aristotle calls categories. The word 'category' literally means 'predicate', and that fact has worried some commentators, especially in the case of substance, since a substance has predicates asserted of it and is not itself a predicate. But a treatment of the subject in *Topics* I.9 makes clear why the term 'category' is used. There Aristotle supposes that we may take a particular thing and ask what it essentially is. The widest answer, the widest predicate that applies essentially to the thing in this way gives its category: substance, quantity, quality and so on. Thus if you take a man and apply this method you get the answer 'substance'; if you take a magnitude of a cubit, you eventually get the answer 'quantity'; and if you take a white colour, you get the answer 'quality'. As a method for arriving at the list of categories it is sadly defective, because it is clear that you have to know what sorts of things there are, what categories of things, in order to know what thing you may start from. But if it is put together with the treatment in the *Categories* one gets some sense of the doctrine.

Aristotle lists ten categories, although in some places he mentions only eight, and the work called the *Categories* sets out to provide an extensive discussion of each of them in turn, trying to distinguish them and point to their peculiarities, beginning with substance. Since they are categories of beings, and, as Aristotle says clearly elsewhere, being does not constitute a genus with species distinguished from each other by defining characteristics or differentia, it is not possible to produce differentia for each of the categories, properly speaking. The text is in any case defective, so that we have a full treatment of only four of the categories. But it follows in the nature of the case that no demonstration of the doctrine is possible. Aristotle simply appeals to our intuitions, *via* considerations that he brings forward, and we are invited to agree that there are these ten sorts of question to ask about a particular substance, with these answers, and so on. If we are persuaded by him, we shall have accepted that the nature of our thought about the world implies that the primary subjects of our thought are particular substances, and that although there are also other kinds of things – colours, shapes, places, etc. – they are dependent on particular substances. Indeed, Aristotle asserts plainly that if there were no particular substances, none of the other kinds of thing would exist.

Some part of the motivation of the doctrine may be a desire to combat Plato, whose theory of Forms Aristotle thought ontologically extravagant. Indeed, one of the arguments that Aristotle uses against Plato in *Metaphysics* I.9 (where incidentally he speaks as a member of the Academy) is to the effect that there ought to be Forms of substances only (and not Forms of, say, beauty and goodness), because the Forms are substances and there ought to be an essential relation between the Forms and the things that participate in them. Aristotle's accusation against Plato, therefore, is that he overpopulated the world with substances, and that some of the things that Plato took to be substances are really qualities or things in one of the other secondary categories. To feel affected by this argument, Plato would have to accept Aristotle's terms of reference, that is to say the doctrine of the categories itself, but that is no objection to thinking that Aristotle's argument has some force.

There is no reference to 'focal meaning' in the *Categories*. The invocation of that doctrine in later works, for instance *Metaphysics* IV.2, and above all VII.1, gives additional credence to the theory of categories. According to that doctrine of meaning, qualities etc. are said to be, because they are dependent on substance. Substance (and the Greek word *ousia* has an etymological connection with the verb 'to be' that the translation 'substance' does not) is called 'what is' in the primary way, and the things in the other categories are so called only because they are *of* substance. This completes the first stage of the general argument.

The second stage starts from the recognition that although by the previous argument the question 'What exists?' gets its primary answer by reference to particular substances, there are differing uses of 'substance' also. Indeed, in *Metaphysics* VII.2 Aristotle typically surveys the various things that people are likely to call 'substance' and from this survey abstracts four main candidates to the title – essences, universals, genera and subjects. It is impossible to go into the complexities of the subsequent discussion, which has in any case defeated whole hosts of scholars who have tried to plot its course. That substances may be identified with the ultimate subjects of our discourse – they are the things that are there to be talked about – is evident from the treatment of the *Categories*. *Metaphysics* VII.3 raises certain difficulties about the notion of a subject by asking how it is to be explained in terms of matter and form. It is far from clear why these notions have to be introduced in this context. Instead of working his way through these difficulties, however, Aristotle turns to the next candidate for the title of substance – essence – raising various questions about the relation of a substance to its essence.

The outcome of this is the claim that only something that is identical with its essence – something the nature of which is exhausted by what it is essentially and so is, as Spinoza was to put it much later, *causa sui*, its own rationale – deserves the title of substance in the full sense. No compound of matter and form satisfies that condition. It is, Aristotle says, logically like a snub nose, where snubness is a property that belongs only to noses and is dependent for its existence and nature on noses; analogously in a compound of matter and form, the form is dependent on the matter and the compound is not simply what the form amounts to essentially. So the argument points towards an identification of substance with form. As we saw earlier, there is reason for saying that, according to Aristotle, reality is primarily exemplified by species or form, species rather than individuals being the really persistent things.

In the subsequent discussion, Aristotle eliminates genera and universals as having a genuine title to substancehood, simply because they are general, and eventually returns to the notion of form *via* a consideration of the question 'What makes a thing what it is?' It is substance that makes a thing what it is, and this is its form. It has sometimes been said that here Aristotle plays on an ambiguity in the notion of substance – the substance of a thing *vis-à-vis* its being a substance. Whether or not that is so, the tenor of the argument has been towards the conclusion that substance, properly speaking, must be particular and identical with its essence. Only God satisfies that criterion, in Aristotle's view. He is pure form, without matter or potentiality, and so his nature is entirely exhausted by what is essential to him; he is also particular. Aristotle does not explicitly point this out in *Metaphysics* VII, but God is described in this way in *Metaphysics* XII, and, as we have already noted, *Metaphysics* VI.1 points to the equivalence of theology and the science of being-

qua-being, of which this has all been a part. At all events we now have Aristotle's final picture of reality. We have an ontology of many different kinds of thing, hierarchically organized in relations of dependence, with God as the being on which all other beings are ultimately dependent, and in whom we are to see what 'being' really and finally amounts to.

I mentioned earlier Aristotle's belief that there is something of the divine in us to the extent that we have reason. He never says, however, that our nature is exhausted by reason. Although in his ethics he presents reason and philosophical contemplation as an ideal to which we should look, he is realist enough to recognize that practical goals demand reference to other aspects of ourselves – our desires, for example. There is the same realism in his ontology; Aristotle never says that there is really only one thing. Nor does he say that there is just one kind of thing. Not even Plato had said that there were really only Forms; there was a sensible world even if it was a mere copy, and a defective one at that, of the ideal world. In the end Aristotle's conception of the relation of the world to God is not dissimilar to Plato's conception of the relation of the world to the Forms. Nor is that surprising, considering the long period that Aristotle spent in the Academy. Aristotle does not disagree with Plato through and through. He simply says, as indeed others too seem to have said, 'Yes, but there are no Forms.'

The soul

Aristotle's conception of the soul, on the other hand, is very different from that of Plato. Plato was no doubt influenced in his conception by the Pythagoreans, and one of the criticisms that Aristotle has to make of the Pythagoreans in this respect is that they offered no explanation of how the soul is related to the body, or how it could manifest itself in different bodies. Aristotle's treatment of the soul in the *De Anima* is typical in that it starts from a consideration of the various beliefs about the soul. The general tenor of the work is, however, very biological. Aristotle takes as fundamental the belief common to the Greeks that the soul is the principle of life. Hence inquiry into the soul is *ipso facto* an inquiry into the different forms of life. Aristotle recognizes the inclination to think of the soul as a substance, but claims that it is substance only in the sense of form. Indeed he defines the soul as the form of a living body equipped with organs; it is form *qua* a capacity to manifest the various activities that life consists in. The basic form of life is to be found in plants, which simply nourish themselves, grow, decay and reproduce; hence the basic form of soul consists in the capacity to do these things, and all forms of life manifest it. With animals there is in addition the capacity for sense-perception and in the case of most, but not all (not limpets, Aristotle thinks), the capacity for movement. In human beings there is all that *plus* the capacity for thought and reason. Hence living things form a hierarchy with man at the top, and it is this hierarchical arrangement which makes it so difficult to give a single illuminating definition of the soul.

This conception of the soul makes any thought of personal survival after death impossible, and on the whole Aristotle is consistent in that. The general approach to the principles that govern life is that because of the organization of living bodies, they have capacities associated with certain organs. These will be realized if there is something that can act as the cause of that realization or actualization. In the basic forms of life which are present in plants it is clear how that works; food, for example, is the cause of the actualization of the capacity for nourishment and thereby growth. In the case of animals and men there have to be objects which actualize the capacities of sense-organs for forms of sense-perception. In perception, Aristotle says, the object is initially different from the sense-organ but becomes like it in the process of perception; or, to put it in terms of an alternative formula that he uses, in sense-perception the sense-organ receives the form of the object without its matter. Aristotle goes into considerable detail about how this works in the case of the different senses, even postulating the existence of a common sense, distinct from the five special senses, to deal with properties of things, such as shape and size, which are perceptible through more than one sense-organ.

Certain objects of perception are essential to a given sense, as colour is to sight, because they are definable in its terms, or *vice versa*, or possibly both ways. But we do, of course, perceive other things, such as people and physical objects, which do not stand in this sort of relation to any special sense, let alone the common sense which I mentioned just now. These, then, constitute incidental objects of perception, just as do those objects of one sense which, Aristotle rightly believes, we can perceive *via* another sense. Thus we can see the bitterness of bile, and the fact that we come to do this as the result of experience, and associate the colour and the taste, does not make it any the less true that we can see bile's bitterness. All these objects are incidental only in the sense that there is no necessary relation between the sense and the objects; Aristotle is not saying that our perception of them is indirect, although he does think that perception of different kinds of object is subject to varying possibilities of error.

Between perception and reason lies imagination, which Aristotle sees as dependent on perception but as involving thought also. Indeed the section of the *De Anima* given over to imagination is concerned with appearances in general, including illusion, not just imagining in the more restricted sense. The treatment of reason or intellect is in many ways parallel to that of sense-perception. That is to say that Aristotle seeks to lay out the relation between this capacity and the relevant objects. Here, however, there are complications, because Aristotle thinks that there are no restrictions on what can be an object of thought. If literally anything can be an object of the intellect, then if the formulae applicable to sense-perception are to be applicable here as well, the capacity cannot be realized in anything at all. Otherwise it would be impossible to think something of that kind, since the bearer of the capacity must be unlike the object before the thought. It follows that there can be no organ for the intellect, and that the intellect is literally 'nothing actual before it thinks'. This is a very awkward view, but it is important to be clear about its basis. Since intellect occurs only in beings that also have sense-perception, intellect is in that sense dependent on sense-perception. Some interpreters of Aristotle want to make it even more dependent, but the thesis that there is no organ for the intellect is derived not from any physiological theorizing, but from the thesis about the unrestricted nature of its capacity.

There is, however, a problem of how in that case the capacity is ever actualized, since there can be no causal principles that explain that actualization. Hence in *De Anima* III.5, in a much disputed, and certainly textually corrupt, passage, Aristotle posits the existence in the soul of a so-called 'active reason'. This always thinks, and is responsible for the actualization of the capacity, the so-called 'passive reason', that we have been concerned with up to now. Because of its nature, the active reason must of necessity have a certain independence from the body, and it survives when the body decays. Some have seen here a return to the idea of personal survival. But that is not what Aristotle intends. The relation of this active reason to us is somewhat like the relation of Aristotle's God to the world. Neither seems personal in any sense that we can understand; they are similar in that they both involve thought, but their main role is in each case to provide a metaphysical underpinning for what they explain. Nevertheless, the existence of such things in human beings distinguishes human beings from the rest of nature, even if they are connected with the rest of nature through the body.

The Ethics and Politics

That same ambivalence affects Aristotle's ethics, as I have already noted, but here there are other complications, because Aristotle insists that men are political animals; to that extent ethics is part of politics

Aristotle's official position with regard to these subjects is that they are practical, not theoretical, sciences, just as the *Poetics* and *Rhetoric* are concerned with productive sciences. A practical science is not a theoretical science about practice, but the art of practice, just as a productive science is not a theoretical science about the production of works of art or speeches, but the art of producing these things. Nevertheless, if we are to acquire the art of producing things of this kind we need to have knowledge of certain background things. Hence the *Rhetoric* contains a considerable amount about various emotions (something almost completely lacking in the *De Anima*), since rhetoric is very much concerned with playing on emotion. Similarly the *Poetics* contains some diagnosis of the role and form of tragedies and comedies, including Aristotle's well-known account of the role of tragedy as producing *catharsis* of pity and fear. But the general aim is still in a wide sense practical.

The same is true in theory of the *Nicomachean Ethics* (which has generally been considered Aristotle's main work on ethics, although some have put in bids for the *Eudemian Ethics*). Aristotle begins with the observation that every action is thought to aim at some good, and goes on to consider whether there is some good which is desired for its own sake and not for any further good. He surveys various opinions on that and concludes that there is general agreement on the end of life, even if people differ on what it consists in. It is *eudaimonia*, generally translated 'happiness', which is a fair translation as long as it is realized that the happiness that Aristotle has in mind is one that attaches to a complete life. *Eudaimonia* literally means 'to have a good daimon, a good guardian spirit'; it is to be well endowed, to be, one might say, blessed, and Aristotle realistically notes that this entails being equipped with at least a modicum of material goods. After some critical consideration of other opinions on this, including that of Plato, Aristotle seeks to elucidate the notion *via* a consideration of the function of man. *Eudaimonia* is associated with the proper fulfilment of that function – with, one might say, human flourishing. This appeal to the notion of the function of man has been much criticized by those who wish to reserve the notion of function either for man-made objects which are designed with a function or for parts of teleological systems, such as the heart in the vascular system of the body. It is not clear whether speaking of a human function is thereby ruled out, and the notion is in any case not original to Aristotle. Plato uses it in connection with justice in the *Republic*.

Aristotle comes to define the good for man – the *eudaimonia* that men aim at – as the activity of soul in accordance with excellence (the best form of life, we might say). The word here translated 'excellence' is *aretē*, the quality that Socrates was so much concerned with. If we translate it 'virtue', we run the risk, as with Socrates, of begging the question. Do we mean by 'moral virtue' the sort of excellence that Aristotle was talking about? Did he himself mean by 'excellence' moral virtue? The difficulty in answering these questions arises from a lack of certainty about what morality actually amounts to. On certain conceptions of morality there is little about morality in what Aristotle has to say. He is simply clear that there is such a thing as the good life in some sense of those words and that a man is thought *eudaimōn*, happy, to the extent that he attains it. If we ask to what we are to look for the standard of goodness, he is clear that nothing of the kind that Plato has to offer will do. Indeed in an early work, the *Protrepticus*, written as a kind of manifesto for the Academy, but surviving only in fragments, he asks forthrightly what standard of this kind we have except that provided by the practically wise man. For the attainment of the good life we need the right character, something which Aristotle believes is produced by training; but we also need practical wisdom, which is generally attainable through teaching.

Hence, when, after a certain amount of moral psychology and consideration of deliberation and choice, he comes to practical considerations about the good life, he defines virtue as a mean between extremes as regards passions and actions. It is a mean which is relative, however, and is to be determined only by a man of practical wisdom. The doctrine of the mean has attracted considerable critical comment. Aristotle arrives at it by analogy with what obtains in various arts, seeing the avoidance of extremes as characteristic of success there. But lying behind such considerations is no doubt the traditional Greek way of thinking about opposites, and the emphasis on measure and proportion that we have seen both among some Presocratics and in Plato. Whatever we think of it – and Aristotle goes into considerable detail in relation to various commonly accepted virtues – the attainment of the mean, it is important to note, presupposes both the right state of character acquired through training and the intellectual virtue of practical wisdom that only teaching can provide. Such teaching will not, and cannot, take the form of demonstration, as may be possible in some theoretical sciences. We have to appeal to examples and to the moral intuitions that people may have, but will not have if they do not have the right character and experience of life. Hence, Aristotle says, ethics is not a subject for young people; they have insufficient experience of life. That claim brings out how practical Aristotle's concerns are.

He works his way through the various virtues more or less systematically and devotes a book to justice, which does not altogether fit into the framework of the other virtues. In this context Aristotle observes that in one sense 'justice' is equivalent to 'the whole of virtue'. That is perhaps the sense with which Plato was concerned. But Aristotle recognizes that there is another sense of justice in which we are concerned with fairness. The *Nicomachean Ethics* contains much else. There is a chapter on intellectual virtues, the importance of which for present purposes lies in its delineation of practical intellect or wisdom. There is a treatment of *akrasia* or incontinence, the falling short from what we know to be required of us. In this Aristotle starts by expressing puzzlement about Socrates' claim that there is really no such thing, but ends with a resolution of the problem that is remarkably Socratic.

There are two discussions of pleasure and its place in the moral life, in which Aristotle's conception of pleasure as an activity bears considerable analogy to his conception of *eudaimonia*. Just as *eudaimonia* is a feature of a whole lifetime, so pleasure is not just a transitory state but a feature of a whole course of action or activity. There is a protracted discussion of friendship and of the place that it has in the good life. Finally Aristotle returns to the good for man, and somewhat to our surprise we find him urging the claim of philosophical contemplation to this title. This is because of his view that what is specific to man is intellect, and that what human excellence must in the end consist in is the virtue of intellect. In the pursuit of that we are closest to the divine. The good for man that we have been concerned with previously is a good that presupposes desire, and the various states that only the body makes possible. Aristotle recognizes all that, but in the end feels the pull towards what he thinks to be the most divine-like activity in us – reason, and its highest manifestation in philosophy.

All that seems miles away from man as a political animal, and so it is, despite the fact that in the closing pages of the *Nicomachean Ethics* Aristotle gestures in that direction and refers forward to the *Politics*. But that work (if single work it is) is severely practical. There is some analysis of various forms of political institution, including, to many people's disappointment, the institution of slavery. There is analysis of various forms of constitution and a discussion, following Plato's, of what an ideal state would be. But much of the discussion is concerned with practical issues of government, including a somewhat Machiavellian treatment of revolutions and their avoidance and suppression. In general the *Politics* is perhaps much more obviously a work in practical science than the *Nicomachean Ethics* is.

The Aristotelian system

In general, Aristotle's philosophy provides a marvellously compendious view of reality, the physical world and human beings. There is little that Aristotle did not consider, and there is much that I have not had space even to mention. Whether or not it is right to speak of an Aristotelian system, as it came to be thought of, he was immensely catholic in his interests and encyclopaedic in his discussions. The detail in Raphael's *The School of Athens*, with Plato pointing up to heaven and Aristotle pointing down to earth, is a caricature of the difference between the two philosophers. They have much in common. Aristotle rejects the Forms utterly; so did, for example, Speusippus, Plato's nephew, who became the second head of the Academy and who rejected other things about Plato, by all accounts in a much more radical way. But if Aristotle in his early life wrote dialogues like Plato, Plato could never have written the mature works of Aristotle. If they were nothing else they were treatises, and Plato did not believe in such things. Aristotle clearly did, and what he wrote is a never-ending source of interest and fascination – and often, despite how things have changed since his time, of illumination.

[6]

The Post-Aristotelian Schools

I have already indicated that both Plato and Aristotle set up schools. These persisted in various forms, perhaps with gaps in their continuity, over centuries, although in the case of the Lyceum we know very little of it after Strato, the successor of Theophrastus, who appears to have introduced a form of atomism. Even before the death of Aristotle, there were other groups of philosophers, who may or may not have constituted formal schools. There were the Cyrenaics under Aristippus, who advocated the pursuit of pleasure as the end of life; and the Cynics under perhaps Antisthenes but certainly Diogenes, who advocated its avoidance. Both thought of themselves as Socratics. There were philosophers who called themselves Megarians, who stemmed from Eucleides of Megara, a contemporary of Socrates; these were an offshoot of the Parmenidean school, and identified the One with the Good. Under Diodorus Cronus and his pupil Philo there were considerable developments in logic, both the logic of propositions and modal logic. They had particular concern with the analysis of hypothetical propositions and the nature of necessity, some of it providing parallels to modern discussions of these issues. How they came to be concerned with these issues is debatable, but they had considerable influence on the Stoics, under whom propositional logic flowered in no uncertain way.

The Stoic school was founded by Zeno of Citium around 300 B.C. in the painted portico or *stoa* in Athens, which gave the school its name. At more or less the same time Epicurus set up his own school in a garden in Athens, and the Epicurean school became known as the Garden. There were now four rival schools in Athens. In addition to these, mention must be made of Pyrrho, who later became thought of as the originator of the Sceptic school, although this was probably not formally founded until the first century B.C. under Aenesidemus. By that time it was therefore possible to think in terms of five philosophical schools, each with its own organization and doctrines. By then, however, the Academy, having gone through a number of sceptical incarnations, had been brought by Antiochus much closer to the Stoa, so that contemporaries held that there was no difference between them. The history of this period is probably one of continual debate, and of argument and counter-argument between rival philosophers, although, as I have already said, we know little of the Lyceum, and the Epicureans kept to themselves to a large extent.

It is often said that the period represents a falling-off from the heights occupied by Plato and Aristotle. It has even been said that in it the conception of philosophy changed, so that philosophers were more concerned with the attainment of salvation in a changing and upsetting world. I doubt if that is true, although the Stoics and Epicureans in particular were very much concerned with the goal for man. It is hard to judge the quality of the philosophy taken as a whole. We do not have anything like the same quantity of surviving texts on which to base a judgement (although some have thought that a very good thing!). Recently a number of scholars have tried to resuscitate interest in the philosophy of the period, and to restore its reputation. It has been said by David Sedley[1] that 'philosophy itself became a specialist subject, unprecedentedly inward looking', so that developments in science, for example, were left to others. To the extent that this is true, the period has some analogy with the history of recent philosophy over the last forty years, where there are no philosophical giants but useful debates between philosophers of rival persuasions. I say 'useful' because it is unwise to depreciate the importance of such debates. Certainly the flowering of scepticism and the responses to it in the Hellenistic period gave rise to epistemology in more or less the modern sense, with its attempt to meet scepticism and to establish foundations for knowledge in what the Stoics called the 'criterion of truth'. It also gave rise, as we have already seen, to considerable advances in logic, and there were also important considerations of issues in naturalistic ethics.

Epicurus

The Epicurean school was the least philosophically interesting one, if debate is considered the important thing. Epicurus was influenced very much by Democritus, and his main theory of the physical world was a strictly atomist one which differed from the views of Democritus only in detail. The school had a reputation for self-involvement and perhaps even secrecy, there being little concern with the affairs of the world generally, but a great deal of concern for the relationships among the philosophers who made up the school. The atomist view – the thesis that everything in the world is made up of indivisible atoms which form larger and larger compounds in the infinite void – was presented not only as

[1] In 'The Protagonists' in *Doubt and Dogmatism*, eds. M. Schofield, M. Burnyeat and J. Barnes (Oxford: Clarendon Press, 1980), a very useful sketch of the history of the Hellenistic period.

giving a correct account of the nature of the world, but also as offering a message for human beings. Epicurus thought that the atoms fall downwards through the void, and that compounds are set up through collisions due to minute swerves from their course by individual atoms. Lucretius, the Roman poet who wrote his *De rerum natura* in poetry about 55 B.C. as an exposition of the Epicurean philosophy, uses the swerve as an explanation of free will too, when the swerve takes place among the atoms of which the soul is made up. It is likely that Epicurus thought similarly; free will is a product of randomness, a solution to the problem of free will in a determinist world which a little consideration ought to reveal as hopeless.

The main message for mankind, however, is summed up in the 'quadrupal remedy' offered by the later Philodemus, a contemporary of Lucretius: The gods have no concern with us, death is nothing to us, pleasure is easy to obtain, and pain does not last long. The gods have no concern with us, in Epicurus' view, because, like everything else, they are composed of atoms, but they live in parts of the void which are empty of atoms, and so are not buffeted by them; they thus have a sort of conditional immortality at the price of being quite apart from human beings. They may be objects of wonder but they cannot interfere with us. Death is nothing to us (Epicurus' own words), because death is simply the dissolution of the atoms of which we (both body and soul) are composed; so there is no after-life to be a cause of concern. Not everyone has found such a view of death consoling (although Schopenhauer, and through him Wittgenstein, embraced it).

Pleasure arises, as indeed pain does too, from the action of atoms on those of the body and soul. Pleasure is thus a natural fact of life, but that pain does not last long in comparison with pleasure[1] can be taken only as an empirical observation, and perhaps a dubious one. Those desires the satisfaction of which leads to pleasures which are simply the removal of pain are both natural and necessary; but there are also pleasures which are natural but not necessary, and pleasures which are neither. It is the pursuit of the first which should be our primary aim. Because pleasure is at bottom a natural phenomenon, even if some pleasures can be classified by some standard as unnatural (and, one supposes, in a different sense of 'natural'), it is in our power to attain the limit of pleasure. All this is meant to show that the good life is realizable and, Epicurus thinks, should be our goal. Morality may be a necessary condition of attaining maximum pleasure, but morality would be nothing if it did not produce pleasure. The final goal of wisdom is *ataraxia* (freedom from anxiety), and there is therefore a sense in which

[1] Cf. Maxim 4, given in Diogenes Laertius: *Lives of the Philosophers*, X.140.

a wise man may be judged happy even when on the rack. The actual life practised by Epicurus, and the one that he thought best, was a relatively private one, based on friendship; morality matters for this simply because it is only thereby that *ataraxia* can be attained. His own death was by all accounts an extremely dignified one, despite intense pain.

Epicurus' epistemology is consistent with the above. Just as in the field of ethics he tries to base everything on what is natural to human beings, especially given his view of what they must consist of, so his account of knowledge (his so-called *kanonikē* – the theory of the canons of judgement) depends entirely on the same account of what is natural. He is said to have stated that all perceptions are true, and there has been some discussion as to what exactly he meant. He must at least have meant that, as he says elsewhere, there is no other source of knowledge or check upon judgement apart from sense-perception. This is produced simply by the action of atoms on those of the sense-organs and the soul. It is true that in perception we also rely on what he calls 'preconceptions', concepts derived from sensations and stored in the mind, but these are not a source of knowledge about the world independent of perception. There is no other source of such knowledge apart from the contact with the atoms in the world that the senses make possible. Epicurus' theory of knowledge is thus completely empiricist, knowledge being dependent at every point on natural and causal processes affecting the sense-organs. When it was necessary to go beyond what the senses tell us, however, Epicurus had apparently no theory as to how we should arrive at the truth. His accounts of celestial phenomena offer a variety of possible explanations of them in a way that suggests that all that he was concerned with was their consistency with sense-perception and nothing more.

The Stoics

There are certain points of contact between Epicurus' epistemology and that of the Stoics, but the latter's view of the world was very different from that of Epicurus. The Stoics emphasized the notion of a continuum, as opposed to the atomism of Epicurus. Body was defined as that which can act or be acted upon, with the result that nearly everything in the Stoic system has to be characterized as corporeal, the exceptions being things such as propositions, which are called 'incorporeals' and exist only as objects of thought. Body is determined by matter and form, the latter providing the rational principles for things – 'seminal principles', as they were often called. These constitute the soul of the world – referred to as *pneuma* (breath or spirit) – so that the world in general has to be seen as living and organic. There is thus room for providence, an idea that received increasing emphasis in later Stoicism, especially in the theory (put forward by Posidonius in the second century B.C.) of cosmic sympathy, whereby all the forces in the world work together. All this is a far cry from the point of view of Epicurus.

It was nevertheless a determinist system, according to which everything has its cause. The Stoics were just as anxious as Epicurus, however, to preserve free will. Chrysippus, the main figure in the Stoa in the second half of the third century B.C., seems to have made a distinction between perfect and principal causes on the one hand, and auxiliary and proximate causes on the other. When we assent to a sense-perception, the existence of the latter is a necessary condition of the assent and thus an auxiliary cause of it, but the principal cause lies in ourselves. Analogously, he said, when a cylinder rolls or a top spins it will not do so without an initial push, but the principal cause of its motion lies in its own nature. In human action, there have to be necessary conditions for our acting as we do, and our action is thus subject to causes; but the principal cause of the action lies in ourselves and our own nature. Such a view is sometimes called 'soft determinism'; it would not satisfy everyone because it invites the question whether our own wills and nature are subject to causes. Why should the so-called principal cause in this case not be subject to cause itself?

The Stoic ideal of the good life was one that was in conformity with nature, but the difference between the Stoic conception of nature and that of the Epicureans leads to a different conception of what living in conformity with nature amounts to. The supremely wise man will aim at being totally in accord with reason. For him, only the ideal of rationality will be good, and only the complete opposite of this bad. Anything in between will be indifferent. Stoics came to recognize, however, that the ordinary man cannot entirely live up to the standard of the sage. Hence among indifferents there were distinguished those which are preferable. Perfect duty, as conformed to by the sage, is in effect conformity with what Kant was to call the good will and is what is required of complete virtue. The obligations of ordinary life are imperfect duties (*officia media*, or *kathēkonta*); to live by them is to live without the complete insight and rationality of the sage. Emotions were thought of as false judgements, so that the Stoic ideal can also be characterized as *apatheia* (freedom from passions). Once again there is a contrast with Epicureanism.

The same applies to their politics. Whereas Epicurus had little to do with society at large, being concerned more with friendship within local communities, the Stoics took over the Cynic idea of man as a citizen of the world. Epicurus had thought of justice as the result of a sort of social contract. The Stoics embraced the idea of natural law and the idea of justice as involving a conformity with nature, and so applicable to all men. It was from the Stoics that the concepts of natural law and natural rights were handed down through the Roman concept of the *ius gentium*, the common law of nations, to the Middle Ages. It was a concept which evidently had appeal to those Romans who found themselves oppressed by emperors such as Nero, and during this period Stoicism, particularly in its moral and political aspects, found many adherents.

I said earlier that in their theory of knowledge the Stoics had points of contact with Epicurus. In the case of most of the philosophers of this period there is considerable emphasis on sense-perception, which has produced the comment that an empiricist approach was common to the different philosophical schools. Certainly it did not occur to anyone to suppose that there was a better source of knowledge than sense-perception. For the Stoics the criterion of truth, as it was put, is to be found in individual sensory intuitions. The explanation of these had, of course, to be different from that offered by Epicurus. Zeno seems to have adopted Plato's model of the wax and the seal, saying that particular things produce impressions on the soul, although Chrysippus was to insist that this should not be taken literally. This produces *phantasiai* (representations or appearances). These might be probable or improbable, and, if probable, true or false. But the criterion of truth lay in those *phantasiai* which were called *kataleptikai*. *Katalepsis* (apprehension) and the *kataleptike phantasia* (the apprehensible or apprehensive presentation) is the certain base on which knowledge rests. The so-called criterion of truth is thus meant to provide the foundations for knowledge, and with this idea begins the search for epistemological foundations which has been characteristic of much subsequent epistemology.

Katalepsis involves a firm grasp on its object. (It might be thought more plausible to think that the presentation grasps us, grips us, and that this is what the intuition consists in, but the most common interpretation has it the other way round.) Zeno apparently illustrated the idea by an image. An open palm, he said, represented the presentation, a slight bending of the fingers assent to it, the clenched fist apprehension, and the grasp of one fist in the other knowledge. Chrysippus certainly thought that assent was in our power, and it might be subject to error. What then of *katalepsis*? Is that in our power? There are clearly difficulties in this; in any case there must be something about the presentation which makes us grasp it. Chrysippus invoked the distinction between principal and auxiliary causes in this context too, the presentation being the auxiliary cause or necessary condition, we ourselves being the principal cause of assent. It is far from clear, however, that this is helpful even for assent, let alone for apprehension proper.

The New Academy

Arcesilaus of the so-called New Academy introduced scepticism into that school around 270 B.C., probably on the grounds that this was a proper return to Socratic practice as suggested by the early Platonic dialogues. He may also have been influenced by Pyrrho, who seems to have claimed that nothing can be known and that the acceptance of this was the secret of the good life, free from care and anxiety. (Pyrrho went to India with Alexander the Great and is said to have conversed with 'Magi and Gymnosophists'; he is also said to have put his scepticism into practice and faced all risks without precaution, 'whether carts, precipices or dogs'!) Pyrrho wrote nothing, but the tradition about him, whether true or not, was preserved by his disciple Timon, who wrote satirical verses in which Pyrrho was contrasted with other philosophers, to the detriment of the latter. However that may be, Arcesilaus introduced a sceptical approach into the Academy and made attacks upon other schools, particularly the Stoics, for their dogmatism. The Stoic doctrine of *kataléptikę phantasia* was an easy target, since it involved in effect an appeal to intuition. Arcesilaus argued, plausibly enough, that it was impossible to tell from any presentation by itself whether it was veridical or not. The content of a *phantasia* is propositional and the causal theory implicit in the story about impressions does not justify the claim to truth implied in the doctrine of apprehension. Arcesilaus probably also employed the Sorites or 'little by little' argument. In this context it probably amounts to the argument that clarity and distinctness in a presentation is a matter of degree; there may be degrees of certainty to be attached to a sense-impression and there is no clear mark which separates those which are veridical from others which are not.

Chrysippus attempted to reply to Arcesilaus, stressing ways in which any one sense-experience could be judged reliable – its conformity with 'common notions', with common sense, and with right reason. We are also told that the 'younger Stoics' claimed that the *kataléptike phantasia* provides a criterion of truth 'provided that there is no obstacle'. The 'younger Stoics' may or may not have included Chrysippus. The view involves a general appeal to the coherence of a presentation with other things. There was thus a general emphasis on right reason and the kind of rationality that the Stoics tried to find in the world at large. The principles of right reason are of course to be found in logic, and this may explain the emphasis on logic in general, and propositional logic in particular, that we find among the Stoics. Apart from their inquiry into the truth-conditions of different propositional forms, including hypotheticals, the chief interest of the system lay, perhaps, in the attempt to formulate and formalize argument-schemata or *tropoi* (moods). They axiomatized the system in the sense that they tried to set out certain argument-schemata as indemonstrable, for instance the *modus ponens* of traditional logic – 'If p then q; but p; therefore q.' Other argument-forms were to be derived from five primitive argument-forms of this kind. The direct descendant of this approach to logic was the theory of *consequentiae* (consequences or implications) of medieval logic, which has its counterpart in so-called 'natural logic' in modern times.

After Chrysippus, a new head of the Academy, Carneades, returned to the attack on the Stoa. The traditional view of Carneades is that he substituted probability for truth, in that he allowed that presentations might be probable although there could be no final criterion of truth. Moreover, he distinguished three grades of probability – the merely probable, the probable and confirmed, and the probable, confirmed and tested. This view makes him into an important figure in the history of the philosophy of science, especially in respect of the consideration about testability. Recently, however, some scepticism has been cast upon this interpretation of Carneades. In the first place, it has been pointed out,[1] the word translated 'probable' is better translated 'persuasive', which gives the issue a more psychological emphasis, rather than an epistemological one. Moreover, Carneades was said by his pupil Clitomachus not to have had any opinions of his own that he could discover; it may be that the views attributed to him arose in the context of exchanges with the Stoics, and that he was using Stoic premises to show that even on their own views a definite criterion of truth providing certainty was not possible. Carneades was known for his willingness to argue on both sides of an issue. Hence his actual position, if there was one, is uncertain.

About fifty years later, somewhere between 90 and 80 B.C., Antiochus broke with the sceptical tradition of the Academy and refounded the Old Academy. He did so in a way that led others to comment that he had brought the Stoa into the Academy, claiming that the Stoic views as well as those of the Lyceum were really all taken from Plato. Panaetius, and after him Posidonius, the leading Stoics of the period, led the way towards a more eclectic Stoicism, so that others found little to choose between the Academy and the Stoa. Eclecticism became indeed typical of the period. Later Stoicism – in, for example, Seneca and later still

---

[1] By Myles Burnyeat in, for example, 'Can the Sceptic Live his Scepticism?' in *Doubt and Dogmatism*, especially pp. 28ff.

the Emperor Marcus Aurelius – is notable for its moral position, the emphasis on dignity and determination in the face of suffering. It becomes mainly a way of life, rather than a philosophy ranging over a wide number of issues. This is true even of Epictetus in the first century A.D., who unlike the other two whom I have mentioned was a professional philosopher.

The Academy had a period of inactivity, such that Cicero – who, though not a major figure as a philosopher, is a useful source for the views of others – claimed that on visiting Athens he could find no indication of the Academy's existence. It later became, in the Middle Academy of the second century A.D. (*c.* 160–80, contemporaneous with Marcus Aurelius), almost mystical as well as eclectic. Albinus and Numenius, the latter being also labelled as a neo-Pythagorean, were concerned with a sort of religious cosmology, derived in part from Plato's *Timaeus* with its emphasis on the Creator craftsman and the world-soul. Numenius was also responsible for the remark that Plato was Moses speaking Greek! The Academy sprang to new life with Neo-Platonism in the third century A.D., and we shall return to that later.

Scepticism

Meanwhile, the dominant Hellenistic philosophy was that of the Sceptical school founded by Aenesidemus around 80 B.C. He may have been a member of the Academy and may have left it when Philo, the head of the school before Antiochus' schism, proved too dogmatic for him. The school looked back to Pyrrho and even claimed a line of descent from him through successive teachers. It is probable, however, that only with Aenesidemus was a systematic sceptical doctrine developed, and this received a more extensive codification from Sextus Empiricus in the second century A.D. Aenesidemus put forward ten arguments or 'modes' aimed at showing that one ought to suspend belief. This is the aim of the sceptical philosophy, since they thought that only suspension of belief could lead to tranquillity of mind. The Sceptics said that, in accordance with the etymological meaning of the word *skepsis*, they were inquirers. Their inquiry, however, led to the conclusion that, since appearances conflict, there is no access to a truth independent of appearances; the proper attitude to adopt, therefore, was *epochē* (suspension of belief). As it happened, they said, this produced *ataraxia* (tranquillity of mind), and they represented this as a chance discovery, drawing an analogy with the painter Apelles who, unable to produce the effect of foam in a horse's mouth, threw his sponge at the canvas and accidentally produced the very effect that he was unable to bring about otherwise.

The ten tropes or modes of Aenesidemus all emphasize what has become known as perceptual relativity. Aenesidemus stresses the differences between appearances because of (1) differences between animals, (2) differences between human beings, (3) differences between sense-organs, (4) differences between the circumstances of perception, (5) differences in the position, distance and place of objects, (6) differences in context and relation to other things, (7) differences in degree of quantity or quality with respect to objects, (8) the relativity of things, (9) differences in the frequency of occurrence, and (10) differences in custom and convention. The general aim of these arguments is to undermine the claim for the possibility of absolute truth about the world. All that we have to go by are appearances, and by that is meant not simply sense-impressions but anything that seems to us to be the case on a given occasion. Going by appearances in this way was supposed to be what governed the life of Pyrrho and brought about tranquillity.

A later Sceptic, Agrippa, who probably lived in the first century A.D., replaced these ten tropes, which are clearly of unequal worth for the purpose intended, by five of his own. These five were, however, of a different kind from the earlier ten. They seem to be considerations which ought to lead an opponent to suspension of belief. There ought to be suspension of belief when there is disagreement, where the considerations lead to infinite regress, where there is relativity in judgement, where judgement depends on assumptions, and where it leads to argument in a circle. In the interval between Aenesidemus and Agrippa there must have been exchanges with opponents whom the Sceptics thought of as dogmatists, with the result that there was emphasis upon the failures of argument which the Sceptics saw in the dogmatists. Indeed a good deal of Sextus Empiricus' works is devoted to such criticisms of others, many of which, it must be confessed, are of very dubious worth. There were arguments of this kind about, for example, the attempt to specify the causes of appearances, especially where the causes in question are supposedly to be found in facts about nature which go beyond appearances.

Later Sceptics again, perhaps in particular Menodotus, an empiric doctor who perhaps taught Sextus Empiricus, were said to have reduced the tropes to two. But what this seems to amount to is a general dilemma with which the Sceptics confronted their opponents. Everything is known either through itself or through other things; but the first is impossible, as the disagreements of the dogmatists indicate, and the second is impossible because either the first horn of the dilemma applies to these other things too or there is infinite regress or argument in a circle. This dilemma clearly depends on the considerations adduced in the earlier tropes, so that these final two tropes look like the summing-up of the multifarious arguments that the Sceptics had had with the dogmatists. Their conclusion was that they 'determined nothing'. The only proper attitude was suspension of belief, being content with appearances, and this, as it happens, they claimed, leads to happiness. Hegel thought that the ancient Sceptics were the only true sceptics, in that the sceptics of his own time wanted to doubt some things only to be dogmatic about other things. There is something in this, or would be if the ancient Sceptics actually lived, as they claimed, by their scepticism. It is more than doubtful if they could have done, or indeed if anyone could.

Neo-Platonism

With Scepticism we really come to the end of the Hellenistic schools, although, as we have already seen, by the time that Scepticism reached its culmination there were already in existence forms of Platonism mixed with other things, which are called Middle Platonism. Apart from Numenius and Albinus, to whom reference has already been made, a form of Jewish Platonism was put forward by Philo, and forms of Christian Platonism by Clement and Origen. The last of these was a pupil of Ammonius Saccas, in some ways a mystery figure, who taught in Alexandria, which became at this point the focus of Greek philosophy. Ammonius wrote nothing, but was the teacher not only of Origen but also of Plotinus, the founder of the so-called Neo-Platonic school. Plotinus (*c*. A.D. 204–69) was born in Egypt and studied philosophy in Alexandria, but he subsequently went to Rome, where his philosophical system was worked out. His main disciple, Porphyry (A.D. 233–304), wrote a biography of him, and made certain developments in the Neo-Platonic system himself. He was also responsible for the arrangement of Plotinus' works in six groups of nine books, so that Plotinus' works became known as *Enneads*, from the Greek word *ennea* (nine).

The Neo-Platonic school became the dominant school of the period, and was even sponsored by the Emperor Julian (the 'Apostate') as a rival to Christianity. After Plotinus' death the school split up, part of it continuing in Syria under Iamblichus and part in Athens under Proclus and subsequently Damascius. In 529 the Emperor Justinian, in the interests of Christianity, forbad teaching of philosophy to be carried out anywhere in the Empire, and the philosophical school at Athens was closed (whether philosophy teaching ceased elsewhere is a matter of dispute). Damascius and others tried to carry on their profession in Persia but found life impossible there. On their return to the Empire they were not penalized for their beliefs, although they could not teach. They devoted themselves to the writing of commentaries, particularly on Aristotle, but in the context of those commentaries dispute of a philosophical nature went on, particularly between Simplicius, the best-known commentator of the period on Aristotle, and the Christian Neo-Platonist John Philoponus. The tradition of philosophical commentary continued into the Byzantine period; it was handed on to the Arabs and was the means of the eventual rediscovery of Aristotle in the thirteenth century, after centuries of ignorance in the west.

The Plotinian system is not really one based on arguments. It is said that Plotinus had no taste for public controversy, leaving that to his pupils. The sixth *Ennead* does contain a criticism of the Aristotelian and Stoic doctrines of the categories, and an attempt both to establish the Platonic 'greatest kinds' as the true doctrine of categories and to fit the other views into the context of that, as applicable to the sensible world but not to the intelligible world. The details of these criticisms are not encouraging for a belief in Plotinus as a philosopher who relies on arguments; they are indeed rather confused. Plotinus' forte lay rather in providing a metaphysical picture of reality of a kind which owes something to Plato, especially in the distinction implicit in what I have already said – that between the sensible and intelligible worlds.

Reality is indeed a continuum expanding outwards from a centre which is the source of power and determines what is derived from it. This process is not to be regarded as temporal; it represents a metaphysical dependence. The lowest degree of power and reality – at the circumference, so to speak – is to be found in matter, which has no positive nature in itself, being definable only by negation. An individual can, as it were, reverse this process through an identification with the source of power, which Plotinus calls the One. This brings out the mystical aspect of Plotinus' philosophy, which was emphasized further by Iamblichus, whereas Proclus stressed the more intellectual aspects. The One is the first of three grades of reality. Plotinus calls these grades *hypostases* (substances, or natures). They are the One, Intellect (*nous*) and Soul (*psuche*). Intellect is derived from the One by emanation (the outgoing process already referred to) and becomes plural both by differentiation into Forms and by differentiation into individual minds. Soul is derived from Intellect and becomes plural by being in all things. It is thus a world-soul which manifests itself not only in obviously living things but in everything else as well, so that Plotinus is committed to a general animism. This works on matter, producing nature, which is the province of practice, not contemplation, which is the responsibility of Intellect. Practice, Plotinus says, is a weak copy of contemplation.

The One is not a person, though it is sometimes spoken of as God. It

is unknowable, but the aim of the mystic, as we have seen, is identification with it. The world of the intellect is the intelligible world of Platonic
Forms to which our own intellects are somehow related. It is the world
of eternity. The world-soul orders the sensible world, Plotinus says, as
a dancer dancing a dance, not by conscious planning. It is responsible
for time, and if there were no soul there would be no time, for soul is
responsible for change and movement, without which, Plotinus
believes – as indeed did Plato and most Greeks – there would be no time
(a view which confuses what is necessary in order to note the passing of
time with a characteristic of time itself). Soul becomes united with matter
by its own will, despite the fact that matter is in a sense the source of
evil. It is so because it is the privation of all form and order, and evil is
thus identified simply with the lack of good. The concept of matter as so
used is of course an Aristotelian, not a Platonic, concept, but this is
typical of Plotinus; he tends to incorporate Aristotelian notions into his
own system.

It is perhaps difficult to make much sense of Plotinus in a short space.
He is presenting a picture of things as deriving from one central source.
It is a picture which is Platonic in inspiration, but is far from him in spirit.
It is so because behind Plotinus lies Middle Platonism and a period in
which quasi-philosophical mystery religions, such as Gnosticism and the
Hermetic movements, held sway. Nevertheless Plotinus knew of his
Stoic and Aristotelian predecessors, as well as Plato. Hence although
there is mysticism in Neo-Platonism there is also genuine philosophy,
though not at a very high level. The system is essentially non-Christian
(there is, for example, no room in it for a doctrine of creation), but
Christians could adapt it so that Christian Neo-Platonism not only was
possible, but actually came into existence. What is essential to Plotinus
is the thought that reality owes its existence and nature to one primary
source and principle, from which derives a world of intelligible Forms
with which we can have some contact *via* our own intellects, and from
which derive again life, time and the sensible world. All this constitutes
the form which is imposed upon formless matter and gives it its rationale
and goodness. We have bodies made of matter, but we have souls and
intellects, and a way is thus in principle open to us for an identification
with the source of being in mystical experience – something that, according to Porphyry, Plotinus achieved four times. (Porphyry himself claimed
to have achieved it once.)

Porphyry himself had little to contribute to the system of thought,
although in a remark about the status of species, when discussing
Aristotle's *Categories*, he spawned the problem of universals which preoccupied the Middle Ages. Proclus (410–85) was a more substantial fig-

ure. He introduced, or at any rate made more prominent within the school, systems of subordinate triads of *hypostases* within the Plotinian major triad, with the aim of filling gaps that he thought existed in it. He also thought that the differentiation into a plurality of things that exists in Plotinus' system at the level of intellect and soul should be present at the highest level too. So he introduced a doctrine whereby the One is differentiated into ones or *henads* (*monads*, we might say, to use the term favoured by Leibniz much later) responsible for a hierarchy of subordinate entities extending downwards to lower levels of reality. This obviously complicates the system immensely and robs Neo-Platonism of the monistic character that it had with Plotinus. One way of putting it is to say that Proclus is Leibniz to Plotinus' Spinoza.

As we have seen, philosophy went on in one form or another into later periods, although because of the circumstances, particularly the political and religious circumstances, of the Roman Empire it became more and more wrapped up in other things. In Byzantium little went on except at the level of commentary. In the western Empire Christianity became the norm and theological and philosophical considerations became intertwined. But, in fact, that had already happened long before Justinian closed the philosophical schools, and to consider the first of the major philosophical figures of the Middle Ages, St Augustine, we must go back before Proclus, or at any rate to his time, in the fourth and fifth centuries A.D.

[7]
Medieval Philosophy I

It is impossible to treat the philosophy of the so-called Middle Ages like that of any other period. We are concerned in effect with a period lasting for ten centuries or more (depending on where one thinks it begins and ends). In that period there are a great many philosophical figures, many of whom we know only by repute; there are far too many to review in detail, and the attempt to do so inevitably produces a sense of having lost sight of the wood because of the trees. There are two further points to be made about it.

First, it is a period which is in many ways backward-looking, towards the giants of Greek philosophy, even when knowledge of Greek had all but disappeared in the west. The habit of commentary on Greek philosophy was carried on in the eastern Mediterranean, under Byzantium, for centuries; indeed any substantial knowledge of Aristotle was preserved through that source only. It was then passed on to the Arabs, and eventually returned to western Europe through them. Plato was usually seen through Neo-Platonic eyes, and initially had greater influence over Christian philosophers. All this was backward-looking in the sense that the forms of philosophy, if not the spirit, the philosophical ideas, if not their use, had their source in Greek thought. Hence in a certain sense the period is not creative, philosophically speaking.

Second, as I have already implied, philosophy became subordinate to Christianity. I do not mean that there is no distinction to be made within it between philosophy and theology, or between reason and faith. Indeed, the question of the relationship between those last two has a large part to play in the debate. It is that philosophy had no longer an independent position; it was pursued in the main by people who were also theologians, central figures in the history of Christianity. It is one mark of the seventeenth-century revolution in philosophy, associated mainly with the name of Descartes, that, however much it owed in its ideas to medieval philosophy, it signalled the regaining by philosophy of the autonomous status that it had among the Greeks.

Much of what I have said about the spirit of medieval philosophy is particularly noticeable in St Augustine and some of the other earlier philosophers of the period; it becomes less evident at the end of the period. It has also to be said that there were investigations of logic during this period, by for example Peter of Spain and William of Ockham, which stand on their own feet. The interest of this has only recently been discovered, along with the development of mathematical logic during the last hundred years, and its freedom from the shackles of traditional 'Aristotelian' logic. Some of this looks back to the logic of the Stoics, but there are elements of real innovation, particularly in the theories of signification (*suppositio*) and inference (*consequentia*). Much of that comes late in the period, however.

Augustine

There are some who think it best to put Augustine in the history of Greek philosophy. He was born in A.D. 354 and he died in 430, so he overlaps with Proclus and is considerably earlier than those Neo-Platonic philosophers who tried to carry on when the Emperor Justinian closed the philosophical schools in the Empire in 529. Moreover, Augustine's conversion to orthodox Christianity from Manichaeanism came largely from reading Neo-Platonic works in a Christian form. There is indeed much Neo-Platonism to be found in Augustine's philosophy. On the other hand, the spirit of much of Augustine's writing is religious, and it is not uncommon to find in them what occurs in his *Confessions*, where a treatment of time and its relation to eternity comes in the course of an address to and praise of God. There is also a plethora of references to the Bible, and religious thinking in general. None of this, I suggest, is really in the spirit of Greek philosophy.

Augustine was born in 354 at Tagaste, in North Africa. His mother, Monica, was a Christian, but he initially found the faith unsatisfactory. He became professor of rhetoric at Carthage, although he claims in the *Confessions* (written at the age of about forty-four) that he first became interested in philosophy at the age of eighteen, when he read Cicero's *Hortensius* (now lost). To his mother's distress he joined the Manichaean sect, but gradually became disillusioned with it. He held posts in rhetoric at Rome and at Milan, where he heard Ambrose, the bishop there. That, combined with a reading of Neo-Platonic works, led to a conversion to Christianity and his entering the Church. On returning to North Africa he first set up a kind of community with friends. His mother died at Ostia on the way there, and the *Confessions* describes a mystical experience of union with God that they both had there shortly before she died. In Africa he was eventually drawn into the priesthood and succeeded Valerius as Bishop of Hippo, where he died in 430 as the Vandals were about to besiege the city.

Augustine has sometimes been seen as an anticipator of Descartes because of his use of the proposition '*Si fallor, sum*' ('If I err, I exist'). But the motivation is quite different. It is indeed true that the proposition constitutes a vital step in the rejection of scepticism, the scepticism of the Greek Sceptics. Augustine is saying that we cannot doubt things in general or suppose them false without accepting our own existence. That is not meant, however, to lead us, as it was with Descartes' parallel '*Cogito, ergo sum*' ('I think, therefore I am'), to a vindication of the scope of knowledge and a claim for the existence of a world apart from ourselves. (It has indeed been plausibly argued[1] that the notion of an 'external world' was not available to Augustine, because the inner–outer distinction depends upon a more radical scepticism about ourselves than had been contemplated at this date.) In Augustine's view the soul is superior to the body, so that even in perception it is not the case, strictly speaking, that the body influences the soul. The soul forms its own impressions in response to what happens in the body and the things that affect that, and makes its own judgements on that basis. (There are similar views to be found in Plotinus.) Perception thus involves an activity on the part of the soul and is in that sense a function of the will. The 'I' the existence of which is sustained by '*Si fallor, sum*' is to be identified with the soul so construed.

At the same time, Augustine did not doubt that we do perceive a world of objects independent of ourselves. How that is possible given the theory that perception is, properly speaking, the work of the soul is one of the obscurities of the Augustinian position, despite his attempts in the *De Musica* and elsewhere to make it coherent. Augustine was in fact more interested in other aspects of the soul's activities, in particular certain thoughts which have the character of indubitability – thoughts involving necessary truths such as those of logic and mathematics. For these 'eternal truths' were taken by him as indications of illumination by God, and the existence of 'eternal truths' was thought by him to give clear indication of the existence of God. Indeed the Platonic or Neo-Platonic Forms were interpreted by him as thoughts in the mind of God. Since such concepts are involved in judgement in general, even judgement about the perceived world, the inference which Augustine draws is that the whole of our knowledge is to one extent or another a product of illumination by God. This is perhaps the central feature of his philosophy.

In a sense, however, the account puts all forms of knowledge on the same level. Despite the active role that is given to the soul, as distinct

[1] By Myles Burnyeat. See his 'Idealism and Greek Philosophy: What Descartes Saw and Berkeley Missed' in *Idealism, Past and Present*, ed. G. N. A. Vesey (Cambridge: C.U.P., 1982).

from the body, the objects of the soul's knowledge are in all cases taken to be independent of that soul. So, Augustine claims, just as what we all perceive is not merely a feature of our sense-organs but something public and independent of each of us, so in the case of other forms of knowledge, including knowledge of eternal truths, what we know must be independent of ourselves. In a sense we know all things in God, if only in the sense that God is the source of that illumination on which knowledge depends. But it is really more than that. For that illumination is also the source of things themselves; all things depend upon the divine mind in the sense that they are the embodiment of divine knowledge. The aim of mankind is to be at one with God, and Augustine believes that therein lies the happiness or blessedness which is also the end of philosophy. From the point of view of knowledge, to be at one with God is to be at one in one's knowledge with the divine knowledge which is its source. This is God's relation to the world as its creator.

That very idea creates a problem. Augustine believed in the idea of a creation out of nothing. But the conception of God that we have just reviewed is much closer to the Neo-Platonic notion of the One as the source of all things through emanation from it. In the Plotinian theory of the relation between time and eternity, time enters the picture only with Soul and therefore life; the domain of Mind and the Forms corresponds to eternity. For Augustine God exists in eternity. How then can we have a doctrine of creation? Augustine's answer is Plotinian with a difference. It is given in a famous passage in Book XI of the *Confessions*. Speaking to God he asks, 'What is time?', adding that he knows perfectly well until someone asks him (a predicament that whole hosts of other philosophers have found themselves in). The problem arises from the notions of past, present and future, the present in particular causing trouble because of the inclination to think of it as a knife-edge between past and future; and yet the past and future, in a sense, are not. On the other hand without the notions of past, present and future we do not have time or temporal passage; in effect we have only eternity.

Augustine's response is to locate the nature of time in the awareness of the passage of time and therefore in the individual soul. There is no time in the sense that involves the passage or flow of time apart from individual expectations, memories and general awareness of time's passage. Time is, as it were, a subjective phenomenon. Hence, when it is said that God created the world out of nothing in the beginning, we speak only from the individual human point of view. In truth God exists in eternity. There is thus no question of what he was doing before the creation of the world or of anything like that. The Neo-Platonic doctrine of a world emanating from a timeless or eternal One is thus squared, or apparently squared, with a Christian doctrine of creation *ex nihilo*, by the supposition that the temporal aspects of the latter story are merely a product of our individual human point of view.

There are additional problems arising from this thesis. God's creation, even if not strictly speaking temporal, is absolute. How is it that there can be developments in the world? How can there even be the sequence of events implied in the Biblical story of the creation, according to which things happened on successive days? To deal with this, Augustine had recourse to a doctrine of 'seminal reasons' (or causes), a notion which has something in common with the Stoic notion of seminal principles. The world is created in such a way that there are in it the seeds for future development when the conditions are right. This seems to imply a determinist view of things. Augustine nevertheless believed that human beings have free will. Man is created with a view to attaining happiness in the vision of and identification with God. Human beings have various impulses which Augustine calls by the name of 'love' (which he sometimes likens to weight), but these are complex, and what men do is not determined by their nature, as is the case with mere physical things. They can therefore (if 'therefore' is the right word) choose not to seek God and thus not attain true happiness. Evil, as with the Neo-Platonists, is a privation of the good, a failure to attain that good which men can in fact attain. None of this is very satisfactory from a theoretical point of view, and the awkwardness results from the abortive attempt to square Christian principles with a doctrine derived from Neo-Platonism.

There is a similar awkwardness in Augustine's view of the role of the state and society. For most of his life he tended to accept society as organized under the Roman Empire as just one facet of human life. The state exists merely to further the individual's well-being through a social order, since the primary aim of the individual is something that involves just him and God. The sack of Rome by the Visigoths in 410 led to something of a re-appraisal on Augustine's part of the role of society. *The City of God*, written towards the end of his life, presents a sharper division between what he calls the heavenly and earthly cities, the city of God and the city of Babylon. They constitute extremes, the former meant for those who are to attain glory with God, the latter for those who are to be confronted with quite the reverse. Neither is in reality society or the state as it actually exists, and in *The City of God* Augustine presents a vision of something that does not actually obtain on earth. What does so obtain is a sort of compromise between the two cities, there to maintain order and material well-being. Augustine's view of society and of political organization is thus a minimizing one, and the ideal of the City of God implied a kind of separation of Church from

State which did not and could not exist as things were in the Roman Empire of his time.

Boethius

The problem of reconciling God's eternal knowledge of his creation with human freedom, which was not properly solved by Augustine, was taken up again by Boethius (*c.* 480–524/5) in his last work, the *Consolation of Philosophy*, written while in prison for treason and shortly before his execution. In his case the problem is explicitly put in the form of how human freedom is to be reconciled with God's *fore*knowledge. Boethius' answer used the same notion of eternity that Augustine had inherited from his Neo-Platonic predecessors. God, because he exists in eternity, does not *fore*see human actions; he sees every temporal event from the point of view of eternity and thus in a kind of eternal present for which all temporal events come together. He sees human actions as free, and there is no obstacle to that from foreknowledge. Whether foreknowledge has in any case anything to do with the question whether human actions are free is a debatable point; for foreknowledge does not necessarily imply determination. If I know now that you will subsequently choose to do one thing rather than another, that does not necessarily imply that you will not freely choose to do that thing. However, it is often thought that foreknowledge is inimical to freedom, and Boethius is no exception in that respect. His 'solution' is ingenious, but it may be thought philosophically beside the point. Whether that is so is still a matter for debate.

Boethius is worth noting in another way too. He was interested in the logic of Aristotle and made translations into Latin of Aristotle's '*Organon*' and Porphyry's *Eisagōgē* (an introduction to Aristotle's treatment of the categories), and wrote commentaries on some of these, particularly Aristotle's *Categories* and Porphyry's *Eisagōgē*. In the last respect he commented upon a remark of Porphyry, mentioned in the preceding chapter, that the status of species and genera was uncertain. Boethius tried to explain what Plato and Aristotle had said on that subject, giving special attention to Aristotle because, as he said, he was commenting upon that philosopher. But he did not try to adjudicate between Plato and Aristotle, as to whether species and genera, and therefore universals, exist in sensible things or whether they exist, as Plato was taken to suppose, in separation from bodies. So Boethius transmitted the problem of universals to later philosophers. Since he was almost the last philosopher in the western part of the Roman Empire to have a comprehensive knowledge of Greek, and therefore the last to have direct knowledge of Plato and Aristotle's works, he was also the funnel by which such knowledge of the ancient world as persisted was passed on, and even then to some extent in a distorted form.

John Scotus Eriugina

The next main figure in medieval philosophy does not come until over three hundred years later, by which time knowledge of the Greek world was almost dead, though something of the tradition lingered. John Scotus Eriugina (born *c.* 810), originally an Irish monk, did have some knowledge of Greek and was able to translate the writings of Gregory of Nyssa (a Church father of the fourth century, who saw the creation of things as proceeding from the divine Ideas, bodies being formed of qualities put together in the form of such ideas – a view which has been seen as a kind of idealism, a point on which there might be much argument). He also translated the works of Pseudo-Dionysius, a writer dating from somewhere around the end of the fourth or the early fifth century, who had much influence on early Christian thought, but who was erroneously believed to be an Athenian convert of St Paul, Dionysius the Areopagite, and had perhaps undue fame thereby. These two writers in particular much influenced John the Scot. In his main work, *On the Division of Nature*, he divides nature, or things in general, into four kinds or phases (and one has to speak of phases, because John views the divisions in part as forming a sequence, the last being the final return to God at the end of things).

The four divisions are nature which creates but is not created (God), nature which creates and is created (the primordial causes or Ideas), nature which is created and does not create (nature in the conventional sense) and nature which is neither created nor creates (the final end of things, the return to God). The calling of the first division 'nature' has led some to see in John a sort of pantheism reminiscent of Spinoza's 'God or Nature', but it is not clear that that is what he intends. John uses ideas derived from Pseudo-Dionysius to describe knowledge of God – the affirmative and negative ways (*viae affirmativae et negativae*) – with a considerable emphasis on the latter. It is an attempt to determine the nature of God in terms of what he is not. This approach goes back to Neo-Platonism and emphasizes the transcendence of God above and beyond natural things. His nature is superessential.

The second division of nature, which is concerned with primordial causes, is an attempt to explain how such a transcendent God can both bring about and manifest himself in a plural world. It provides a link, or attempts to do so, between the first and third divisions of nature. Among the primordial causes is to be found the Idea of man – a primordial man, free but lacking most of the characteristics that go with the body and life in a material world. John gives an allegorical account of the Biblical story of the creation, in which Adam's fall is the coming into being of material man, and the whole material world with him. The final division of nature can only be regarded as the last stage of such a process, construed sequentially – the final return to God, which nature desires, and a kind of rest in God. It is clear that John's account is highly mystical in character. It has been seen as a great metaphysical construction, and construed as a picture it has something of that quality. Its motivation is however primarily religious.

The Arabs

We move on another two hundred years, by which time the emphases had changed. There was greater interest in logic. For example, both Abelard and John of Salisbury wrote works with titles deriving from logic or dialectic. It is not altogether easy to explain this shift of emphasis, although some of the interest in the status of universals or species and genera and how these are expressed in language had something to do with the doctrine of the Trinity and the relation of the three persons in one. Meanwhile, but quite unknown in the West, there was a flowering of philosophy in the Arab world, with a revived knowledge of and interest in Aristotle, albeit an Aristotle intermixed with Neo-Platonism. Alfarabi is the earliest of the better-known Moslem philosophers of the tenth century. He used Aristotelian ideas to argue for the existence of God, claiming that in God existence and essence are to be identified; God is identical with his essence and is the source of the being of other things. The greatest Moslem philosopher of this period, however, is Avicenna (Ibn Sānā), who produced a vast system of philosophy based on Aristotle *via* Alfarabi. In his view, God is again a necessary being and the source of other things, since they emanate from him as the result of his self-knowledge. He also postulated a number of intellects deriving from this, including ten intellects in a heavenly realm beyond the fixed stars, responsible for the movement of the heavenly bodies according to a modified Ptolemiac system. It is impossible in a short space to give an adequate account of the complexity of the system, although one of the central points of it is the emphasis on the active intellect or reason which Aristotle had postulated.

Elaborations on that and its relation to the so-called passive intellect were carried further by the twelfth-century Arab philosopher Averroes (Ibn Rushd), whose writings were known to Aquinas. I shall return to him later. Another Arabic philosopher of the tenth and eleventh centuries who is perhaps worthy of mention is Al Ghazali. He was primarily a religious figure, anxious to resist what he saw as the departures from orthodoxy embraced by his predecessors. One doctrine for which he is notable, however, is a view of causality which makes him something of a predecessor of Hume, in seeing the relation between causes and effects as contingent only. But he embraced this view for reasons which make him closer to the eighteenth-century occasionalists. He wished to defend the possibility of miracles performed by God and indeed the causal agency of God in general. Attribution of causes and effects is based on the constant conjunction which we perceive between certain events, but the causal efficacy, properly speaking, is due to God.

Abelard

Abelard and the logicians of the eleventh and twelfth centuries in the west knew nothing of this. In the west, that period saw the beginning of philosophical argument about the status of universals, deriving from the remarks that had been passed on from Porphyry by Boethius, as we saw earlier. Abelard (1079–1142) was taught by Roscelin of Compiegne, whose writings have not survived, but who is reported as having maintained that a universal was a mere word (*flatus vocis*). Roscelin also appears to have maintained a 'three-god' version of the doctrine of the Trinity, on the grounds that every existent thing is particular – a doctrine for which he was accused of heresy, so that he had to retract his theory. The opposite camp of extreme realism over universals was occupied mainly by William of Champeaux (1070–1120), although St Anselm, to whom we shall return in another connection, was also a realist. Abelard brought forward telling criticisms of William of Champeaux, asking how an identical substantial species could be found in two places simultaneously. Abelard's own theory is somewhat obscure. He has traditionally been thought a conceptualist on the grounds that despite his opposition to extreme realism he also denied that universals were words (*voces*), using instead the term '*sermo*'. Contemporaries, including John of Salisbury thought that he was a nominalist all the same (for does not '*sermo*' mean speech?). Finally, although he denied that universals were things, reserving that term for particulars, he did not deny that our general thoughts have something to do with what is in the world; for he put forward a theory of abstraction from things, based on the occurrence of general images which represent what is common to them. Once again, however, Abelard does not seem to have thought of images as things themselves.

The truth is that Abelard's main concern was as a dialectician or logician, and what he wanted to bring out was the logical status or role of predicates. Predicate-expressions do not stand for anything in themselves; their role must be seen in what they contribute to the proposition of which they are a part. One commentator[1] has seen a similarity to the views of the twentieth-century logician Gottlob Frege in this respect. According to both philosophers, to ask what kind of *object* a predicate picks out is a mistake, since the logical role of predicates is not to pick out an object. Frege says that predicates refer to concepts, but Abelard does not allow even that. If a predicate has a meaning or content, that content can be spelled out only *via* its role in a proposition in which we assert something of a thing. It might be said, therefore, that Abelard does not have a theory of universals, since any theory of universals tends to identify the content of a predicate with an object, whether real nature, word or mental entity, and Abelard rejects all these. If Abelard was a conceptualist he was one in a rather sophisticated sense, and it is not surprising that others with a more traditional framework of ideas saw him differently – as a nominalist, or even as a moderate realist.

Anselm

I have already referred to Anselm (1033–1109) as a realist over universals; his main claim to fame lies elsewhere, however. Anselm was born in Piedmont in Italy, but eventually became Archbishop of Canterbury, where he staunchly defended the rights of the Church against the King. He was also a defender of the place of reason in relation to faith, and it is this spirit which embues his two works, *Monologium* and *Proslogium*, in which he sets out to produce rational arguments for the existence and nature of God. The *Monologium* sets out certain *a posteriori* arguments, that is to say arguments which at some point rely on a premise derived from what we know from experience of the world. These arguments look back to similar arguments to be found in Plato and Aristotle. Anselm argues – as did Aristotle in an early work, the *De Philosophia* – from degrees of goodness, claiming that there must be something which constitutes perfect and absolute goodness (and wisdom too), and which is the cause of the goodness of other things; that thing, which of course is God, is the exemplar of the real universal, goodness. Anselm argues analogously in the case of existence, maintaining that although, as is usually the case, things exist only through other things, there must be something that exists in and for itself – which is God. The outcome of these arguments (which anticipate arguments put forward in St Thomas

[1] Martin M. Tweedale: *Abailard on Universals* (Amsterdam, New York, London: North Holland, 1976).

Aquinas' so-called 'Five Ways') is not only, in Anselm's view, that there must be a God, but also that he is to be identified with absolute goodness, wisdom, being, etc. The arguments are not formally valid, since they depend on the idea – common to many other philosophers, including Aristotle – that there *must* be a final term in a scale of degree or dependence. They also depend on factual premises, as we have noted.

The *Monologium* brings out the conception of God with which Anselm worked. The *Proslogium* in effect presupposes that conception, but sets out an independent argument, the so-called 'ontological argument', which has met with repeated discussion ever since. Anselm presents the argument in the context of an address to God. It is in effect that God is that than which no greater can be conceived (the conception of what is meant by 'God' that is derived from the *Monologium*); that conception must be of something that exists not only mentally, but also independently of the mind (for something that exists only mentally is not as great as something that has independent existence also); therefore God must exist (for we have the concept of God, and it is part of that concept that he exists, and indeed must exist, independent of our concepts). Even the fool who says 'There is no God' should see that his very denial of God is a contradiction; for the very conception of God that he employs has the existence of God as an implication. As that formulation of the issue makes clear, the argument is an attempt to show that the existence of God follows from his mere conception. It is an argument that, if described in that way, seems implausible. It has been the subject of attack for centuries, but for some reason it keeps coming back and it is constantly claimed that it, or something like it, can be defended.

There was an immediate objection to it from a monk, Gaunilo, who insisted that similar argument would show that a perfect and most beautiful island must exist, if existence is taken to follow from perfection. Anselm replied in return, arguing that the two cases were not similar. The reply has a certain cogency, especially when it is recognized that the considerations of the *Monologium* lie behind what Anselm has to say in the *Proslogium*. At a much later date Leibniz argued against a version of the ontological argument put forward by Descartes that we do not know that the idea of God as an absolutely perfect and infinite being does not involve a contradiction; and if it does, the idea of a God so conceived would not be the idea of a being that could possibly exist. Later still, Kant was to argue that existence was not a predicate, so that the idea of a being who has all predicates in perfection could not be the idea of a being one of whose attributes was existence. It has been argued that that consideration does not apply to necessary existence, because whatever else God may be conceived to be, he cannot be conceived (as

Hume was indeed to suggest he might) as a being whose existence might be simply contingent, so that he might exist at one time and not at another. However all that may be, Anselm's argument was not adopted by many of his immediate successors, and Aquinas, for one, rejected it.

The rediscovery of Aristotle

At about the same time and earlier, there was a flowering of Arab civilization in Moorish Spain. One of the products of this was Averroes, of whom mention has been made above. Averroes (1126–98) was a convinced believer in the philosophy of Aristotle, known of course in Arabic translations. Averroes (Ibn Rushd) wrote extensive commentaries on the Aristotelian works, maintaining what is for the most part a reasonably orthodox Aristotelian philosophy, with fewer of the Neo-Platonic elements that existed in Avicenna's philosophy. Nature is a continuum extending from the pure form and pure actuality which is God, to (at the opposite extreme) pure matter without form. One thesis maintained by Averroes is of note, if only for the reason that he later came under criticism from Aquinas in the latter's *De Unitate Intellectus*. This is a thesis concerning the distinction made by Aristotle between the active and passive intellects, the former of which has an independence from the body and does not perish with it. Averroes maintained that the passive intellect had the same kind of survival as the active intellect, although neither of them was in any sense personal, except in their combined manifestation in the body – the so-called acquired intellect. There is thus no room for any form of personal survival, and this made Averroes a target for Aquinas' criticisms, even apart from the question whether it was a correct interpretation of Aristotle.

Another product of Moorish Spain was the Jewish philosopher Maimonides (1135–1204), who left Spain and eventually died in Cairo. His *Guide for the Perplexed* was again an attempt to give theology a philosophical foundation in the philosophy of Aristotle. From this time onwards into the thirteenth century Aristotle became the dominant influence on philosophy, and Aristotle's works were rediscovered in detail in the Christian West. There were Latin translations of Arabic translations, and these were perhaps the first main source of knowledge of Aristotle. Gradually, however, there came into existence translations directly from the Greek of works that were not previously known in the west (which is to say more or less the whole of Aristotle's works apart from the logical ones). Some of the translations from the Greek may have been available before the Latin translations from the Arabic, and these came to provide a check upon the not always very good Arabic translations. One of the main translators in the thirteenth century was William of Moerbeke, a friend of Aquinas; the latter had little if any Greek and was enabled to write his commentaries by these translations.

St Bonaventure (*c.* 1221–74), the first thirteenth-century figure to note, but one who perhaps stands out more as a theologian than as a philosopher, had a more limited acceptance of Aristotle than others of the time. In many ways he was an Augustinian. He accepted a good deal of Aristotle's natural philosophy, but did not think that it was an adequate foundation for theology. Indeed he did not see philosophy, or indeed reason in general, as capable of telling the whole story. So for these purposes he went back to Augustine and the more Platonic points of view that Augustine embraced. A great many of Bonaventure's philosophical positions represent in consequence something of a compromise. In his account of sense-perception, for example, he accepts the Aristotelian thesis of the effects upon the sense-organs, and the production of a sensible species. In the end, however, he wants to stress, as did Augustine, the power of the soul to act upon the body, even if he offers no clear account of how this happens. Bonaventure's views are in general not only a compromise, but an unhappy one.

Medieval Philosophy II

Aquinas

In the previous chapter I have already encroached upon the thirteenth century in speaking of Bonaventure. There is reason, however, for separating off the three thirteenth- and fourteenth-century thinkers with whom I shall deal in this chapter: Aquinas, Duns Scotus and William of Ockham. Their stature and comprehensiveness is quite unlike any of those from the Middle Ages with whom we have had to deal so far. Aquinas was the great synthesizer, able to use the newly rediscovered Aristotle to produce a philosophical system by which reason could be set alongside faith. There are for Aquinas revealed truths, and where philosophical considerations conflict with revelation – as is the case, for example, when Aristotelian principles lead to a denial of a first creation – Aquinas has no hesitation in siding with faith. Nevertheless in natural theology and elsewhere reason is paramount, and Aquinas thought that the Aristotle of whom he first learned through his teacher Albertus Magnus provided the rational principles for a complete philosophy which faith could call to its aid. As we saw in the previous chapter, Aquinas knew his Aristotle not from original sources, but in translation; moreover it was still necessary to sort out which of the received works were truly Aristotle's. Hence his knowledge of Aristotle is relative to the times and circumstances in which he lived. Nevertheless for Aquinas Aristotle is 'the Philosopher'.

The synthesis which he produced came under criticism eventually from Duns Scotus and Ockham. They were Franciscans and he was a Dominican. Historically speaking, therefore, the great synthesis to be found in particular in his two *Summas*, the *Summa contra Gentiles* and the *Summa Theologiae* (with their series of questions, considerations *pro* and *con*, and final answers) did not persist. All the same it is Aquinas who has come down to us as the great scholastic philosopher, and Duns Scotus and William of Ockham have, whether or not with justice, a lesser standing. Aquinas' life (1225–74) was neither long nor very eventful, apart from a period in which his family imprisoned him in their castle, wishing him to further their political aims and not become a member of the Dominican Order. He persisted, however, gained his freedom, and went to Paris to study under Albertus Magnus, whom he accompanied to

Cologne from 1248 to 1252. The rest of his life was divided between Paris and Italy, and was given up to teaching and writing. He died while on a journey to the Council of Lyons. Apart from the two *Summa*s, there are a large number of other works by him, including commentaries on Aristotle which must be high on the list of the most boring works ever written; presumably because of the limited access to Aristotelian texts, Aquinas had to describe in meticulous and relentless detail what Aristotle said, and exposition heavily outweighs comment.

Aquinas' account of the natural world is almost strictly Aristotelian, based on the reciprocal principles of matter and form, things occupying various degrees between the extremes of prime matter and pure form. Aquinas had a concern, which perhaps Aristotle never had, however, with what has become known as the principle of individuation – the question of what ultimately distinguishes any two things. Matter, simply as stuff, cannot do that; nor can form, since that is general. Aquinas therefore introduces the notion of *materia signata quantitate* – matter marked out in respect of quantity. Two things, even things of the same kind, are to be distinguished from each other by their being made of a certain stuff occupying a certain delimited space, even when they are not distinguishable by other means. God, being pure form, needs no such criterion of distinguishability. But Aquinas identified the intelligences which Avicenna, following Aristotle, had postulated as the causes of the movement of the spheres bearing the heavenly bodies, with angels. These he thought could have no matter either. Angels could be distinguished only by difference in form. Since the notion of form corresponds to that of a species, each angel constitutes in effect a distinct species. It is not perhaps a happy idea, but neither is that Aristotelian idea of beings consisting of pure form.

Aquinas is generally said to have added something of his own to this framework of ideas – the distinction between essence and being or existence, which appears in an early work *De Ente et Essentia*, and is used continually thereafter. Aristotle would of course have recognized *a* distinction put in those terms. The categories are kinds of being, whereas things or beings have essences to the extent that they belong to species of which certain things must necessarily or essentially hold good. There is thus a connection between essence and form or species. Aquinas imposes on this another Aristotelian distinction, that between potentiality and actuality. I say 'imposes', but even for Aristotle there was an association between form and actuality on the one hand and between matter and potentiality on the other. One of the Aristotelian words for actuality is '*energeia*', usually translated as 'activity' or 'act'. It is this notion of 'act' which Aquinas invokes in order to explain what he means by 'being', by contrast with essence. One might put the matter in another way by saying that the being or *esse* of a thing is the realization of the nature that it has; without that realization the nature would be potential only.

That is not a very perspicuous idea, although it is one that Aquinas seems to have in mind. It would make sense to a modern philosopher if it were taken to mean that there is a distinction to be made between the *concept* of a thing and its realization or actualization in reality. But for Aquinas, as for Aristotle, the nature or essence of a thing is not a matter of what concepts we have of it; it is a matter of what there is in reality, since Aquinas is a realist. Aquinas seems to be using the distinction between the potential and its actualization to make, in realist terms, the distinction between the concept of a thing and the realization of that concept. It might be argued that, from an Aristotelian point of view, that is a misuse of the Aristotelian distinction between actuality and potentiality. It is certainly a different and non-Aristotelian point that is being made. Much later, in this century, we find Quine saying that to be is to be the value of a variable; one might say that for Aquinas a comparable slogan would be that to be is to be the act of an essence or nature. But there can be variables without their being given a value; the trouble with the 'Aquinas' slogan is that there cannot actually *be* essences except as realized in things, and therefore except as in act. Realism over essences entails that. Aquinas is surely trying to make a non-realist point, involving a distinction between concepts and their instances, in realist terms.

None of this applies, in any case, to God, since he is pure form and pure act, without any potentiality. Hence in his case his essence and his *esse* are the same. Aristotle too asked whether things are the same as their essences and answered that this is so only in the case of substances in the primary sense; and this amounts to saying that it is so only in the case of God. Aquinas agrees with that but wants to say something more: that God's *esse* is the same as his essence, and there is nothing in his nature which is not actualized, in act. Aristotle would have agreed with the conclusion, because in his view God is pure actuality, his nature being pure thought, but he would not have put it in terms of *being*. In any case, as a Christian, Aquinas wanted more of God than Aristotle allowed.

What access, however, do we have to the actual nature of God? There are of course negative things, that he is not this, that and the other thing, mention of which goes to make up the *via negativa* (way of negation), characteristic of mystics in their approach to God. When it comes to positive attributes, however, Aquinas thinks that we can approach God only through attributes that apply to the world that we know. Since God stands above and beyond all that, those attributes apply to him only analogically; in other words, they do not apply to him literally but only by analogy with ordinary things. For these purposes Aquinas takes over and extends the Aristotelian considerations about equivocation. For Aristotle, analogy was one type of equivocation, one that was distinguished from what has become known as 'focal meaning'. Aquinas counts both of these as analogy, the latter being analogy of proportion, the former analogy of proportionality. There is analogy of proportion when the resemblance between the things between which there is analogy involves a difference of degree, so that the one might be regarded as the highest degree of exemplification of what is exemplified only in a lesser degree in the other. That is what Aristotle's doctrine of focal meaning comes to in the end.

It follows, according to Aquinas, that we cannot have complete and full knowledge of the nature of God, and it is impossible for reason, as exemplified in philosophy, to rectify that situation. It is different with knowledge of God's existence. Aquinas does not accept the ontological argument for the existence of God as put forward by Anselm. In the *Summa contra Gentiles* in particular he rejects that argument on the grounds that it involves an invalid move from existence in thought to existence in reality. It is of course the whole point of the Anselmian argument to make that move, but Aquinas rejects it all the same. There are no further *a priori* arguments for God's existence; so we are left only with *a posteriori* arguments, arguments from the nature of the world as we experience it. Aquinas mentions five such arguments (the so-called 'Five Ways') although he gives greatest attention to the first. The arguments go back in various ways to the Greeks, and to Aristotle in particular. The first argument is in effect Aristotle's argument for a prime mover. There is motion in the world, and this is the actualization of potentialities; but such an actualization depends upon something to bring about the actualization. This idea presupposes a chain of actualizations which cannot continue *ad infinitum*, and so must come to a stop in something purely actual, an unmoved mover, which is God. The argument is, strictly speaking, invalid, as is the Aristotelian version. It presumes that there must be a complete explanation for what happens, and that chains of actualization cannot continue *ad infinitum*. That the supposed prime mover is indeed God is a further assumption. Kant was to argue that all such arguments need the ontological argument, and the conception of God that that assumes, to reach the final conclusion.

The second argument proceeds similarly on the basis of efficient causation, arguing that there cannot be an infinite series of efficient causes.

The third argument, the so-called argument *a contingentia mundi*, argues that the fact that things in this world come into being and cease to be shows that they are only contingent; but contingent beings can exist only if there is something which exists necessarily and which is the reason for their existence, and this is God. The fourth argument is in effect the Aristotelian argument from the *De Philosophia*, that where there is a better there must be a best; degrees of perfection and goodness in the world imply the existence of a best and most perfect thing, which is God. The fifth and last argument is the teleological argument, or argument from design; indications of purposiveness in the world imply the existence of a designer (although a designer need not, strictly speaking, be a creator, as the Demiurge of Plato's *Timaeus* was not). None of these arguments is compelling in the demonstrative sense, because they all involve assumptions that can be resisted. The extent to which they give additional plausibility to a belief reached on other grounds or simply by faith is a matter for individual judgement.

It is important to realize that, according to Aquinas, the word 'God' is not strictly speaking a proper name; there might have been more than one God. For Aquinas there is naturally, given the above, only one. He maintains that the most appropriate name for God is the one given to Moses from the burning bush: I am that I am. This name clearly indicates the identity of existence with essence in God, something that is not true of anything else. According to Aquinas, God freely created the world out of nothing, a point on which, as we saw earlier, faith conflicts with the doctrine of Aristotle. Equally – and again this is a matter of faith, not of philosophical proof – God created the world in the beginning, even if he himself is eternal. But God's will is subject to his intellect, just as, Aquinas maintains, is the case with men, whom God created in his image. This is the doctrine of the primacy of the intellect over the will, a doctrine that subsequently came in for criticism, especially from Duns Scotus.

For Aquinas, however, it is part of the view that in creating the world God acted to communicate his goodness. That view brings with it the problem of the existence of evil. God, being good, cannot will evil; nor indeed, Aquinas thinks, can man. Evil is simply a consequence of what is willed as good, and Aquinas here adopts the view which goes back to Plotinus, that evil is just the privation of good, not something positive in its own right. Evils, both natural and moral, exist for the sake of a more positive good. God created such a world with foresight, but for the sake of that good. Whether that is a satisfying account of the rationale of evil is a matter on which debate still continues. Some may think that the view of evil as a privation involves playing down the possibilities of real evil, but the view is perhaps the price that one has to pay for belief in a benevolent creator.

Aquinas' account of the individual human soul is, with certain modifications, very Aristotelian. He views the soul as the form of the living body, although that is a view which presents obvious difficulties for belief in the soul's immortality, which, as a good Christian, Aquinas had to accept. In order to defend immortality Aquinas has recourse to what Aristotle says about reason, taking this to show that reason has a spiritual nature, whatever is true of other faculties of the soul. I shall return later to the exact role that Aquinas gives to reason, both the active and the passive reason as Aristotle had distinguished them, in connection with his theory of the acquisition of knowledge by human beings. Aristotle had argued that reason in general must be independent of any organ, because, given his understanding of the way in which the faculties of the soul function, the possession of an organ for reason would limit what reason was capable of thinking; it could not think anything which had the nature of that organ. He had also posited the existence of an active reason to explain how the potentiality that the passive reason – the kind of reason we have been concerned with so far – consists in could be actualized.

Aquinas takes over these points, using them to argue for the thesis that the rational soul, the kind of soul that includes reason, must be immaterial. But he argues that it is the whole human soul that survives death, even the faculties which depend, as is the case with sense-perception, on the body for their actualization. In separation from the body, faculties remain as potentialities, although they lack the bodily conditions which make their actualization possible. The rational faculty demands those conditions only to the extent that it depends on sense-perception for its content; and Aquinas maintains the doctrine of *nihil est in intellectu quod non prius in sensu* (there is nothing in the intellect which was not previously in sense-perception), whether or not Aristotle held it. The active intellect does not demand bodily conditions at all. Whether this is a satisfactory account or simply incoherent is best left to individual judgement.

From a psychological point of view, however, the soul is merely a collection of faculties or potentialities which function by being actualized by something. For Aquinas, there are the usual five individual senses, and what Aristotle called the 'common sense', to which Aquinas attributes various functions according to an interpretation of Aristotle that has become almost orthodox, although in my opinion wrong.[1] In addition to this he speaks of four internal senses, which are really non-

[1] See my *Aristotle's De Anima II and III* (Oxford: Clarendon Press, 1968) on this.

rational capacities: *imaginatio*, the power of conserving sensory images or *phantasmata*; *vis aestimativa*, the power of apprehension, possessed by animals, that something is for example useful or hostile; *vis cognitiva*, a similar power possessed by human beings; and *vis memorativa*, the power of retaining or conserving those apprehensions. Apart from these, and the power of movement, appetite and reason, there is also will (*voluntas*), as far as human beings are concerned. The object of the will is the good, which Aquinas, following Aristotle, identifies with happiness, with the gloss that true happiness is to be found only in God. We have already seen that for Aquinas evil is the privation of good and is not in itself an object of the will.

Before going further into Aquinas' ethics we must first consider what is in effect Aquinas' cognitive psychology, his account of the acquisition of knowledge and the part that reason plays in this. (We do not find in Aquinas any epistemology concerned with the justification of claims to knowledge in general, any more than we do in Aristotle.) Aquinas is an empiricist in the sense that he thinks that all our concepts, all our understanding of things, are derived from sense-perception (as I indicated in my earlier reference to the doctrine that there is nothing in the intellect that was not previously in sense-perception). He was also a moderate realist in connection with the theory of universals, in the sense that he believed that there has to be a foundation for our conception of what is general – of, in his terms, species – in the world in which we find ourselves. Aquinas starts from what is in effect a causal theory of perception, which, as I have observed elsewhere,[1] he may have derived from the Greek Atomists. But it is a theory which is meant to explain what Aristotle meant when he said that in sense-perception we receive the form of the object without the matter. I think that Aristotle meant that to be taken at the level of physiology, but Aquinas wants it to be psychology too.

In general Aquinas insists on the identity of knower and known in any form of apprehension of the world. That doctrine cannot be taken literally, however, because in perceiving a stone, for example, I do not become that stone, nor does that stone come to be in me in its physical or natural nature. Aquinas thinks that it nevertheless comes to be in me in *esse intentionale* (intentional being), that is, as being what the apprehension or intending of the mind (*intentio animi*) consists in. To have an apprehension of a stone is for that stone to exist in me, not in *esse naturale* (natural being), but in *esse intentionale*, and thus not in a material way, but in an immaterial way. It might be suggested that this

[1] See my *Sensation and Perception* (London: Routledge and Kegan Paul, 1961), pp. 47–51.

explanation is simply playing with words; so it is, without the surrounding theory. It has to be remembered in any case that it is, strictly speaking, the *form* of the stone, without its matter, which comes to exist in me in this way. What, however, is the surrounding theory? It is that the object sets up *phantasmata*, or likenesses, in the sense-organs. But if these are to do the work that is necessary they have to be mental too.[1] We are told that the active reason abstracts the form or species from the *phantasmata*, so that it issues in the passive reason as a *species expressa* (expressed, rather than impressed or imposed (*impressa*)) or *verbum* (word). Aquinas calls this the *conversio ad phantasmata*, or – using an analogy taken from Aristotle, but which the latter probably meant differently – the illumination of the species. That *species expressa* is the occurrence in *esse intentionale* of the form of the object. All this sounds like rather dubious psychology which has resort to inner agencies or *homunculi*, but it could conceivably be interpreted in terms of the functions that have to be performed for apprehension of an object as a such and such to take place.

Another aspect of the account is that it can be interpreted as trying to do justice, in a moderate way, to the aspects of different theories of universals. Realism is retained, in that there can be no conception of a such and such (something general) unless the world is such that abstraction from images of it of species is possible. On the other hand, only concrete objects exist in the world and these are such and suches to the extent, and only to the extent, that abstraction from their images is possible. At the same time the active reason must be capable of illuminating what is so abstracted, revealing to the mind the nature of the such and such. Thus there must be, so to speak, concepts, or aspects of the intellect which amount to that, and the fact that these have verbal expression does justice not only to the demands of conceptualism but to those of nominalism too, as long as those demands are not imperialist. The theory, in other words, brings in aspects of all three main theories of universals.

If syncretism were thought desirable, this would be an admirable result, provided that the theory is coherent. Whether it is so is a matter for debate, the main difficulty being the link between the causal, and presumably purely physical, account of sensation with which the theory starts, and the later story about the different mental functions that are performed in order to provide apprehension of objects as such and suches. Without a coherent theory at this point the assertion that the objects of perceptual awareness exist in us in *esse intentionale* is empty.

[1] See J. Haldane: 'Aquinas on Sense-Perception', *Philosophical Review*, XCII, 1983, pp. 233–9.

One final point needs to be noted on this score. It is a consequence of the claim that the intellect always works in this way, that all the concepts that we have are derived ultimately from sense-perception, however indirectly. Thus there can be no direct apprehension of immaterial beings as long as the soul is connected with the body. There is *a fortiori* no direct apprehension of God, nor direct understanding of his nature. But that we have already seen to be Aquinas' view anyway. We can have understanding of God only by analogy, and on this point Aquinas is completely consistent.

Aquinas' ethics is again Aristotelian with modifications. We have already seen that on his view men always will the good or what they see as such, and that the good is happiness. Aristotle had said that happiness was an activity of the soul in conformity with virtue, and had treated the virtues as habits and acquired by habituation. So is it with Aquinas. But although there was a certain ambiguity in Aristotle over the identification of the good for man, according to whether man was treated as a social animal or as a being in which divine-like reason was paramount, Aquinas introduces another ambiguity. For what Aristotle called happiness Aquinas thinks of as merely temporal happiness, as distinct from perfect happiness, which is identifiable only as the vision of God and is attainable, properly speaking, only in the next life. Nevertheless, by espousing the great bulk of the Aristotelian ethics – including the doctrine of virtue as a mean, leaving it to reason (what Aristotle called practical reason) to determine how the mean is constituted and how one should act in order to attain the end of life – Aquinas emphasized once again the part that reason and the intellect play in life. Will is nothing without reason, as the doctrine of the primacy of the intellect over the will spells out.

Aquinas is also notable for a theory of natural law. Aristotle's moral theory is naturalistic in the sense that it sees the good for man in terms of what is part of human nature, and of what is natural for men to aim at, as rational beings. Men as political animals and in society are governed by human laws, which are, in a sense, a sort of image of the divine law that governs the universe. But individuals can be regarded in themselves as an analogous system subject to laws which govern the relationships between their parts. The law that governs this is natural law, and it lays down what must be done and not done to further the ends of man. As such, this law, as is the case with human laws, is prescriptive, but the basis of what is prescribed is to be sought in what is natural (or supposed to be natural) for human beings. Aquinas thus attempts to derive the moral laws that govern human conduct from a conception of human beings and what is natural for them. Whether this sort of 'ought' can be derived in any way from this sort of 'is' is still the subject of debate among philosophers.

Since men are political animals as a fact of nature, the state is also a natural institution which exists to further the ends of those who are part of it. Individual men are nothing without the state, but equally the role of the state is to further the ends of individuals. Human law must therefore be based upon or in some sense subordinate to natural law, which is itself, as we have seen, a sort of image of divine law. Given this hierarchical arrangement, it follows that there is a sense in which the state must be subordinate to the Church, to the extent that the latter's function is to further the ultimate end of men's union with God. Once again certain aspects of Christianity are imposed upon a generally Aristotelian framework of ideas. With some exceptions, this is the general pattern with Aquinas. It is a great synthesis of mainly Aristotelian ideas, but given the Christian, theological, context in which they are put the result is inevitably a compromise.

Duns Scotus

To move from the writings of Aquinas to those of John Duns Scotus (*c.* 1266–1308) is, stylistically, to move from clear to extremely muddy water. Scotus is a difficult writer and a difficult thinker, and the involution of his style made his name the origin of the word 'dunce'. He received the honorary title of 'Doctor Subtilis', which is no doubt a more polite way of indicating the same thing. On the other hand, the nineteenth-century American philosopher C. S. Peirce thought of him as one of the 'profoundest metaphysicians that ever lived'. A true assessment of him is not made easier to arrive at by the facts that many works attributed to him have come to be thought spurious, and that the main ones tend to have nothing of the clarity of form possessed by Aquinas' *Summas*. The two main works are perhaps the commentary on the *Sentences* of Peter Lombard (a collection of theological opinions held by the Church fathers, composed in the first half of the twelfth century, which received much attention and many commentaries) known as the *Ordinatio* or *Opus Oxoniense* and the *Quaestiones quodlibetales* (records, presumably edited, of responses to questions and objections on any subject put in the course of a formal disputation in Paris), a work written at the end of his life. They do not make easy reading.

Duns Scotus was almost certainly born in Scotland. He entered the Franciscan order, studied at Oxford, and lectured there and subsequently in Paris. He underwent a period of exile from Paris when he may have lectured at Cambridge, but later returned to Paris. Finally, in

1307 he was transferred to the Franciscan study-house at Cologne, where he died in the following year. Scotus, like Aquinas, wrote commentaries on Aristotle. He was to a certain extent critical of Aquinas in relation to Aristotle, and he had a tendency to look back past Aquinas via Avicenna to Augustine. Many of the criticisms expressed in his writings are, however, directed at unspecified contemporaries, a fact which may have excited students, but makes interpretation difficult for us.

Scotus' proofs of the existence of God are extremely complex, in part because of a sensitivity to the question how an *a posteriori* proof, of the kind used by Aquinas in the 'Five Ways', could be demonstrative if its premises were based on matters of fact that were for that very reason not necessarily true. He tried to get around that point by making the premises have to do with possibilities – for that certain contingent facts are possible might be something that was necessary. His most complex proof of this kind has to do with God as first cause and infinite being, the final step being to argue that an uncaused cause (necessary to avoid an infinite regress of causality) could not be both possible and incapable of being caused unless it was also actual. Even this brief outline of the argument gives some indication of its complexity. The main point in this area over which Scotus objected to Aquinas concerns the doctrine of analogy. Scotus thought that 'being' was univocal, and that the same applied to other so-called transcendental terms, such as 'one', 'true' and 'good'. If this were not so, knowledge of God would be impossible. We derive our understanding of the meaning of such terms from experience of sensible things; if the terms acquired a different meaning when applied to God we should have no way of understanding that different meaning. On the other hand, Scotus admits that, although in applying such terms to God we express general knowledge of him, we do not thereby have knowledge of him in his individuality and perfection.

In this connection, Scotus made use of a notion for which he has acquired some notoriety, although the notion did not originate with him. This is the notion of a *distinctio formalis a parte rei* (formal distinction on the side of the thing), a distinction which has to do with the form or essential characteristics of a thing and which is in that sense objective. ('Formal' should not be interpreted as 'logical' or 'merely formal'; a formality is an objective aspect of a thing which is less than that thing's total nature or essence.) Scotus, like certain other philosophers of his time, wanted something in between a real or ontological distinction, where the things distinguished can actually exist separately, and a merely conceptual distinction, where the things distinguished are separable only in thought, without being able to exist separately. In the intervening case, the distinction must in some sense be imposed upon thought because of its basis in reality. According to the Aristotelian theory of the soul, which Scotus accepted in its essentials, reason cannot exist separately from the other faculties (waiving for the moment any objections arising from considerations about active reason); there is nevertheless a real distinction between the faculties which is not simply a matter of how we happen to think of them. This is an example of the formal distinction which Scotus had in mind. It is a quite genuine distinction and one that there is not much cause, in itself, to dispute. It becomes interesting only when it is implied that the distinction is a necessary one, where the necessity is *de re* (in things, not merely a conceptual necessity).

The situation may be different with the uses to which Scotus wanted to put the distinction. For he holds that there is a formal distinction in this sense between the divine attributes, which are in fact inseparable from each other in God; and it is because of this that God is one. This consideration, when generalized, introduces another characteristic idea that Scotus put forward. He was a realist over universals to the extent of believing that there must be some objective basis for attributing a common nature to a number of individuals, even if common natures do not exist in the world except in individuals. Hence the distinction between the common nature and the individuality of a particular thing is a formal distinction, because it is not just a distinction in thought, even if common natures cannot exist separately from individuals. The individuality of a particular thing Scotus called its *haecceitas* (thisness), a notion which Leibniz was to revive. He rejected the Thomist thesis that the principle of individuation is provided by *materia signata* (by, in effect, spatio-temporal position), maintaining that there must be something intrinsic to the individual that gives it its individuality. This haecceity may not be known by us and we may not appeal to it in distinguishing things, but it exists and is known to God. What exactly this comes to in Scotus is rather obscure. For Leibniz, the individuality of any given thing was guaranteed by the claimed facts that no two individuals have all their properties in common and that the number of properties of any given thing are infinite. Scotus in effect rejects that. The distinction between a thing's haecceity and the common nature that it may share with other things is for him a formal distinction.

Scotus takes Aquinas as holding that we have only indirect knowledge of particulars because of the need for the process of *conversio ad phantasmata* (although whether this is a correct interpretation of the implications of Thomist doctrine is open to doubt). He too sees the intellect as interacting with phantasms, but he holds, as William of Ockham was to hold also, that we have intuitive cognition of the existence of objects.

Knowledge of their natures, their common natures, is dependent on the workings of the intellect in relation to phantasms, whereas knowledge of their haecceity is not possible in this life; knowledge of their existence, however, is a matter of intuition. Scotus, again like Ockham, also distinguishes between intuitive and abstractive cognition, the latter being concerned with an object in abstraction from its existence or non-existence. But it is the possibility of intuitive cognition, free from the workings of the intellect, that is important. Except that it is confined simply to the existence of things, it corresponds to the 'knowledge by acquaintance' that Russell was to insist on in this century. Scotus also sees a place for intuition in the recognition of the certitude of some truths.

We have already seen something of Scotus' 'Aristotelian' view of the soul. Once again he sees a certain incoherence in the Thomist position on it, at least to the extent that the more the soul is seen as the form of the body, the less it becomes possible to prove its immortality. Not that he doubts that it is immortal; this is yet one more place where the limits of what can be proved become apparent. Scotus took a much more positive view of human freedom, however, wishing to give the will an absolute freedom, and not one merely relative to what the individual sees as the ends to be pursued. Hence he asserts the primacy of the will over the intellect, in contrast with the opposite relation maintained by Aquinas, in a way that goes back to Augustine. The same doctrine drives him in the direction of the thesis that what one ought to do morally is dependent on what God wills. Although he does not fully assert that things are good to the extent that God wills them (for he does appeal to right reason and considerations of fittingness), he certainly has a tendency in that direction.

William of Ockham

William of Ockham (*c.*1285–1349) carried on many of the tendencies manifest in Scotus, but was also opposed to him on some issues, especially Scotus' realism and his notion of the formal distinction. Ockham is often thought of as one of the great exponents of nominalism; and so in a way he was. But it is impossible to arrive at an assessment of that without considering Ockham's contributions to logic. Indeed logic and the theory of meaning are central to Ockham's philosophy in a way that they are not to the others whom I have been considering in this chapter. One of the most important of his works is the *Summa Logicae*, the first part of which is concerned with the theory of terms, in a tradition that goes back to Abelard, but which had been developed in the thirteenth century by such logicians as William of Sherwood (or Shyreswood) and

Peter of Spain. Ockham went on in the second part of his work to consider the syllogism and the theory of consequences – a form of the logic of propositions and inferences made in their terms which goes back to the Stoics, and which was also pursued by Walter Burleigh, a Franciscan rival to Ockham. But these last matters have less general philosophical importance, however important they are for the history of logic.

Ockham was born in Surrey, entered the Franciscan order and studied at Oxford. He knew well the views of Scotus but it is unlikely that he was actually taught by him. His lectures on the *Sentences* gave rise to accusations of heresy by the Chancellor of the university, and he was summoned to Avignon in 1324 to answer the charges before being awarded his teaching licence. He remained in Avignon for four years, after which a commission proclaimed some of his articles heretical, though no action seems to have been taken on this score. During this period he was philosophically active, but in 1327 he took the side of Michael of Cesena, the General of the Franciscan Order, against the Pope at Avignon on the question of apostolic poverty. In 1328 Cesena and Ockham, with two others, fled from Avignon and put themselves under the protection of the Emperor Louis of Bavaria, who had set up an anti-Pope in Rome, and now moved to Munich. Ockham went with him and was excommunicated by the Pope at Avignon; in Munich he produced a number of pamphlets on papal power and argued for political representation even in the Church. The Emperor changed his position, abandoning Cesena and Ockham, and the latter appears to have sought some form of reconciliation with the then Pope and his Order. He seems to have died in the Black Death in 1349.

Ockham is of course the originator of 'Ockham's razor' or principle of parsimony, and although it is not clear whether he actually used the words in which it is usually expressed ('entities should not be multiplied beyond necessity') he certainly said things very like that. It is also clear that, to use the words used later by John Locke, he thought that everything that exists is particular. To understand how he could maintain that and still give meaning to general terms, it is necessary to say something about his logic of terms and about the theory of cognition that goes with the understanding of those terms. Terms, as they occur in language, are signs which are the linguistic expression of states of mind (*intentiones*), which are natural signs of whatever they signify. To make this work over names in the ordinary sense Ockham has to presuppose a form of cognition which involves a grasp of those things which names pick out. Thus, as with Scotus, Ockham puts forward an account involving intuitive cognition of individuals and a distinction between this and abstractive cognition. This theory is put forward in the *Commentary on the Sentences* and also in the *Quodlibeta*, two important works by Ockham which can be set alongside the *Summa Logicae*.

Intuitive cognition is a form of apprehension of an object present to us such that the knowledge of it can be evident; abstractive cognition is apprehension of an object apart from the conditions of its existence. It is important that the two forms of cognition can take the same objects; the difference is purely a matter of the circumstances or conditions of the apprehension. The objects can be of any kind. An intuition is perfect when it is constituted by an immediate experience, imperfect if past experience has to be brought in as well. Thus, there is no suggestion, as with Scotus, that intuitions of things must in this life be confused because of our inability to apprehend the haecceity of the thing. All abstractive cognitions are derived from intuitive cognitions, just as according to Hume, much later, all ideas are derived from a corresponding impression. They depend upon the setting-up of an acquired capacity or *habitus* to conceive the object.

Ockham seems at first to have assumed that the objects of abstractive cognitions must always be particular things, just as is the case with intuitive cognitions; but in the *Quodlibeta* he states that, however an abstractive cognition is formed, one cannot exclude as its objects things that would have produced an exactly similar result. Thus the move from an intuitive cognition to an abstractive cognition is a move from direct apprehension of a single object (a form of acquaintance with it) to the possession of a concept. But that concept is merely the act of understanding those things of which it is a concept. Those things may be similar, but they do not have anything literally in common; they are, Ockham says, similar simply in virtue of what they are in themselves. The object of a concept, what the concept is a natural sign of, is simply those individuals which fall under it. These constitute its signification.

When one turns to linguistic terms one has to note, first, a distinction between categorematic and syncategorematic terms. The latter correspond to purely logical terms the role of which is just to connect terms which are categorematic; and *these* mean things in one or other of the categories and can function as subjects or predicates. Categorematic terms can be distinguished into those of first and second intention. Terms of first intention are those which are signs of non-linguistic items, and terms of second intention are those which are signs of other linguistic signs or the concepts which are the corresponding natural signs. Terms such as 'universal' are terms of second intention in this way, and in Ockham's view those who embrace realist theories of universals fail to see that. Among terms of first intention there is also a distinction between those which are absolute and those which are connotative. Absolute terms or names signify what they signify primarily in all cases, while connotative terms or names signify one thing primarily and another secondarily.

Ockham's explanation of this in the *Summa Logicae* is not very clear. One example of a connotative name is the word 'similar', because in calling something similar we are relating it to something else, and that something else is signified by the term secondarily, whereas the thing to which the term is first applied is signified primarily. Ockham thinks, however, that the category of connotative terms is much wider than simply relational expressions; any term that can be construed only by reference to something else is connotative. Indeed on the 'Platonist' view to which Ockham is opposed, any predicate term (such as 'wise') is to be construed as connotative, because although it is applied to the subject (for instance Socrates), it also makes an oblique reference to an abstract entity, wisdom.

That, however, is precisely the view that Ockham wishes to reject. He thinks that a predicate term such as 'wise' signifies simply those things to which it applies, and when we say 'Socrates is wise', the subject and predicate terms signify the same thing. In considering sayings, however, we have, strictly speaking, moved into another domain apart from mere signification; we have moved to a concern with what Ockham calls 'supposition'. This, he says, 'is said to be a sort of taking the place of another'; the term in a proposition takes the place of what it 'supposits' for. But supposition is a property of a term only when it is in a proposition. Normally the term will supposit for what it signifies; but it is possible for a term to be used non-significatively, as when it is used to speak about itself, when we are concerned with the word rather than what it signifies, or when it is used to speak of the concept expressed by the word.

These last two cases of supposition are called material and simple supposition respectively; the first kind of supposition is called personal supposition. Of this last Ockham says that a term never supposits for a thing in any proposition unless it can truly be predicated of that thing. Hence when we truly predicate 'wise' of Socrates, the term 'wise' supposits for, stands in the place of, Socrates. It follows that there is a sense in which the doctrine of supposition (of which there are other complications into which I shall not enter) presupposes the notion of predication and a view about the function of propositions. Hence when we are told that the predicate term supposits for whatever is there to function as subject, we are told something not only about the signification of the predicate term – its relation to what it picks out – but also about its logical role in the context of a proposition. That logical role prevents the predicate term being taken as the name of an abstract entity.

What, however, of abstract names such as 'courage' or 'whiteness'? Ockham's account of these is complicated, and I cannot go into details. Abstract names look like absolute terms, and Ockham admits that in the case of terms such as 'whiteness', which signify sensible qualities of things or substances. In the case of terms from other categories he wants to give an account of what is said in the use of an abstract name, which shows that its use is dispensable in favour of forms of speech that have no apparent reference to abstract entities. Such an account is reductive in the sense that it reduces apparent talk of one thing to talk of another. It is essential for Ockham that such an account be given, for otherwise, whereas reference to sensible qualities might be taken as reference simply to the substances that have them, in that the terms in question supposit for them, reference to things in other categories will involve reference to abstract but real entities or universals. In fact, Ockham believes, there exist only substances and sensible qualities of them; and nothing in the facts of language or of thought, which relies on natural signs, really suggests otherwise.

It is fairly easy to see why such an extreme, 'empiricist', view might be taken as offensive to certain religious beliefs, and perhaps as heretical. Ockham was extremely critical of the traditional proofs of God's existence. The requirements of demonstration – that it presupposes necessarily true premises – puts severe limitations on its scope. Ockham thought that such premises had to do with what follows conditionally from what or, as with Scotus, with what is possible. Such propositions, whether they are evident in themselves (because of the signification of the terms that they contain) or from experience, are insufficient for the purpose of demonstrating God's existence. The distinction between what is evident in itself and what is evident from experience has pre-echoes of the positivist distinction between what is analytically necessary and what is simply *a posteriori*.

Science can proceed because of the possibilities of generalization that are involved in the move from intuitive to abstractive induction; but the validity of such moves depends upon the acceptability of the assumption that there is a common course to nature. On the other hand, knowledge of what is the cause of what is based simply on observation of concomitances or regular sequences of events. The assumption of a common course to nature, which amounts to something like belief in the uniformity of nature, remains for Ockham merely an assumption, although, like Hume, Ockham did not dispute its truth. Final causation, on the other hand, he saw as little more than a metaphor. It is evident enough what restrictions all this puts on the possibility of even *a posteriori* arguments for the existence of God, even the Scotist ones based on causality; for the employability of considerations about causality beyond what one can observe is a mere assumption. None of this is to say that he thought that there was no good reason to believe in God; but the considerations in favour of belief rest in the end on faith.

Similar considerations apply to Ockham's views about the nature of the soul and about immortality. He thought that there were no philosophical reasons to believe in a rational soul which could be distinct from the body, saying that he did not care what Aristotle thought on the matter, and that Aristotle in any case spoke on it with indefiniteness. Once again immortality is a matter of faith. As regards the nature of the soul he was inclined to the Franciscan doctrine of a plurality of forms corresponding to different faculties; and he rejected the Scotist doctrine of the formal distinction, both because of its realist basis and because he thought that the idea of an identical thing having formally an objective difference within it offended against the idea of strict identity. The argument here corresponds in some respects to that of Leibniz, who argued that if two things are identical there cannot be things that are true of the one and not of the other. Nevertheless, once again Ockham accepted some form of unity of the self as a matter of faith, while arguing that all we can know of it from experience is that we do think and will. He reaffirms the doctrine of the primacy of the will, putting a great emphasis on the complete freedom of the will both in ourselves and in God.

God could command us to hate him, and we have an obligation to obey, although in doing so we should in effect be showing our love of him. If that is a paradox, it is not one that Ockham thought led to a logical contradiction. But our own moral goodness lies entirely in free exercise of our own will in a good way. Goodness lies entirely in a good will, as in effect Kant was to say later. Ockham's ethics plays, however, a very minor part in his philosophy. His main interests were logical, although his epistemological emphasis on intuitive cognition of particulars is of fundamental importance in its opposition to the main trend of Thomism.

There were other Ockhamists and other philosophers of other persuasions in the fourteenth century. The general empiricist attitudes shown by Ockham and to some extent by Scotus had also been reflected in some early interest in issues which are in a genuine sense scientific – in Robert Grosseteste (*c.* 1175–1253) and Roger Bacon (*c.* 1212 to the end of the thirteenth century) for example. The period that followed Ockham saw many further developments in science and also – what some have seen as connected with that – a reflowering of Platonism. But philosophy as such did not reach the same heights. Whatever the Renaissance did for other areas of man's endeavour, it was not a high point of philosophy. Hence in effect Ockham is the last peak of medieval philosophy. When philosophy emerges again in a major way it is in a more secularized form.

[9]
The Renaissance

It may seem a paradox that a period that saw the flowering of much else –
of science, of art and of literature – was a period in which philosophy was
at a low ebb. It is nevertheless a fact. At the same time it cannot be denied
that the rise of science in particular – especially in the person of Galileo –
had a profound influence. When philosophy rises to a height again in the
seventeenth century, above all in Descartes, natural science has become
a dominant influence. Descartes also provides a break with much that
has gone on before. Some of his language and ways of thinking look
back to scholasticism, as the style and institutional background of the
philosophizing characteristic of the Middle Ages has come to be called;
but his main ideas constitute something of a revolution in philosophy,
the origins of which, like those of many revolutions, are not altogether
clear. In the intervening period after Ockham, scholasticism went on, but
it was no longer the force it had been. The main figure in that movement
was Francis Suarez (1548–1617), who had some influence on the subsequent history of scholasticism as well as, in all probability, on Descartes.
The main interest in the Renaissance period, however, lies elsewhere.

At the end of the last chapter I mentioned the rediscovery of Plato.
This was a product of the general Renaissance concern with Greece and
Rome, and the flowering of Greek studies generally. Marsilio Ficino
(1433–99) translated all the dialogues of Plato along with other Greek
works, including Neo-Platonic writings; but his interpretations of them
involved an admixture of Christian thought together with Hermetic
ideas (associated with Hermes Trismegistus, the 'thrice-great' Hermes, to
whom various theosophical and occult views had been attributed in the
early centuries A.D.). Hence, although Plato's writings became available
again in their entirety, Plato's thought was still interpreted in a way that
mixed it up with other things, particularly Neo-Platonism. It is doubtful
whether Plato and Neo-Platonism were properly distinguished until the
development of German classical scholarship in the late eighteenth and
nineteenth centuries. Ficino preached an ascent to God *via* contemplation, the immortality of the soul, and a doctrine of 'Platonic love'
based on Plato's *Symposium* and *Phaedrus* with additions drawn from
ancient views of friendship and the notion of courtly love drawn from
Dante and others. None of this is philosophically important in its own

right, but it had considerable influence on a whole host of other thinkers, and set a pattern for construal of Platonism that was to last for a very considerable time.

The most important figure of the early Renaissance was, however, Nicholas of Cusa (1401–64). He too derived much from Platonism, and saw in Neo-Platonism a doctrine which implied a way of knowing or intuition which can go beyond reason, the latter being bounded by the principle of non-contradiction. Although we are finite, we have a way of thereby getting to the infiniteness of God, to which reason cannot attain. In Nicholas' view, it is not just that God is infinite, even absolutely and positively infinite; God somehow transcends the principle of non-contradiction so as to form a unity which combines all opposites. This notion of a coincidence of opposites is Nicholas' key idea. It is an idea precedents for which can no doubt be found in Neo-Platonism, especially in Proclus' commentary on Plato's *Parmenides*. For Nicholas, if we say that God is *maximus*, the greatest, we must also say that he is *minimus*, the least, because in him opposites are somehow reconciled. We, of course, cannot see how this is possible; we have to approach God by the *via negativa* (way of negation), stressing the differences, gradually and by degrees, between him and what we are aware of in the world.

God is transcendent in that the world somehow depends on him, but he is also in a sense immanent in the world, although in a way, as Nicholas was to insist, that did not make pantheism true. The world, in consequence, is infinite too, although not in the positive way that God is. It is not a limited sphere and in consequence has no centre and no circumference. The earth is not the centre of the universe, nor is it absolutely at rest. It can well be understood what a break this view entailed with the cosmological view of the Middle Ages, although it took Copernicus (1473–1543) and more particularly Galileo (1564–1642) to give the view substance as part of a scientific cosmology. For Nicholas, however, the world has God as its centre, and because God is immanent in it, it too is a unity in plurality, derived from the coincidence of opposites which God involves. This is clearly a form of mysticism, but one that, as applied to nature, had its influences on later philosophies of nature, particularly in German Romanticism.

A fairly immediate example of that is to be found in Jakob Boehme (1575–1624), a Lutheran mystic, for whom God was the *Ungrund* or Abyss, an undifferentiated absolute, which is 'neither light nor darkness, neither love nor wrath, but the eternal One'. He claimed to see this and more in a mystic vision. The idea of the mystery of the abyss may have been derived from Paracelsus (1493–1541) who, strangely, combined medical practice and theorizing with alchemy and astrology, as well as mystical theological views. The best-known philosopher to be influenced by Nicholas of Cusa, however, was the Italian Giordano Bruno (1548–1600), who was eventually arrested by the Inquisition and burned at the stake in Rome. His views were clearly thought of as heretical, as, of course, were those of Galileo later, although for different reasons. Bruno, like Ficino, was much influenced by the Hermetic writings, but he was also – perhaps oddly, in the circumstances – influenced by Copernicus, going beyond him indeed in positively rejecting the geocentric view of the universe. He took this, however, as confirmation of the views of Hermes Trismegistus, and despised Copernicus for being a mere mathematician. His dialogues on *Cause, Principle and Unity* assert the principle of the unity of All in the One. The world is infinite and he uses Nicholas of Cusa's idea of the coincidence of opposites in regard to it. The world is the expression of a world-soul, and Bruno's theory in this respect is a strange mixture of Epicurean atomism with this idea of a world-soul. From this is derived a doctrine of monads (animate atoms) which anticipates in some ways the later doctrine of Leibniz. In other ways – for example, in his view of God as completely transcendent and yet as manifested in the world and as nature – there are anticipations of Spinoza's view of 'God or Nature'. Bruno's philosophy is clearly a mixture of things, but, as in others of the period, mysticism and Hermeticism are large constituents in the mixture.

It should be clear from what has been said so far that the scientific view of the world which was beginning to emerge had a very varying influence on the philosophers of the period. Galileo himself was of course known for various scientific pursuits and inquiries, involving, for the first time in any major way, experimentation – as is the case with his experiments with rolling balls in order to verify the law governing the uniform acceleration of falling bodies. He thought of the universe as governed by mathematical principles, but he also took an essentially mechanistic view of the world. He accepted an atomism which embraced the distinction between what became known as the primary and secondary qualities of things: those properties which Democritus had said belonged to atoms, and those, such as colour, which did not and were taken to be subjective. It is perhaps not surprising that atomism experienced a recrudescence during this period. The main exponent of the doctrine – in a form which goes back essentially to Epicurus, though with some Christian admixtures, especially in relation to God and the soul – was Pierre Gassendi (1592–1655). Gassendi's reputation remains largely because of his criticisms of Descartes. An English counterpart in embracing atomism was Thomas Hobbes (1588–1679), who expounded his version of the theory in his *De Corpore*. Hobbes' claim to fame, however, rests more on his theory of man and in particular on his theory of the state – the great Leviathan. I shall return to that later.

Francis Bacon

Perhaps the greatest exponent of the implication of the new science was Francis Bacon (1561–1626). As the titles of his greatest works – *The Advancement of Learning* and the *Novum Organum* (a deliberate challenge to Aristotle) – indicate, Bacon's main concern was to set out the correct methodology for the acquisition of knowledge. He is thus less concerned to set out a theory of the world than to chart the path that science should follow. Indeed he put forward the vision of what he called the 'House of Solomon', which was a sort of research institute with members having different roles, conforming to his view of the methodology of science, so that learning might be pursued more quickly and efficiently. He was bitterly opposed to the idea of final causes and, in his opposition to it, thought of himself as bringing about the overthrow of Aristotle. A final cause, he said, was like a virgin consecrated to God; it produces nothing! At the same time some of the language in which he expressed himself was, fundamentally, Aristotelian. Thus he spoke of his rules for determining causes (as Hume was later to put it) as methods for discovering the forms of things. The forms of things are in effect the laws which govern their behaviour, and the method which must be pursued to discover these is essentially inductive, not deductive. But induction must be governed by rules; otherwise there will occur what he thinks previous thinkers were guilty of – rash and over-hasty recourse to generalizations.

The trouble is, Bacon thinks, that there are natural prejudices to which men are liable, and these get in the way of the advancement of true learning. These prejudices must be set aside. It is therefore incumbent on the philosopher to make clear what they are. Hence his doctrine of what he called 'idols' – the idols of the tribe, of the cave or den, of the market-place and of the theatre. The setting out of these fallacies is parallel to the setting-out and diagnosis of sophistries in traditional logic – as in Aristotle's *De Sophisticis Elenchis*. The idols of the tribe are the errors to which men in general are liable, because of human nature – errors arising from, for example, a too-ready reliance on the senses, feelings or received beliefs. In speaking of the idols of the cave or den, Bacon was making a reference to Plato's simile of the cave, where the prisoners take shadows for the only reality. But Bacon gave that image an individualist slant. Each of us, he said, has his own cave or den, which 'interferes with and distorts the light of nature'. In other words an individual's personal disposition, his private theories and his personal point of view are liable to produce a distorted view of things, and Bacon declared that we should distrust anything that produces in us a point of view which is particularly satisfying.

The idols of the market-place are errors arising from language, from the ambiguity, emptiness or misleadingness of words, from indeed anything that so arises from intercourse between men. Finally, the idols of the theatre are false beliefs arising from the acceptance of various systems of philosophy – systems which, like stage plays, do not present a real or correct view of the world. They may, Bacon believes, be systems such as Aristotle's, which are sophistical and have taken men away from experience; or systems which, like those of some contemporary scientists, rely on too few empirical observations or experiments in constructing theories; or systems which, like that of Plato, mix up philosophy with theology. Not that Bacon objected to religion in itself; it was merely important that it should be kept in its place.

Having set aside these errors and prejudices, Bacon's plan was to set up a great programme for the pursuit of proper scientific knowledge, the aim of which was to discover the forms of nature, the underlying structures and laws which govern phenomena. This great programme he called the *Instauratio magna*: it would have various parts and its culmination would be a new science of nature. The key element in it, however, would be a new inductive logic or methodology of science. Bacon rightly distrusted induction by simple enumeration – the use of generalization from a collection of favourable instances – and insisted on the greater force of the negative instance (*maior est vis instantiae negativae*) as a method of elimination of improper candidates for the title of the forms that explain phenomena. In other words, the aim of the exercise was to eliminate various possible explanations of a phenomenon in order to arrive at the one actual explanation which Bacon believed was there to be discovered, because nature is founded on a limited number of forms or generating causes. A disconfirming instance serves that end much more than any number of confirming instances.

To that end Bacon put forward the idea of three tables of investigation – those of presence, absence and degrees. If, to use Bacon's favourite example, one wants to find the form of heat, one collects in the first table various instances of heat, the aim being to eliminate what they do not have in common: that is to say, what is not present generally when heat is present. In the second table one collects together cases which are like those in the first table, but which do not go with heat. For example, in the first table one may have listed the rays of the sun, which produce heat; in the second table one might therefore include things such as the rays of the moon or stars, which do not produce heat. On that basis one can then eliminate all those things which are present when heat is absent. Finally, in the third table, one collects cases where heat is present in varying degrees, to see whether these things vary with the degrees of heat; if they do not, they can be eliminated. The hope is that the employment of the three methods together will finally eliminate all candidates for the underlying cause of heat except the actual one, which Bacon thinks is motion.

Bacon does not think that the interpretation of the tables is unproblematic and he goes on (or planned to go on, since the work is incomplete) to specify other considerations which would help the process of induction and lead to certainty. The main sort of consideration which he does set out is the appeal to 'prerogative instances', cases in which some peculiarity determines the issue, such as their uniqueness, or their making explicit a crucial difference between two possible forms or natures in connection with the phenomenon in question. Nevertheless, despite the complexity of the search for causes, Bacon did think that there was a method for eliminating all but one of the finite number of possible forms for a given phenomenon, and that nature was such that the method could lead to certainty.

The stages of the overall method to be found in the three tables have sometimes been seen as anticipations of J. S. Mill's methods of agreement, difference and concomitant variations, as set out in his *System of Logic* in the nineteenth century. There are differences between the two, however, both in the details and in their presuppositions. For example, Mill's aim in his method of difference was to find a *single* difference between instances in which a phenomenon occurs and instances in which it does not, and so identify the cause of the phenomenon with that distinguishing item. That is not Bacon's aim, because his method is more strictly eliminative than Mill's. On the other hand, a method of elimination does depend upon the assumption that there is a finite number of possibilities and that there is a single thing which constitutes the nature of the phenomenon being investigated. Bacon made those assumptions, and it was because he considered them tenable that he thought it possible, as suggested for the House of Solomon in the *New Atlantis* for a number of people to be given distinct roles in a cooperative enterprise concerned with the collection of instances in accordance with the general method. Science has not worked out like that, nor has it turned out to be in any clear sense Baconian. Bacon pressed upon James I, however, the idea of a college for the pursuit of science, and his idea led to the founding in due course of the Royal Society and similar organizations elsewhere.

It is clear that, in spite of his disparagement of past philosophers, Bacon's conception of nature presupposes a definite metaphysics. His use of the very word 'form' indicates that. Nature is deterministic, the result of a finite number of generating mechanisms associated with particular law-like natures or essences. In all that, there are echoes of previous theories, despite the newness of his methodology. His writings also suggest a connection between the forms to be discovered and the primary qualities of things. It will be remembered that Galileo identified these with the physical nature of things to the exclusion of secondary qualities. Bacon also had an interest in atomism, but was inclined not to believe in the possibility of a vacuum, and found other empirical phenomena difficult to square with atomism. Hence the details of his metaphysics are not set out with any definiteness or perhaps even consistency.

This is in some ways a reflection of the character of the man. As well as being a philosopher, he became Lord Chancellor and Viscount St Albans, spent much of his life in the affairs and intrigues of the court under Elizabeth I and James I, and devoted a great deal of time to the attempt to get royal favour, partly in order to further his schemes for science. He was not very successful in that, and was in the end expelled from court after being found guilty of taking bribes (to which he pleaded guilty while claiming that they did not affect his judgements!). He died, perhaps characteristically, after catching a chill from going out into the snow in order to conduct an experiment on the preservative effects of cold on a chicken. He was, however, a man of vision and a product of the 'new age' which the new science was introducing.

Hobbes

A clear effect of that new science was a certain obsession with method. It is obviously there in Bacon and, as will appear in the next chapter, it was there in Descartes. Few saw in the new science the need for the emphasis on induction that Bacon insisted upon, and most others saw the need for a greater emphasis on mathematics in general and geometry in particular. Hence the suggestion of Descartes that knowledge should be set out in geometrical fashion, with axioms, definitions and derived theorems – a suggestion that was taken to its extreme in Spinoza's *Ethics*. That conception of things influenced others in a less direct and explicit way. Hence I shall take as my last example of this influence the philosophy of Thomas Hobbes (1588–1679).

It may seem odd that I chose to include Hobbes in this chapter, but leave his near-contemporary Descartes until the next. Is Hobbes, despite his dates, a figure who belongs to the Renaissance in a way that Descartes does not? Perhaps not, but Descartes, as we shall see, introduced a new approach to certain aspects of philosophy in a way that makes him a genuine revolutionary as Hobbes was not. Hobbes' philosophy of nature, as found in his *De Corpore*, is materialist and atomist in a way that puts him with Gassendi. His view of man is largely consistent with that. His views about religion, which some have seen as atheistical, were similar to, but more radical in their implications than, those of Gassendi. To all this precedents can be found in earlier atomism. Hobbes' political philosophy, with which his name is chiefly associated, began to be formed (particularly in his *De Cive*) at the beginning of the Civil War, and *Leviathan*, his greatest work, was published in 1651, during the Commonwealth. He explicitly acknowledged the effects of these historical events on his thinking. But versions of the social contract view of the relationship between individuals and the state can be found much earlier, in Plato and Greek Atomism for instance. Hence, despite the influence of the new science and methodology, Hobbes' philosophy can be viewed as the culmination of previous ways of thinking which were brought to prominence during the Renaissance. Although Hobbes' political thinking had immense influence on others, the rest of his philosophy was far less influential, and, one might say, had no immediate followers.

It would in any case be wrong to see even Hobbes' political philosophy as existing in a vacuum of thought in that area. Hobbes probably knew of the views of Machiavelli (1469–1527), whose *The Prince* had, though recognizing the advantages of a free republic, nevertheless insisted on the necessity of monarchic despotism for good order, and – somewhat cynically in most people's opinion – advised the prince how that was to be maintained. Hobbes' sovereign is equally absolute and his function is to keep the peace and preserve order. Richard Hooker (1553–1600), who was to influence John Locke, put forward in his *Laws of Ecclesiastical Polity*, within the context of a view of natural law which looked back to Aquinas, the idea of civil government being based on the consent of the governed. Others too put forward the idea of contract as the foundation of political obligation, and Grotius (1583–1645) associated this with a full-blown theory of natural law, founded on the nature of man without recourse to the idea of God. It is the natural law which is, for example, the source of the obligation to keep promises, the source of the law itself being the nature of man as a social animal. All these ideas have their reflection, in one way or another, in Hobbes.

The first part of Hobbes' *Leviathan* is entitled 'Of Man'. It attempts to provide the premises from which the next part, 'Of Commonwealth', is to be derived in the spirit of Hobbes' love of geometry. In many ways it is in tune with atomistic doctrines, and it is certainly materialist. From 1634 until 1637 Hobbes had been in continental Europe, where he became associated with the circle of philosophers attached to the Abbé

Mersenne and met Gassendi; he also visited Galileo. He returned to England before the Civil War but fled to France in 1640, where he eventually became for a short time tutor to the future Charles II. *Leviathan* was published while Hobbes was still in France, although he returned to England that same year (1651).

For Hobbes all thought is derived ultimately from sense-perception, so that he is to that extent an empiricist, just as Epicurus had been. Objects produce motions in sense-organs, and thereby affect the brain and heart (to which Hobbes attached almost as much importance as did Aristotle), producing an 'endeavour' which 'because *outward*, seemeth to be some matter without'. Imagination is decayed sense and memory is a function of imagination. Thought is dependent on memory in turn. Hobbes attaches a special importance to speech and language, its use being 'to transfer our mental discourse, into verbal', words functioning thereby as signs, rather as was the case with William of Ockham. Hobbes also asserts that names are the only universal things, and because of this he is generally classified as a nominalist. He does not, however, show the same subtlety over these matters, and about the nature of language in general, as Ockham had done. Nevertheless, Hobbes is fully alive to the possible abuses of language and to the ways in which words can deceive and mislead. Reason, he says, is 'nothing but *reckoning*, that is adding and subtracting, of the consequences of general names agreed upon for the *marking* and *signifying* of our thoughts'.

There are also motions coming from within, which Hobbes calls, as already mentioned, 'endeavour'. These are the source of voluntary motions and account for desire and the passions generally. Will is 'the last appetite, or aversion, immediately adhering to the action'. The ends of action are simply those things that bring motion to an end; if the vital motions are allowed to take place without hindrance, we have pleasure; if not, displeasure. We regard as good what furthers our desires, and felicity is '*continual success* in obtaining those things which a man from time to time desireth'. There is no such thing as continued tranquillity of mind in this life, because life is just motion and there can never be freedom from desire. On all this is built Hobbes' theory of human motivation.

The fact that men have the same motivation and a rather similar power leads to enmity between them, and thus to war; and in war of this kind the life of man is, in one of Hobbes' most famous phrases, 'solitary, poor, nasty, brutish and short'. Such is the state of nature, conceived of not as something that actually holds good anywhere or has actually done so (despite some gesturing on Hobbes' part to what may be the case with 'the savage people in many places in America') but as what would be the case if there were no means of preserving peace, simply as a result of man's nature. 'The passions that incline men to peace,' Hobbes says (*Leviathan*, ch. 13), 'are fear of death; desire of such things as are necessary to commodious living; and a hope by their industry to obtain them.' Because of this, reason suggests what Hobbes calls 'convenient articles of peace, upon which men may be drawn to agreement'. These are what are otherwise called 'Laws of Nature'. It is this idea which leads to the idea of a social contract.

A natural right, Hobbes says, is the liberty that each man has to use his own power, and liberty is simply the absence of external impediments. In a state of nature every man has the natural right to everything, 'even to another's body'. The result of this is that nobody has security. So, it is a 'precept, or general rule of reason' that 'every man, ought to endeavour peace, as far as he has any hope of obtaining it; and when he cannot obtain it, that he may seek, and use, all helps, and advantages of war'. There is a second law to be derived from this – that 'a man be willing, when others are so too, as far-forth, as for peace, and defence of himself he shall think it necessary, to lay down this right to all things; and be contented with so much liberty against other men, as he would allow other men against himself'. Hence in Part II, 'Of Commonwealth', Hobbes sees the generation of a commonwealth, in the interests of peace and security, as a convenant 'of every man with every man, in such manner, as if every man should say to every man, *I authorize and give up my right of governing myself, to this man, or to this assembly of men, on this condition, that thou give up thy right to him, and authorize all his actions in like manner*'. Having thus given up his right to the sovereign, however constituted, no man has the right to rebel against the sovereign except on the one condition that the sovereign, the Leviathan, does not do what he was set up to do – preserve peace and security. This is the case with a 'commonwealth by institution'; in the case of a commonwealth by acquisition, where sovereignty has been acquired by force, the covenant is between the subjects and the sovereign, on the same condition.

This means that the obligation to obey the sovereign rests upon a covenant, and the obligation to maintain the covenant rests upon convenient articles of peace, which themselves rest upon the facts of human motivation when men live together – or so Hobbes would have us believe. It means that political obligation rests upon a moral obligation, but this rests on merely prudential principles (which is really all the convenient articles of peace are), which derive their force from certain supposed facts about human nature. It is noteworthy that Hobbes in effect says that Laws of Nature, the natural law that so many previous philosophers had appealed to, are merely prudential principles; they are natural laws only in that they are supposedly derived from facts about nature, about human nature. Many philosophers would claim that this chain of derivation is invalid at more than one point. One cannot derive a moral principle from a merely prudential one, nor that from facts about nature. But at the end of Hobbes' argument the obligation to obey the sovereign remains a merely conditional one, and is not absolute. One should obey the sovereign as long as he preserves peace and security. But what sort of 'should' is that? The answer to that question remains obscure in Hobbes' system.

It should be noted that the first two parts of *Leviathan* amount to only half the book. The rest is given up to 'Of a Christian Commonwealth' and 'Of the Kingdom of Darkness'; it is not much read. Hobbes had in fact added another *proviso* to the statement of the obligation that subjects have to the sovereign; they owe simple obedience 'in all things wherein their obedience is not repugnant to the laws of God'. We need therefore to know those laws of God. They are, Hobbes says, either the laws which concern the natural duties of one man to another, or those which concern the honour to be paid to the Divine Sovereign. These latter issues, like everything else, are to be determined by the civil sovereign. In a Christian commonwealth the head of the Church and the civil sovereign will be the same. Part III of *Leviathan* is meant to show that the same conclusion is to be derived from the revelation provided by the scriptures. Part IV is concerned with opponents of this view – Catholicism and some forms of Non-Conformism, together with forms of superstition, both religious and philosophical. It is an extraordinary book.

Argument concerning the basis of political obligation went on among subsequent philosophers, especially in connection with the idea of a social contract. Different political situations tended to alter the tone of this, and there can be no doubt that Hobbes was profoundly affected by the political circumstances of his time. But the attempt to found political obligation on an account of human nature in accordance with a generally materialistic view of nature as a whole was not repeated with quite the same flavour and fervour, even in the rather different materialist context that Marx argued for. It is no exaggeration to say that Hobbes represents the end of an era.

[10]
Rationalism

It is conventional to divide the philosophers of the seventeenth and eighteenth centuries into Rationalists and Empiricists. Rationalism is a title which is given, roughly speaking, to the Continental philosophers of the period, empiricism to the so-called British Empiricists: Locke, Berkeley and Hume. It is a very rough and sometimes inaccurate categorization. There are some aspects of Locke's philosophy, for example, which are decidedly rationalist in the sense that they put weight on reason or the understanding, as distinct from the senses or sense-perception. On the other hand, there were a number of Continental philosophers in the period, particularly philosophers in France who were influenced by Locke – for example Condillac, and some of the philosophers associated with the *Encyclopédie* under Diderot, and later Maine de Biran – who were empiricist in tendency. The history of philosophy is rarely tidy.

Nevertheless, there is some reason in making a distinction between the kind of philosophical movement initiated by Descartes and carried on with varying degrees of thoroughness by Spinoza and Leibniz, and the more empirical philosophy that began with Locke and was carried on by Berkeley and Hume in Britain. It may be that some of these philosophers would not have accepted the relevant title, and Berkeley, for one, is in a way more notable for a certain form of metaphysics – idealism – even if that was built upon an empiricist epistemology. I shall, in the following, accept the conventional division, which is at best one that reflects general tendencies of thought, because it has a certain convenience; but it must always be remembered that it is not entirely accurate.

In this chapter I shall therefore deal with Descartes, Spinoza and Leibniz, with a sideways look at one or two of the Cartesians. In the next chapter I shall consider the British Empiricists, Locke, Berkeley and Hume, with, as a sort of addendum, Thomas Reid. I shall reserve for the following chapter a brief consideration of a number of other figures of the eighteenth century, mostly more concerned with ethics and political philosophy than with the epistemology and metaphysics of those who are usually considered the major figures. I have in mind the moral sense philosophers in Britain, the French 'encyclopedists', and Rousseau and Vico.

Descartes

René Descartes (1596–1650) was born at La Haye, near Poitiers. He attended a Jesuit college at La Flèche, and perhaps the University of Poitiers. He then joined the army, for, as he put it, educational reasons, served in the Netherlands and Germany, and was present at the battle of Prague. He began writing while in the Netherlands, and during his army career he had one night certain dreams which suggested to him that his destiny was to found a complete science of nature based on mathematics. After the battle of Prague he left the army, travelled, and then settled in Paris. In 1628 he returned to the Netherlands, where he stayed for twenty years. At about this time he wrote his *Regulae* (*Rules for the Direction of the Mind*) and after further studies completed by 1634 a work entitled *Le Monde*, which he then suppressed when he heard of the condemnation of Galileo for teaching the Copernican system, as his own work did. That action was not untypical of Descartes' attitude to authority, which affected his subsequent publications. In 1637 he published his *Discourse on Method*, followed by works on optics, physics and geometry. These works were published in French, apparently in the hope of gaining popular support. When in 1641 he published his *Meditations on First Philosophy*, together with objections by various philosophers collected by Mersenne and his own replies, he wrote again in Latin, but the work was translated into French with Descartes' approval. It has come to be thought of as his central work, but his hope that by it he would elicit approval from the theological and philosophical establishment was unfulfilled, and he met with much hostility, a fact that somewhat coloured his philosophical attitudes. In 1644 he published his *Principles of Philosophy*, again in Latin – an attempt to present his whole system, but in a didactic way. Finally in 1649 he was persuaded by Queen Christina of Sweden to live in Stockholm and teach her philosophy, and he died there in 1650, having published the *Passions of the Soul*, in French, in 1649.

Despite his rather ambiguous relations with the authorities of his day, there is no doubt that Descartes is a true philosophical revolutionary, even if some of his philosophical language looks back to his scholastic predecessors. Perhaps the key notion in his philosophy is that of 'ideas'. Descartes is not totally clear, or even consistent, about what he means by that term, but in one of the letters he says that by it he means all that is in our mind when we conceive a thing, however we may conceive it. The emphasis upon ideas thus implies an emphasis upon human understanding, and an inquiry based upon ideas is an inquiry into what 'we' think. From an individual point of view this could be put in terms of what 'I' think. There is thus a sense in which the search for truth, which

Descartes often puts as the goal of his inquiry, is one based upon what each of us can discover in himself or herself.

The *Regulae* (which remained unpublished until 1701) and the *Discourse on Method* could be represented as attempts to lay down recipes for the pursuit of knowledge in general. The method that Descartes advocates is an analytical one, no doubt inspired by his mathematical studies. He thus emphasizes the necessity of trying to isolate the simple, and then, but only then, trying to build the complex on its basis. The aim of the whole exercise is to arrive at certainty. Moreover, this is put forward not just as a method for philosophy, but as a quite general method which all pursuit of knowledge should follow. The *Discourse on Method*, which is written in a very autobiographical style, sets out in this spirit four rules: (1) 'to accept nothing as true which I did not clearly recognize to be so'; (2) 'to divide each of the difficulties under examination into as many parts as possible'; (3) to carry on reflections in an order 'beginning with objects that are the most simple and easiest to understand, in order to rise little by little, or by degrees, to knowledge of the most complex'; and (4) to be so thorough and general as to be 'certain of having omitted nothing'.

Apart from the analytical basis of these rules and their general concern with arrival at certainty, there is nothing particularly startling or revolutionary in them. In Part IV of the *Discourse*, however, Descartes represents himself as having lighted upon what is perhaps his most celebrated idea: the indubitability of the truth, 'I think, therefore I am' (*Cogito, ergo sum*, so that the truth has received the title of the '*Cogito*'). Moreover, he arrives at this as a result, first of the observation that we are often deceived in what we perceive and think, and second of a more positive policy of doubting things in general. This general policy (the so-called 'method of doubt') is also spelt out in the *First Meditation*, with the additional consideration that there might be a malignant demon who systematically deceives us. Descartes thinks that the one thing that survives such systematic doubt is the '*Cogito*', or, as he puts it in the *Second Meditation*, ' "I am, I exist" is necessarily true whenever I utter it or conceive it in my mind'. In the *Discourse* he swiftly concludes from that in turn that he is a substance whose essence or nature consists in thinking and is thus wholly distinct from the body, the essence of which consists in extension. The *Meditations* argument takes rather longer and is subject to certain qualifications.

It was objected to Descartes at the time that something like the '*Cogito*' had been employed by Augustine, although with a different purpose. But one thing that marks off Descartes' procedure is that he arrives at his conclusion *via* a consideration of what he himself thinks: it involves, one might say, a kind of self-examination. In the *Discourse* again, he claims to derive from it a further rule 'that the things which we conceive very clearly and very distinctly are all true', although there are problems over the identification of such objects. Hence the idea of one's own existence and thereby of one's own nature is one that must be both clear and distinct. On the whole Descartes tends to take the notions of the clarity and distinctness of ideas for granted, although in the *Principles* I.45 he explains clarity by analogy with vision in terms of how objects strike us, and says that something is distinct when it contains nothing that is not clear. Leibniz was to offer a more formal account of these notions, but Descartes leaves it at that. The account, however, brings out yet again how Descartes' approach depends upon what is evident to the individual. It is this individualist basis of Descartes' philosophical inquiry that is the notable and indeed revolutionary thing.

The exact logical status of the '*Cogito*' has been much discussed by commentators, both contemporaries of Descartes and more recent philosophers. In reply to objections, Descartes insisted that the '*Cogito*', in spite of its form, is not to be taken as an inference; its truth is something that we perceive by the 'natural light'. The procedure involved in the method of doubt suggests that Descartes is saying that I can doubt – that is, I can suppose to be false – all else, but the one thing that I cannot suppose to be false is that I am doing that. It is not clear, however, that that, if true at all, expresses more than a psychological impossibility. On the other hand, there is clearly something paradoxical in the denial both of one's own existence and of one's involvement in thinking (since denial surely involves just that). Yet, as Gassendi pointed out in his objections to Descartes' *Meditations*, my existence seems to follow just as directly from the truth of 'I walk' as from that of 'I think'. Descartes pointed out that there is a difference in that the truth of 'I walk' is not itself evident – one could be wrong about the fact that one is walking – in the way that the truth of 'I think' is. If one is thinking, that fact is, so to speak, self-presenting. Nevertheless, it has to be pointed out that the best that that offers is that if one is looking for something that one cannot doubt without absurdity, then one cannot doubt that one is doing that very thing, and thus is thinking. I say 'best that that offers', because that does not provide a certain and indubitable truth that could function as a premise from which other truths could be derived. Yet that is just what the argument of the *Meditations* suggests is required, as we shall see shortly.

Before we turn to that, it is necessary to make a further point about terminology. I said earlier that for Descartes an idea is whatever is in our mind when we conceive a thing. Likewise, the notion of thought that we have been operating with so far is one that corresponds reasonably well to our ordinary use of that word. It is sometimes said, however, that 'thought' (*cogitatio*) covers anything that involves consciousness, and that '*cogitatio*' or '*pensée*' should be translated 'consciousness'. It is true that at *Principles* I.9, for example, he says that by thought he understands all that so takes place that we are consciously aware of it, and goes on to say that thinking includes understanding, willing, imagining and even perception. But when concerned with the question of his nature as a thinking thing, he seems to take a narrower view of thought, and in the *Sixth Meditation* he says that perception and sensation are *modes* of thinking. Given his use of the term 'mode' this means that they depend on thought in the sense that they cannot occur without it, while thought can occur without them. It is this narrower use of the term 'thought' and the emphasis upon it that justifies the ascription of the label 'rationalist' to him. The notion of an idea, on the other hand, is sometimes restricted by him in another way. Thus in the *Third Meditation* he says that the term 'idea' applies properly only to those thoughts that are 'as it were, images of things'. To the extent that we are concerned with ideas, therefore, we are concerned with representations of things, and the doctrine that the mind in general, and perception in particular, is concerned with ideas is commensurate with the doctrine sometimes referred to as the representative theory of the mind or of perception.

In the light of this, or perhaps in the lack of light provided by this, let us turn to the general argument of the *Meditations*. The *First Meditation* expounds the general argument based on the method of doubt, appealing to, among other things, the supposed lack of a conclusive method for distinguishing dreaming from waking experience. It comprises a form of scepticism, except that Descartes uses the sceptical arguments with the definite aim of finding something in the end which provides certain knowledge. Descartes is no sceptic in a genuine sense, and the doubt that he engages in he calls 'hyperbolic'; it is not a genuine doubt. The *Second Meditation* is entitled 'Of the nature of the human mind, and that it is more easily known than is the body'. At the outset he invokes the '*Cogito*' though only in the form that the proposition 'I think' is 'necessarily true whenever I utter it or conceive it in my mind'. As I indicated earlier, to leave matters there would be quite insufficient for his purposes. So, he asks, 'What am I?' He suggests that all those properties of myself which depend on the body (and he does not deny that they *are* properties of myself) might be such that ideas of them are produced in my mind by a malignant demon, so as to deceive me. This applies not only to corporeal characteristics but also, for example, to perception which depends upon the body. It is only in relation to thinking that I am certain that I exist;

and the answer to the question 'What am I?' is 'A thinking thing'. It is only in this that I have a clear and distinct idea of myself.

As we have seen, thinking covers will and perception, but in being aware of myself simply as a perceiver I do not have a clear and distinct idea of myself. The one thing that I can be certain of in perception is that I *seem* to see light, hear a noise, etc.; indeed Descartes adds that it is this seeming to see, etc., which is properly called perceiving, and it is nothing else but thinking. There is much to argue about in that. Is my seeming to see a light properly characterized as thinking there is a light in the sense of 'thinking' that Descartes seems to have in mind (according to which 'think' does not just mean 'believe')? Is it the case that whenever something seems to me to be such and such I either believe or think that it is such and such? Nevertheless, Descartes takes himself to have shown that he is a thinking thing with a variety of thoughts.

The rest of the *Second Meditation* follows a rather curious course. He seeks to show that we may have a clear and distinct idea even of corporeal bodies through a mental intuition, but that the idea that we have of our mind is even more clear and distinct. Since we know of the nature of bodies through the intellect alone, it is supposed to be obvious that the intellect can know itself even more easily and clearly. Gassendi protested about this stage of the argument, and perhaps rightly. The earlier stages of the argument, which seek to show that we can know the nature of bodies by an intuition of the intellect, have acquired a certain notoriety. Descartes appeals to the example of a piece of wax, which is perceived as having certain sensory properties. When the wax is melted, however, those properties disappear, although the wax remains, and remains as 'something extended, flexible and movable'. The latter two properties reduce to variations of extension, so that it is extension that is the key factor. But, he claims, we do not perceive this as we did the properties that belonged to the unmelted wax; nor is it known by the imagination, since the variations of extension possible in its regard may go beyond what I can imagine. So, we know of the nature of the wax – its extension – through the mind alone. There is much that is defective with the argument as presented. Not all the properties of the wax need disappear when it melts, for example, and the final claim about the mind's intuition seems something of a jump. Elsewhere, however, Descartes brings forward considerations of a more general kind that may give some support to his conclusion, and it is in any case the *Fifth Meditation* that offers a general theory of matter.

Given that I am a thinking thing with a variety of ideas, it still has to be shown that those ideas correspond to anything, so that I can justifiably conclude that there actually exists a material world independent of me –

the so-called external world. Descartes' general strategy in the remaining *Meditations*, as far as this is concerned, is to rule out the possibility of the deceiving demon, by establishing the existence of a non-deceiving God who is responsible for the ideas that I have. Hence the *Third Meditation* is devoted to a proof of God's existence, and the *Fourth* to considerations about truth and error. In fact, Descartes brings forward two proofs of God's existence, the second in the *Fifth Meditation*. The one used in the *Third Meditation* is a version of the cosmological argument. Descartes classifies ideas into those which are innate, those which are, as he puts it, adventitious, and those which are factitious or made by oneself. To use ideas that we have to prove the existence of God, it is necessary to show that the idea that we have of God is one of an actual God. On the causal/representational view of the mind that Descartes espouses, this means that it is necessary to show that God is the cause of the idea that we have of him; it is not an innate idea, deriving from my own nature, as Descartes supposes the idea of truth, for example, to be, nor is it something simply made up by myself.

He starts from the presupposition that the idea of God is the idea of a perfect and infinite being. He then invokes a general principle that when X causes Y there must be at least as much reality or perfection in X as in Y. Where we are concerned with the causes of ideas, we need certain other refinements in addition. Descartes says that the cause of an idea must possess at least as much reality as the idea both formally and objectively. The terminology, which is scholastic in origin, has caused interpreters difficulty because its meaning is the opposite of what an immediate intuition might suggest. The formal reality is the reality that something has in itself (because of its form); the objective reality is the reality that something has in respect of its object. In the case of the cause/effect relation the cause must either have as much reality as the effect, in which case the reality is in it formally, or it must have more reality, in which case it has it eminently. Descartes argues that the idea of a perfect being must have a cause which has formally at least as much reality as that idea has objectively. That cause cannot be whoever has the idea; it cannot be Descartes himself, because he has obvious imperfections. Hence there must actually exist a perfect being to be the cause of that idea of him. The argument has generally been judged unsatisfactory. Apart from the presuppositions of the argument, and the dubious scholastic apparatus, there is the question whether we do have an idea of God which might be said to have this kind of perfection.

In the *Fifth Meditation*, in a somewhat different context, Descartes seeks to prove the existence of God by a form of the 'ontological argument', maintaining that existence must be a property of a being who is conceived of as possessing all attributes in perfection. He claims indeed that one cannot conceive of God except as existing, any more than one can conceive of a mountain without a valley. It was to this version of the argument that Kant responded by asserting that existence was not a predicate, not a property of a thing in the way that Descartes supposes. Whether that claim is right in its generality, it certainly cannot be the case that something's existence follows from its conception. Apart from anything else, as Leibniz maintained, it depends on whether that conception is coherent or involves a contradiction.

However that may be, Descartes takes himself to have proved the existence of God and goes on in the *Fourth Meditation* to try to show that God is not a deceiver. Or rather he tries to show, in effect, that he cannot be, since the possibility of error is due to our ability to assent to what is false, and assent is a function of our will. God has given us free will partly for this reason. God is not a deceiver, in the sense that we are not deceived in the natural inclination which we have to take our ideas as having a reality corresponding to them. Error arises from what we ourselves make of that. The trouble with this is that it now seems that we might withhold assent to anything, including that of which we have clear and distinct ideas, with the result that no belief need be incorrigible. In the end, our assurance that our clear and distinct perceptions are true, and that we are not engaging in mistaken assent to the wrong thing, must depend on the simple view that God is not a deceiver. But that is a separate issue from what is implied in the doctrine of the sources of error. What needs to be shown is that in the case of some perceptions we cannot be in error, we cannot misuse our will; that God *would* not deceive us is neither here nor there. In any case the whole doctrine gives rise to what has become known as the 'Cartesian circle'. We need God to preserve the force of clear and distinct ideas, but the proofs of God's existence depend on the identification of certain clear and distinct ideas. Descartes tried to reply to this by saying that it was not the force of clear and distinct ideas in themselves that we need God to preserve, but the conclusions that we draw while relying on memory without attending in the present to what is clear and distinct. It is very doubtful whether such a reply meets the point.

In the *Fifth Meditation*, apart from the proof of God's existence already referred to, Descartes seeks to found on that knowledge of God the very existence of science as he conceives of it. The nature of matter is that extension which was invoked in the passage about the wax, but now Descartes argues that it is extension that is the essential nature of matter, and that knowledge of it comes from geometry. It is the so-called primary qualities of objects that are expressible in geometrical terms and which constitute material reality. Secondary qualities, such as colour, are purely subjective, and the *Dioptric* offers an account of the physics and psychology of perception to explain how that is so. But in geometry we have knowledge of the objective properties of things. Descartes had originally suggested that the malignant demon might deceive us even over the truths of geometry and mathematics generally. Now he claims that because we know that God is not a deceiver, we can rely on geometry and mathematics, and because of geometry in particular we have knowledge of the physical world. Thus 'all science depends upon the knowledge alone of the true God'. I shall not enter here into a consideration of Cartesian physics in general. Much of it became discredited with further developments of science. It may suffice to point out that since matter's essential nature is extension, there can be no void or vacuum, and matter must constitute a continuous plenum.

Despite what I have said in the preceding paragraph about the possibility of science, Descartes does not consider himself to have shown at the beginning of the *Sixth Meditation* that material things exist. He claims that he at least knows already that they *can* exist in so far as they are considered as objects of geometrical proofs, since in that way he conceives them very clearly and distinctly. For God has the power of producing everything that he is capable of conceiving in distinction. Moreover we have a natural inclination, through the imagination, to be persuaded of the existence of material things. It is perception that provides us with information about material things; but perception depends upon the body and is also passive in the sense that it depends upon the agency of something else, which we suppose to be material things. What are the grounds for the belief that the latter supposal is in fact correct? Descartes' answer to that question is complicated, because it involves also his final answer to the question 'What am I?'. It is that I am a thinking thing distinct from the body, although nature teaches us that we are in that body, not, as he puts it, as a pilot in a ship, but in such a way as to form a unity with it.

Descartes' argument for the absolute distinctness of myself, or my mind, and my body, is that I have a clear and distinct idea of myself as a thinking thing, and I have a separate clear and distinct idea of the body as an extended thing. All that I clearly and distinctly conceive can be produced by God exactly as I conceive it, and that is sufficient to show that if I clearly and distinctly conceive them as different they are different. They have different essences, and therefore have no necessary connection. So, he says, 'it is certain that I am entirely and truly distinct from my body, and can exist apart from it'. That is so because I am my mind. That argument must not be taken as showing that I do in fact exist apart from my body. It is directed simply to showing that I as a thinking thing and my body are different natures, and it rests on the epistemological point that what is clearly and distinctly conceived as different is in fact different in nature. The acceptability of the conclusion depends entirely on the acceptability of that premise.

Nevertheless, we do have faculties like those of imagination and perception, which, Descartes says, are modes of thinking, in that they involve ideas, but also depend on the body. They are possible only if there is some kind of connection between the mind and the body. It is indeed sensations such as pain, hunger and thirst which, he says, teach us that I am not in my body as a pilot in a ship; there must be a closer connection than that. It was this point that perplexed the Princess Elizabeth of Bohemia, and Descartes replied in correspondence with her, speaking of a quasi-substantial union between the mind or soul and the body. The questions that all this gives rise to make up what has come to be known as the mind–body problem; it is a problem which Descartes has in effect bequeathed to us. But as he raises it, it is not simply a question of what relation is supposed to exist between mental states and events and their bodily counterparts; it is one of how two substances with utterly distinct natures can be connected as experience suggests they are.

Descartes' final argument for the existence of material things, given his account of perception, depends on the same principles about causality as were invoked earlier. We know that the ideas produced in perception, being passive, are not produced by ourselves. They must therefore be produced by something that has at least as much reality as the ideas themselves have; or, to be more exact, they must be produced by something that has formally at least as much reality as the ideas have objectively. They must therefore either be produced by their objects themselves or by God. But it cannot be God, since he is no deceiver. Hence they must be produced by material things themselves, as we have a natural tendency to believe. Hence the argument depends once again on the point that God is no deceiver, and *a fortiori* on the previous dubious arguments for the existence of such a being. It has to be noted that Descartes does not take the argument as showing that perception is always veridical. On the contrary, it is only those ideas which are clear and distinct that we can suppose to be so veridical. Hence exact and accurate knowledge of material things is reserved for what is possible *via* geometry. In everyday life we are liable to error constantly, and, as Descartes says in concluding his *Meditations*, 'we must recognize the infirmity and feebleness of our nature'.

I have concentrated on the *Meditations* because the work presents a continuous piece of philosophical argument in a style that is in itself new.

It is certainly the central work in Descartes' philosophy. What is new about the approach to philosophy is, as I said at the beginning, its claim to secure an epistemological and metaphysical underpinning for our knowledge of the world on the basis of what the individual can construct from his own consciousness. The emphasis on what has become known as 'privileged access' is notable, in the form of the claim that we have a clearer and more distinct idea of our own minds than we do of anything else, although Descartes believes that a clear and distinct idea of the nature of matter is also possible. The latter is secondary to the former in the course of the argument, which goes from oneself to God and only then to the material world. The thought that one should approach the world and our knowledge of it in this way has been immensely influential, and it is perhaps only in very recent times that it has become subject to question. Descartes is not a solipsist; he does not think that everything is a function of his own mind. But his approach is one that has leanings in that direction, and there is plausibility in the claim that the idealism that was to appear, in Berkeley for example, could occur only given the framework of Descartes' philosophical ideas. In modern times it has been suggested that those ideas and their individualistic standpoint could make sense only given a public framework – something that Descartes ostensibly casts doubt upon in the method of doubt.

I must add as an addendum that in his last work, the *Passions of the Soul*, which contains a detailed dissection of the emotions, Descartes puts forward the suggestion that the mind is connected to the body through the pineal gland, which is, he says, its seat. Through it animal spirits in the nerves are affected, and they affect it. Descartes also thought that the possession of the soul or mind in the sense specified is peculiar to human beings. Animal bodies are in effect machines and it is only the soul in human beings which marks them off from animals. This is the origin of what Gilbert Ryle has called the notion of a 'paramechanical cause', which he sees as the central Cartesian view. In truth it is not that – not, at all events, by the standard of the *Meditations*.

Earlier I spoke in a way that may seem disparaging about Descartes' contributions to science, saying that they became discredited. So they did, but at the time they were part of a great intellectual ferment out of which was born modern science. Numerous major figures in the history of science were rough contemporaries of Descartes. He himself was not an experimentalist, but the framework of his ideas, the emphasis on mechanics and belief in the law of the constancy of motion, was immensely fertile. The new movement in physics had its culmination in Isaac Newton's *Principia* (1687). It would be quite wrong to underestimate the influence of the developing science on the philosophy of the period. But it would equally be wrong to underestimate the influence of Cartesianism on contemporary and subsequent intellectual movements. It must be evident that in some ways Descartes' philosophy was dependent on the scholasticism of the past – its use of the notions of substance and essence, for example. But the spirit was new; and it was the individualism, whatever its source, which was the crucial element in that. Moreover the fact that numbers of the leading intellectuals of the age felt called upon to respond to Descartes' *Meditations* shows something about the status that was felt to attach to Descartes' ideas.

Cartesianism and Occasionalism

I have already referred briefly to Father Marin Mersenne, who acted as a sort of convenor of discussions between the leading philosophers of the period. A rather more important figure was Antoine Arnauld (1612–94), who, as a young priest, contributed to the objections to the *Meditations*. He later became involved in correspondence with Leibniz, and was certainly a major element in the reaction to Descartes. Arnauld was a member of the movement set up at the abbey of the Port-Royal, by in particular Cornelius Jansen, Bishop of Ypres (1585–1638). In opposition to the Jesuits, Jansen expounded an Augustinian doctrine of the sovereignty of divine grace, and of the limitations of reason, as opposed to faith, in respect of God. Another prominent member of the movement was Blaise Pascal (1623–62), a distinguished mathematician, who took a Jansenist view of the relation of theology to philosophy. In his posthumously published *Pensées*, he put forward the celebrated idea that in relation to God the heart has its reasons; reason proper has a more limited place. He also put forward the idea which has become known as 'Pascal's wager' – that belief in God is the best bet, because if God exists he will reward the belief, and if he does not exist no harm will have resulted from the belief. It is perhaps a curious attitude for a theologian to adopt, and the premises of the argument are not beyond objection. Pascal is not really a major *philosophical* figure, despite his contributions to knowledge in other ways.

Arnauld has a bigger claim to note, because he was the main author of the so-called *Port-Royal Logic* (*La Logique ou l'art de penser*, 1662). Formal logicians would not recognize this work as a substantial part of the history of logic; it looks back to the theories of signification that were prominent in the late Middle Ages, and seeks to clarify the notions of substance, attribute, mode, etc., as these notions were used in the seventeenth century, by Descartes among others. It is notable for making the distinction between the comprehension and extension of terms – between the ideas that a general term expresses and the things to which it is applied – a distinction which was to assume greater importance in later philosophy of logic. Moreover, in the account offered of what are called 'complex terms', such as 'the King of France', the *Port-Royal Logic* raises considerations which are relevant to twentieth-century discussions of what Russell called 'the theory of descriptions'. It does so by considering how the addition of words such as 'of France' restricts the comprehension of the term 'King' so that its extension can be one individual. In cases where the added words are merely implicit, as when one speaks simply of 'the King', the *Port-Royal Logic* appeals to the notion of equivocation, claiming that the intellect has the tendency, in error, to substitute a determinate subject for what is really confused. The language in which all this is expressed has much in common with that of Descartes.

None of these people was, strictly speaking, a Cartesian, although they were all influenced by Cartesianism. The main Cartesian with a status of his own is Nicholas Malebranche (1638–1715), who is particularly associated with the doctrine known as 'Occasionalism'. We have seen that there was an ambiguity in Descartes' account of the relation between body and mind, and of the role of God in our knowledge both of our own body and of bodies around us. Arnold Geulincx (1624–69) put forward the view that it is impossible for bodies which are so different in nature from the mind to affect the mind. What happens is simply that on the occasion of certain physical events God puts into our mind ideas of them. Hence Occasionalism puts a greater weight on the part played by God than was the case even in Descartes, and denies the possibility of the *quasi*-substantial union between mind and body at which Descartes had hinted. Malebranche accepted the same view, but gave it an Augustinian gloss by claiming that in consequence we see all things in God. Indeed Malebranche began life as an Augustinian theologian, and was converted to Cartesianism on reading Descartes' work on *Man*. It is, however, an unorthodox Cartesianism. For one thing, apart from the Occasionalism and the special role given to God, Malebranche denied that we have a clear and distinct idea of the nature of our soul while admitting that we do have such ideas of extension, figure and movement. We know of the mind or soul only by an 'inner sentiment' or *conscience*, and thereby know that it is a thinking thing; but it is quite another matter to say that we have a clear, let alone a distinct, idea of it.

Malebranche's two main works, apart from the theologically orientated *Conversations chrétiennes*, were *De la recherche de la vérité* and *Entretiens sur la métaphysique et sur la religion* (*Dialogues on Metaphysics*). *The Search for Truth* is much preoccupied with the errors to which we are liable. Malebranche claims that the senses were given to us not in order that we might see things in themselves, but only for the conservation of the body. There are traces of that view in Descartes, but Malebranche takes it much further. We know in respect of physical things only that of which we have clear and distinct ideas – their extension, figure and movement – and even then, properly speaking, we know only what God puts into our minds by way of ideas. But Malebranche is not an idealist; he does not deny that there are things beyond our ideas. Ideas which are clear and distinct correspond to these things. Nevertheless, an account of what the senses tell us is, in his view, a record of error. Our eyes, he says, 'generally deceive us in all that they represent to us'. We can be certain that we have sensations; error arises when we make judgements about the things ostensibly responsible for those sensations, and that error must, in the nature of the case, be systematic. For the things in question are not in fact responsible for the sensations.

These sensations are put into our minds by God according to the bodily conditions, and as the latter vary so do the sensations. The idea of the relativity of perception to bodily conditions plays a large part in Malebranche's theory of sense-perception. For the conservation of the body we need to be able to perceive how far things are from us and how big they are, etc. Optics shows, he thinks, how the eyes are deceived. To explain how we are able to correct those errors we need to appeal to a theory about how our judgements override misleading sensations. Such judgements are not what he calls 'free judgements', as ordinary judgement is. We are not aware of making any such judgements when we succeed in seeing correctly the size of things which are at a distance from us – to give one example of our ability to override what optics suggests we should not be able to do. So Malebranche invokes the idea of 'natural judgements' or 'judgements of sense', although he hastens to add that these judgements are really complex sensations, in which one component corrects the other. Once again, these judgements or complex sensations are put into our minds by God. Indeed at the end of the *Recherche* I.9.3 he says that God makes these judgements in us 'in consequence of the laws of the union of the soul and the body'. God puts into our minds all the judgements which we could make ourselves if we knew in a God-like fashion, 'optics, geometry, and all that takes place at the time in our eyes and in our brain'. Malebranche's account of various illusions is of considerable interest, but the general account of perception cannot be said to be happy. The claim that knowledge is restricted to that of which we have clear and distinct ideas is, however, very rationalist.

Spinoza

The philosopher in whose views rationalism receives its most systematic and rigorous expression is undoubtedly Benedict de (or Baruch) Spinoza (1632–77). Spinoza was born in Amsterdam of Jewish parents who had come there as refugees from the Inquisition in Portugal. He had an orthodox Jewish upbringing, but developed sceptical beliefs and was eventually excommunicated from the synagogue. He made a living as a lens-grinder while entering into discussions of the 'new philosophy' of Descartes with a group of enlightened Christians. In 1660 he left Amsterdam to live in seclusion in various small villages, and wrote there the *Treatise on the Correction of the Understanding*, although he did not publish it. He did publish the *Principles of Descartes' Philosophy*, in which that philosophy is expounded in geometrical order, together with an appendix called *Metaphysical Thoughts*; but an introduction written by a friend claimed that the book did not conform to Spinoza's own views. The *Theological-Political Treatise* was published anonymously in 1670. But his main work, *Ethics*, was not published until after his death. All the major works are in Latin.

Spinoza refused an offer of the Chair of Philosophy at Heidelberg in 1673, because he wished to live without official commitments, as he thought a philosopher should. He died of consumption, to which dust from his lens-grinding must have contributed, in 1677. During his lifetime he had some correspondence with Henry Oldenburg of the Royal Society in London, and with the great scientist Christian Huygens, and through them became known to other scientists; but his seclusion kept him unknown to the world in general. When his works were published after his death they were initially greeted with incomprehension, and Spinoza had no direct influence on others, although Leibniz knew him and to some extent reacted to his views. He is a supreme example of what many think a philosopher should be, a man dedicated to the working out of his philosophical ideas.

It is of some importance that Spinoza's main work was called *Ethics*, although one who comes to read it for the first time may be inclined to think that the title is a misnomer. It consists of five parts, in each of which the subject matter is set out in geometrical fashion, with axioms, definitions, and propositions which are said to be proved from those axioms in accordance with the definitions. The first part is ostensibly concerned with God, although it is in fact a highly metaphysical presentation of a theory concerning the nature of reality. The second part is concerned with the nature of the mind; the third with the emotions. So far then we have metaphysics and the philosophy of mind. Parts four and five are in turn concerned with 'Human servitude, or the strength of the emotions' and 'The power of the intellect, or human freedom'. They seek to provide a recipe for the attainment of a form of blessedness, which, Spinoza says, is identical with virtue itself. This was the aim with which Spinoza set out his system. Even the early *Treatise on the Correction of the Understanding* presents the aim of the inquiry in a similar way; it is not, like Descartes' *Regulae*, merely a methodological treatise about the way to attain truth. It is the *correction* of the understanding that is important, and Spinoza sees in his account of reality and of man's place in it the way to a better understanding, which will also bring blessedness. Spinoza provides in this way a striking contrast with Descartes, who had little concern with things ethical. There is perhaps a religious element in Spinoza's thought which is somewhat lacking in Descartes', despite the fact that Descartes was a determined Catholic and Spinoza a lapsed follower of Judaism.

The geometrical form of the exposition shows a determination to follow out the method that Descartes had theoretically held to be *the* method for the pursuit of knowledge, but to which he paid in practice little more than lip-service. Spinoza attempts to provide by its means a unified theory in which everything has its place. The terms of which Spinoza provides definitions in Part I are terms taken from the tradition of philosophy derived from Aristotle – terms such as 'substance', 'attribute', 'mode', 'God' and 'cause of itself' (*causa sui*). The axioms seem relatively uncontroversial, and no doubt Spinoza thought that they were evidently true. 'Substance' is defined as 'that which is in itself and is conceived through itself', and by 'attribute' Spinoza says that he understands 'that which the intellect perceives as constituting the essence of a substance'. It is worthy of note that Spinoza approaches these things *via* what can be conceived or perceived by the intellect. To that extent, the Cartesian tradition of appealing to the mind and its ideas persists. 'God' is defined as a being absolutely infinite, that is a substance consisting of infinite attributes, each of which expresses eternal and infinite essence. Spinoza no doubt believed, and with some justification, that that was how God was conceived in the theological tradition. It is nevertheless true that his conception of God is a very philosophical one. As it turns out, the main function of God is to be the first cause and in that way the cause of itself.

Spinoza does not explicitly explain 'cause', but the definition of 'cause of itself', as that the essence of which involves existence, or that the nature of which cannot be conceived except as existing, indicates that by 'cause' he means something like 'rationale'; he does not have in mind simply our everyday conception of 'cause'. It is for that reason that he can offer as one of the axioms the proposition that from a given determined cause the effect follows of necessity. Hence, if, as turns out to be the case, everything is taken to have its rationale in a first cause, it will follow from that necessarily. Any system which entails that everything has its rationale in this sense in something or other must be one in which determination by that thing, and so determinism, is the rule. So it is with Spinoza. He claims that it follows from his axioms that there is only one substance, which is God. Descartes had said in the *Principles* (I.51) that 'in truth, there can be conceived only one substance which is absolutely independent, and that is God'; and he had gone on to say that the term 'substance' applies to God and his creatures equivocally. Spinoza, in effect, takes the first part of that absolutely seriously and concludes that there is no substance but God. Proposition XIV of Part I of *Ethics* asserts that 'Except God no substance can be granted or conceived'; and Spinoza takes that to follow from the infinity of God and from a further prop-osition that he thinks he has proved – that two or more substances having the same nature or attribute cannot be granted. For the nature or attri-bute of a substance determines its essence. If two substances were to have the same essence nothing would distinguish them, and so Spinoza concludes that it would make no sense to suppose that they were two.

What we ordinarily think of as substances cannot therefore be such. In Spinoza's view they have to be regarded as modes or modifications of the one substance, that is to say they are in it and are to be conceived only through it. All things are thus in a sense in God, and God is the immanent cause of all things. Hence, as I have already noted and Proposition XXIX of Part I makes explicit, 'In the nature of things nothing contingent is granted, but everything is determined from the necessity of the divine nature in order to exist and work in a certain way.' God necessarily exists; he is one alone; he exists and acts entirely from the necessity of his nature; he is the cause of all things and they exist in him and are predetermined by him, not from his free will or beneficence, but as the result of his absolute nature or infinite power – to paraphrase slightly the summary given in the opening words of the Appendix to Part I of *Ethics*. Spinoza is a thoroughgoing monist in the sense that he allows the existence of only one substance, one self-cause which is the cause of everything else, in that everything else is merely a modification or attribute of that sub-stance. The one substance is also infinite, with infinite attributes and modifications. It is no surprise that it is given the name of God.

Part II claims to start again with new definitions and axioms, as do the remaining parts of the work. I shall not, from here onwards, pay attention to that fact, but treat the argument as if it were continuous, which in a way it is. Part II is supposed to be about the nature of the mind, but it begins in effect with the Cartesian distinction between thought and extension. These are both attributes which we think belong to things; but they must really belong to God. Individual thoughts are modes that express the nature of God, which must therefore include thought as an attribute; the same holds good of bodies and the attribute extension. It is at this point that Spinoza's views were seen as shocking, because the God in which all things exist is – quite contrary to the views of Malebranche, who ostensibly embraced the same doctrine – material as well as capable of thought. Later, in Part IV, Spinoza uses the phrase for which he has become famous (or notorious) – 'God or Nature'. These are alternative names for the same thing – a view which seems to entail a sort of pantheism. But if God has infinite attributes, and thought and extension are distinct attributes, God must have them – and the rest follows, if anything does.

In fact Spinoza is even more radical than that. He says that thinking substance and extended substance are, contrary to Descartes, really the same thing comprehended through alternative attributes. Analogously a mode of extension and the idea of that mode are really the same. Spinoza concludes that the order and connection of ideas is the same as the order and connection of things. The human mind is simply part of the infinite intellect of God, and consists first and foremost of the idea of an existing thing, namely the human body. Other things are perceived as they affect the body. Hence Spinoza's answer to the body–mind problem is that mind and body are essentially connected, since the latter is simply the object of the ideas which constitute the former. If we put it in that way, we are, of course, confining our attention to what are in fact *modes* of the one substance, and we are considering their relation accordingly; *sub specie aeternitatis*, as Spinoza sometimes puts it, they are simply parallel aspects of the same thing.

Because other things are perceived as they affect the body, no idea of a modification of the body involves adequate knowledge of an external body – an adequate idea being defined in the definitions as one which, in so far as it is considered in itself without relation to an object, has all the intrinsic properties and marks of a true idea. (The phrase 'without relation to an object' is important; Spinoza does not think it possible to compare ideas with their objects to ascertain their truth.) Conversely, because our ideas of the body arise through its being affected by external bodies, we have no adequate ideas of our body either. Indeed Spinoza says that, whenever the mind perceives a thing according to the common order of Nature, it has no adequate ideas, but only confused ones, of itself, its body and external bodies. This is *not* to say that it cannot have a clear and distinct idea of itself, merely that it cannot do so in this way, and this is the only way in which one can have ideas of the body. So the

Cartesian principle that we can have clear and distinct ideas of the mind in a way that we cannot of the body is preserved, although scarcely in a Cartesian way.

On the basis of this, Spinoza distinguishes between three kinds of knowledge (there were four in the *Treatise on the Correction of the Understanding*). There is, first, knowledge from vague experience, which we have when we generalize from casual and confused experience, and knowledge from signs, which we have when we rely on memory of what we have read or heard. These constitute a knowledge of the first kind, which Spinoza identifies with opinion and imagination. (The *Treatise* separates the two species which Spinoza here brings under a single head.) The second kind of knowledge is identified with reason, and is said to be dependent on the possession of common notions and adequate ideas of the properties of things. Common notions are ideas of things which are common to all things and cannot – so Spinoza thinks – be other than common to all men. They involve ideas of extension and of modifications of it, ideas which lie at the root of science and objective reasoning in general, and which must be adequate. Knowledge of the third kind is intuition. Spinoza says that this kind of knowledge 'proceeds from an adequate idea of the formal essence of certain of the attributes of God to an adequate knowledge of the essence of things'. But he illustrates it by reference to an example which involves simply seeing that a certain relationship holds between numbers. The *Treatise* here speaks of perceiving a thing through its essence alone. Spinoza goes on to say that only the second and third kinds of knowledge are necessarily true, and that reason regards things as necessary and perceives things under a certain species of eternity (*sub quadam aeternitatis specie*). There can be no doubt, however, that it is the third kind of knowledge which he regards as most important, and which is involved in the insight into the nature of reality to which he was laying claim.

The third part of *Ethics* contains an account of the nature of the emotions, and provides a detailed analysis of particular emotions and their differences. Spinoza's main motive, however, is to give an account of the passions and passivity as seen against the mind's essential activity. At the end of the section he gives a general definition of the emotions, saying that an emotion is 'a confused idea through which the mind affirms a greater or less power of existing of its body or some part of it than before, and given which the mind itself is determined to think of this rather than that'. There is much in that definition, but the association between passivity and confused ideas on the one hand, and between activity and clear ideas on the other is notable. At the beginning of the discussion Spinoza introduces a new thought, which he claims to derive from what has already been shown – the thought that 'everything in so far as it is in itself endeavours to persist in its own being'. This endeavour, he says, is called will when it has reference to the mind alone, and is called appetite when it refers to the mind and body simultaneously. It is this which explains changes that take place in the mind. It must be noted, however, that emotions do not merely affect the ideas that we have; emotions *are* ideas. They are confused to the extent that the mind is affected by the body and by things that affect the body. They are clear and adequate to the extent that the ideas are part of the mind's endeavour to persist in its own being. We experience pleasure when our power of preserving our being is enhanced, and pain when that power is diminished.

I shall not enter into further discussion of Spinoza's account of the particular emotions, subtle though that account often is. The fourth and fifth parts of the *Ethics* are the parts which, in the light of the preceding, set out the ends of man and how they are to be achieved. The fourth part is entitled 'On Human Servitude, or the Strength of the Emotions', and the fifth part is entitled 'Concerning the Power of the Intellect, or Human Freedom'. The titles indicate what Spinoza believed we should do, given our nature, as modifications of God or Nature. Freedom and blessedness come from the use of the intellect to acquire adequate ideas, and thus from activity, rather than the passivity that is inherent in emotion. For in having adequate ideas I think rationally and logically, and then one idea has its cause in another because the latter is its ground. ('Cause' and 'logical ground' become, to our modern understanding, conflated here.) Spinoza says at the beginning of Part IV that he means by servitude the lack of power that humans may have in moderating and checking the emotions. For if a man is submissive to his emotions he is not in power over himself. He is subject to things that are largely external, and he does not fulfil the *conatus* or endeavour which is his real nature. For that endeavour with which anything endeavours to persist in its own being is actually the essence of the thing itself (as Proposition VII of Part III makes clear).

The essence of the human mind is thought, and its endeavour is to persist in its power of acting through ideas that are as far as possible adequate. To be subservient to the emotions is to prejudice that power. Freedom derives from an understanding of oneself and one's emotions; the greater that understanding, the greater one's understanding of things in general, and the greater one's understanding of God. The intellectual love of God, which results from that, involves knowledge of the third and highest kind. As Spinoza says (V.38), the more the mind understands things by the second and third kinds of knowledge, the less will it be subservient to the passions, and the less will be its fear of death. Freedom lies in the power that the intellect has to transcend the passivity that reveals itself in the emotions and in the power to acquire an understanding of the nature of things in general, which is both the understanding and the love of God. Such is the message of Spinoza's philosophy. In it freedom becomes the acceptance of absolute determinism, in full awareness of it; but the activity that this involves diminishes the passivity that we display in being subject to the emotions, and so diminishes the subservience to emotion that Spinoza saw as the threat to human freedom itself.

There is of course a paradox in all this. Many philosophers have seen freedom as possible only if human beings can be an exception in some way to a determinist interplay of causes and effects. For Spinoza there is no possibility of such an exception. We are all modifications of God or Nature, and what we are follows from what God or Nature is. In his view, freedom consists in not being subject merely to how external objects affect us, and in not being subject to the influences of the passions. We must follow the endeavour which is our own nature. In the end, freedom lies in the intellectual love of God. But, it may be asked, is not the question whether we shall actually achieve that settled by the absolute determinism which Spinoza maintains? We are as we are because we are modifications of God or Nature. How can we choose whether or not to conform to the principles that Spinoza urges us to accept? Whether we shall do so or not is already determined. If that is freedom we shall achieve it only if we are destined to do so; it is not a matter of our own choice.

This is a fair comment. Other philosophers have sought to reconcile freedom and determinism by providing an analysis of what it is to do something freely, according to which the notion of freedom is restricted to freedom from external impediment. We act freely if we are free from hindrance, restriction and the like. That is not Spinoza's way with the problem, although he insists that we must be free from subjection to the passions, above all perhaps from subjection to the fear of death. It may well seem that salvation must be for Spinoza, as it was later for Schopenhauer, a matter of grace; we shall achieve it if that is how it is to be. There lies the great paradox. Both philosophers assert that salvation can come only from a true understanding of things, including an understanding of ourselves. They both offer an account of what that understanding consists in, and they both urge that understanding on us. It remains true that there must, for both philosophers, be a sense in which whether or not we shall attain that understanding does not lie in our power. They both hold that if we are to attain it, we must do so by shedding what makes us individuals, and by acquiring an impersonal knowledge involving an identification, as far as is possible, with what Spinoza, although not Schopenhauer, calls God.

On the way to this conclusion, Spinoza provides a somewhat destructive account of the basis and nature of our ordinary moral judgements. In the Definitions of Part IV 'good' is defined as that which we certainly know to be useful to us, and 'bad' as that which we certainly know will hinder us so that we have a smaller share in some good. Moreover, the preface to that part of the work says that the terms 'good' and 'bad' indicate nothing positive in things considered in themselves, but rather modes of thinking or notions which we form from the mutual comparison of things. Spinoza's account of what saying that something is good or bad means has some similarity in this respect to that of Hobbes. Spinoza does not allow any other sense of the term as applied to persons. Men are good and bad, more or less perfect, only to the extent that they approach or recede from the idea that we have of man as a type. Hence, he does not allow to these words any sense which we might think of as specifically moral. Moreover he defines 'virtue' in such a way that it means the same as does 'power', saying that 'virtue, in so far as it refers to man, is the essence or nature of man itself, in so far as he has the power of bringing about something which can be understood through the laws of that nature alone'.

The concluding proposition in the book says that blessedness is not the reward of virtue, but virtue itself. So it is, on Spinoza's account of the meaning of these words; for the activity which constitutes the nature of man is that intellectual love of God which is itself blessedness. Spinoza's use of the terms involved is entirely naturalistic in the sense that he uses these apparently moral words simply to describe what happens as a fact of nature; he does not give them a specifically evaluative sense in a way that also makes them distinctively moral. Although we can describe Spinoza as concerned with the end of man, we should recognize that he means by 'end' simply what man in his true nature really is; it is only the passions and the influence of external things that prevent that nature being realized. The wise man, he says in his concluding remarks, is scarcely moved in mind, but conscious of himself, God and things by a certain eternal necessity, never ceases to be, but always enjoys a true acquiescence of mind. The achievement of that may be difficult, but 'all excellent things are as difficult as they are rare'. The puzzle however remains; how can one set out to overcome the difficulty, if all is determined?

Spinoza's treatment of moral terms such as 'good' is naturalistic to the extent of removing the distinctively moral content from their meaning. The same applies to his treatment of the notions of obligation and duty, in connection with man's relation to society and the state. Spinoza's *Theological-Political Treatise* probably owes much to Hobbes. Certainly the apparently strange combination of political and theological issues is the same, and Spinoza has the same concern with the proper interpretation (as he sees it) of the Bible and other religious texts; for, like Hobbes, he sees this as central to the political organization of his time. He says in the preface that his concern is to persuade men to give up superstitions and prejudices in favour of the natural light of reason, and that the role of political organizations should be to make that possible. On the other hand, beliefs should be free, and any attempt by the political power to regulate belief is likely to give rise to disorder. Hence Spinoza preaches a definite liberalism combined with a belief in the natural light of reason. He thus differs from Hobbes in urging freedom of belief, provided that it does not give rise to sedition, and he does not think that matters of belief can be left in the control of the sovereign.

Like Hobbes, Spinoza sees the sole role of the state or sovereign as the maintenance of the security of the individual. But, as must be evident from the preceding, he saw the interests of the individual differently from Hobbes – in a more positive way, one might say. Hence, in classifying different forms of political institution Spinoza is not, as Hobbes was, totally on the side of monarchy; indeed quite the reverse. The source of the sovereign's authority is nevertheless a social contract on the part of the people. But whereas Hobbes used that idea to derive from 'convenient articles of peace' an obligation to obey the sovereign, Spinoza treats the notion of obligation in a totally prudential, and fundamentally non-moral, sense. The only thing that justifies the continuance of the sovereign power is the preservation by it of men's security and of the possibility of pursuing the end of man in a Spinozistic sense. If that is not done, the contract has no force; there is no point in the sovereign saying that a promise has been made. Whether someone has the right to do anything is entirely a matter of whether he has the power to do it. The obligation or duty to obey the sovereign is nothing more than the advisability of doing so as long as he has the power to protect the individual and preserve his well-being in the Spinozistic sense.

The overriding characteristics of Spinoza's philosophy are its claim to rigorous consistency and its thoroughgoing working-out of the consequences of an initial position. Whether every proposition in his system does follow from its immediate premises is a matter for argument; but it is undoubtedly the case that nearly everything turns on the initial premises, and in particular on the conception of substance. In that conception Spinoza has much in common with Aristotle, who claimed, as we have seen, that only God is substance in the primary way. For Spinoza, however, only God is substance – full stop. Hence the monism, the determinism, and the suggestion that what we ordinarily think of as distinct things, including ourselves, are not really distinct, but simply modifications of the one substance which is God or Nature. It is an impressive intellectual construction, but it is not surprising that many who have taken it seriously have thought it abhorrent. For others, and again not surprisingly, it is a magnificent philosophical conception.

Leibniz

In most ways there could hardly be two men so different as Spinoza and Leibniz. Spinoza was to some extent a recluse, and a man totally devoted to the working-out of his philosophical system without the obligations of a public post; Leibniz was a very public figure, a man of affairs and a courtier, who had dealings and correspondence with nearly every person of intellectual eminence in his time. He was a distinguished mathematician in his own right and discovered (as did Newton independently) the differential and integral calculus. He travelled incessantly, but during the last forty years of his life he was in the service of the house of Brunswick, by whom he was commissioned to write their history. But under George Louis of Brunswick, the eventual George I of England, he fell out of favour, and he died in Hanover, at the age of seventy, in comparative isolation.

Gottfried Leibniz (1646–1716) was the son of a professor of moral philosophy at Leipzig. As a boy he worked on a great many things, often on his own, but he eventually entered the University of Leipzig. His doctoral dissertation, which he wrote at the age of twenty, was on law; it was rejected at Leipzig because of his youth, but he was granted the doctorate at Altdorf. Law and politics were subjects that occupied him throughout his life, but they were just two of the vast range of subjects that he covered. He entered the service of the Elector of Mainz in 1668 and travelled to London on his behalf in 1673, where he met Oldenburg, and exhibited to the Royal Society a calculating machine which he had devised. He tried to set up other academies in various places, and was successful at Berlin, where he was elected President for life. At one point in his travels he met Spinoza and made notes on his *Ethics*.

He was phenomenal in the range of his interests and activities. However, he published only one book on philosophy during his life-time – the *Theodicy*, a work concerned with natural theology, and written as a result of discussions with Sophie Charlotte, daughter of the Electress Sophia of Hanover, and later Queen of Prussia. But he wrote, without publishing them, a great number of philosophical works of various kinds and lengths, including the *Monadology*, the summary of his mature philosophy, and what many think his greatest work, the *Discourse on Metaphysics*. He also wrote a chapter-by-chapter reply to Locke's *Essay Concerning Human Understanding*, entitled *New Essays Concerning Human Understanding*, which he left unpublished on Locke's death in 1704. Much of Leibniz's philosophy is, however, to be found in correspondence with other distinguished men, particularly Arnauld and Samuel Clarke (who wrote as a mouthpiece of Newton).

The fact that his philosophy was formulated in these ways led Bertrand Russell in *The Philosophy of Leibniz*[1] to assert that Leibniz had two philosophies, the public and the private, and that he did not publish the private philosophy because of his desire to retain the favour of princes and other influential persons. Russell also maintained that his private and true philosophy was derived from logic. There may be an element of truth in the claim that Leibniz was over-concerned with getting recognition and honour from those in power, but it is also necessary to remember what power could do. The claim that Leibniz's real philosophy is founded on logic has been rejected by other scholars, although logic and its principles were of undoubted importance to him. He contributed to the development of logic, having in mind the aim of producing a *characteristica universalis*, a universal logical and mathematical language, which would make possible the solution of a whole range of problems. With it we should be able simply to say 'Let us calculate'. Such an ambition has not been realized, despite the advent of computers.

Given the nature of his writings it is impossible to treat Leibniz as I have treated Descartes and Spinoza, by consideration of a continuous piece of argument. Russell asserted that Leibniz's philosophy was based on five premises, which were inconsistent; but not every commentator would agree on that. In his mature philosophy Leibniz came to believe that the world consists of an infinite plurality of simple substances, which he called 'monads', each of which is like *le moi* or the *ego* in ourselves. He thought that these monads were organized in a hierarchy, with God as the dominant monad. Each monad has its own line of development due to what Leibniz called its appetition, which is responsible for the changes of states in the monad. Each monad reflects the world from its point of view, but has no effect upon, and is not affected by, any other monad. Space and time are merely ideal.

[1] B. Russell: *The Philosophy of Leibniz* (London: Allen and Unwin, 1900).

In effect, each monad is a Spinozistic unitary substance, and at one point in his correspondence Leibniz makes the curious admission 'If it were not for the monads Spinoza would be right'. He thinks that common sense indicates that there must be a plurality of substances. They cannot all be identified with God. What holds good of any monad is determined, but there is a sense in which there is nevertheless free will. On the other hand, these substances cannot be identified with ordinary things, any more than Spinoza's one substance can be. Ordinary things are not real substances; they are merely *phenomena*, although, as he puts it, well-founded phenomena. It should be clear from this that although Leibniz is a rationalist he is not the supreme rationalist that Spinoza was; there is in his theory too large a place for common sense.

Like other rationalists, Leibniz takes it for granted that the basic things that exist in the world are substances. That is the Aristotelian inheritance. Unlike Aristotle, however, Leibniz takes it that if a substance is the basic form of existence it must be absolutely simple. For if it were complex, it would be secondary to whatever it is composed of. Yet a substance must have an identity; indeed, it must have an essence. The problem is how something that is absolutely simple could have the multiplicity of properties that makes up its essence. Leibniz spent some time looking for a model for such a 'simplicity in complexity'. At one time in his life he played with the idea that the ultimate substances were 'massy points' – entities which were simple in the way that points are, in having no spatial dimensions, but which had nevertheless the physical properties of mass and what follows from that. The problem was how there could be such a thing and how an extended world could be derived from such substances – a problem which he associated with what he called the 'labyrinth of the continuum', the problem of how a continuum could be derived from indivisible points. The mathematical problem involved in the latter was solved by denying that lines *are* composed of points; rather, points are the limiting but ideal extremities (to use Leibniz's own word) of the process of dividing a line. But massy points could not be treated in that way; otherwise there would be no substances. Leibniz ostensibly solves the problem by identifying the ultimate substances with monads or spiritual entities, and by denying that the problem of the continuum applies to such entities.

This may seem a rather curious solution of the problem. It is in effect to say that if one identifies the ultimate substances of the world in a certain way the problem does not arise. But the solution has its consequences. Spiritual substances cannot stand in spatial relations;

hence space cannot be real, but only a phenomenon, an appearance, even though it is a well-founded phenomenon. It is well-founded because the appearance of space follows from the nature of monads in a way that will become apparent below. Leibniz lighted upon the monad as his model for a true substance – one which has an absolute simplicity and unity, and is not, as he puts it, like a sack of pistoles (that is, a sack of coins) or mere collection – because he thought, as other philosophers have done, that the 'I', the *ego*, must be regarded as a simple thing forming a true unity. An *ego* was also capable of having a multiplicity of properties, and it seemed to him that something of that sort was the obvious model for a combination of simplicity with a multiplicity. Indeed he thought that the model made it possible for each monad to have an *infinity* of properties, just as we are capable of having an infinity of perceptions, in being related to other things in an infinite number of possible ways. Leibniz in fact used the notion of a 'perception' to express the relation that a monad can have to the rest of the world, that is to say to other monads. Each monad, he said, reflects the world from its point of view, and does so *via* an infinity of perceptions.

At the same time, Leibniz insisted that monads must be, as he put it, windowless, and it follows from this that the monad's perceptions cannot be regarded as real perceptions of the world. Rather they constitute states of the monad which correspond to the states of other monads by what he called a pre-established harmony. The pre-established harmony also explains the relations between the states of the dominant monad which constitutes the soul in each of us and those of the monads which make up our body. Whereas Spinoza had said that the body is the object of our ideas and that the mind and the body are simply two aspects of the same thing, Leibniz thinks that they are two different things; they do not affect each other, however, and stand in relation to each other only in virtue of a pre-established harmony laid down by God. Why, however, do monads have to be windowless?

The reason for this lies ultimately in a logical doctrine which is perhaps most clearly expressed in the *Discourse on Metaphysics*. There Leibniz says that in every true proposition the predicate is contained in the subject and claims that this is 'what the philosophers call *in-esse*'. Elsewhere he distinguishes between truths of reason and truths of fact. Truths of reason are those which Kant was to call 'analytic'; they can be analysed into identical propositions, of the form 'A is A', *via* chains of definitions of the terms involved. That is to say that if one substitutes for the terms of any necessarily true proposition terms which are definitionally equivalent to them the proposition will eventually be reduced to one the denial of which will evidently produce a contradiction. Thus such propositions are founded on the principle of non-contradiction. Contingent propositions are not so founded and their basis must, if they are true, be another principle, which Leibniz calls the principle of sufficient reason.

A third related principle which has sometimes been equated with this is what is known as the 'principle of the best'. Our world, Leibniz says, is simply one of an infinite set of possible worlds which God could have created. Such worlds must not only be logically possible; they must be what Leibniz calls 'compossible', their components must fit together. God chooses which world to create on the principle that it must be the best compossible world. That is a sufficient reason in itself for the existence of the world and of the substances which make it up. Nevertheless, when Leibniz says that if a proposition is true there must be some sufficient reason for its truth, he does not mean merely that God has so created the world that the proposition is true and that God always chooses for the best. He means also that if we look for the rationale for the truth of the proposition concerned we shall find one. (Hence Leibniz's appeal to the principle of sufficient reason is not simply the crude optimism about this being the best of all possible worlds that Voltaire satirized in *Candide*.)

In some of his writings, however, Leibniz says that truths of fact can after all be given an *a priori* basis. This seems to conflate the apparently clear distinction between truths of reason and truths of fact. Indeed, Russell claimed that Leibniz believed that every true proposition is analytic, this being the final form of the principle of sufficient reason, whereas the principle of contradiction or non-contradiction states that every analytic statement is true. This version of the matter has been embraced by other commentators. What Leibniz said was that God had so created the world that everything that was true of a substance was necessarily true of it, because it followed from its individual essence (and in this context he reinvoked the Scotist notion of *haecceitas*). God has what Leibniz called a complete concept of each thing. Because that concept must individuate the thing in question, in distinction from any other thing, it must be infinitely complex; for the properties that make up a given thing must be infinitely many, especially if relational properties are included. Being infinite, God can complete the infinite analysis of the essence of an individual thing, and knows, because he has created the world in accordance with the complete concepts of things, that everything that is true of each individual thing holds necessarily of it. We, on the other hand, being finite, cannot complete the analysis, and all that we can know is that *if* a proposition about a substance is true it is necessarily true. In order to judge whether it is true, we have to depend on the principle of sufficient reason.

This last point brings us back, after what may seem a digression, to the thesis that in every true proposition the predicate is contained in its subject. It is not an isolated remark confined to the *Discourse on Metaphysics*; it is frequently repeated in, for example, the correspondence with Arnauld which arose out of the *Discourse*. Leibniz's claim that it constitutes a doctrine corresponding to 'what the philosophers call *in-esse*' is a mistake. It is not the view of the scholastics, or of Aristotle, that the predicate of a true proposition is contained in the subject in a sense which implies the necessity of the truth of the proposition. Kant was to define an analytic proposition as one in which the concept of the predicate is contained in the concept of the subject; to say that something is actually in the subject is to say something different, and does not imply the inclusion of one concept in another, as would be required for the proposition to be conceptually necessary. For it to be true that Adam fell, falling must have inhered in Adam. There is a very considerable gap between that and the assertion that the concept of Adam (if there is any such thing) includes the idea of falling. It is that latter claim that is involved in Leibniz's view that in creating this world – the best of all possible worlds – God had the complete concept of Adam to the extent of knowing that he was to fall of necessity. In fact, therefore, the doctrine of what is implied by a true proposition, if correctly understood, does not support and is not supported by the doctrine that in the complete analysis of the concept of Adam what is truly predicable of Adam must appear as necessary. (There is a further question of whether it is legitimate to speak of concepts of individuals, but that is another matter; the question is on a par with whether there is such a thing as the haecceity of an individual.)

Despite possible doubts concerning which doctrine came first in the order of Leibniz's thinking, it does appear that the foundation of his views is the doctrine of what is involved in a true proposition. The view that there are complete concepts of things goes together with another of Leibniz's doctrines – the principle of the identity of indiscernibles, or, as he often puts it, the principle that no two substances can differ *solo numero*. If there is a distinct complete concept of every individual substance, any two substances must differ in respect of some aspect of those concepts; they must differ in respect of some property and cannot be merely numerically different without that. Since Leibniz's day there has been much discussion of this principle, and it is probably the case that most philosophers today would agree that it cannot be *necessarily* true. Yet it *must* be necessarily true on Leibniz's view, because it follows from the other principles which he holds to be necessarily true. It may be a point of some interest that the supposed necessity of the principle did not stop Leibniz from seeking empirical evidence in its favour. He pointed to considerations such as that the leaves on a tree are all different, and appealed to similar supposed evidence derived from what could be observed through the newly discovered microscope.

Another consequence of the principle that in every true proposition the predicate is contained in the subject is that whatever will be true of an individual is already implied by the concept of that individual. This appears to entail determinism of a Spinozistic kind. But to accept what Spinoza supposed to follow from that would have been anathema to Leibniz. It should be noted that in Leibniz's view every substance has an appetition (an inbuilt activity which determines the changes of state of that substance). The appetition of a monad which is a soul determines what holds good of it without reference to anything outside it, although by the pre-established harmony its perceptions will correspond to the states of other monads which make up its body. Leibniz sees in this the source of freedom in human beings. What a human being does has in every case a sufficient reason, but, he says, those reasons incline without necessitating.

He made a similar response to Arnauld, who objected that Leibniz's views made impossible the attribution of freedom to God, because, once Adam is created, all that is in the concept of Adam, including all that will happen to him, is fixed. Leibniz replied that this was to confuse absolute and hypothetical necessity. There is no absolute necessity that Adam should fall and so on; these events are necessary only on the hypothesis that God has freely chosen to create a world of this kind, because it fulfils his purpose to create the best of all possible worlds. The truth in all this is that the kind of determinism that is entailed by Leibniz's doctrines is not a *causal* determinism. If one is looking for the cause of what happens, in the ordinary sense of 'cause', the doctrine of what is involved in the complete concept of Adam does not establish that; it establishes that what happens does so of logical necessity. It is still possible to ask whether Adam did this or that freely and say that what caused him to do this or that was not, strictly speaking, necessitating, even if it is granted that if it is true that he will do this or that it is necessarily true that he will. Leibniz is in effect saying that the issues of freedom, causal determinism and what might be called logical determinism are all different. Not all philosophers would accept that, but it is an arguably valid point all the same, whether or not logical determinism is a tenable position in itself.

As we have seen, he believed that every soul is a monad which is dominant in relation to a complex of monads which constitute the body. Such monads have no real relations to each other, and in particular no causal relations. The idea of pre-established harmony applies here. Arnauld objected that Leibniz was positing a permanent miracle brought about by God when he created a world in which such a harmony obtains. Leibniz replied that a miracle was an exceptional event in a regular course of events, and that something that held good all the time was not a miracle. Another point is that monads, being spiritual entities, cannot have physical properties; they merely have perceptions which represent their supposed, but really phenomenal, relations to others. It is sometimes said that it was customary at the time to use the term 'perception' in a much wider sense than is usual now. However that may be, the term 'perception' is a natural one to use of a spiritual entity which reflects the world from its point of view. Can monads that make up bodies, however, have perceptions in any literal sense? Leibniz insisted that they did, distinguishing between perception and apperception, the latter involving the kind of conscious awareness that takes place in ordinary human perception. This implies the possibility of unconscious perception. Leibniz adduced several arguments for the possibility of this, not all of them very good. His most important argument turns on the idea of '*petites perceptions*'. He drew attention to the fact that when we hear the sound of the sea we hear a conjunction of a large number of noises given out by different waves; we do not hear those distinct noises consciously. The one conscious perception is made up, he said, of a number of '*petites perceptions*' which are not conscious. Clear perceptions involve apperception; confused perceptions involve at least in part perceptions which are *petites* or unconscious.

That idea also lies at the root of his account of matter. A monad has an active force, the appetition towards clear perceptions; this, Leibniz says, constitutes the form of the monad or, to use the Aristotelian term, its *entelechy*, and gives the monad its unity. Confused perceptions constitute the matter of the monad – what Leibniz calls *materia prima*. Its nature is simply resistance, and that forms the basis of extension, which cannot be a real property of a monad; it is a phenomenal property derived from the mutual resistance of monads when indistinguishable. A complex of monads of this kind exhibits *materia secunda*, the matter presupposed by the physics of his time; this is associated with corresponding active forces, particularly what Leibniz called *vis viva* (live force) which he identified with kinetic energy. Leibniz believed in the constancy of *vis viva*, as opposed to the constancy of motion in the universe presupposed by Descartes. Indeed Leibniz's whole conception of matter is opposed to that of Descartes; given the conception of monads and that of force, the essence of matter could not, in his view, lie in extension.

There are many other aspects to Leibniz's philosophy. I shall touch on two more. The first follows on naturally from what I have said about matter and extension. On the Cartesian view, since extension was the essential property of matter, there could be no extension without matter, and thus no vacuum. On Leibniz's view there could be a vacuum, although he denied its existence in fact. Given, however, the fact that monads are windowless, and the consequent fact that there cannot be real relations between them, there cannot be spatial relations, and these must be simply well-founded phenomena. Similar considerations apply to time, since what we think of as the temporal states of a monad are simply parts of what is *in* it, and are necessary to it. Hence, Leibniz defined space as the order of coexistence and time as the order of succession: they are both purely relational. In saying that, Leibniz put himself in opposition to Newton, who in the Scholia to the Definitions in his *Principia* maintained the existence of absolute space and time, considered as infinitely extended continua with properties of their own. In reviewing in the *Nouveaux Essais* what Locke had to say on the same theme, Leibniz makes it clear that he takes Newton to be maintaining that space and time are infinite substances, and in the *Correspondence with Clarke* he criticizes Clarke, as the mouthpiece of Newton, on that basis.

His main argument adduces the principle of sufficient reason: if space and time were as Newton supposes, God would have no sufficient reason for creating the universe here rather than there, or at one time rather than another. This in effect says that no sense can be given to 'here' rather than 'there' and of the idea of one time rather than another, if there is no way of making those distinctions in terms of what otherwise exists. In an infinitely big box there is no way of determining positions within it by reference to properties of the box. Newton might well have thought that this begged the question. Why should not God simply create the universe somewhere in space without there being a prior determination of that position? In other words, why should the question of what makes sense depend on the possibility of verifying the truth of what is said? To suppose that it does is to presuppose a verificationist theory of meaning. (Leibniz's opposition to Newton on this point must not, incidentally, be taken as grounds for seeing him as a precursor of Einstein. The latter is concerned with the relativity of dynamics to alternative coordinate systems within nature; that is not Leibniz's concern, but with the nature of space and time from a philosophical point of view.)

Leibniz's system has elements that connect him with Spinoza, but he was unable to accept Spinoza's rejection of the common-sense observation that there are many things. The thesis that there is an infinity of absolutely simple things arose from a combination of the Spinozistic view that substance is basic and *causa sui* with the belief in an extended world of physical and mental substances. This produced the doctrine of monads. But the view that everything about a monad is internal and necessary to itself, and all the consequences of that view, seem to depend crucially on the mistaken doctrine, as Leibniz construed it, that in every true proposition the predicate is contained in the subject. It does not strictly follow from the view that everything is internal to a monad that if that monad is a human mind all ideas and knowledge that it has are innate, although Russell thought that Leibniz ought to hold that. He certainly held that some ideas and some knowledge were innate – for example, knowledge of eternal truths, such as the principles of logic. Nothing prevents its being the case, however, that a monad should acquire knowledge in the course of its history. What is necessary is that it should do so, if that is part of its individual essence; it is not necessary that it should start with that knowledge.

The second point involves the position of God, given the above. Leibniz's conception of God is not that of Spinoza. In his view, God is the dominant substance; indeed, in one or two places he refers to him as a monad. God is responsible for the world, and because he chooses for the best, the world is the best of all the possible and compossible worlds that he could have chosen. Hence the monads exist because of him, and could cease to exist because of him – although it is difficult to think of this being a creation and destruction, given Leibniz's view of the ideality of time. Leibniz invokes several supposed proofs of God's existence, but is critical of Descartes and Spinoza for their reliance upon the ontological argument. For, he says, the argument depends on the assumption that the idea of God, as a being whose essence implies his existence, is a logically coherent idea, and is thus a possible idea; and this has not been shown. Not that Leibniz disputed the idea of God. In his view, God's existence does follow from his essence, and he thought that he could show that such an idea of God is a possible one. But for these purposes he had to rely on other arguments, such as the cosmological argument, the argument from design, and an argument from the existence of eternal truths, these being supposed to be thoughts in the divine mind. None of these arguments is any better than similar ones used by other philosophers. Hence, although the existence of God is crucial to Leibniz's scheme, there is another weakness in the scheme at this point. None of this is surprising, but although Leibniz's system does not perhaps have the grandeur and relentlessness of Spinoza's, it remains a fascinating metaphysical theory.

Leibniz's philosophy was handed on in a weakened form by Christian Wolff (1679–1754). Leibniz wrote mainly in Latin and French, but Wolff wrote in German, and partly because of that Wolff's philosophy became more or less the received metaphysics in Germany in the period before Kant. He put a great deal of weight upon the principle of sufficient reason, but he gave up the idea of a general pre-established harmony between monads, restricting that harmony to the relation between mind and body. Whatever influence Wolff exerted on the course of the history of philosophy, the changes that he made to Leibniz's metaphysics robbed that theory of its centre.

[11]
British Empiricism

Locke

Locke, Berkeley and Hume are conventionally called the British Empiricists. As a general indication of a trend in their thinking the title is a reasonable one, although their central concerns were not in all respects the same. However, Locke certainly established a position or positions to which the other two reacted.

John Locke (1632–1704) was the son of a West Country lawyer who had been a Parliamentarian in the Civil War. After school at Westminster he went to Christ Church, Oxford, where he eventually became a Senior Student, and taught Greek and moral philosophy. He then became interested in medicine and after some years obtained a licence to practise. This brought him to the attention of the first Earl of Shaftesbury, Lord Ashley, and Locke entered his service in 1667. Shaftesbury fled to the Netherlands in 1683, because he was in danger of being impeached for treason, and he died there. Locke followed him to the Netherlands in fear of being incriminated, and remained there until 1689, when the 'Glorious Revolution' had led to the overthrow of the Stuarts. During this period he wrote his *Essay Concerning Human Understanding*. On his return to England he took up an appointment in the Civil Service, but he became very involved in controversies resulting from his publications, particularly the *Two Treatises on Civil Government*, which he wrote in part as a defence of the 'Glorious Revolution'. He lived during the last few years of his life in the household of Sir Francis Masham at Oates in Essex, where he died.

Locke's *Essay* is very much an epistemological work. He is conscious of living in the age of Newton, and in a period in which science was developing rapidly. Indeed, he describes himself in the 'Epistle to the Reader' which prefaces the *Essay* as an underlabourer, saying that it is ambition enough to be so employed, 'clearing the ground a little, and removing some of the rubbish that lies in the way to knowledge'. This is a very modest description of his aims, but the work is really much more than this, attempting to establish in a general way the limits of the human understanding. Locke says that a discussion with friends on 'a subject very remote from this' led him to try to pursue the issue. In the Introduction to Book I he says that his purpose is 'to inquire into the original, certainty, and extent of human knowledge, together with the grounds and degrees of belief, opinion and assent', without meddling with the 'physical consideration of the mind'. His method, he says, is the 'historical, plain method'. All this makes it sound as if he is concerned with developmental psychology as well as the theory of knowledge in the traditional sense, but this is misleading. He is in fact concerned, as I have said, with the limits of the human understanding, a preoccupation which was to become common in the philosophy that followed his.

The *Essay* has four books entitled respectively 'Of Innate Notions', 'Of Ideas', 'Of Words' and 'Of Knowledge and Opinion'. These titles give a reasonable idea of the contents of the work. The first book contains a sharp attack on the notion of innate ideas. It is generally put in that way, but on the face of it Locke is concerned with two things: (1) whether there is any innate knowledge of principles; and (2) whether what he sometimes calls the *materials* of that knowledge, the ideas on which the knowledge is based, are innate. That distinction between knowledge and ideas affects the whole *Essay*, because Book II is given over to a discussion of ideas and their source, and it is left to Book IV to discuss knowledge, and propositional knowledge in particular.

Locke apologizes for the use of the term *idea* at the end of I.1.1, saying that it is 'that term which, I think, serves best to stand for whatsoever is the object of the understanding when a man thinks'; and he adds that it expresses 'whatever is meant by *phantasm*, *notion*, *species*, or whatever it is which the mind can be employed about in thinking'. We cannot have an idea without being conscious of it. The traditional interpretation of Locke takes him as understanding by the term roughly what Descartes meant by it, and in consequence takes him as embracing a representative theory of perception and of the mind in general. Some recent commentators[1] have insisted that in Locke's view ideas had more of the character of acts of mind. There are indeed passages in which Locke seems to identify ideas with perceptions, although that does not clinch the matter, because by 'perception' he could mean either the faculty or act or its object – what is perceived. Locke was not over-precise in his use of terms, or indeed in his thinking in general.

In Book I, Locke attacks the view that there are innate speculative principles, such as the principles of identity and contradiction, and that there are innate practical principles, such as those of morals. It would appear that many in Locke's time held that there were such innate principles, and based their claim on the supposed universal assent to them. Locke denies that such principles are universally assented to, and points

---

[1] Especially perhaps J. Yolton: *Locke and the Compass of Human Understanding* (Cambridge: C.U.P., 1970).

to the fact that they are not appreciated by children and idiots. He argues similarly over moral principles, with perhaps greater ease. He admits that there may be innate *capacities*, but asserts that the only grounds for maintaining that a *truth* is in the mind is that it is actually understood. Given this, he has a somewhat easy task with his opponents. He goes on to reinforce his conclusion by arguing that there can be no innate ideas either; if the materials of knowledge cannot be innate, neither can knowledge itself. His argument largely depends upon a consideration of putative counter-examples, such as the ideas of identity and God. It is not a thorough argument and on the whole Locke is content to appeal to what he takes as obvious. He may be right in his conclusions, although the idea of innate knowledge has been resuscitated in recent times by Chomsky and other linguists who follow him.

In Book II Locke sets out to classify ideas, and seeks to show that they are all derived from experience. In the latter respect, Locke has sometimes been accused of being concerned with psychology rather than philosophy. Certainly his account sometimes looks like an exercise in the psychology of concept formation. In fact, however, he is concerned more with what is possible than with what actually happens; he is arguing that the understanding cannot be conceived of as functioning unless it is organized in a certain way. This fits in with his concern with the limits of the understanding. Locke says that the answer to the question of the source of our ideas is 'in one word, from *experience*'. But experience furnishes ideas in two ways, as he makes clear in II.1.3–4. There is, first, sensation, by which the senses 'from external objects convey into the mind what produces there those perceptions'. Second, there is reflection, 'the perception of the operations of our own mind within us', from which we derive ideas of those operations, such as perception and thinking. (It is worth noting that whatever Locke meant by 'idea', the inner/outer distinction which he inherited from Descartes is evident in these remarks.) There is no other source of ideas. On the whole, Locke insists that in getting ideas of sensation the mind is passive, and at II.1.25 he likens the mind to a mirror in this respect. But he is not quite consistent in this, sometimes referring to the part played in sense-perception by operations of judgement and attention.

Locke then turns to another way of classifying ideas, distinguishing between those which are simple and those which are complex, the latter being built up from the former. In embracing an atomism of ideas of this kind, Locke may have been influenced by the science of his day, although it is a very pervasive theory in the history of philosophy in one form or another. Locke gives a number of examples of simple ideas, such as whiteness and softness, but on the whole he takes it for granted that readers will all understand what a simple idea is; it is one which is not formed from other ideas. A simple idea, and what is understood in it, does not depend on having any other ideas. One might put the point in another way by saying that a simple idea is one such that the corresponding term gets its meaning from what it applies to and nothing else; or, in more modern jargon, it is definable only ostensively, by direct reference to its object. It is supposed that the content of what we perceive when we perceive whiteness, if we have a simple idea of it, cannot be given except by pointing to that colour. In a sense, however, the very attempt to state this shows its falsity, for (as Wittgenstein and other philosophers have indicated) we have in the circumstances contemplated to know that it is the colour to which we are pointing, and not some other aspect of the object: and that presupposes other knowledge and understanding. There are no such things as simple ideas in the sense that Locke supposes. Nevertheless the simple/complex distinction pervades the whole of British Empiricism and the thought of other philosophers influenced by it. It is not an understatement to say that it has been disastrous for epistemology.

When one turns to complex ideas the waters are muddied because Locke offers two different accounts of them in different editions of the *Essay*. In the first edition he classifies complex ideas in terms of their objects; there are ideas of substances, modes and relations. Substances are independently existing things; modes are 'dependences on, or affections of substances' (II.12.4), in so far as these ideas are not simple; relations are complex ideas which consist in 'the consideration and comparing of one *idea* with another'. Modes may be either simple or mixed. The simple ones are those which 'are only variations, or different combinations of the same simple *idea*, without the mixture of any other'. Under this head Locke considers spatial, temporal and numerical ideas, including the idea of infinity, all of which he supposes to be derived from combinations of simple ideas. We get the idea of infinite extension, for example, by supposing the simple ideas of extension and duration reduplicated without end. Mixed modes are those the ideas of which are derived from combinations of *different* simple ideas; Locke instances the idea of beauty. In the fourth edition of the *Essay*, published in 1700, Locke offers in addition a different basis for classifying ideas, as if it were just the same as the original one, or at least consistent with it, which it is not. He now says (II.12.1) that complex ideas are arrived at by combination, ideas of relations by comparison, and general ideas by abstraction (a doctrine that has to wait until Book III for its exposition).

Certain points of detail in all this need to be noted. First, in the course of his treatment of simple ideas of sense he makes an important distinction between primary and secondary qualities. It is not in its general form a new distinction. It came into prominence after the Renaissance with Galileo, and Locke probably derived it from Descartes and from scientists of his day, such as Boyle. The primary qualities of things are, he says, those qualities 'such as are utterly inseparable from the body, in what state soever it be' (II.8.9), and which the 'mind finds inseparable from every particle of matter'; they are solidity, extension, figure, motion or rest, and number. The secondary qualities, such as colours, smells, tastes and sounds, are, he says, qualities 'which in truth are nothing in the objects themselves but powers to produce various sensations in us by their primary qualities'. There has been much discussion among philosophers as to whether the distinction is a genuine one. To the extent that it corresponds to Aristotle's distinction between special and common objects of the senses – primary qualities being perceptible through more than one sense, secondary qualities through one sense only – it seems a quite genuine distinction. Whether Locke is right in saying that primary qualities are essential to something's being a body, whereas secondary qualities are not, is much more disputable.[1]

Whatever may be said of the distinction in itself, further consideration needs to be given to Locke's claim that secondary qualities are merely powers associated with primary qualities to produce ideas of them in us. That is in effect to say that the ideas of secondary qualities are merely subjective; they do not represent anything in bodies which are like them, as ideas of primary qualities do. All ideas of perception are caused in us by bodies, and to that extent Locke embraces a causal theory of perception. Nevertheless, he believes that the ideas of primary qualities actually correspond to something in bodies, whereas ideas of secondary qualities do not. The standard objection is to ask how he knows that. For how can we have access to bodies independently of ideas so as to be able to compare them with ideas? Locke's justification of belief in the objectivity of primary qualities involves an appeal to the success that science has in dealing with them, but that does not really meet the point.

Similar considerations apply to his treatment of complex ideas of substances. He says that our complex ideas of substances are made up in large part of powers – powers to produce ideas in us and to produce changes in other bodies, of which the primary qualities of bodies are the foundation. Indeed when he comes to consider the 'names of substances' in Book III.6, he makes a distinction between the real and

[1] But see Jonathan Bennett's discussion in his *Locke, Berkeley, Hume: Central Themes* (Oxford: Clarendon Press, 1971), ch.4.

the nominal essence of things (a distinction which has been resuscitated by some recent philosophers). The nominal essence of a thing is what is essential to that thing, if considered in terms of some system of classification which allocates it to a species. The real essence of a thing is its underlying constitution, which makes it appear as it is and gives us the ideas that enable us to allocate to it its nominal essence. Locke claims that we know that things have such real essences, although we must be ignorant of what they are because our senses are not accurate enough to detect them. (Recent philosophers have appealed to scientific theorizing in the attempt to by-pass this consideration.)

Hence, in classifying and naming substances we have to rely upon their nominal essences – what we know as essential to them through the ideas that we have of them. But, as he says in II.23.11, 'Had we senses acute enough to discern the minute particles of bodies and the real constitution on which their sensible qualities depend, I doubt not but they would produce quite different *ideas* in us.' Nevertheless, our ideas of substances are simply complex ideas formed of numbers of simple ideas, although a great part of the complex consists of powers. Locke refuses to accept the idea of something which is merely the support of qualities, a substratum, a 'something I know not what', a view of substance which he attributed to the scholastics. Substances are merely collections of qualities, although they have an unknowable physical constitution which would, if known, explain why the collection exists.

Locke held similar views about spiritual substance. In II.23.5 he makes what may appear somewhat derogatory remarks about the notion of a spirit, but maintains both that we have the idea of a substance 'wherein *thinking, knowing, doubting*, and a power of moving, etc., do subsist', and that we cannot conclude the non-existence of spirit because we are ignorant of its nature any more than we can conclude the non-existence of body. He was criticized by Edward Stillingfleet, Bishop of Worcester, for his treatment of substance in general and for his ambiguous treatment of the notion of spirit in particular, because, the Bishop maintained, it left open the possibility that the nature of the soul might be material. Locke replied rather cautiously in correspondence, but he does not seem to have doubted the existence of the soul as a thinking thing.

The notion of power comes into play here too. The chapter on power (II.21) distinguishes between passive and active powers and he uses the latter notion to express his views on freedom of the will. He says that this in fact belongs to men, not the will, which is 'a power to direct the operative faculties to motion or rest in particular instan-

ces'. Liberty is 'a power to act or not to act, according as the mind
directs', and it is desire, as the result of 'some present uneasiness',
which determines the will to any change of operation. Hence Locke's
solution to the problem of the freedom of the will is to say that such
freedom should be attributed, not to the will, but to *human beings*,
who have it in virtue of active powers that they possess. Nothing about
determinism makes it false that they have that power.

The part of Book II which has perhaps produced most discussion
is that concerned with personal identity – an issue which it would not
be too misleading to say Locke raised for the first time. The discussion
occurs in the course of a chapter (II.27) devoted to identity and
diversity in general. Locke associates identity with the continued existence of a thing according to its nature. In dealing with the identity of
human beings, he distinguishes between person, man and substance.
The identity of a man depends upon identity of his body, however
that is determined. By identity of substance he has in mind identity of
spirit *qua* thinking thing. But Locke does not believe that the notion
of a person is equivalent to either of these notions, and he is prepared
to contemplate the idea of persons exchanging or sharing bodies. There
are indeed genuine questions about the criteria of personal identity
(about the circumstances in which we are prepared to apply the notion
of 'the same person') which philosophers still discuss. The questions
are commensurate with the question of what sort of concept that of a
person is. Locke comes to the conclusion that the identity of a person
is determined by identity of consciousness, which he then identifies
with identity of memory. At the conclusion of his discussion he says
(II.27.26), '*Person*, as I take it, is the name for this *self*. Wherever a
man finds what he calls *himself*, there, I think, another may say is the
same person. It is a forensic term, appropriating actions and their
merit, and so belongs only to intelligent agents, capable of a law, and
happiness and misery.'

Although the questions raised are interesting, there are problems
about Locke's answers. They were subject to more or less immediate
objections. Bishop Joseph Butler objected, in his dissertation on personal identity, that Locke's account was circular, in that having the
same memories presupposes being the same person. Thomas Reid, in
his *Essays on the Intellectual Powers* 3.6, said that Locke confused
personal identity with the evidence for it. He also claimed that Locke's
view was contradictory, because as a result of lapses of memory a man
could, on that view, both be and not be the same person he once was.
It is indeed strange to base decisions about the identity of a person on
what he or she can remember. Moreover, if Locke's final words are

interpreted as saying that we can base decisions concerning identity on ascriptions of responsibility, rather than *vice versa*, his views can have very unacceptable consequences.[1] Nevertheless, the issues raised by Locke about personal identity have proved fascinating ones to successive philosophers.

Book III of the *Essay* is concerned with language, the importance given to which may be a legacy of Hobbes. Locke's views on signification and meaning are relatively crude, for he says simply that words signify ideas, and considers hardly anything else in language apart from individual words. It is in this context, however, that he introduces his doctrine of abstraction and abstract ideas. At the beginning of Book III.3, Locke maintains that all things that exist are particulars. How then do general terms get their meaning? Locke says that general terms are 'applicable indifferently to many particular things' (III.3.11). But if the meaning of words consists in their signifying ideas there must be general ideas for general terms to signify. In consequence, Locke supposes that we separate from ideas 'the circumstances of time and place, and any other *ideas* that may determine them to this or that particular existence' (III.3.6). He calls this process abstraction and the results of it are abstract ideas. At this point, the indeterminateness in Locke's conception of an idea becomes extremely pertinent. Berkeley objected to the idea of a triangle that was neither equilateral, isosceles nor scalene; if an idea is anything like an image or representation, that objection is telling. If an idea is an act of thinking, then (as it is clearly possible to think of a triangle without thinking of it as equilateral, isosceles or scalene) the situation is different. In a certain sense Locke was a conceptualist in his theory of universals – thoughts are the only general things. That view is not satisfactory; after all, if one abstracts from a number of things it is because they have something in common. But there is nothing mysterious in the notion of abstraction itself; the problem in Locke's case is what can be meant by an abstract *idea*.

By the end of Book III of the *Essay* we have been given Locke's views about the materials of knowledge, and Book IV sets out his account of knowledge itself. It constitutes a relatively small part of the book, and is not very satisfactory in general; it is certainly not obviously empiricist in tendency. Hence, if it is the conclusion that Locke meant to arrive at in setting out on his journey, the journeying was clearly far more important than the arrival. Locke defines knowledge as 'nothing but *the perception of the connexion and agreement, or disagreement and repugnancy, of any*

[1] For this and other considerations, see my *Metaphysics* (Cambridge: C.U.P., 1984), ch.9.

[2] See on this my *Metaphysics*, ch.5.

of our ideas' (IV.1.2). This seems to confine knowledge to ideas, and even on the view that ideas are acts of mind that seems unacceptable. Locke seems to think, however, that he can square that view with the belief that we have knowledge of separate existences. In Chapter 2 of the book he speaks of degrees of knowledge, distinguishing between intuitive knowledge, demonstrative knowledge and sensitive knowledge of the particular existence of finite beings without us. These represent degrees of knowledge, because they vary in clarity. Intuitive knowledge involves comparing two ideas; demonstrative knowledge involves examining the relation between two ideas through the intervention of others; and sensitive knowledge involves perception of the existence of particular things. But does not the last go beyond ideas? To the extent that all these degrees of knowledge have to do with existence, do they not *all* go beyond ideas? For Locke maintains (IV.9ff.) that we have intuitive knowledge of our own existence, demonstrative knowledge of God's existence (by a variety of proofs), and sensitive knowledge of particular things.

In the first chapter of the book Locke classifies the forms of agreement or disagreement between ideas that knowledge involves into four kinds: identity or diversity, relation, co-existence or necessary connection, and real existence. It is once again the last that causes trouble. It is tempting to hold that when Locke speaks of real existence as a form of agreement between ideas he means that we perceive the agreement between such and such ideas and that of existence, and that we do so because we are caused to think in that way by whatever causes our perception. That would not be an answer to the question of what entitles us to move from ideas to their causes, but on the view under consideration that question need not arise. We could take Locke as saying that we just do have knowledge of things when we are caused to perceive the agreement between certain ideas and the idea of existence. Perhaps that is what he did think, but if so he expressed himself badly, because real existence is presented as being in itself one kind of agreement between ideas. In spite of this perhaps not untypical lack of clarity, and possible incoherence, Locke's *conclusions* are relatively clear. His account of intuitive and demonstrative knowledge sounds rationalist, but the intuitive knowledge that I have of my own existence and at least some supposed demonstrative knowledge of God's existence have a form of experience as a basis. In the case of the other forms of intuitive and demonstrative knowledge that Locke allows, the position is not clear.

There is much else in Book IV of the *Essay*: a version of the correspondence theory of truth, a theory of probability, an account of faith and reason, and other things. It is probably the part of the *Essay* which is least read, however. That may be a pity, because there are individual remarks on particular issues which are illuminating. But after the relative sophistication of the discussion of the materials of knowledge in the first three books, the last book comes as something of a disappointment. The first three books, however, have been profoundly influential.

Locke wrote next to nothing on ethics, although certain ethical observations are to be found in the *Essay*, including the remarks on freedom of the will. He had more to say on political philosophy, and his views in this area have the same kind of sanity, combined at times with a certain casualness and lack of total consistency. Apart from a *Letter Concerning Toleration*, he wrote two *Treatises on Civil Government*. The first is an attack on Sir Robert Filmer's *Patriarchia*, which defended the idea of the divine right of absolute monarchy on the basis of hereditary descent. The second *Treatise* has a more permanent interest and the principles laid down in it influenced, through Montesquieu, the setting-up of the American Constitution. Locke was clearly influenced by Hobbes, but had a quite different view of human nature from his. He was also influenced by Richard Hooker in embracing a doctrine of 'natural law' and 'natural rights', as was noted in Chapter 9.

Locke accepts the idea of a state of nature, although with a certain ambiguity as to whether there is or ever has been such a state. He claims, however, that all men are naturally in such a state unless in a civil society. The historical question of the existence of such a state does not matter; Locke is trying to establish what the natural condition of men must be if there is no civil society. The state of nature, he says, is one in which there is liberty, but not licence. It is in effect governed by laws of reason, according to which people have a right to the preservation of life, liberty, health and possessions. Hence, no one has the right to transgress another's rights in these respects. On the other hand, everyone has the right to punish another for any evil that he has done; everyone has 'the executive power of the law of nature'. Thus Locke holds that the state of nature is by no means as unpleasant as Hobbes supposed, because men are rational beings and will have some respect for rights. The state of nature nevertheless has many inconveniences, because individuals act on their own behalf. Hence the social contract, by which men put themselves under an obligation to others of the society, 'to submit to the determination of the majority'. There is no absolute sovereign; Locke wrote at a different period from Hobbes. His concern is simply with the basis of civil government, the aim of which is not only to preserve peace, but also to make possible the enjoyment of property.

This reference to property is one of the distinguishing marks of Locke's theory. In the state of nature it is supposed that there is a natural right to property, on the condition that something is a man's property if he has mixed his labour with it. This arises, Locke thinks, from the fact that everyone has a right to his own person and body, and thus to the use of his body in labour. In the state of nature, land and creatures are common, but they become a man's property when he mixes his labour with them. This was an influential idea; it connects the idea of individual freedom with property-ownership, although, as Marx was to insist, it is unrealistic in a society which depends on things other than property-ownership and where access to certain goods is possible to some people only. What happens, in any case, in succeeding generations? Locke thinks that men have a right to inheritance, but what happens to people who become disinherited for some reason, and where the distribution of goods in limited supply is manifestly unfair? These are issues that are still with us. There is also the question of why an original contract is binding upon succeeding generations. To deal with that problem Locke introduces the doctrine of 'tacit consent'. If one remains in a civil society this provides grounds for saying that one has consented tacitly to the government. Locke supposes that if someone did not wish to consent he could withdraw from the society and live elsewhere – another idea that has become progressively unrealistic.

It is clear that there are great practical difficulties in the working-out of Locke's ideas, and the question about the extent to which merely living in a society constitutes consent to the government is a real one. The practical machinery of democratic government is supposed to take care of some of these difficulties, but does so only up to a point. One view of Locke's that has been put into practical effect is that there must be separation of the powers; this is now written into the American Constitution. The functions of the legislative, executive and federative powers must be kept separate (the last power being concerned with treaties, transactions and war with other communities). Although the legislative is the supreme power while the government exists, power remains with the people if self-preservation demands its use; so revolution is possible. In this way Locke defends the revolution of 1688, with sanity if not with total realism.

Berkeley

I shall return later in this chapter to the influence that Locke had on French thinkers. The most immediate influence that Locke exerted was on George Berkeley (1685–1753), who was born near Kilkenny in Ireland, and eventually became Bishop of Cloyne there. He took his B.A. at Trinity College, Dublin, where he studied a variety of subjects, and became acquainted with the works of Locke and Malebranche; he also came to know something about Newton. Berkeley became a Fellow of Trinity College in 1707, although he combined this with entering the priesthood and became a priest in 1710. He wrote the main works through which he has become famous, and in many people's eyes notorious, while holding the fellowship. These are *An Essay towards a New Theory of Vision*, *A Treatise Concerning the Principles of Human Knowledge* (generally known as *The Principles*) and *Three Dialogues between Hylas and Philonous* (in which Philonous – lover of mind – wins over Hylas – matter – to Berkeley's views).

In 1713 Berkeley went on leave to London, where his views were received with some ridicule. This was a typical response. Swift is reported to have suggested that a consequence of his idealism ought to be that he could walk through closed doors; and Dr Johnson, as nearly everybody knows, kicked a stone, saying, 'I refute it *thus.*' Perhaps as a result of this reception, Berkeley took the opportunity of becoming chaplain to Lord Peterborough, and toured France and Italy with him. He published his *De Motu*, a treatise on mechanics, in 1721, and in the same year returned to Ireland. He was made Dean of Derry in 1724, but never took up residence in Derry, being concerned at this time to get government support for the setting-up of a College in Bermuda, largely for missionary purposes. He became impatient with government delays and in 1728, having married, he went to America, where he settled on Rhode Island. While there, he established contact with Yale College and had some correspondence with a Dr Samuel Johnson of Yale – a different Dr Johnson from the famous one. He also wrote a defence of Christianity, called *Alciphron* (published in 1732). Government support for his project never materialized, and in 1731 he returned to England. He was appointed Bishop of Cloyne in 1734, returning to Ireland to take up the appointment. He retired in 1752, went to Oxford and died there in the next year.

Berkeley wrote various works in his later years, none of which is of philosophical importance. His final work, apart from letters and further reflections on the work itself, was *Siris* – a strange book, which begins with a consideration of the virtues of tar-water for medicinal purposes (something that Berkeley put to practical use among the local population in Ireland), but goes on to consider, in terms of the idea of a great chain of being, the nature of the universe, ending with God and the doctrine of the Trinity. For some reason the work was a great success at the time; but although it has sometimes been suggested that it is the consummation of Berkeley's philosophy, it is now little read and not much regarded. Reference must also be made to one other source of information about Berkeley's ideas, the *Commonplace Book* or *Philosophical Commentar-*

ies. This comprises a pair of notebooks written in 1707–8, in preparation for his main works, publication of which began in 1709.

The view for which Berkeley has become famous (or notorious) is idealism – the theory that reality consists in ideas, and that there is nothing, apart from God and other spirits, 'without the mind'. The doctrine is summed up in the *Principles* in the slogan '*esse est percipi*' (to be, as far as material bodies are concerned, is to be perceived). If that view is so expressed, it does not quite amount to idealism; it simply asserts that the only things that exist are things that are perceived. To arrive at idealism we need the additional premise, on which Berkeley explicitly relies, that the only objects of perception are ideas. In the first of the *Dialogues* Berkeley makes a distinction between immediate and mediate perception, claiming that all that we immediately perceive are the proper objects of the senses: light and colours, sounds, smells, tastes etc. When we hear a coach in the street, we immediately hear sounds, which suggest to us a coach. Immediate perception is inference-free, and thus immediate in that it involves no intellectual process, simply the direct operation of the senses.

The claim that there is any such thing as immediate perception in this absolute sense may be disputed, especially given that Berkeley claims as another characteristic of immediate perception that we cannot be mistaken over its objects. The notion of the proper objects of the senses also needs examination; it corresponds in some way to the Aristotelian notion of the special objects of the senses, although Aristotle did not make the corresponding epistemological claims in the way that Berkeley did. In Berkeley's case this way of thinking has a history, which begins in the *New Theory of Vision*. I shall return to this later. The immediate issue is the connection between it and idealism.

Berkeley assumes that these immediate objects of perception are sensations, and that these in turn are ideas. Why? It must first be noted that Berkeley takes over from Locke the whole doctrine of ideas, interpreted as things that take place in the mind. Whatever Locke meant by the term 'idea', Berkeley takes him as referring by it to a mental entity akin to an image; ideas would be representations of things, if only there were things for them to represent. As the *Principles* makes clear, not all ideas are sensations (there are, for example, ideas of the imagination), but all sensations are ideas. Indeed Berkeley, perhaps somewhat carelessly, often uses the terms 'idea' and 'sensation' as alternatives.

All this might suggest that when Berkeley says that the only objects of perception are ideas he is simply following out the implications of Lockean terminology. The situation is, however, more complicated than that. In the early part of the first *Dialogue*, for example, Berkeley invokes additional arguments to support his view. When Locke made his distinction between primary and secondary qualities, he asserted the subjective nature of the latter. In doing so, he used arguments relying on the relativity of perception – the fact that how we perceive the secondary qualities of objects is relative to circumstances. How warm we feel an object to be depends on how far we are from it, how warm our own body is, and so on. When a fire is very near to us it may produce pain. Why, Locke asks, should one think that the 'idea of warmth' produced by the fire is in the fire, but the pain is in us? Such an argument fails to distinguish between warmth and feelings of warmth. Nevertheless Locke used arguments of this kind to conclude that all secondary qualities have the same status as pains: they are in us, not in objects.

Berkeley accepts this argument and extends it, not only by adding to it as regards secondary qualities, but also by arguing that exactly similar considerations apply to primary qualities. The relativity of perception holds good of them too; the size and shape that we see objects as having depend on the circumstances. Hence if secondary qualities are subjective (merely ideas in the mind) primary qualities must be so too. On the point about the relativity of perception Berkeley is surely right; but he was not right to accept the Lockean argument for the subjectivity of secondary qualities. Hence he was not right to conclude that primary qualities are subjective, either.

Moreover, the fact that secondary qualities are anthropocentric, in the sense that their significant ascription to objects is possible only for beings with human forms of sensibility or something like it, by no means entails that they are subjective. Still less does it entail that the qualities are themselves merely sensations or ideas in the mind, although many philosophers and supposedly philosophically minded scientists have believed otherwise. Nevertheless, Berkeley does accept that they are merely sensations, and he argues that because there is no good reason to make a distinction between them and primary qualities in this respect, the same applies to primary qualities. It must therefore apply to all properties of objects, and so to objects themselves. For it is a cardinal point of Berkeley's empiricism that there cannot be anything to objects except what the senses tell us of their properties. The only objects of perception are ideas; the being of objects is to be perceived; hence objects are really just ideas. Such is Berkeley's idealism, apart, as we shall see later, from spirits.

Berkeley's *New Theory of Vision*, his first work, is still some way from that conclusion, although it takes important steps towards it. It is in the main a work on optics, in the tradition of Descartes' *Dioptrics*, extracts from which Berkeley included as an appendix to the second edition of his work. He does not refer to Malebranche's discussion of optics, merely expressing puzzlement about Malebranche's doctrine that we see all things in God. Berkeley begins by saying, 'It is, I think, agreed by all that Distance, of itself and immediately, cannot be seen.' His reason for this assumption is, in effect, that the retina of the eye is a two-dimensional surface, with no possibility of the projection on to it of the third dimension.

It might be replied, and has been replied by the modern psychologist James Gibson,[1] that facts about the distances of objects are recorded on the retina *via* a projection of the texturing of the ground which objects occupy and which intervenes between them and us. Berkeley would have thought that beside the point, as is evident from the words 'Distance, of itself and immediately, cannot be seen'. There is much that requires examination in the phrase 'of itself and immediately', but in effect Berkeley is saying that since the retina of the eye is a two-dimensional surface it is unintelligible how the perception of distance could be provided by its means, without reference to anything else. For that to be a real problem, however, we should have to accept the views that there is immediate perception and that its scope can be inferred from the character of our sense-organs. That presupposes that there is a form of perception which involves nothing else but the operations of the sense-organs, without any part being played by the understanding. That view is very much open to dispute. It is perfectly true that if sensations are correlated with features of sense-organs, there can be no *sensation* of distance. The question is what this implies for the *perception* of the distance of objects; and the answer to that question is 'Nothing'.

Given his premises and point of departure, Berkeley has no difficulty in disposing of other suggestions about the origins of the idea of distance, such as the visual angle occupied by objects and the sensations which go with the turning, accommodation or converging of the eyes. The crucial elements in Berkeley's own theory are to be found in sections 41–51 of the *New Theory*. In them, Berkeley makes two points: (1) that the idea of distance can be derived only from touch, and that because of the association in our experience of certain visual ideas or sensations with certain tactual ideas or sensations, the former come to *suggest* the latter; (2) that the immediate objects of sight are 'not without the mind'.

Berkeley concludes from the former point that the answer to the problem set in his time by Molyneux – whether a man born blind would, if his sight were restored, immediately perceive the distance of things, or things as at a distance – is 'No'. He would need experience to connect the ideas of sight with the ideas of touch. The problem is still discussed

[1] See his first book, *The Perception of the Visual World* (Boston: Houghton Mifflin, 1950).

today, but it is not easy to determine the answer by any empirical means because of the habits built up by the blind in their reliance upon touch and other senses, and because of the conditions under which any restoration of sight must take place. For philosophical purposes, however, the second point is perhaps the more important. Berkeley says that 'at this time it seems agreed on all hands, by those who have had any thoughts of that matter, that colours, which are the proper and immediate object of sight, are not without the mind'; and he argues that if that is true of colour it must be true of figure and motion too *qua* seen. He concludes that the proper objects of sight are not to be regarded as images of anything outside the mind. The situation, he suggests, is different over objects of touch.

In the *Principles* sections 43–4, he withdraws the latter suggestion, saying that the objects of touch are equally in the mind. All the immediate objects of perception are ideas. When we perceive something mediately, as we do when we perceive a coach by hearing, certain auditory ideas suggest other ideas, visual and otherwise, which go to make up our complex idea of a coach. Things are just collections of ideas, which we have put together in experience. Towards the end of the *New Theory* Berkeley puts forward the idea that the proper objects of vision constitute the 'Universal Language of Nature' whereby we learn how to regulate our actions and maintain the well-being of our bodies. In the third edition of the work the phrase was altered to 'universal language of the Author of Nature'. The same thought appears in the *Principles* (sections 66 and 108), although in the second edition Berkeley weakened it and spoke merely of God providing us with signs. It is, as we shall see, crucial to Berkeley's conception of God in his scheme of things.

The *Principles* begins, however, on another tack. For the Introduction is given over to a sweeping attack on the Lockean theory of abstract ideas. Berkeley seems to interpret Locke as maintaining that one arrives by abstraction at ideas which have the form of images and yet have none of the characteristics of the particulars from which they are abstracted. He has fun at Locke's expense, taking him to hold that it is possible to have an image of a triangle which is neither equilateral, isosceles or scalene, and that it is possible to have an image of something of indeterminate colour, etc. This attack is no doubt unfair to Locke, who did not mean by 'idea' what Berkeley takes him to mean. In the second edition of the work, Berkeley added at the end of section 16 of the Introduction, 'And here it must be acknowledged that a man may consider a figure merely as triangular, without attending to the particular qualities of the angles, or relations of the sides. So far he may abstract: but this will never prove, that he can frame an abstract general inconsistent idea of a triangle.' Locke might well have accepted that quite happily.

Berkeley, on the other hand, suggests that the source of what he sees as the fallacy is to be found in words and in the supposition that 'every name has, or ought to have, one only precise and settled signification' (section 18). Because of this, he thinks, every general term is taken to signify an abstract idea. In the place of that view, he suggests that ideas and the corresponding words become general by signifying indifferently a great number of particular ideas. As Hume was to say, they are particular in their nature but general in their representation. An idea is general 'by being made to represent or stand for all other particular ideas of the same sort'. Similar things hold good of words; the generality of a word lies in its use or function. Some have seen in this a notable contribution to the theory of meaning, but it pales into significance if it is set alongside the theories of, say, Abelard or Ockham. In any case, what is it for ideas to be of the same sort, and what is it to see that things are of the same sort? As a contribution to the theory of universals, Berkeley's nominalism or imagism is relatively crude.

Why, however, is Berkeley so keen to dismiss the doctrine of abstract ideas? He gives in the Introduction only the merest hint of an answer to this question, but it is probable that he thought that, if it was possible to use abstraction in the way that Locke supposed, it might be possible to abstract from things all their sensory properties, leaving only their matter. In other words, Berkeley saw a connection between the doctrine of abstraction and the Lockean view of substance, conceived as implying the existence of an underlying matter to which the senses cannot attain. There is no evidence that Locke himself made that connection, but the dismissal of the idea of matter was certainly a central aim of Berkeley's philosophy. Matter was an unknowable 'something I know not what', and Berkeley thought that unintelligible, because it could never be made manifest to us by way of ideas. The danger in the doctrine of abstract ideas was that it might be thought possible by their means to make it manifest to us. So abstraction had to be dismissed as well. This may make Berkeley's argument sound unduly calculating, but there is no doubt that once given the premise that we perceive only ideas the rest was taken to follow. In the main part of the *Principles* (sections 4ff.) he returns to the question of abstract ideas, saying there that abstraction might be thought to make it possible to distinguish the existence of sensible objects from their being perceived, which he believes impossible.

Berkeley starts the main part of the *Principles* by asserting once again that the objects of human knowledge are confined to ideas. He now adds that such ideas can be 'imprinted on the senses', 'perceived by attending to the passions and operations of the mind', or finally 'formed by help of memory and imagination'. He goes on to say that there is also something which knows or perceives such ideas. 'This perceiving, active being is what I call *mind, spirit, soul* or *my self*.' Ideas cannot exist 'otherwise than in a mind perceiving them'. There are, therefore, ideas and spirits, and if substances are things which persist through changes, then the only substances in Berkeley's system are spirits. Physical things, as we ordinarily know them, are merely bundles or collections of ideas.

Such a view is closely related to the view sometimes called phenomenalism (that material objects are collections of actual or possible sense-data), except that Berkeley makes no reference to *possible* ideas. In section 48, when trying to meet the objection that his view entails that things are annihilated every moment and created anew, he says 'Wherever bodies are said to have no existence without the mind, I wou'd not be understood to mean this or that mind, but all minds whatsoever.' Hence, to say that a body persists is really to say that the ideas of it are either in my mind or in someone else's, and at least in God's mind. For ideas cannot exist without spirits which have them. To be is either to be perceived (in a sense that entails that to be perceived is to exist by way of idea), as is the case with ordinary things, or it is to perceive etc., as is the case with spirits.

Berkeley goes on to reject the distinction between primary and secondary qualities, and to dismiss as unintelligible the notion of matter, both in general and as the support of ideas – for ideas themselves can give us no possible knowledge of it. Berkeley's argument is frankly verificationist: speaking of matter is unintelligible because there could be no way of verifying its existence. He then argues for the thesis that the only possible causes of ideas are spirits. Ideas, he says, are manifestly passive; they are 'visibly inactive'. So the only possible cause of changes in the succession of ideas must be an 'incorporeal, active substance or spirit'. We find that we can change certain ideas in our minds at will, which indicates that the mind can be active. But ideas of sense do not depend upon the will. So they must be produced by some other spirit – by God. Ideas of sense may be distinguished from those of the imagination in that they are 'more strong, lively and distinct' – a point that was to be taken up by Hume. But they also have an order and coherence, due to laws of nature, which we discover through experience. Such laws of nature are due to God and testify to the goodness and wisdom of that 'governing spirit'.

This constitutes the main fabric of Berkeley's theory as expounded in the *Principles* sections 1–33. He spends sections 34–84 trying to meet various objections to his idealism, most of which can be dealt with relatively easily if his premises are accepted. Many of the objections purport to arise from the point of view of common sense, and the general ridicule that Berkeley's views received arose largely from the belief that his views were so opposed to common sense. Berkeley himself thought that his views were totally in conformity with common sense, at any rate if the implications of his philosophy were correctly understood. At the end of the *Dialogues*, Philonous is made to say, 'I do not pretend to be a setter-up of new notions. My endeavours tend only to unite, and place in a clearer light, the truth which was before shared between the vulgar and the philosophers: the former being of the opinion, that *those things they immediately perceive are the real things*; and the latter, that *the things immediately perceived are ideas, which exist only in the mind*. Which two notions put together, do, in effect, constitute the substance of what I advance.' And the *Dialogues* conclude with Philonous saying, 'Just so, the same Principles which, at first view, lead to Scepticism, pursued to a certain point, bring men back to Common Sense.' This is an accurate enough account of what Berkeley meant to convey, although it may be argued whether the vulgar and the philosophers do hold what is attributed to them. Nevertheless, his philosophy was taken by others as utterly opposed to common sense. Hence the responses of Swift and Johnson.

In the rest of the *Principles*, from section 85 onwards, Berkeley sets out what he takes to be the admirable consequences of his doctrine. He considers the part of his doctrine concerned with ideas first. He maintains that his view removes the possibility of scepticism, since if there is nothing for ideas to be copies of, there is no room for scepticism on whether they correspond to reality. That is a form of scepticism that many have thought Locke's view a prey to; it is not, of course, the only possible form of scepticism. Berkeley seems to be saying that his theory is at least better than Locke's in this respect. The second advantage which he claims for his view is that it precludes atheism. The position of God in Berkeley's system is obvious, but he now claims that it is the assumption of matter that is the foundations of atheism. He seems to have in mind here the views of '*Epicureans*, *Hobbists*, and the like', although he does mention other considerations. Thirdly, he says that his views free us from various difficulties that arise from belief in abstract ideas. He seems to have in mind the puzzlement that we are liable to get into if we have truck with abstractions such as time and happiness, when these notions are divorced from their application and their use in the ordinary course of events.

Berkeley goes on to expound what he sees as the advantages of his view for physics and mathematics. In the case of physics the target of his criticisms seems to be Newton. He attacks first what he sees as appeals to occult qualities, particularly in the notion of gravitational attraction.

Berkeley will have nothing of such ideas (such 'hypotheses and speculations'), and speaks of the admirable simplification of physics that results from their abandonment. We should see the laws of nature simply as uniformities which we can discover through observation, not through any form of demonstration. The 'Author of Nature' gives us signs to read – the language of God to which reference was made earlier. In sections 110ff. Berkeley makes explicit reference to Newton and to his notions of absolute time, space and motion in particular. Berkeley claims that there cannot be anything but *relative* time, space and motion, because observation could not tell us of anything else. His views of science are thus totally positivist.

His account of mathematics is similar and indeed formalistic also: that is to say that he thinks that, at least in the case of arithmetic and algebra, 'we regard not the *things* but the *signs*, which nevertheless are not regarded for their own sake, but because they direct us how to act with relation to things, and dispose rightly of them' (section 122). Indeed he says (section 120): 'Hence we may see, how entirely the science of numbers is subordinate to practice, and how jejune and trifling it becomes, when considered as a matter of mere speculation' – not a sentiment that was likely to endear him to pure mathematicians.

The view of geometry offered in the *Principles*, however, is different. For Berkeley considers geometry to be the science of actual extension, and therefore an empirical science. For this reason he speaks scathingly of the idea of infinity as applied to lines. Geometry is concerned with lines drawn on paper or the like, and such lines must have a finite length. There is no question of lines being divisible *ad infinitum* either. For there can be no idea of something infinitely small. There must be a *minimum visibile* (a least perceptible size) and that is all that a point is. Whether a line is capable of bisection will depend on the number of points, so construed, that it contains.

Such a view has disastrous consequences for geometry, and Berkeley was aware of that fact. In the *De Motu*, however, he briefly presents a view of geometry which brings it more into line with his view of the other branches of mathematics; and in the *Analyst* (1734) he attacks the idea that the differential calculus implies real infinitesimals, on the grounds that mathematicians are inconsistent in their use of them, treating them at one point as if they were quantities having positive size, only to treat them as if they were equivalent to zeros at another. Because this represented another attack on Newton it enraged Newton's supporters; but in this respect Berkeley was on the side of the angels, as the subsequent history of mathematics was to show.

Berkeley thought of himself, however, as on the side of the angels

throughout, as well as on the side of common sense. The *Principles* ends
with considerations about the consequences of his doctrine for the conception of spirits in general and of God in particular. Since spirits are
active, Berkeley denied that we can have ideas of them, although in the
second edition of the *Principles* he added at various places passages in
which he asserted that we nevertheless have *notions* of them, and that
we have direct knowledge of their existence in our own case. We know
of other spirits, however, only through the ideas that they produce, and
knowledge of them is not immediate. Spirits are naturally immortal in
that there is nothing in nature which could destroy them. This holds good
even more of God, because God is the Author of Nature. His existence
and nature are evident, Berkeley believes, in the ideas that he produces.

This, he thinks, is not prejudiced by the existence of evil and pain in
the world. Some of the 'inconveniences' result from the fact that God
operates in such a way that nature conforms to the 'most simple and
general rules'. Berkeley thinks that we should take a different view of
pain if we were to enlarge our view so as to take in the various ends of
things, 'the nature of human freedom, and the design with which we are
put into the world'. In general, therefore, his arguments for the existence
of God, to the extent that there are any, are the cosmological argument
and the argument from design. These arguments and his responses to the
problem of evil are similar to those of whole hosts of other philosophers,
and are as convincing or as unconvincing as they are.

Berkeley had little to say about ethics or politics. What there is suggests
that he saw both of these as subservient to religion. His claim to fame,
however, rests on the fact that he was perhaps the first philosopher to
put forward a full-blown idealism. Although that idealism is founded on
a form of empiricism, it does not simply follow from the thesis that all
our knowledge or all our ideas are derived from experience. The crucial
principle in Berkeley's philosophy is the doctrine that we perceive only
ideas. That doctrine is, in an extended form, sired by Locke out of
Descartes. Or to be more exact perhaps, it is the doctrine that Berkeley
thought Locke ought to have produced himself.

Hume

The precise philosophical position of David Hume, the last of the three
British Empiricists, is less clear. Many have seen Hume's philosophy as
one which takes the principles of the other British Empiricists to an
extreme in scepticism. Another view, which Hume suggested himself, is
that it is an attempt to apply to the mind the principles that Newton
applied to the physical world, and to produce a science of human nature;

according to the resulting theory nature, rather than reason, is the main source of our beliefs about the world. In the *Treatise of Human Nature* I.iv.2, Hume says, about beliefs in the existence of bodies independent of our minds, 'We may well ask, *What causes induce us to believe in the existence of body?* but 'tis vain to ask, *Whether there be body or not?*' A good deal of Hume's philosophy can be seen in that light: as an attempt to explain our beliefs in this and that, but not to justify those beliefs.

David Hume (1711–76) was born in Edinburgh, of a family of poor landed gentry. He attended Edinburgh University, being destined for the law, but was seduced from that by a 'passion for literature'. After a short but abortive period in business in Bristol, he went to France and there wrote the *Treatise* in three volumes. This was published anonymously in 1738–40, and (in the words of his posthumously published autobiography) 'fell dead-born from the press'. He had returned from France in 1737, and, judging his work to be a failure, he lived with his mother and brother until 1745, publishing in the meanwhile a collection of essays. After an unsuccessful bid for a chair at Edinburgh and a year's appointment as tutor to the Marquis of Annandale, Hume became secretary to General St Clair, accompanying him on an abortive expedition to Brittany and on diplomatic missions.

He published the *Enquiry Concerning Human Understanding* in 1748 and the *Enquiry Concerning the Principles of Morals* in 1751. These were more favourably received than the *Treatise*, but did not get much attention. In 1752 Hume became librarian to the Faculty of Advocates in Edinburgh and turned his attention to history; as a result he became better known as a historian than as a philosopher. He became a leading figure in the literary world of his time. From 1763 until 1769 he was in Paris, for the most part as secretary to the embassy there. In 1775 he realized that he had cancer of the bowel, and faced death calmly and courageously, retaining the wit, affability and sociability that he had always had. His *Dialogues Concerning Natural Religion* were, like his autobiography, published after his death. It is no exaggeration to say that Hume's true merits as a philosopher were not really recognized until many years later, although Kant claimed that it was a reading of Hume (it is not clear how much) that woke him from his 'dogmatic slumbers'.

The *Treatise* was a young man's book, and very much a treatise in its aims and ambitions. The *Enquiries*, although (as is commonly said) better written, were more concerned to put over Hume's philosophical views to the world of letters. The first *Enquiry* is much briefer even than the first part of the *Treatise*; it omits many issues raised in the *Treatise*, such as space, time and personal identity, but contains a section on miracles which has no parallel in the *Treatise*. Nowadays the *Treatise* is more read, and probably rightly. It contains three books entitled respectively 'Of the Understanding', 'Of the Passions' and 'Of Morals', and it is probably true to say that the second book is less read than the other two.

Book I begins with a distinction between impressions and ideas, and in making this distinction Hume claims to be restoring the word 'idea' to its original sense 'from which Mr *Locke* had perverted it, in making it stand for all our perceptions'. The word 'impression' suggests that things make an impression on the senses, but Hume does not really accept the implications of the term in that respect. In perception we are aware only of sensations, and these are the impressions in question. Hume is still working within the Cartesian heritage. Impressions may be either simple or complex, and every simple idea is derived from and is a copy of some simple impression, complex impressions and ideas being compounded of simple ones. The doctrine that every simple idea is derived from some simple impression is the centre-point of Hume's empiricism, and it is crucial for his philosophy. Impressions, like Locke's ideas, can be either of sensation or of reflection, although Hume's account of reflection seems different from Locke's; in either case they are distinguishable from ideas by their superior 'force and vivacity', and *by that alone*. That is another very important principle, and one inherited in effect from Berkeley; one cannot distinguish between impressions and ideas by reference to anything outside them, only by internal properties such as their liveliness.

Notoriously, Hume allows one possible exception to his principle that ideas must be derived from a corresponding impression. He allows that it may be possible by extrapolation to have the idea of one particular shade in a series of shades of colour when one has had no experience of it. But he thinks that the idea of such a missing shade of blue, for example, is 'so particular and singular, that 'tis scarce worth our observing, and does not merit that for it alone we should alter our general maxim' (I.i.1). It has been the subject of much discussion whether Hume is right in this judgement. Moreover, if all simple ideas (other than this) are to be taken as copies of simple impressions, how does one distinguish between ideas of memory (which presumably repeat an original impression) and ideas of the imagination (which do not)? Hume cannot, on his own principles, say that they can be distinguished because the ideas of memory correspond to the events that have occurred. Hence, he claims again that the only distinguishing mark lies in the superior liveliness, force and vivacity of the ideas of memory (although, as he recognizes in I.iii.5, the positions of the two ideas in this respect can become interchanged in the course of time, so that what force and vivacity amount to is merely our tendency to believe what goes with some ideas as opposed to others).

There are no abstract ideas, and on this subject Hume takes further what Berkeley had to say on it. Hume's version of the doctrine is to say that '*some ideas are particular in their nature, but general in their representation*' (I.i.7); and he claims somewhat dubiously that, 'shou'd we mention the word, triangle, and form the idea of a particular equilateral one to correspond to it, and shou'd we afterwards assert, *that the three angles of a triangle are equal to each other*, the other individuals of a scalenum and isosceles, which we over-look'd at first, immediately crowd in upon us, and make us perceive the falsehood of this proposition . . .' The source of this tendency is what Hume calls 'custom': something that has a special importance in his philosophy. The general principle that underlies it is that of the association of ideas, which governs the tendency of the mind to pass from one idea to another because of resemblance, contiguity in time or place, or the relation of cause and effect. Association of ideas, Hume says (I.i.4), is 'a kind of ATTRACTION, which in the mental world will be found to have as extraordinary effects as in the natural, and to shew itself in as many and as various forms'. In other words, in the principle of the association of ideas (a principle which is not, of course, original to him) Hume is claiming to find the principle which will make him the Newton of the mind.

The formation of complex ideas is one example, Hume says, of the effects of this principle. There are complex ideas of relations, modes and substances. But Hume thinks that our ideas of substances (and also thereby modes) are merely collections of simple ideas united in the imagination; for there is no impression of sensation from which the idea of substance can be derived, and impressions of reflection 'resolve themselves into our passions and emotions' (I.i.6). So there is no impression of substance, and ideas of substances are merely collections of ideas that 'are at least supposed to be closely and inseparably connected by the relations of contiguity and causation', although they are commonly ascribed to a fictitious unknown something.

The account of relations is more complex. Hume first distinguishes between ordinary relations between ideas, which, he says, obtain only when two ideas are connected together in the imagination by the principle of association, and philosophical relations, which, he says, are adduced only in philosophy 'to mean any particular subject of comparison without a connecting principle'. There are seven such philosophical relations: resemblance, identity, spatial and temporal relations, proportion in quantity or number, degrees in quality, contrariety and causation. At the beginning of I.iii.1 Hume subdivides these into two classes: 'such as depend entirely on the ideas, which we compare together' and 'such as may be chang'd without any change in the ideas'. The four philosophical relations of the first kind – resemblance, contrariety, degrees in quality and proportions in quantity or number – are the only objects, he says, of knowledge and certainty. Of the other three, it is only causation which 'produces such a connexion, as to give us assurance from the existence or action of one object, that 'twas follow'd or preceded by any other existence or action'. Hence the importance of causation, on which Hume spends a considerable amount of time in a treatment for which he is justly famous.

In distinguishing the two classes of philosophical relations Hume is making, in terms of relations, the kind of distinction that Leibniz made between truths of reason and truths of fact. The two kinds of relation are in fact logical relations and matter of fact relations. In putting causation into the latter category Hume is firmly distinguishing between causes and reasons in the logical sense – something that Spinoza, for example, failed to do. Before going on to review Hume's discussion of causality it will be as well to consider where we have come and why, and also to consider briefly Hume's treatment of space and time.

Much of Hume's discussion of impressions and ideas sounds as if it is psychology. The issues are really ones of meaning and significance allied to epistemology. The *Enquiry* makes it clear that Hume, like the other philosophers of his time, was concerned with the limits and scope of the human understanding. The empiricist claim is that all that we can understand must be based on sense-experience; no supposed idea, no term in our language, can have significance unless it is somehow derived from sense-experience. Hume's atomism of impressions and ideas has its linguistic counterpart in the thesis that all meaningful terms must be explicable by reference to terms that get all their significance by direct application to experience. The supposal that there are such terms has *its* counterpart in the thesis that all simple ideas (those in terms of which all other ideas are analysable) are derived from simple impressions. Hence, the issues are not really about what the mind can or cannot do as a matter of psychology; they are about what is and what is not intelligible, what the understanding is capable of comprehending.

Hume's treatment of space and time need not detain us long. It is not one of the best parts of the *Treatise*. In some respects he may have been influenced by an article on Zeno in Pierre Bayle's *Dictionary*.[1] He rejects the suggestion that our ideas of space and time involve infinite divisibility on the grounds that whatever is capable of being divided *ad infinitum* must have an infinite number of parts. No idea could consist of an infinite number of other ideas. Apart from the supposition that ideas of extended things must themselves be extended, the argument rests on a mistaken premise in supposing that anything divisible *ad infinitum* must have an

[1] For which see Chapter 12, p. 210.

infinity of parts. Like Berkeley, Hume thinks that there must be a minimum perceptible as regards size, and therefore argues that anything extended, whether spatially or temporally, must be divisible into indivisibles. He then goes on to argue that such indivisibles cannot themselves be extended; for, like Zeno, he holds that anything that has extension must have parts. Therefore the least perceptibles cannot have extension, although they may have other properties such as colour. Hence there are non-extended things which are nevertheless coloured – a very odd view.

In any case, if these are the parts of which extension in space (and correspondingly in time) is composed, how can extension be constructed out of such non-extended parts? Hume's answer is that an impression of extension must be an impression of the *order* or *manner* in which the indivisible but non-extended parts are disposed. This amounts to a relational view of space (and *mutatis mutandis* of time), but one in which the relations hold between non-extended points which nevertheless have other properties such as colour. There are in this echoes of Leibniz's 'massy points', but none of Leibniz's tendency to say that the relations involved are merely phenomena, although *phenomena bene fundata*. Hume does little to grapple with the real problems involved.

Fortunately we can put these issues on one side and return to that on which Hume's discussion is justly famous: that of causality. It is important to note that Part III of Book I of the *Treatise*, which is concerned with these matters, is entitled 'Of Knowledge and Probability'. For Hume, knowledge goes with certainty, and he holds that only the non-matter-of-fact relations provide that. When we go beyond them we are concerned with probability only. This is a view which many philosophers have held and some still do; we cannot have certainty with regard to matters of fact. The supposition is in fact quite false; there are many, many things about which we can be certain. The belief to the contrary is nevertheless endemic.

Hume describes his problem over causation as that of finding out the origin of our idea of cause, because he thinks that to understand an idea we need to know its origin. But in speaking of origin he is not really concerned with genetic psychology; in effect he wants to know how the idea of cause is to be understood and thinks that for this we need to know the components from which it is derived, that is, what is necessarily implied in it. Two things that he finds necessarily involved in it are that the cause and effect must be contiguous and that the effect must follow the cause in succession. (Both of these have been disputed: might there not be action at a distance, and might not a cause be at least simultaneous with its effect?) The other characteristic that he finds involved in the idea of cause is that there is a necessary connection between cause and effect.

But he can arrive at no clear notion of the nature of this necessary connection. In consequence he suggests that we must 'beat about all the neighbouring fields' in the hope that good fortune will enable us to find what we are looking for.

The two questions which he sets out to answer in beating about the neighbouring fields are: 'For what reason we pronounce it *necessary*, that every thing whose existence has a beginning, shou'd also have a cause?' and 'Why we conclude, that such particular causes must *necessarily* have such particular effects; and what is the nature of that *inference* we draw from one to the other, and of the *belief* we repose in it?' (I.iii.2). Hume deals with the first question by denying that there is any intuitive certainty over the principle involved. He does not deny that every event has a cause, merely that there is any logical necessity in that idea. If we believe in the necessity of a cause it must be on the basis of experience – another very important principle, which has been extremely influential. Hume suggests that if we can answer the question how experience gives rise to the principle of the necessity of a cause we may be able thereby to answer the second question stated above.

The subsequent course of Hume's argument is long and not entirely easy to follow. He first asserts that the experience which enables us to make an inference from one object to another, and thus from effect to cause, is that of the constant conjunction of those objects. On the basis of such constant conjunction in experience we move from a present impression to the idea of something as the cause. It is in effect *custom* that takes us from the impression of one thing to the idea of another, and the constant conjunction of objects in experience is therefore one other element, apart from contiguity in space and succession in time, that we may add to our conception of the causal relation, which is, it must be remembered, a philosophical relation. It now appears, Hume says (I.iii.6), that that philosophical relation is founded on a natural relation between an impression and an associated idea, and it is only because of this that 'we are able to reason upon it or draw any inference from it'. It is indeed this very same set of characteristics which enters into our idea of belief. Belief, Hume says, is merely a lively idea related to or associated with a present impression. To have a belief about something is therefore to have a lively or vivacious idea of it, to which we are brought by custom, because of an association between the idea and a present impression. That association is a product purely of the constant conjunction in past experience between this impression and another impression to which the idea corresponds. It is not a matter of any form of demonstration or reasoning.

The extreme empiricism involved in this claim is evident enough. The scope of reason is reduced drastically by it, and some philosophers would hold that it is overdone. It has been noted by commentators that when in I.iii. 15 Hume sets out rules by which to judge of causes and effects, he cannot adduce anything corresponding to the rules of elimination which Bacon put forward on the principle of the greater force of the negative instance. What Hume has to say hardly does justice to what goes on in scientific theorizing. Nevertheless, the doctrine that our attribution of causes is based upon the experience of a constant conjunction between objects or events was historically of the utmost importance, in that it finally marked out clearly the distinction between causes and reasons construed as premises from which conclusions can be deductively drawn. Not many philosophers today would accept what Hume has to say about belief, however. In the first place, belief that such and such is the case is propositional. That fact is hardly represented in speaking of a lively idea. In the second place, it is difficult to accept that all beliefs are formed in the single way that Hume supposes. Indeed, Hume's way of putting the issues makes it difficult to distinguish between a belief and a pressing thought brought about by association of ideas. Even at the level of psychology Hume's account seems inadequate.

Despite all this, it must be insisted that Hume's account of the foundation of our causal inferences was revolutionary and immensely influential. He fills out the account in a number of succeeding chapters, dealing with, among other things, probabilistic reasoning. It is not until section 14 that he returns to the idea of necessity which we have when we think of two objects connected together by the causal relation. The account so far was meant to explain how it is that we can go beyond our present impressions. In fact it provides no *justification* for our doing so; it merely explains why we do. That it does this is typical of Hume's whole programme, and it will appear later that Hume makes a similar move when concerned with belief in objects in general.

Nevertheless, given that we believe that some sort of necessity attaches to the causal relation, and given that that necessity cannot be found in objects or in impressions and ideas themselves, Hume is left with the questions what the idea of that necessity amounts to, and from what it is derived. His answer to those questions is that the idea of necessity is an idea of reflection, not an idea of sensation, and that it is derived from the constant conjunction that underlies our belief in causes – that is to say, that it is the idea corresponding to the impression we have of being taken from one item to another. That impression is a *feeling* of necessity derived from the 'determination of the thought to pass from causes to effects and from effects to causes'. Necessity is 'something, that exists in the mind, not in objects'. The impression from which the idea of necessity is derived is simply the impression of 'the propensity, which custom produces, to pass from an object to the idea of its usual attendant'.

This in effect completes Hume's lengthy account of causality. He sums the matter up in I.iii.14 by offering two definitions of *cause*, according to whether the causal relation is treated as a philosophical or as a natural relation (in spite of the fact that he had originally said that it was a philosophical relation). On the first definition, a cause is 'An object precedent and contiguous to another, and where all the objects resembling the former are plac'd in like relations of precedency and contiguity to those objects, that resemble the latter'. That definition might be thought insufficient, because it says nothing of the association between cause and effect (something which belongs, properly, to a natural relation). So he offers as a second definition 'A CAUSE is an object precedent and contiguous to another and so united with it, that the idea of the one determines the mind to form the idea of the other, and the impression of the one to form a more lively idea of the other'. That sums up his account of the matter.

Part IV of Book I of the *Treatise* is entitled 'Of the Sceptical and Other Systems of Philosophy'. He gives some consideration to ancient philosophy and what he calls 'modern philosophy' (by which he means on the whole the philosophy of Locke). There is also a section on the immateriality of the soul, in which Hume rejects the whole notion of the soul, as well as its immateriality. In that section too there is a certain discussion of the notion of substance, a notion with which Hume will have nothing to do, except to say in a telling way that if by 'substance' is meant *something which may exist by itself* his perceptions are substances 'as far as this definition explains a substance'. This is significant because it is true that the only self-subsistent things in Hume's system are individual impressions; the trouble is that they do not have a persistent existence, despite what Hume supposes the vulgar to believe on the matter, and so provide no basis for the identity of objects, or indeed of the self which is supposed to have the impressions in question.

For this reason, in setting out further worries about personal identity in the Appendix to the *Treatise* Hume says that he is unable to make consistent two principles that he also wishes to maintain: that *all our distinct perceptions are distinct existences*, and that *the mind never perceives any real connexion among distinct existences*. He thinks that there is a particular cause for concern over this in connection with personal identity; but the problem is in fact general. If individual impressions are distinct existences, and there is no possibility of finding a real connection between them, there is nothing in what is given to the mind that can justify our belief in the persistence of bodies. Moreover, Hume thinks that Berkeley's views do not provide any answer in this respect. Hume would reject the notion of God as used by Berkeley, but he thinks in any case that Berkeley's conclusions do not amount to a defence of common sense. In a footnote to section XII, Part I, of the *Enquiry* he says that Berkeley's arguments '*admit of no answer and produce no conviction*'; they are in reality sceptical.

But that is in effect Hume's answer too, and in relation to ordinary life he recommends 'inattention' (that is, to the philosophical considerations). In the conclusion to Book I of the *Treatise* he speaks of what nature can do in this respect. A dinner, a game of backgammon and conversation with friends can make philosophical speculations appear 'cold, and strain'ed, and ridiculous'. This seems far from satisfactory; it is surely something of a *reductio ad absurdum*. And so it is – a demonstration of the absurdity of the epistemological principles on which the system is built. It is to Hume's credit that he had the courage to follow the argument where it leads, as Socrates said we should. But if we are concerned with the justification of our belief in bodies and the self, the argument must lead to scepticism. That is why the quotations from *Treatise* I.iv.2 above are so pertinent: 'We may well ask, *What causes induce us to believe in the existence of body?* but 'tis vain to ask, *Whether there be body or not?*' Hume's answer to the first question involves an appeal to the imagination. It is this which makes the vulgar, as Hume would have it, confound perceptions and objects, so attributing a continued existence to the former, whereas philosophers and scientists adopt the 'philosophical system' distinguishing between perceptions and objects, only the latter having continuity. (It should be noted that Hume's account of the difference between the vulgar and the philosophers is different from Berkeley's, since Hume is more preoccupied with problems of identity and continued existence.)

The imagination relies upon two features of perceptions. There is, first, their coherence – the fact that different sets of impressions fit together, so that objects seem to have an identity and interdependence which are not affected by gaps in the series of perceptions when we are absent from the scene. This apparent regularity, however, goes beyond any data which the senses directly provide, even when these are supplemented by the effects of custom or habit, based on constant conjunction of perceptions. So, Hume says, the imagination 'is apt to continue, even when its object fails it, and like a galley put in motion by the oars, carries on its course without any new impulse'. But he agrees that the principle that the mind carries on finding uniformities among objects in this way is 'too weak to support alone so vast an edifice, as is that of the continu'd existence of all external bodies'. So he adduces in addition the idea of the constancy of impressions; there is a uniformity in the order of impressions of objects, and such impressions continue in the same order after interruption. For that reason, we are inclined to fill in the gaps by supposing a single real existence accounting for them. These two characteristics of impressions explain, according to Hume, our tendency to believe in the continuity and identity of objects. But they do not justify such a belief, and Hume ends *Treatise* I.iv.2 by saying that ' 'Tis impossible upon any system to defend either our understanding or senses . . . Carelessness and in-attention alone can afford us any remedy.' Hence, scepticism remains ineradicable, and the idea of subsistent objects is a kind of fiction.

Similar conclusions follow from his treatment of the self. In this case, Hume denies that there is any impression of the self from which the corresponding idea can be derived, asserting in a famous passage that whenever he examines himself he can only find perceptions. Kant was to argue in reply that it makes no sense to suppose of the existence of a perception which is not *someone's* perception. Hence the existence of a subject or self is presupposed in the very idea of a perception. That thought, however, is foreign to Hume's system, for it goes against the idea of the basic and substance-like existence of impressions. Hume does, indeed, suppose the existence of impressions which are 'unowned' – a very strange idea, but one which is a consequence of the system.

Hume might be accused of not looking in the right place for the idea of the self. Nevertheless, he thinks that the most that one finds in oneself is a bundle of impressions and ideas united by resemblance, contiguity and causal relations. The mind, he says, is a 'kind of theatre, where several perceptions successively make their appearance . . . there is properly no *simplicity* in it at one time, nor *identity* in different'. Hence, the idea of the simplicity and identity of the self is a kind of fiction. This is, once again, a product of the imagination, although it is influenced by the three characteristics of resemblance, contiguity and causal relations which impressions in a series may exhibit. It is an uncomfortable conclusion, and Hume recognizes that fact in the Appendix, where he suggests that what he has said is not enough to make us attribute to a bundle of perceptions 'a real simplicity and identity'. In the case of objects, it seemed to Hume enough to explain why the imagination makes us attribute to them a unity and identity; in the case of the self, he was left with the feeling that that was not enough. He was surely right in this.

Thomas Reid thought that Hume's argument was valid, but that the conclusions were unacceptable. The fault must lie, therefore, in the premises, and in the account of perceptions in particular. Reid was right in this. It is the initial epistemological position and the principles associated with it (two of which, Hume admits in the Appendix, are impossible to reconcile) that lead Hume to his radically sceptical conclusions. It has been debated whether Hume intended to be a sceptic or whether his prime aim was, rather, to found epistemology and metaphysics on the nature of the human mind as he saw it. But his explanations of how we come to believe what we do as a result of our nature are too weak. This becomes crucial over the self, but similar considerations apply throughout Hume's philosophy, even in the case of what has given him the largest claim to fame – his treatment of causality. The first *Enquiry* ends with a notorious purple passage: 'If we take in our hand any volume; of divinity or school metaphysics, for instance; let us ask, *Does it contain any abstract reasoning concerning quantity or number?* No. *Does it contain any experimental reasoning concerning matter of fact and existence?* No. Commit it then to the flames; for it can contain nothing but sophistry and illusion.' The argument turns on what is sometimes called 'Hume's fork' – an 'either/or' based on the distinction between the two kinds of philosophical relations. It presents a dichotomy similar to that espoused by modern logical positivists: propositions are either logically true or empirically verifiable, otherwise nonsense. But for Hume's own metaphysical conclusions this is perhaps of less importance than the doctrine of impressions and ideas on which it all rests.

Book II of the *Treatise* is concerned with the passions, which are, on Hume's reckoning, impressions of reflection. It includes a survey of a range of emotions, including sympathy, which is important for Hume's conception of morals. Hume distinguishes between the causes and objects of the emotions, between the idea 'which excites them, and that to which they direct their view, when excited', and it is these characteristics which enable him to distinguish the various passions to which we are subject. Will is merely the internal impression that we feel when we knowingly give rise to a new motion of the body or new perception of the mind. Hume argues as if it is agreed by everyone that all our actions are subject to causes, in that desires in particular bring actions about. He is thus a decided determinist. But he argues that this is quite compatible with belief in freedom of the will, as long as we distinguish between 'liberty of spontaneity' and 'liberty of indifference'. We do act freely in the first sense, and the fact that our actions are subject to causes is no obstacle to that; we should recognize that freedom in this sense is opposed to compulsion. There is no freedom in the sense of liberty of indifference, 'which means a negation of necessity and causes'. Hume is therefore a compatibilist over the freedom of the will; such freedom is quite compatible with determinism. Many other philosophers since his day have espoused the same view; it has not satisfied everyone, but there is much in its favour.

It is in this Book too, and in this same context (II.iii.3), that there occurs one of Hume's more celebrated remarks relevant to morals: that 'Reason is, and ought only to be the slave of the passions, and can never pretend to any other office than to serve and obey them.' In other words, reason can have no practical effects, and there is no such thing as practical reason, properly speaking; if reason is to have any bearing on practice it must be because of some accompanying desire or passion. Conversely passions can be called unreasonable only when accompanied by some judgement, and then, strictly speaking, it is the judgement that is unreasonable. Hence Hume can say that apart from this, ' 'Tis not contrary to reason to prefer the destruction of the whole world to the scratching of my finger.' Many people have found these remarks scandalous. But Hume is not saying that one *should* prefer the destruction of the world to the scratching of one's finger, or indeed that it is reasonable so to do. What he says about its not being contrary to reason so to prefer has as its premise the hypothetical assumption that the passion in question is 'neither founded on false suppositions, nor chuses means insufficient for the end'. It is only in relation to considerations of that sort that questions of reasonableness or the reverse arise. Nevertheless, Hume puts a great deal of weight on desires as the motives for our actions, and supposes that there is a severe limitation on what reason can do. Some passions, he says, are calm, as opposed to violent; but we must not confuse calmness with reasonableness.

It is pleasure and pain, Hume thinks, that lie at the root of the passions which determine us to action. These are the things that most concern us, and we approve those actions which produce happiness (which Hume does not differentiate from pleasure) in others. The source of the latter sentiment is sympathy, which produces 'our sentiment of morals' in the case of most, if not all, virtues. Thus, like other philosophers of his time, Hume had a theory of moral sentiments, which lie in men's nature. Hume is both a hedonist and a utilitarian, in the sense that he saw pleasure and pain as the springs of action, and held that our estimate of the rightness or wrongness of an action is a function of the extent to which we believe that the action produces happiness or pleasure. He needed, however, to explain how, in spite of the motivation of our actions on his account, we can come to regard some things with moral approbation, some with the reverse. For he was anxious to deny that rightness or wrongness are to be regarded as properties of actions themselves, independent of our feelings towards them. To think of actions as right or wrong is just to have feelings of approval or disapproval towards them. The moral sentiments are merely a sub-class of such feelings, and they are to be distinguished by the part that sympathy plays with regard to them, sympathy itself being derived from the idea that we have of an emotion in another which produces a like emotion in ourselves. Such moral sentiments are common to all men, and are founded on a common human nature.

There are some virtues, however, which Hume calls artificial, in that they 'produce pleasure and approbation by means of an artifice or contrivance, which arises from the circumstances and necessity of mankind' (*Treatise* III.ii.1). The prime example of this is justice, and Hume spends a considerable amount of time on it. Our moral approval of justice (that is, the feeling of approval that we have towards it) does not arise directly from the sympathy that we have towards others. We approve of justice because we approve of some system of conventions set up by men, such that actions in conformity with the rules involved are in the public interest. Such actions are not always to our own interest, and the motivation towards them cannot be what it is in the case of natural virtues. Their motivation must lie in the educative role that conventions play in our lives. The force of such conventions cannot lie in any contract, founded on promise-keeping, that such conventions presuppose, for the keeping of promises and contracts is an example of the very thing the explanation of which we are trying to find. Hume is indeed opposed to any idea of natural law, as a principle of justice, and to the idea that the principles of justice are founded on any form of social contract. He speaks disparagingly of the idea of a state of nature, and thinks the idea of a social contract a fiction. Whether or not societies originated from consent, this is not the present source of people's obligation to them. Hence, we do not approve of justice and what it entails for that reason. We approve of it because of the advantages that we see to derive from it. Self-interest, educated by family life, leads men to abide by the rules of justice, which contribute to general utility. Hume thought indeed that such obedience to the rules of justice must be inflexible; the existence of society and the advantages that accrue from it depend on such obedience.

Hume's moral theory is naturalistic, in that it appeals to certain supposed facts about human nature. It is subjectivist in that it denies that moral rightness and wrongness are objective features of the world. (There is indeed a famous passage in *Treatise* III.i.1 in which Hume speaks of moralists smuggling in an *ought* when they have been talking about what *is* or *is not* the case – a passage which has led philosophers to speak of the impossibility of deriving an *ought* from an *is*, and which is still the subject of controversy.) It is utilitarian in that it sees the criteria of our judgements of goodness and badness in the amount of happiness produced by the actions in question. Whether all these things can be combined in such a way as to produce an acceptable ethical theory is a matter for debate.

It remains to look in brief at Hume's philosophy of religion. The *Dialogues Concerning Natural Religion* are concerned primarily with arguments for the existence of God on the basis of experience, with *a posteriori* arguments to that effect. As with many dialogues, it is not entirely clear with which character the author is to be identified, if any. But Hume's sympathies are with critics of what a chapter in the first *Enquiry* calls the 'religious hypothesis', and in particular with critics of the argument from design. On that the *Dialogues* take further the argument of the *Enquiry*, pointing to the fact that an appearance of purposiveness does not entail the existence of a designer. Things in the world (animals, for instance) reveal evidence of teleology although they have not been created by any designer, so why should we suppose that the world in general is the product of a designer? Although dispute about such arguments continues, Hume's criticism of them is a classic of its kind.

The same applies to the treatment of miracles in the first *Enquiry*, although here Hume reveals a faith in laws of nature which might seem surprising, at any rate to a relatively casual reader of the treatment of causality in the *Treatise*. For he insists that a miracle must be a violation of laws of nature, and on that basis he argues that 'no testimony is sufficient to establish a miracle, unless the testimony be of such a kind, that its falsehood would be more miraculous, than the fact, which it endeavours to establish'. Hume thinks that no testimony to a miracle has ever amounted to a probability, let alone a proof. But his final conclusion allows the *possibility* that miracles might occur and that there might be sufficient testimony to that effect, although he adds, perhaps oddly, that in that case philosophers 'ought to search for the causes whence it might be derived'. Nevertheless, he is quite adamant on his general principle if it is qualified in one particular way – 'that a miracle can never be proved, so as to be the foundation of a system of religion'. For past testimony concerning religious miracles has been so subject to violation of truth that it is more probable that any new testimony to such a miracle will be a violation of truth than that it will be proof of a violation of the laws of nature. Hume was known in his time as 'Mr Hume, the atheist', but his arguments

on such religious matters are still philosophical. Hume's general reputation as a philosopher has varied in the period since his death, but in
his willingness to 'follow the argument where it leads' he was very
much a philosopher in the Socratic sense.

Reid

I have already mentioned the fact that Thomas Reid (1710–96) was a
severe critic of Hume, suggesting that what he took to be Hume's
absurd conclusions were due to erroneous premises, in particular the
doctrine of impressions and ideas. Read was born at Strachan in
Scotland. He was educated at Marischal College, Aberdeen, and
became librarian at the university there until 1736, when he resigned
the post and visited England. In 1737 he entered the ministry, as many
of his family had done in the past. Despite the fact that he had
published only one philosophical paper, he was in 1751 appointed as
professor of philosophy at Aberdeen, where he wrote his *Inquiry into
the Human Mind on the Principles of Common Sense* (published in
1764). In that same year he became professor at Glasgow, following
Adam Smith, but in 1780 he resigned the post in order to devote
himself to his writings. He published his *Essays on the Intellectual
Powers of Man* in 1785, and the *Essays on the Active Powers of Man*
in 1788. Reid had a disciple Dugald Stewart (1753–1828), to whom we
owe details of his life. A later follower was Sir William Hamilton
(1788–1856), although by this time Reidian views were mixed up with
those of Kant. There were other philosophers in Scotland in this period
who were critical of Reid, however, particularly Thomas Brown (1778–
1820).

Since he was a *critic* of British Empiricism, there is a sense in which
Reid does not belong in this chapter; but Reid's philosophy is so
related to that of the British Empiricists that it is appropriate to
consider him now. Reid objected to the whole 'way of ideas' on various
grounds. In particular, he thought that it led to conclusions that flew
in the face of common sense. Hence his attempt to establish a philosophy on the basis of the principles of common sense. Reid's reaction
to the British Empiricists in this respect is very similar to that of
G. E. Moore to the idealists at the turn of the present century. Like
Moore's reaction, Reid's was very much an assertion of realism. Like
Moore too, Reid was opposed to the subjectivism and naturalism in
morals which Hume proposed, putting in its place the idea that the
first principles of morals are self-evident and the objects of moral
intuition. He also defended a positive view of human free will. But it

is in his account of perception and its distinction from sensation that Reid's real claim to fame and originality lies. That account of perception is itself an answer to the British Empiricists.

Reid defines a sensation as an act of mind that 'hath no object distinct from the act itself', and he takes the sensation of pain as the paradigm of such sensations. One might quibble about Reid's use of the term 'act', but for the rest he seems right, although even he was to indicate that we might in certain circumstances fail to note the occurrence of sensations because of inattention. Perception differs from sensation in that it is related to other objects, and involves, apart from the occurrence of sensations: (1) 'a conception or notion of the object perceived'; (2) 'a strong and irresistible conviction and belief of its present existence' – a conviction and belief which he goes on to say is (3) immediate and not the result of reasoning. Perception is thus concept-dependent and epistemic, but the belief that results from it is not the result of inference or reasoning. Details of the analysis might be disputed, but the distinction that is made between perception and sensation is clear.

It is equally clear how different this account of the matter is from those which he is criticizing. The qualities of objects cause in us, he says, the relevant sensations, and these are natural signs of those qualities. Reid insists that almost all perceptions have accompanying sensations, and he says that sensations *suggest* to us the perception of the quality that produces them – thus adopting Berkeley's use of the term 'suggest' for this purpose. In the case of what Reid calls 'natural and original perceptions' this suggestion is a fact of nature, but experience makes possible acquired perceptions. Moreover, Reid attempts to explain the details of the Berkeleian theory of distance perception in these terms. The original perception of a sphere takes it as circular but two-dimensional; but as a result of experience natural and original perceptions of this kind suggest to us an acquired perception of the sphere as genuinely spherical.

The details of all this do not matter, perhaps, as much as the general framework into which they are put. It is arguable that Reid is the first philosopher to make a clear distinction between perception and sensation, and as a contribution to the philosophy of perception this makes his philosophy quite remarkable. There is nothing in Reid's account corresponding to Hume's impressions or later philosophers' sense-data, and his account shows that there is no need for such things; indeed they involve incoherence in conflating things of quite different kinds. Reid thinks of his account as a defence of common sense, and so in many ways it is, especially if it is compared with the views of those whom he attacks. It has greater importance, however, as an analysis of perceptual experience and what is involved in it. Strangely enough, Reid had comparatively little influence in this respect on the general course of philosophy, apart from his immediate followers, although Schopenhauer approved of much that he took Reid to be saying. It is perhaps time that philosophers, particularly those interested in perception, went back to him.

[12]
The Enlightenment

Although it is normal to put Locke, Berkeley and Hume together, as manifesting, despite their difference, a generally empiricist philosophy, these philosophers, or at any rate Locke and Hume, can be regarded as part of a general intellectual movement that took place in the eighteenth century, generally referred to as the 'Enlightenment'. It was a movement characterized by a tendency to apply the methods of the new sciences of the age of Newton to other intellectual and philosophical problems. No doubt it would not have taken place if Descartes had not introduced his new individualist approach to philosophy, but directly it owed more to Locke. It was also a movement which was often, though not always, anti-religious and free-thinking; and in France in particular, some of the *philosophes*, as they were called, risked and suffered imprisonment as a consequence. There is a sense in which Hume fits into the movement very well, especially in the field of morals. In this chapter, I shall survey briefly the debate in Britain over the idea of a moral sense, and the thought of the French *philosophes* associated with *L'Encyclopédie*, the French Encyclopaedia, edited by D'Alembert and Diderot, much of which was sensationalist in its epistemology and materialist in its metaphysics, together with the political thought of Rousseau and the social and historical thinking of Vico.

The idea of a moral sense
The idea of a moral sense was first introduced by Anthony Ashley Cooper, third Earl of Shaftesbury (1671–1713), a follower of Locke. In many ways, Shaftesbury's views were a reaction against the so-called Cambridge Platonists, for example Ralph Cudworth (1617–88) and Henry More (1614–87), who represented a kind of late flowering of Neo-Platonism without any real claim to originality or greatness. More held that there were self-evident moral truths, knowledge of which was the province of reason. Shaftesbury maintained on the contrary that moral discernment was the function of a moral sense. We distinguish what is bad from what is good by *seeing* their difference, in the same way as we see, and thereby distinguish, what is beautiful from what is ugly. What, however, are we seeing when we perceive something or someone as

virtuous? Shaftesbury's answer to that question lay in the idea of harmony: a harmony between man's passions and inclinations, and a harmony between those of one individual and those of other men. Conscience is the expression of the feeling of sympathy which we have for others; in the virtuous man this is the mark of the harmony that exists between himself and others. Given that sympathy, men have a natural inclination to benevolence.

Shaftesbury was attacked by Bernard de Mandeville (1670–1733), particularly in his *Fable of the Bees*, which argued that virtue and public good are in fact based on egoism and selfishness, not (as Shaftesbury maintained) on benevolence and public feeling. Indeed, Mandeville claimed that society can be conceived as *founded* on the fact that each individual seeks his own interest. This opposition between Shaftesbury and Mandeville was the beginning of discussion of an issue which occupied the attention of several of the British Moralists, the relationship between self-interest and benevolence.

That issue does not, however, make a large appearance in the writings of Shaftesbury's immediate, and arguably greater, follower Francis Hutcheson (1694–1746). Hutcheson's first book (1725) was entitled *Inquiry into the Original of our Ideas of Beauty and Virtue*, but it is in fact a compendium of two works, one on moral good and evil, the other on aesthetics. The treatments of the two subjects are parallel, so that Hutcheson provides a fairly complete working-out of the supposed similarity between an aesthetic and a moral sense. Indeed his answer to the question why we approve of benevolence, rather than self-interest, is an aesthetic one. It is just that these moral features arouse in us the appropriate feelings. Moreover, the sufferings of others produce in us feelings of pain which are the source, through sympathy, of benevolence towards others. Benevolence is thus, as with Shaftesbury, a natural impetus towards action which is common to men. The implication of this is that what is characterized as a sense is the source, not only of feelings of approbation and disapprobation, but also of action. It is not at all clear how it could be this. Nevertheless, in Hutcheson's view benevolence is, so to speak, the whole of virtue, and benevolence is founded on the moral sense. His philosophy is, however, wider than this simple formula might suggest. He is the originator of the phrase which became famous in the context of nineteenth-century utilitarianism, 'the greatest happiness for the greatest numbers' – an idea which he saw as the key to social welfare. He might therefore be said to be the originator of utilitarianism itself.

It is Bishop Joseph Butler (1692–1752) who stands out as, apart from Hume, the greatest moralist of the period, and he had a firm grasp of the issue between self-interest and benevolence. Indeed one might say that this issue was his central concern. His solution of the problems involved was to argue that self-interest or self-love and benevolence coincide. Butler argued that we have a number of particular propensities. Although the satisfaction of these propensities results in pleasure, it is a mistake to suppose that pleasure itself is the sole end of human action. Thus psychological hedonism – the doctrine that we all and always pursue pleasure – is rejected. Benevolence is one of our propensities, but it is not thereby the whole of virtue because it is only one propensity among others. Self-love, on the other hand, cannot be identified with mere selfishness or egoism in a crude sense, because it should be concerned with our total happiness. What Butler described as 'cool self-love' involves reflection in a rational way upon our particular propensities, and upon how they can best be satisfied without our giving ourselves up to passions and desires in a way that must bring about our ruin. The aim of cool self-love must therefore be to bring about our happiness by means of an appropriate but not unbalanced satisfaction of the propensities which we have. But, as we have seen, among those propensities will be that towards benevolence; hence we cannot achieve true happiness without benevolence, and in that way benevolence and self-love coincide.

Butler put forward these views in a number of *Sermons* published in 1726. It is clear that Butler is attempting to found ethics on a view of human nature. It is a view of human nature that is unlike that of, say, Hobbes in rejecting hedonism, in rejecting the idea that pleasure is the sole spring of action; it appeals nevertheless to the thought that we do have a number of propensities and passions, the satisfaction of which will produce pleasure and thereby happiness. That is an important distinction, one between the suggestion that we are always moved by pleasure and the suggestion that we are moved by a number of other things such that their satisfaction does in fact produce pleasure. It is to Butler's credit that he made the distinction; it is one that is still not always recognized.

There remains, however, the problem of how we are to decide between the satisfaction of the various propensities which we have. I have mentioned already the rational reflection upon those propensities that is the essence of cool self-love. We need more than that, however, if cool self-love is to be given any principles, in terms of which decisions can be made about how happiness is best achieved. In this respect Butler invokes the idea of conscience, which he sees as having a peculiar authority in relation to rational choice. It is, he says, 'a superior principle of reflection' which has a steadfastness against the momentary appeals of the passions. It acts in the interest of cool self-love, so that duty and interest can coincide, if not in this world then in the next. It is perhaps no surprise to find Butler, as a Christian bishop, making this appeal to conscience. To some extent he can be criticized for not explaining further the source of its authority, but it is noteworthy that in appealing to it he was appealing to something that he saw as part of human nature. It is natural for human beings to feel the demands of conscience, just as they feel the demands of particular passions and propensities.

Hume, as we have seen, rejects in his theory of moral sentiments the idea that there is any superior principle of this sort. There are indeed calm passions, but calmness is not *ipso facto* reasonableness. Hume in fact supplies no principles of moral reasoning, and his whole theory of morals is opposed to the suggestion that anything of this kind can be supplied. On the other hand, Hume would have said, and did on occasion say, that the authority that Butler saw as attaching to conscience is no different from that which we feel as attaching to all our sentiments. Butler, in other words, does not explain why the principles of moral reasoning should have force with moral agents. Reason has not yet been shown to be practical. It was left to Kant to try to show how it could be.

Hume's theory of moral sentiments was taken further by Adam Smith (1723–90) – perhaps better known as a political economist – who argued in *The Wealth of Nations* (1776) that society is best preserved both socially and economically by self-interest. In his *Theory of the Moral Sentiments* (1759), however, he produced a subtle account of the moral sentiments, in which sympathy once again plays a large part. He also put great weight on the idea of an imaginary impartial spectator of our actions, in terms of whose judgements the propriety of actions is to be assessed. This impartial spectator is a substitute for Butler's conscience, and provides a shadow of moral reasoning proper.

Opposed to these conceptions of morals was Richard Price (1723–91), a Unitarian minister, and author of *A Review of the Principal Questions and Difficulties of Morals* (1758). Price owed much to Cudworth and the Cambridge Platonists, and was in general tendency a rationalist. He produced criticisms of Locke and Hume, arguing that many of our ideas cannot have the empiricist origins that they maintained they had. Hence he laid claim to the idea that reason itself must be the source of many of our ideas, and of many principles which we believe ourselves to know. The distinction between right and wrong, in particular, is to be attributed to the understanding, not to sense-perception. The principles of morals are known by a form of rational intuition. In this, Price's views have some similarity to those of G. E. Moore, H. A. Prichard and W. D. Ross in this century. The ideas of right and duty are simple ideas which do not admit of further analysis, and the principles of morals that are built upon them are known by intuition as self-evident. Such a view is, unless further worked out, little more than a reaction to the inadequacies of a moral sense position; it leaves questions about practical reason untouched. As we saw in the last chapter, Reid too held the view that the principles of morals are self-evident, although he did not in general embrace Price's rationalist epistemology. It is not a view that is intellectually satisfying; its appeal to intuition leaves too much in mystery, and leaves un-worked-out the relation between moral truths and practice.

The philosophes

Some of the same tendencies can be seen at work in France, although they took a somewhat different form. I have already spoken of the general cast of thought that pervades the French Enlightenment. In some respects it goes back to Pierre Bayle, whom I mentioned in the last chapter as perhaps influencing Hume. Bayle (1647–1706) was a sceptic. His *Dictionnaire historique et critique* (*Historical and Critical Dictionary*, 1695–7) is in form a biographical dictionary, dealing critically with a whole host of relatively unknown persons. This gave Bayle the opportunity of criticizing and opposing a large number of beliefs and theories put forward by them. As a work of reference it was too idiosyncratic, but it was very influential in the eighteenth century, largely because of the spirit in which it was written. Although his own sceptical views were largely negative he provided ammunition and an impetus for the Enlightenment in general.

Perhaps the centrepiece of the French Enlightenment is the *Encyclopédie*, edited by Denis Diderot (1713–84) and Jean D'Alembert (1717–83). Contributors to it included, apart from the editors, François Voltaire (1694–1778), Charles, Baron de Montesquieu (1689–1755) and Jean-Jacques Rousseau (1712–78). It had a chequered career, receiving opposition from the Jesuits, and it was suppressed for a while. It set out to display the totality of knowledge as it was then conceived, but its spirit was empiricist, anti-religious, to some extent materialist, and certainly humanist. It was meant to be the epitome of the 'age of reason'.

Locke's influence on this was profound in more ways than one. Montesquieu took over from Locke the doctrine of the separation of the powers, which he thought was incorporated into the British constitution. He laid great weight on the Aristotelian idea of man as a political animal, adding to it an emphasis on the part played by the particular societies in which men are to be found. He also combined a belief in eternal moral laws with a social relativism as far as values are concerned – two views which it is difficult to square. But the main way in which Locke influenced the encyclopaedists was through his epistemology, an influence which was added to by Hume. In general the epistemology of these thinkers was empiricist and sensationalist: that is to say that they tended to put forward a theory of the mind which based everything on discrete sensations provided by the senses. So, as with Locke, knowledge was thought to be derived entirely from sensation together with reflection upon that.

This view is to be found in Étienne Bonnot de Condillac's *Traité des sensations* (*Treatise on Sensations*). Condillac (1715–80) tried to show how all the mind's operations could be analysed in terms of the occurrence of sensations and their derivatives. Judgement, for example, was explained in terms of two sense-impressions occurring together. It will be evident that there must be some crudity in this analysis, but the point was to explain the workings of the mind in terms of what occurs automatically and passively, once given sensation. Diderot complained that this view was too close to that of Berkeley and implied an idealism which Condillac did not want. Hence Condillac had also to show that the processes in question could give rise to knowledge of an external world, the existence of which was not prejudged in the epistemological apparatus.

Condillac tried to use the idea of a marble statue with the inner complexity appropriate to a human being, to explain what could give rise to such knowledge – what, that is, would have to be built into such a statue to make knowledge of more than mere sensations possible. He found the answer in terms of feelings of solidity, which kinesthesis made possible. This was supposed to provide impressions of exteriority, and Condillac believed that the ideas of a world and of space and time could be derived from these. This last idea was taken further and modified by a later thinker, Maine de Biran (1766–1824), to whom reference has been made earlier. Biran thought that passively received sensations, even those of the kind that Condillac postulated, were not enough to provide knowledge of the world. For this reason he laid weight on what he called an *effort voulu* (willed bodily movement). It was only resistance to this, and not merely the contact with the body that Condillac had in mind, which could explain the impression of exteriority. The objection to all this derives from the unsatisfactoriness of the premise on which these views depend – the belief that we are immediately given only private, inner sensations. The influence of Descartes, mixed up with that of the British Empiricists, is obvious.

The same sensationalist epistemology is to be found in the writings of Claude-Adrien Helvétius (1715–71), combined with a materialism and psychological hedonism which was judged scandalous by the authorities, with the result that he had to retire from the royal service. He also joined a complete determinism to a belief that human nature could be transformed by an enlightened system of education, through processes which are akin to conditioning (a view which makes him an eighteenth-century B. F. Skinner). Diderot likewise believed in a form of materialism and presented such views in *Le Rêve d'Alembert* (*D'Alembert's Dream*). The most extreme of such thinkers in this respect, however, was probably Julien Offroy de la Mettrie (1709–51), as is indicated by the title of one of his main works, *L'Homme machine* (*Man the Machine*). Like Helvétius, and before him, he believed in a strict determinism and an ethics which is founded on hedonism moulded by social influences. None of these thinkers can be said to reach a high point of philosophy, but despite differences in detail they present a framework of ideas that is of a piece. Men are animals, the behaviour of which is to be explained in terms of the new sciences; knowledge is based on sensation and modified thereafter on mechanical principles; society makes education and re-education possible if only political institutions allow this. The influences of the British Empiricists are large in all this, but there is a sense in which it is second-hand. The *philosophes* are important for the history of ideas and the history of culture, but they do not mark an important stage in the development of philosophy as such.

Rousseau

Rousseau is in a way connected with the *philosophes*, being a contributor to the *Encyclopédie*. In general, however, he exhibits a different spirit, and certainly presents a picture of human beings which is different in many ways from theirs. He seems to have been an impossible man: suspicious, hypochondriacal and sometimes quite unscrupulous. He was born in Geneva in 1712, and had a rather complicated early life, including a period as general factotum and lover of a Madame de Warens. He came to Paris in 1742 and made a livelihood in various ways. He lived with an illiterate serving girl by whom he had five children, all of whom were handed over to a foundling hospital. Acquaintance with Diderot led to the contributions to the *Encyclopédie*. In subsequent writings he was critical of the part played by society in human affairs. His main works are *The Social Contract* (1762) and an essay on education, *Émile* (1762); these two works brought fame but also immediate persecution, and he had to flee from France to Switzerland. He then wandered about and for a time sought refuge with Hume, who found him impossible because of his hypochondria and paranoia. He eventually returned to France, where he died in 1778.

Rousseau's conception of human nature is a romantic one, as is witnessed by his famous remark that man is born free but is everywhere in chains. He does not think that natural man or the state of nature is as Hobbes supposed. Man is not governed by the same pushes and pulls; he is not a psychological egoist. Men do have feelings of sympathy towards others, and there is thus a sense in which even in the state of nature (which Rousseau does not conceive of as a historical state of affairs) men are social beings. They are also naturally good. But social life proper, in which there develop the institutions of property and forms of skill and art, leads without the institutions of government to various forms of oppression and slavery. Hence the need for the state, which emerges from a social contract. In actual societies there tends to be oppression, and Rousseau's account of the social contract as the foundation of political life is meant to be an account not of what actually happens in contemporary society, but of what *should* happen. It is an account of what should happen if the common good is to be attained. Rousseau says that the function of the social contract is, paradoxically, to bring it about that men give up their freedom absolutely so that they may become freer than before. How can this be? The secret of that lies in the concept for which Rousseau has become famous, that of the General Will.

Through the social contract the people give up their rights and freedom to the sovereign, which may of course be the people themselves. In doing so, they thereby distinguish between their individual wills and the general will, which is that of the sovereign people. The general will is a will for the common good, as distinct from the individual goods that individuals may will. This general will is to be distinguished, Rousseau insists, from the 'will of all'. The sum of individual wills may not in fact be for the common good, although Rousseau maintains that, in a democracy, the differences between the individual wills may somehow cancel out, leaving a result which is an expression of the general will. How this can be is one of the great problems in Rousseau's philosophy.

The ascription of a general will to a sovereign people involves the personification of the sovereign and the state, an idea that was to be taken further by Hegel. There are certain parallels in this respect between Rousseau's thought and Plato's. The latter set the unity of the state above all else, embracing the idea that only where a city is a unity formed by the different classes working together under the guidance of the Guardians can the good of that city as a just state be achieved; and he went into great detail over the social institutions necessary for the achievement of that aim. Rousseau thinks in terms of political institutions rather than social institutions, but the aim is somewhat similar. The aim of political institutions is to achieve the common good; and, by participation in them *via* the contract, people will share in that common good, so becoming freer than before. Nevertheless, in doing so they submerge their individual wills into something greater, which necessarily expresses what they, so to speak, really want.

It is a romantic doctrine, but it is a dangerous one too. For if it is to have any application the general will must be determinable. In Plato the unity of the state is a unity under the wise guidance of the Guardians, and the crucial question is what that wisdom consists in. Similarly in Rousseau the crucial question is what the common good consists in, and what therefore is the general will. To presume that there is such a will, something that people *really* want, as distinct from what they want individually, is not only a mystical doctrine; it invites the identification of the general will with some individual's conception of it, and ahead of that lies the totalitarian state.

Rousseau himself would have been horrified at the suggestion that his ideas could have such implications, although the *Social Contract* ends with the suggestion that there are certain beliefs which form part of 'civil religion' and which people must hold or be punishable by death. For the most part, however, Rousseau was an extreme democrat who believed that government should be determined by an assembly of the people, and who rejected any suggestion of representative government. His conception of the state makes it a cross between a Greek city-state and what he took to hold good in the Geneva of his time. How such a political institution was to determine the common good remains impenetrably obscure all the same. It is sometimes said that Rousseau was not a proper philosopher. He was certainly part of the Enlightenment, in his hope that machinery could be devised for the attainment of human welfare – a *philosophe*. Unfortunately, his muddled optimism is liable to misuse, as subsequent history, both intellectual and practical, was to show.

Vico

For the last philosopher to be mentioned in this chapter, it is necessary to go back a little in time. Giambattista Vico (1668–1744) is a figure who falls outside the main stream of the thought of his time, and he does not fit easily into the history of the period. He was the son of a bookseller in Naples, where he attended a Jesuit college, and eventually attained the relatively minor post of professor of rhetoric in Naples. He failed to get the chair of civil law there, and lived most of his life in relative poverty and neglect. His main work is the *Scienza nuova* (*New Science*). Vico's conception of the new science was anti-Cartesian. He did not accept the claims that were central to Descartes' philosophy, particularly those embodied in the '*Cogito*' and the appeal to clear and distinct ideas. Although mathematics has a kind of certainty, this does not carry over to physics or any science of the physical world. Mathematics has the kind of certainty that it has because it is a human creation, and thereby satisfies the principle that is central to Vico's thought, that truth (*verum*) is coincident with what is made (*factum*).

Because of that principle, Vico laid weight upon human institutions and creations, and saw history and historical understanding as the key to a sure understanding of the world in general. These were matters which Descartes had ignored or depreciated, and Vico's views were in that sense not only unorthodox but revolutionary. Historical understanding involved rejecting *a priori* conceptions of human beings, and accepting the necessity of trying to get into the minds of past men. The key to that was the study of language, myth and tradition. This emphasis on, and conception of, history influenced Johann Herder in Germany in the late eighteenth century, and Benedetto Croce in Italy and R. G. Collingwood in England in this century. But the general line of thought has been taken up and developed by humanist and sociological thinkers. Hence, Vico is not just perhaps the first philosopher of history, but also the originator of the thought that later emerges in the idea that reality is a human or social construction.

Unfortunately that idea is a muddle. If one thinks that truth entails certainty (and that is in itself a mistake), there might conceivably be something to be said for the thesis that the one thing an individual knows with certainty is what he himself does. Each person knows what he does, because he is the originator of his own intentional actions, and an act counts as intentional only if it is done knowingly. That was a thought on which Schopenhauer, for example, relied. It is true only with certain qualifications, because, given that we have bodies and that our bodily actions involve interaction with a physical world, the success of a great many of our actions – whether we succeed in performing them – depends on how the world is. There is, however, more to be said for such a thesis than for the thesis that we know with certainty of our own creations, because, apart from what we might call thought-creations, we create only what can be made out of something that already exists, and that limits the possibilities of creation. The word '*factum*' is ambiguous between what is made and what is done, and it might be thought that Vico was playing on that ambiguity. It is not clear, however, that anything of that kind is the case. If that is so, one has to conclude that his claim for the coincidence of *verum* and *factum* is simply wrong. He remains an intriguing figure, even if out of the main stream. He is of the time of the Enlightenment, but not really part of it.

[13]
Kant

Immanuel Kant (1724–1804) is the great giant of eighteenth-century philosophy, and arguably the great giant of philosophy in general. Despite that, his life was almost eventless. He was born in Königsberg in Prussia, where his father was a saddler. After what was in effect a grammar school education, he eventually went to the university at Königsberg. After a period as Privatdozent, during which he was very poor, he became professor of logic and metaphysics at the university, and remained in that post until three years before his death. He remained a bachelor, though he is said to have liked company, especially that of ladies who were good-looking and educated. He was reputed to have been a lively lecturer, although nobody would guess that from his published works, which are difficult and dry, both in style and in content. He went for regular daily walks, to the extent that people could tell the time from them. He hardly moved outside Königsberg for the whole of his life. It is difficult to know what moral one should draw from all this, but by common consent Kant's greatness as a philosopher overrides all else.

Kant wrote a number of early minor works, which have become known as pre-Critical writings. Then, after a period of silence, he published in 1781 his *Critique of Pure Reason*, a second edition of which was published with substantial revisions in 1787. The *Critique of Pure Reason* was in fact the first of three *Critiques*, the second being the *Critique of Practical Reason* (1788), which is concerned with ethics. He had published in 1785 a *Groundwork of the Metaphysics of Morals*, a much shorter work, which has received a good deal more attention than the second *Critique*. The third *Critique* – the *Critique of Judgement* – was published in 1790 and was concerned in large part with aesthetics, but also with teleology. In 1783 he had also written the *Prolegomena to any Future Metaphysics*; it was published between the two editions of the first *Critique*, and was meant to make his views more accessible. Kant also wrote on, among other things, religion, politics and what was then called anthropology – the empirical psychology of the time. The core of his work is, however, to be found in the three *Critiques*, particularly the first.

Transcendental idealism

The title of the first *Critique* in a way reveals its aim. Kant, as was noted in an earlier chapter, said that it was Hume who woke him from his dogmatic slumbers. It is not entirely clear how much Hume he had read, but it was enough for him to feel doubt about the received philosophy of his time, which was largely Leibnizian, through the influence of Christian Wolff. It raised in his mind the question 'How is metaphysics possible?', and the answer of the first *Critique* is that if speculative metaphysics attempts to go beyond the limits imposed by the nature of the human understanding, it is not possible. Such attempts merely end in contradiction or analogous incoherences. Any future metaphysics must therefore be limited to what lies within the bounds of human understanding. Kant's own 'critical philosophy' exhibits the form such a metaphysics must take, if at all. The emphasis upon the limits of the understanding is inherited from Hume and the other British Empiricists, and Kant derives from them too a good deal of epistemological apparatus. His own epistemology is, however, not empiricist, but seeks to drive a wedge between the empiricism and the rationalism that preceded him. That is evident from the opening words of the Introduction to the first *Critique*[1]: 'There can be no doubt that all our knowledge begins with experience . . . But though all our knowledge begins with experience it does not follow that it all arises out of experience' (B1).

It is not clear that any of the empiricists we have already considered said that all knowledge arises out of experience, although they did say that all *ideas* are derived from experience. Kant did not accept even that; along with rationalists such as Leibniz, he believed that some of our ideas are *a priori*, independent of experience, in the sense that their content is not derived solely from what is given in experience. Nevertheless, the opening quotation makes quite clear his position on knowledge. Experience is a necessary condition of the possibility of knowledge, but it is not a sufficient condition. On the other hand, the faculty of understanding, in virtue of which we make judgements about the world, by bringing experiences under concepts, needs the faculty of sensibility to provide those experiences. Kant's declared aim is to undermine claims for a supposed faculty of pure reason which could arrive at truths about the world or about reality independent of experience. Nevertheless, when we make judgements about the world, the understanding is dependent on certain formal and *a priori* concepts or categories, and these are the source of

---

[1] I shall refer to it as *CPR* from now onwards, quotations being taken from the admirable translation by Norman Kemp Smith (London: Macmillan, 1929). Passages marked 'A' are taken from the pagination of the first edition, those marked 'B' from the second edition.

principles that have to be observed in bringing experiences under concepts in judgement, if those judgements are to be objective.

This is the bare skeleton of Kant's thought, and it is likely to be relatively meaningless without at least some of the flesh. Nevertheless, the two extreme positions to which Kant is opposed should be clear: that all concepts and all knowledge are derived from experience; and that not only some concepts, but some knowledge too, can be absolutely independent of experience. (It would be unrealistic to take as the extreme in the second case the thesis that *all* concepts and *all* knowledge are independent of experience; no one could plausibly hold *that*.) His own epistemological position implies an acceptance of the empiricist doctrine that we are given information in impressions. Kant calls those impressions representations (*Vorstellungen*) or sensible intuitions. The content of a representation constitutes its matter, but every representation has a spatiotemporal form also. This is *a priori* in the sense that the spatiality and temporality of the representation are not, so to speak, constructed out of other impressions which, as Hume made clear, would have to be unextended or point-like. Spatiality and temporality are *presupposed* in the having of a representation. Although such representations have a content, they do not amount to knowledge unless they are brought under concepts in judgement. It is judgement that is epistemologically basic. In a famous remark Kant says: 'Thoughts without content are empty, intuitions without concepts are blind' (B75). The empiricists had said little if anything about judgement, and the importance of Kant's emphasis upon it should not be underestimated.

Nevertheless, Kant's acceptance of a large part of the empiricist epistemological apparatus, particularly the thesis about representations, affects the rest of his philosophy. For, if sensibility provides us with representations only, we have at best only an indirect access to the so-called external world. The view implies a form of idealism. Kant's thesis is that we must suppose that representations are somehow due to what he calls things-in-themselves, but we can have no knowledge of these. Indeed, there are places in his writings where he speaks of the idea of a thing-in-itself as a limiting concept – a concept which we must presuppose for the sake of completeness, but the content of which is purely negative. Given this, Kant's position is neither a Berkeleian idealism, which he criticizes in the part of the *CPR* entitled 'The Refutation of Idealism', nor a straightforward realism. Kant calls his position 'transcendental idealism'.

The word 'transcendental' must be distinguished from 'transcendent'. To suppose that there was knowledge that was transcendent would be to suppose that knowledge could go beyond the limits of experience; and that Kant thinks impossible. Knowledge is transcendental if it is 'occupied not so much with objects as with the mode of our knowledge of objects in so far as this mode of knowledge is to be possible *a priori*' (B25; cf. B352–3). So, to say that idealism is transcendental is to say, in Kant's own words, 'that appearances are to be regarded as being, one and all, representations only, not things-in-themselves, and that time and space are therefore only sensible forms of our intuition, not determinations given as existing by themselves, nor conditions of objects viewed as things-in-themselves' (A369 – Kant omitted this passage from the second edition).

The problem is how to interpret this so as to make it different from Berkeleian, empirical idealism. Kant says that transcendental idealism is consistent with empirical realism. According to this latter view there is a a distinction within experience between things such as material objects and space and time, and merely mental things, such as sensations, images and dreams. From this point of view the former things are real, and the merely mental things are not. But from the point of view of the conditions of possible experience the things that seem real – the 'appearances' of the passage quoted above – are ideal; they are, as it were, functions of the human mind and sensibility, as contrasted with things-in-themselves. Our ordinary contrast between appearance and reality is to be made within representations alone.

Kant emphasizes transcendental idealism and its consistency with empirical realism particularly in connection with space and time, which he regards as the *a priori* forms of experience. From the point of view of experience, space and time are real, not mere appearances; they constitute nevertheless the *a priori* form of experiences, of sensible intuitions, and they do not apply to things-in-themselves. In the Preface to the second edition of the *CPR*, Kant compares his point of view with that of Copernicus' reversal of previous accounts of the relation between observers on earth and the heavenly bodies. His own so-called 'Copernican revolution' involves conceiving objects as conforming to our 'faculty of intuition' rather than conceiving intuition as conforming to objects (B xvii). If that is so, objects are no more than what our sensible intuitions represent to us; they *are* representations subject to the *a priori* conditions that the forms of space and time determine.

Transcendental idealism therefore presupposes a distinction between what Kant calls *phenomena* (appearances) and *noumena* (intelligibles). Objects as they reveal themselves to experience are phenomena. As far as our experience is concerned, noumena, as objects, constitute a mere possibility, for if they were to be a real possibility for us there would have to be an intuition of them. There is no such thing as far as we are concerned, which is why the concept of a noumenon should be taken negatively, not positively. Nevertheless, phenomena exist *because of* things-in-themselves, and these are noumena. The question then arises, to what conditions phenomena have to conform in order to be objective, as opposed to merely subjective. That question occupies the greater part of the section of the *CPR* known as the 'Analytic'; this expounds a theory of judgement and its presuppositions, and also a theory about the self or subject which makes such judgements. To be expressible in objective judgements, experience must be so organized as to be of an object and belong to a subject. These are the two sides, objective and subjective, of what Kant calls the 'transcendental unity of apperception'. But just as there is no access to noumena lying behind phenomena, so there is no access to a noumenal self, a real self, to which phenomena are appearances. Yet, as we shall see, Kant thinks that moral thought and, in particular, considerations about human freedom, demand reference to such a noumenal self. It remains something of which there is no experience. The only self that can be experienced is the empirical self, which is simply all the introspectible, mental features of which each of us can be aware.

The synthetic **a priori**

The Introduction of the *CPR* presents a certain amount of apparatus, particularly the distinctions between *a priori* and *a posteriori* judgements and synthetic and analytic judgements, and the connections between the two. I have already spoken of Kant's notion of the *a priori* as independent of all experience. The notions of the *a priori* and *a posteriori* are epistemological notions. A judgement is *a priori* if its truth can be known without reference to experience; it is *a posteriori* if it cannot be so known. The 'can' is important in this account, as is the fact that the *a posteriori* is defined negatively in terms of the failure of the condition applying to the *a priori*. Moreover, if a judgement is *a priori*, its verification demands no direct reference to experience; but, as the opening words of the Introduction (referred to earlier) make clear, the knower must have experience in general. Kant goes on to maintain that necessity and universality are 'sure criteria of *a priori* knowledge', so that a judgement is *a priori* if (and perhaps only if) it is universal and necessary. It is not clear that Kant is right in this.[1]

The distinctions so far considered have a history in previous thought going back to Aristotle, and in this respect Kant is merely putting refinements upon ideas that he has inherited from others. The distinction between the synthetic and the analytic is all his own, although Leibniz

---

[1] See my *Theory of Knowledge* (London: Macmillan, 1971), ch.9.

and Hume made distinctions that are in the same family. Kant says that an analytic judgement is one in which the concept of the predicate is contained in that of the subject, although covertly; if the predicate lies outside the concept of the subject the judgement is synthetic. The latter kind of judgement is ampliative in that it adds to the concept of the subject, while an analytic judgement is explicative in that the act of predication unfolds, as it were, what is already thought in the subject. Kant gives as examples of analytic and synthetic judgements respectively 'All bodies are extended' and 'All bodies are heavy'. Elsewhere he adds that an analytic judgement is such that its denial involves a contradiction (as was the case with Leibniz's 'truths of reason'), whereas this is not the case with a synthetic judgement. There are difficulties with Kant's formal definitions of the analytic and the synthetic, of which subsequent philosophers have made much. Most later philosophers have, however, respected the spirit of Kant's distinction, if not the letter.

Kant also sees connections between this distinction and that between the *a priori* and the *a posteriori*. Analytic judgements are all *a priori* – which seems right. But Kant thinks that synthetic judgements may be either *a priori* or *a posteriori*. Empiricists have accepted quite willingly the idea of synthetic *a posteriori* judgements or propositions, because there is nothing wrong with the idea that experience can provide knowledge of new pieces of information. They have, however, balked at the idea that there can be synthetic judgements the truth of which can be known without reference to experience. Kant's central problem, therefore, is how synthetic *a priori* knowledge is possible. He thinks that speculative metaphysics makes claims to synthetic *a priori* knowledge, although in fact it provides nothing of the kind. There *are* nevertheless synthetic *a priori* truths, in mathematics and in the principles that state the presuppositions of objective experience (such as the principle that every event has a cause). Each of these claims has been the subject of much argument. It has not generally been in dispute that mathematics provides *a priori* knowledge, but empiricists have maintained that its propositions are analytic. It has been questioned whether propositions such as 'Every event has a cause' are even true, and – to the extent that they are – whether they are *a posteriori* rather than *a priori*.

The 'Aesthetic'

The first part of the main fabric of the *CPR* is entitled the 'Transcendental Aesthetic'. Kant's use of the word 'aesthetic' is intended to indicate that he is concerned with sensibility and its forms. The section is mostly given up to a consideration of space and time, which Kant regards as the *a priori* forms of sensibility. Space is the form of outer sense (the experience of objects external to us), while time is the form of both outer and inner sense (because our inner experiences, as well as our experiences of outer objects, involve time). Space and time are each given so-called metaphysical and transcendental expositions. The latter are concerned with the part that space and time play as necessary conditions of the possibility of mathematical knowledge. I shall come to the metaphysical expositions later.

Kant maintains that geometry presupposes an intuition of space, and that arithmetic presupposes an intuition of time. Whatever may be said in favour of the first claim, the second has been almost universally rejected. The number series involves a progression, but it is not a temporal progression. On the other hand, to say that arithmetic involves an intuition is to say that it is not simply a matter of relations between concepts, and that there is something about it which makes application to the world possible. If Kant had said that arithmetic depends upon an intuition of plurality, through which numbers and counting get application to sets of things, he might have been judged right. Similar considerations apply to geometry and an intuition of space. One might view geometry as the metrical unfolding of a certain conception of space, but if geometry is to have application to the world more is required than a mere conception of space. There must be grounds for thinking that that conception has application. In Kant's language, that is provided by an intuition, a perception of the spatial character of the world.

Kant is often criticized over what he has to say about geometry. It is claimed that he assumed too readily that Euclidean geometry is *the* geometry of space, and that the subsequent development of non-Euclidean geometries has proved him wrong. This is, arguably, beside the point. It is essential to Kant's account of these matters that geometry involves a certain conceptual structure and an intuition. He might reasonably have claimed that, given our sensibility, our intuition of space is such that Euclidean geometry is the one which has the most obvious application to things within our experience. Nothing rules out the possibility that other geometries might fit better things outside our immediate experience, or indeed things that exist for creatures with a different sensibility. (Einstein's espousal of a non-Euclidean geometry within the General Theory of Relativity implied the applicability of such a geometry only on a cosmic scale.) In fact, the claim that an *a priori* intuition of space is a necessary condition of the possibility of geometry says nothing in itself about the *kind* of geometry in question. It must also be noted that Kant sometimes says, not just that there is an *a priori* intuition of space (and similarly of time), but also that they each *constitute* an *a priori* intuition. This is part of the transcendental idealism, according to which objects have to be construed as experiences, as intuitions. Kant's fundamental point is that space and time are in some sense objects themselves.

That point is spelled out in the metaphysical expositions of space and time. Under this heading Kant makes four points, although in the exposition of time he unfortunately brings in an extraneous fifth point. The four points are: (a) the concept of space is not an empirical concept, but an *a priori* one that is presupposed by all outer experiences (at least, this is what he seems to mean, although he actually says that *space* is not such a concept). The claim over time is similar except that there is no need to make the qualification involved in the use of the word 'outer', because *all* experiences involve time. On this point Kant seems right; it is impossible to abstract a concept of space from individual experiences, as Locke supposed; to have the concept of an extended object some concept of space is already presupposed. (b) Space is a necessary *a priori* representation, which underlies all outer intuitions, so that we can think of space as empty of objects, but we cannot represent to ourselves the absence of space. The situation over time is the same as in (a). Apart from the point about space *being* a representation, Kant is arguably right here too, although by no means all commentators have thought so. (c) Space and time are intuitions, not concepts – a point already mentioned; they are not merely ways of *thinking* about the world, they are ways in which the world *is*. Kant adds as a corollary, although one which has been disputed, that space and time are each essentially one. (d) Space and time are represented as infinite *given* magnitudes. Spatial and temporal intervals are not just potentially extendible *ad infinitum*, so that they can be thought of as possibly going on in that way. To perceive a spatial or temporal interval is to perceive something which is part of an infinite whole and is perceived as such. Once again, what Kant says on this is a matter of controversy.

The 'Aesthetic' presents us, therefore, with a conception of experience such that each experience has a content, in that it is *of* something, but such that it also has a necessary spatial and/or temporal form. Strictly speaking, however, that alone does not amount to knowledge. For this we need judgement, and experiences or intuitions have to be brought under concepts. But judgement is used in imagination or fancy just as much as it is in objective experience. Hence, the next question is what conditions have to be satisfied for an experiential judgement to be objective, where by 'objectivity' is meant, not truth, but being a candidate for truth. To answer that question is the task of the 'Analytic'.

The 'Analytic' and the deduction of the categories

The course of the argument in this part of the *CPR* is immensely complicated. The first part of it consists of what Kant calls the deduction of the categories. By 'deduction' he means something like 'justification', and a deduction of categories is an argument aimed at the justification of claims for their necessity, where by 'category' Kant means a general and formal concept of a way in which experiences may be unified in judgement. The aim is to show what formal *a priori* concepts are presupposed by the very possibility of judgement about objective experience, and why. When this is finished, Kant argues that something else too is required to link this purely formal understanding with experience – what he calls a 'schema'. From this there emerges a set of *a priori* principles which, it is claimed, are presupposed in all objective judgements about experience – principles such as that every event has a cause. The setting out of these principles completes the argument of this part of the *CPR*. I can do no more than gesture at the details of it.

The 'deduction of the categories' has two parts or aspects: a transcendental deduction and a metaphysical deduction. The former is supposed to show the general need for such categories as a condition of possible objective experience; the latter is supposed to show what the actual categories are. In the first edition of the *CPR*, Kant sets out, as the first part of the transcendental deduction, what is known as the 'threefold synthesis'. As a condition of objective judgement and experience the 'manifold of experience' has to be brought together and unified in three ways.

First, there is the synthesis of apprehension in intuition: the manifold of experiences has to be distinguished and brought together as a unity if it is to be represented as a manifold. We must, that is, perceive a group of experiences as belonging together. Second, there is the synthesis of reproduction in imagination. When we perceive a group of experiences as a single manifold and thus allow the possibility that they are experiences of one object, we must be capable of bearing in mind experiences which have occurred earlier in the sequence when we are concerned with later items. Kant takes this to be a function of the imagination, although the first two syntheses are in fact inseparable. Third, there is the synthesis of recognition in a concept. The manifold must be given a true unity as an experience of a single thing; a concept provides this principle of unity. The process as a whole, the three-fold synthesis, constitutes transcendental apperception – that form of consciousness which is a necessary condition of objective experience. The synthesis must, however, be in accordance with a rule, which prescribes how it is to be brought about successfully, with the result that there is a single object for a single consciousness. Such rules have their basis in general, formal concepts of the principle of unity in judgement; and these are categories.

The second-edition version of the 'deduction' of the categories lays perhaps greater weight upon the nature of the apperception involved. What Kant now calls the synthetic or transcendental unity of apperception is said to have two sides – subjective and objective. In a famous phrase Kant says that 'it must be possible for the "I think" to accompany all my representations' (B131). For representations to be possible items in judgement, they must be capable of being objects of thought for the subject whose representations they are, and that is because all my representations are *necessarily* mine. Hume had supposed as possible the occurrence of impressions or ideas the ownership of which might be in question, because, given what impressions and ideas are (that is, *quasi*-substantial entities), it is a contingent matter to which bundle they belong. Kant is in effect saying that such a suggestion is absurd. Experiences and other items of consciousness cannot, logically, go unowned; all constituents of my consciousness are necessarily mine.

The thesis of the objective unity of consciousness asserts correlatively that it cannot be a contingent matter to what bundle, *qua* object, impressions are thought to belong. The transcendental unity of apperception, Kant says (B139), 'is that unity through which all the manifold given in an intuition is united in a concept of an object'. Kant's implication is that these two sides to the unity of apperception are correlative. Consciousness of something as an object implies self-consciousness and *vice versa*. This is an important result in itself, and enough to provide a counter to Humean thinking, according to which both the concept of a self and the concept of an object are products of the imagination – concepts the application of which can have no justification. Kant can be taken as replying that the work of the imagination involves judgement, and the very conditions of the possibility of this presuppose the points at issue. The manifold of representation is necessarily unified in these two ways, the subjective and objective ways mentioned. It is a further question, debated by commentators, whether Kant claims even more than this: that the very thought of something as subjective or merely ideal presupposes, not just the thought of an object, but the actual existence of objects. Something like that is asserted in a later section of the *CPR*, known as the 'Refutation of Idealism'. It is not clear that it is asserted in the Transcendental Deduction.

The outcome is nevertheless the same as that of the first-edition version of the argument. The synthesis presupposes rules and there must be formal concepts corresponding to those rules. In the second edition, however, Kant emphasizes more strongly that these formal concepts or categories have application only to experience and takes that as following from the argument of the deduction. We have not been told as yet, however, what these categories are. It is the claim of the Metaphysical Deduction to provide that information. Unfortunately, Kant's claims in this respect have been almost universally repudiated, in spite of occasional valiant attempts to restore them. Kant appeals to the table of judgements derived from traditional formal logic, according to which judgements are in form universal, particular or singular (what is called their quantity), affirmative, negative or infinite (their quality), categorical, hypothetical or disjunctive (relation) and problematic, assertoric or apodeictic (modality). From this Kant derives a table of categories under the same heads; unity, plurality and totality; reality, negation and limitation; inherence and subsistence, causality and dependence, and community or reciprocity; possibility/impossibility, existence/non-existence, and necessity/contingency.

It is pointless to go into this further, because the whole basis of the argument is wrong. What Kant wants is a set of concepts which are the source of the rules for the synthesis of experience in judgement if that judgement is to be objective – the categories to which experience must conform if it is to be objective. Even if traditional logic were right in its claim to provide a systematic account of the forms of judgement *qua* judgement, that would have nothing to do with what Kant is trying to provide. Thus the claim to provide a key to a systematic theory of categories is mistaken, and any arguments for specific categories will have to be treated on their merits. For this reason expositors of Kant tend to jump at this point to his discussion of such matters as causality in the 'Analogies'.

It should be noted, however, that the categories, if derived merely from considerations about judgement, ought to be purely formal. For example, the idea that might conceivably be derived from the conception of a judgement as hypothetical is the dependence of one thing on another: if p then q. The relation of p to q is that of ground to consequence. Causality is a much more specific notion than that, because it is concerned with a particular kind of dependence. In order to explain the move from the purely formal category to its specific form, Kant introduces the idea of a schema. This is a function of the imagination which involves time in various ways. That is not perhaps a readily intelligible notion, but Kant insists that the necessity of a schema for concepts is quite general, and that the schematism of our understanding 'is an art concealed in the depths of the human soul' (B180). In the case of empirical concepts it involves the use of an image.

The point is this: we might, to use Kant's own example, have the concept of a dog to the extent that we could give a formal account of what a dog is – an animal of a certain kind with certain attributes. It is logically possible that we should know all that, but be quite unable to identify any dogs, because we are quite unable to apply this formal understanding to experience in such a way as to be able to recognize instances. The problem that Kant presents here is quite real. The relation of the formal understanding to the recognitional capacity cannot be specified in such a way that the gap is filled by the specification of further formal rules. We need a different kind of understanding, apart from the purely formal one, so that the formal understanding is capable of being filled out in experiential terms. It seems clear that this does involve the imagination in some way, although the idea of a schema does not perhaps provide a clear view of how the task in question is accomplished.

The 'Analytic of Principles'

The final part of the 'Analytic' consists of an attempt to justify the various principles according to which objective experience must be organized, each principle involving reference to a schematized category, such as a general concept in its application to experience. According to the scheme laid down in the Metaphysical Deduction there are four sets of such principles, which Kant calls respectively Axioms of Intuition, Anticipations of Perception, Analogies of Experience, and Postulates of Empirical Thought. The first two sets he calls mathematical principles, in that they are concerned with the structure of experience; and the second two sets are called dynamical, in that they are concerned with the conditions of possible existence. The Axioms and Anticipations say respectively that all intuitions are extensive magnitudes, and that 'in all appearances, the real that is an object of sensation has intensive magnitude'. The Analogies have ostensibly to do with necessary connections between perceptions, and the Postulates have to do with the conditions, as far as experience is concerned, of the possibility, actuality and necessity of things. Only the Analogies have received any extended discussion from commentators, because only with them is there any consideration of what – as Hume would put it – can take us from one perception to another. In other words it is here that the claim to substantial synthetic *a priori* knowledge becomes crucial.

As Kant says in his summary of the Analogies (B262), 'They are simply principles of the determination of the existence of appearances in time, according to all its three modes, *viz*. the relation to time itself as a magnitude (the magnitude of existence, that is, *duration*), the relation in time as a *successive* series, and finally the relation in time as a sum of all *simultaneous* existence.' The Second Analogy has attracted most discussion, because here Kant appears to try to answer Hume and to show that it is a synthetic *a priori* necessity that every event has a cause. The First Analogy is concerned to show the necessity of a permanent or persistent substance. Kant begins as if he were arguing for the necessity of persistent substances (the kind of thing that Hume seemed to deny in arguing that there were only bundles of perceptions). It soon becomes evident, however, that he is really concerned with conservation principles, such as the principle of the conservation of matter. The substances for the permanence of which he wants to argue are stuffs or forms of matter. His general argument is that only with something permanent can there be the experience of temporal succession. That is as may be, but it is no argument for the persistence of matter or stuffs, as opposed to the persistence of particular substances, particular *things*. It looks as if issues in the philosophy of physics have intruded here.

The Second Analogy has received very extensive comment. Kant's argument is based on a contrast between two examples of successions of experiences; as the examples are hypothetical, the point he is trying to make seems to be a conceptual one. He is trying to set out what is involved in the concept of a set of experiences which are objective, as opposed to what is involved in that of a set of experiences which are subjective. The examples are the sequence of experiences involved in (a) the perception of a ship going down a river, and (b) the perception of a house. In the first case, he says, the sequence is irreversible, but in the second case the order of perceptions can vary, depending on what one looks at first. Kant then claims that irreversibility must mean that there is a necessary conformity with a rule or law; and law-governedness implies cause and effect. Hence a necessary condition of the possibility of one's perceptions being perceptions of an objective process is that the process and the perceptions be subject to a law of cause and effect. All events involving objects of objective perception must have a cause.

Opinions on the success of Kant's argument in this respect have been variable. If the argument is as I have set it out, it must be the case that we are supposed to see from the examples that the characteristics of an objective sequence of experiences are different from those of a subjective one. The most important question is whether the examples are good enough for the purpose. The sequence of perceptions derived from looking at a house is dependent on our will, in that it depends on what we choose to look at first. In that respect it is not like a sequence of fantasies or flights of the imagination. Schopenhauer pointed out that Kant ignored the movements of our eyes in relation to the house; these ought to be for him just as much a matter of perceived fact as the movements of the ship. Schopenhauer also pointed out that we could reverse the order of the perceptions of the ship, if only we had enough strength to pull the ship up river, as we have strength to alter the position of our eyes. It might nevertheless be argued that there is something in Kant's argument, even if the examples are not good enough; an objective sequence of perceptions is not order-indifferent, whereas a subjective sequence may be just that. Moreover, if we are to make sense of an objective sequence it must be subject to a rule; we could not make sense of a random sequence. That, however, is perhaps rather less than Kant intends to show.

It does not amount, certainly, to the thesis that every event has a cause, merely that there must be some causal order in the events that we perceive. Schopenhauer objected to both Hume and Kant on these matters, saying that Hume thought that all consequence is mere sequence, whereas Kant thought that all sequence is consequence. That is just a slogan, of course, but it sums up some of the points at issue. There have been other criticisms of the detail of Kant's argument. Kant needs to show, in contraposition to Hume, that causal inferences are not merely an exercise of the imagination; there are good grounds for making such inferences about the world as it falls within our experience. One way of doing that would be to show that objective experience must be such that we can make sense of it, and that to the extent that that is so it must be subject to laws of some kind. It is doubtful whether more than that can be attained by this sort of argument. In the Third Analogy Kant argues that all substances must stand in interrelationship. In other words, he connects the notion of substance (now construed as things, not stuffs) with that of causality or law-governedness. Schopenhauer was to say that the necessity of causality could be argued for only in connection with substances. The permanence of substances depends upon their mutual relationships according to law. There is perhaps more to this sort of consideration than there is to the bare proposition that every event has a cause; but the Third Analogy has received much less attention than the Second.

Apart from some considerations about the relationship between phenomena and noumena, to which reference has already been made in speaking of the negative role to be attached to things-in-themselves, and apart from a 'Refutation of Idealism', in which Kant claims to refute Berkeleian idealism in favour of his own transcendental idealism, this ends Kant's positive argument about the understanding. He has shown, or has claimed to have shown, what is involved in the workings of the understanding in relation to sensibility, and what is of necessity presupposed in that.

The 'Dialectic'

The section of the *CPR* that follows is known as the 'Dialectic'. In it Kant claims to show what happens when reason tries to go beyond the bounds of experience and make claims to metaphysical truths about reality itself. Reason gives rise to what Kant calls 'Ideas' – pure concepts of reason. Because we have reason, it is natural that we should have such Ideas. They arise when we try to think in terms of an unconditioned or absolute unity, not the conditioned unity with which the understanding is concerned, which is conditioned because it is relative to possible experience. It is inevitable that we should try to think of reality in an unconditioned way. All argument is conditioned in the sense that it depends on premises, which are the conditions under which alone the conclusions can be asserted. But reason inevitably wants to arrive at premises unconditioned by any further argument, any further premises.

Once again, Kant thinks that one can derive the Ideas of Reason, or Transcendental Ideas, systematically from a consideration of traditional logic – on this occasion, from the forms of syllogistic argument. The categorical, hypothetical and disjunctive syllogisms are supposed to be the basis for a tripartite division between Transcendental Ideas. These Ideas are regulative in that, being an inevitable product of the workings of the faculty of reason, they govern the ways in which we think, when we go outside the realm of possible experience. Those ways of thinking are nevertheless illusion, and the tripartite division between Ideas therefore corresponds to a tripartite classification of the illusions of speculative metaphysics.

Such metaphysics, Kant thinks, has been characteristically concerned with God, freedom and immortality, but Kant's system offers a framework in which such metaphysical thinking, and metaphysical illusion, is to be ordered. The three classes of transcendental ideas can, he says (B391), be arranged in order, 'the *first* containing the absolute (unconditioned) *unity* of the *thinking subject*, the *second* the absolute *unity of the series of conditions of appearance*, the *third* the absolute *unity of the condition of all objects of thought in general*'. They are concerned with the thinking subject (and thus with the illusions of speculative psychology), the world as the totality of appearances (and thus with the illusions of speculative cosmology), and God as the 'highest condition of the possibility of all that can be thought (the being of all beings)' (and thus with the illusions of speculative theology). When these ideas are applied in this way outside the bounds of possible and conditioned experience, they give rise to certain pseudo-rational inferences, or dialectical syllogisms, which are really defects of reason. These Kant calls Paralogisms, Antinomies and Ideals of pure reason.

The Paralogisms are concerned with the attempt to identify as a substance the subject which has the unity of apperception – and, moreover, as a substance which is simple, which has an identity through time, and which is somehow related to objects in space, particularly the subject's own body. There are indeed four paralogisms concerned respectively with the self as substance, as simple, as having a unity or identity through time, and as having relations to bodies in space. Kant says (B411) that the whole of rational psychology is summed up in a syllogism: 'That which cannot be thought otherwise than as subject does not exist otherwise than as subject, and is therefore substance; A thinking being, considered merely as such, cannot be thought otherwise than as subject; Therefore it exists also only as subject, that is, as substance.' He maintains that such a syllogism is fallacious because 'thought' is taken in the two premises in different senses. In the first premise we are concerned with what can be thought in general, whereas in the second we are concerned with how a subject can think of itself.

It might be said that the word 'subject' is also being taken in different senses, in that in the first premise it means subject as opposed to predicate, whereas in the second it means the subject who thinks. It is not quite clear, however, that Kant takes it in that way, and in a footnote he says, 'In thinking my existence, I cannot employ myself, save as subject of the judgement,' which seems to say something about the role of 'I' in 'I think'. However that may be, Kant takes himself to have shown that the only legitimate conception of the 'I' is that involved in the 'I think' of the unity of apperception. Our tendency to identify it with a simple substance, such as a soul, is wrong if understandable. Thomas Reid said, in criticizing Locke on personal identity, that the self is the only truly simple substance – a monad. Kant did not have Reid in mind, being more concerned with Leibniz and his followers, but Reid's remark sums up the position to which Kant was opposed. It is important, however, that Kant thinks that he can show why we are naturally inclined to think that way, even if it is wrong.

The illusions of speculative cosmology are set out in the form of four Antinomies. An antinomy is an argument which seeks to show that two apparently inconsistent propositions can be derived from the same premises; an antinomy may be resolved either by showing that the premises from which the contradictory conclusions are derived are themselves contradictory (as is the case in a *reductio ad contradictionem*) or by showing that the conclusions are not contradictory after all. Kant's aim is to show that if reason tries to concern itself with the absolute unity of what is responsible for appearances, it inevitably gives rise to such contradictions, because it goes beyond the conditions of possible experience. The First Antinomy is concerned to show, first that the world has a beginning in time and is limited in space, and second that it has no beginning in time and no limits in space. The Second Antinomy is concerned to show that every composite substance is composed of simple parts (*à la* Leibniz), and that there are no simple things in the world. The Third Antinomy argues, first that causality in accordance with laws of nature is not the only kind of causality applying to appearances, and that it is necessary to assume another kind of causality, that of freedom, and second that there is no freedom and that everything in the world takes place in accordance with laws of nature. Finally, the Fourth Antinomy argues, first for the thesis that there belongs to the world a being that is absolutely necessary as a cause, and second for the antithesis that there is no such absolutely necessary being.

It is impossible here to go through the arguments of the Antinomies; they are exceedingly complex and have generated an immense amount of discussion on the part of commentators, including discussion on whether Kant's arguments presuppose the truth of the Critical Philosophy. It should be noted, however, that Kant's attitude to the four antinomies is not the same throughout. In the *Prolegomena*, he calls the first two antinomies mathematical, and the second two dynamic. In the first two *both* conclusions are supposed to be false, and he terms the opposition between them dialectical, as opposed to analytical. It is very unclear how a pair of contradictories can both be false, although in the case of the specific examples invoked both positions are to be rejected if one accepts Kant's system. It was this notion of a dialectical opposition that Hegel seized upon in developing *his* dialectic. In the second pair of antinomies, however, Kant's view is that the conclusions are not really incompatible, and that the falsehood lies in representing what is compatible as contradictory.

In the Fourth Antinomy, for example, Kant provides a resolution by arguing that there is no contradiction between the positions that there is no absolute cause of phenomena in accordance with laws of nature and that there is an absolute cause in things-in-themselves. There is a similar resolution of the Third Antinomy in that, despite causality in accordance with laws of nature, freedom is a presupposition of the idea of moral obligation, and thus of practical reason. Of course if freedom is only an Idea – something that we must think of in relation to ourselves – Kant would be saying only that practical reason presupposes our *thinking* of ourselves as free; it would not necessarily amount to the thesis that freedom is a reality. Some of what Kant has to say, however, suggests the stronger thesis. Moral thinking and experience give access to ourselves as things-in-themselves to which there belongs a freedom which is transcendental – an agency which is not, properly speaking, causal. We shall return to this suggestion later.

In considering the illusions of speculative theology Kant considers the traditional arguments for the existence of God, considered as directed to the existence of what Kant calls an *ens realissimum* (most real thing). Kant finds many fallacies in these arguments, but one central point that he makes is that even if the cosmological argument (the argument from the contingency of the world) were valid it would prove at most the existence of an absolutely necessary being (such as was invoked in the Fourth Antinomy). Similarly, the physical–theological argument (the argument from apparent design in the world, an argument for which Kant shows some sympathy) would show only the existence of a creator. Neither would show the existence of God or of an *ens realissimum*. Hence, he claims that for these purposes both arguments presuppose the ontological argument for the existence of God (and he seems to think that these three arguments are all that are available).

Kant's treatment of the ontological argument is famous. He takes the argument as proceeding from the claim that the very concept of God as a perfect being involves his existence; otherwise he would not be perfect. Kant's criticism is summed up in the assertion that existence is not a predicate. All existence claims are synthetic, not analytic. In asserting something's existence we always go beyond the concept of that thing, and, in a famous example, Kant claims that in speaking of one hundred real or existent thalers we add nothing to the one hundred thalers. 'The conceived hundred thalers are not themselves in the least increased through thus acquiring existence outside my concept' (A599, B627). It has been disputed whether Kant is right in saying that existence is never considered as a predicate of anything. It remains true that it is impossible to argue from the thought of something to its existence. Kant's treatment of the ontological argument has acquired something of a classical status, but attempts to resuscitate the argument still go on.

It should be noted, however, that if a proof of the existence of God is impossible, so is a disproof. The illusion lies in thinking that *anything* can be established in this area. The idea of God is an Idea of Reason, and – like other such Ideas – has a regulative role only. Such a role is, in Kant's view, quite legitimate, as is that of what is crucial for his system – the idea of a thing-in-itself. The Ideas comprise the thoughts that we must arrive at if we try to think of the world in the widest and highest terms; there is no harm in that unless we also think that in them we have a complete picture of reality. Moreover, Kant thinks that the Ideas have great heuristic value if we treat them in an 'as-if' way; that is to say, if we think about the world as if it were governed by what is implied by the Ideas, without thinking that thereby we offer a complete account of how the world is constituted. Kant speaks at length about this view of the Ideas, although any estimate of the real utility of any use of the Ideas must necessarily be arguable. With this conception the real substance of the *CPR* ends.

Kantian ethics

Although the ideas of a real self, of freedom and of God are problematic from the point of view of pure reason, this is not the case, Kant thinks, from the point of view of practical reason. Indeed, practical reason – the sort of reason which we employ in considering what we ought to do – presupposes a noumenal self, a transcendental freedom, and God as the condition of the attainment of the highest good. This and many other things are the concern of the *Critique of Practical Reason*, although the *Groundwork of the Metaphysics of Morals* provides perhaps a clearer, and certainly more succinct, account of what is central to Kant's ethics. In the latter book (on which I shall rely) he represents what he is engaged in as a three-step process. There is first a transition from common rational knowledge of morality to the philosophical; second, there is a transition from popular moral philosophy to what he calls the metaphysics of morals; and third, there is the transition from that to a critique of pure practical reason. It is noteworthy that Kant presents his moral philosophy and the critique of practical reason that is derived from it as a kind of abstraction from our ordinary moral consciousness. That consciousness is, according to him, one that puts a premium on the notion of obligation, of duty, or the 'ought'. How far Kant is a child of his time and culture in this respect is a matter for argument.

Kant starts with a famous remark that nothing in the world or out of it can be considered good without qualification except a *good will*. In assessing the moral worth of an action, that is the only thing that we need attend to – not the other talents or conditions of happiness of the agent. To have a good will is to act solely from duty and for the sake of duty; and to do that is to act not only in accordance with but *from* what Kant calls a moral maxim. Hence, the moral worth of an action done from duty depends upon the maxim or principle which determines it. Duty, he says, is the necessity of acting from respect for law. Inclinations towards an object and the effects or consequences of one's action have nothing to do with it, and one should follow law or principle even against one's inclinations. Many have seen this as a very austere moral viewpoint, but it follows directly from Kant's conception of a good will and the notion of duty which that involves. It must also be remembered that Kant sees this viewpoint as one that is involved in ordinary moral consciousness. Morality just is this respect for law or principle – something that is possible only in a rational being. The rational principle that must therefore govern the will is that I should never act otherwise than so that '*I can also will that my maxim should become a universal law*'.

In the second section of the *Groundwork*, Kant claims to provide this with a metaphysical basis. He does this by appealing to the notion of practical reason, through which in general the will is determined by principles of reason. If the will were unaffected by inclinations it would be what Kant calls a 'holy will'. But human beings are not like that; hence the force of moral principles is that they are felt as imperatives – demands upon the will, possibly against inclination. Kant believes that if such imperatives can be derived from the notion of practical reason in general they will have been shown to be objective as well as necessary, and they will have been shown to be *a priori* and synthetic. In the case of the principles of the *CPR*, their objectivity was supposed to be shown by their being revealed as conditions of possible experience. It is less than clear what corresponding move is possible for the imperatives of practical reason. Kant seems rather to have assumed that showing that such principles are the demands of reason in general is enough to show their objectivity – whatever that means in this context.

He distinguishes, however, between two kinds of imperatives. Hypothetical imperatives are those which have to be fulfilled *if* something else is to be the case. We must do such and such *if* we are to attain certain ends. A categorical imperative has no such 'if' attached to it; its demands are non-hypothetical. The maxims or principles that should govern our moral action are of the categorical kind. It is not just that we ought to keep our promises *if* such and such results are to be attained; we ought to keep them without qualification. Hence the flouting of a categorical imperative ought to involve a kind of incoherence of reason, akin to asserting a contradiction. Indeed, Kant apparently argues in that way when considering examples of moral principles, saying that if it were thought that one could simply break promises when one pleased, this would amount to a contradiction. For in these circumstances promising would become empty and thus impossible.

It is far from evident, however, that this would be anything like a contradiction. Kant suggests that the form of a categorical imperative is that one should act only on a maxim which can at the same time be willed as a universal law, this being, as we have seen, the rational principle that must govern the will. This, it should be noted, is not a maxim or principle of action itself; it lays down the form that such maxims must take. Hence the person who argues that it is all right to break one's promises if one wishes is setting up as a universal law of action that breaking promises is acceptable. If there were such a universal law and it was followed, it is likely that the institution of promising would cease to exist, because of its emptiness. It is not clear, however, that the man who so wills has committed anything like a contradiction. This means that the force of practical reason remains unclear, and argument about it and its utility has gone on ever since.

There has also been continual argument concerning the adequacy of the formal characteristics of the categorical imperative for distinguishing *moral* principles or maxims from principles of other kinds, including those which are hypothetical. Are all and only moral principles those which can be willed as a universal law? However that may be, Kant also suggests that the categorical imperative can be expressed in other ways. He says, first, that it can be formulated as the principle that one should so act as to treat every rational being, whether in oneself or in another, always as an end and never as a means – for rational nature exists as an end in itself. He next invokes the idea of the will of every rational being as a universally legislative will, an idea which he also expresses in terms of the notion of the autonomy of the will, as opposed to heteronomy. This leads him to a version of the categorical imperative which asserts that the maxims of action should be willed as laws of nature in a kingdom of ends, or that all maxims ought by their own legislation to harmonize with a possible kingdom of ends as with a kingdom of nature.

A rational being belongs as a member to the kingdom of ends when prescribing universal laws in it, through the autonomy of the will; but he is also subject to such laws, and it is as being such a member that the individual moral being must determine the principles on which he should act. Kant claims that these three versions of the categorical imperative amount to the same thing, providing in turn the form, matter and complete characterization of all maxims in accordance with the categories of unity, plurality and totality. Few have been able to see how the three versions could really be construed as three versions of the same thing, and the appeal to the categories does not help. Hence, even if – as may seem plausible – the three versions of the categorical imperative sum up a conception of morality that can indeed be abstracted from a common moral consciousness, the claim to have established a metaphysical basis for that conception of morality seems altogether more shaky.

The third part of the *Groundwork*, and indeed a great deal of the other writings of Kant in this area, is concerned with freedom. The Kantian claim that 'ought' implies 'can' is well known. But the very idea of the autonomy of the will, which is involved in the theory of the categorical imperative, is enough to indicate to Kant that freedom is a very real condition of our ordinary moral experience. Since that experience is real and the moral law is something that human beings autonomously legislate for themselves, the choice whether to act in accordance with that law is real too. So there must be real freedom, in spite of the fact that human beings are subject to laws of nature, like everything else. This is possible only if that freedom is transcendental, and that implies that it belongs to something which is a noumenon, not a phenomenon. Hence, in spite of everything that was said in the *CPR*, Kant takes practical reason to show the existence of a noumenon in our own nature. We are at bottom noumena, and it is this that guarantees our freedom.

Apart from doubts as to how it is possible that the facts of moral experience should lead to a categorical conclusion which was forbidden by the *CPR*, it is not really clear what it all amounts to. In more recent treatments of the freedom of the will (such as that by G. E. Moore in this century), it has been suggested that the freedom that is a condition of moral responsibility amounts to the position that we can do things if we so choose. It has sometimes been objected to this that we need to know also whether we can choose; we need to know, not only that we could have done otherwise if we had chosen, but that we could have chosen otherwise. Kant's answer is in effect that once given the choice, the rest is subject to causes, like everything else that is phenomenal. The free choice itself, however, is the product of a noumenon in a way that we cannot understand further, except that it is not subject to the conditions of space and time. Whether that is the sort of freedom that one wants, whether the mystery that the account inevitably involves is a price that one is willing to pay, is perhaps almost a matter of taste. The argument over the freedom of the will still goes on, and perhaps always will. It is clear that the attribution of moral responsibility to someone for a certain course of action presupposes that that person in some sense chose to do whatever he did. Choice is a reality. Whether that has to be explained, if explained it is, in Kant's way is another matter.

At all events, the existence of free will is one of three postulates of practical reason that Kant thinks can be abstracted from a consideration of moral action and moral choice. The other two involve the immortality of the soul and the existence of God, notions that the *CPR* had claimed could exist only as Ideas, so that there could be no proof of their realization. Immortality is required, Kant now suggests, because holiness, the complete conformity of the will with the moral law, involves a perfection to which man can approximate only *via* an infinite progression; the latter is possible only if we assume that the rational being that man is has an infinitely long existence, and this means the immortality of the soul. Perhaps the less said about this argument the better; apart from the worries that the considerations about infinity may produce, the possibility of perfection, if it exists, does not entail that conditions must exist for its realization. Much the same applies to the argument for the existence of God. Kant thinks that God's existence is necessary as a condition of the achievability of the highest good. It is clear that the argument for immortality needs the postulation of God's existence as a condition of its realization. But Kant needs an argument in the reverse direction too, and that he does not, and cannot, provide.

The Critique of Judgement

The third *Critique*, that of judgement, makes very important, indeed fundamental, contributions to aesthetics, but it does not have the same standing and organization as the other two *Critiques*, and has been given less attention accordingly. The judgement that the *Critique of Judgement* is concerned with is something that Kant saw as intermediate between, and mediating between, the understanding and practical reason; its domain is the faculty of feeling. The pleasure that it involves is supposed to be a function of a relation of fittingness between our cognitive faculties and nature, to the extent that we find purposiveness in it. For this reason the overriding concern of the third *Critique* is with the purposiveness of nature, which reveals itself firstly in beauty and secondly in teleological processes generally. The second part of this *Critique*, therefore, elaborates on the interest in the idea of design in nature which Kant manifested when considering the argument from design for the existence of God in the first *Critique*. Such a notion of purpose or design can only be, accord-

ing to the *CPR*, a regulative Idea. Kant's aim is thus to show how, given
the faculty of feeling, it is both natural and useful to find evidences of
purpose in nature. Such a concern is of much less interest than that of
the first part of the third *Critique*, where Kant considers beauty and sees
it as involving 'purposiveness without purpose'.

In many ways the problems that Kant sees in aesthetics are similar to
those of the other two *Critiques*. In his view, aesthetic judgements need
not be merely subjective. Our attitudes to beauty in nature, and secondarily to art (for Kant attached less aesthetic importance to art than to
nature, and thought of music as the least important art), are not just
matters of taste, as are merely sensuous pleasures. Hence aesthetic judgements are in principle capable of objectivity, and Kant's central question
is therefore how objective and universally valid aesthetic judgements are
possible. He initially presents the issue in the form of an antinomy – that
of taste. The problem is to reconcile the conditions of judgement and of
feeling. Unlike feeling, judgement normally involves concepts; but if that
were how it was in the aesthetic realm, a decision on the validity of a
judgement could be made in terms of the conditions of applicability of
those concepts – and that does not seem to be how it is. On the other
hand, without concepts there seems no room for anything that might be
called judgement, and no room for anything beyond the subjective
aspects of taste. The judgement that others ought to feel as I do with
respect to instances of beauty must be synthetic *a priori*, and the question
therefore arises once again how that is possible.

Kant's answer comes *via* the consideration that the object of an aesthetic judgement is a particular which is regarded for its own sake, in
abstraction from any interests that the observer may have in regard to it.
It is that abstraction which makes possible a legislation for others when
I make an aesthetic judgement about a particular. It is made possible,
Kant thinks, by the special role that the imagination has in this connection. Imagination, it will be remembered, was involved in the doctrine of
the schematism of concepts in the *CPR*, but there the exercise of the
imagination was constrained by the rules that concepts imply. In the case
of aesthetic judgement, Kant maintains, the imagination is free. It is the
free play of the imagination, or free interplay of the imagination and the
understanding, that marks off the aesthetic judgement. The concepts
involved in this are indeterminate. In contemplating an object aesthet-
ically I do not judge that it is a so and so; rather I see it *as* a so and so.
Hence, I can give reasons for the aesthetic judgement that I make, without implying that they have to do with anything beyond the relation of
that particular object to my sensibility and feeling.

The beauty of an object thus depends upon its relation to the harmonious interplay of imagination and understanding, and that relation must itself be a harmonious one too. Hence the purposiveness without purpose that we find in examples of beauty, and particularly in what Kant calls 'free', as opposed to 'dependent', beauty. Beauty is free when it presupposes 'no concept of what the object ought to be', and Kant instances the beauty of flowers as an example of this. Opposed to this is the beauty of, for example, a building, where we inevitably have some idea of its purpose. It is therefore free beauties which manifest purposiveness without purpose *par excellence*. They do so, however, only because creatures like ourselves, with the faculties which Kant finds in us, see such purposiveness in them. It is arguable that in this Kant is imposing a certain *criterion* of aesthetic judgement, one that puts a premium on organization and harmony, on the conditions for a judgement being aesthetic at all. Certainly it is difficult to see what he has to say taking in the wilder forms of art; and even his attitudes to nature seem very eighteenth-century ones. Nevertheless, Kant's treatment of the issues of aesthetics is a valiant attempt to deal with the problems, and there is no doubt that the first part of the *Critique of Judgement* is a classic, perhaps *the* classic, work in aesthetics.

I have left out one notion which plays a significant part in that aesthetics – the notion of the sublime. That too is perhaps a very eighteenth-century concept. Edmund Burke had distinguished between the beautiful and the sublime in 1756, and Kant quotes what he has to say in a later German translation. He regards Burke's account as 'physiological' (that is, merely psychological), and his own account is meant to be transcendental. The eighteenth-century interest in the sublime has, however, an ancient ancestry in Longinus' work *On the Sublime*, a Platonist work of the third century A.D. Experience of the sublime occurs, Kant thinks, when we are overwhelmed by the infinite or boundless greatness of the world. By comparison with beauty the sublime involves for that reason a certain formlessness. Strictly speaking, Kant says, nothing in nature can have that boundlessness in which we find the sublime. Objects that are seen as sublime incite the mind 'to abandon sensibility and to busy itself with ideas that involve higher purposiveness'. The boundlessness lies in effect in our Ideas of reason.

Kant introduces other refinements into his account of the sublime, distinguishing for example between the mathematically and the dynamically sublime, according to whether the movement of the mind that is brought about involves the faculty of cognition or that of desire. The all-over account is complex, but the main point of the sublime is that it takes us towards a recognition of the supersensible. There is indeed a sort of link between it and the intimations of the divine described in the second part of the third *Critique*. From the point of view of aesthetics, however, the theory of the sublime is, as Kant himself says, a sort of appendix to the treatment of the aesthetic perception of the beautiful.

The import of Kant's philosophy

The *CPR* is the greatest of Kant's works, and most of the rest of his philosophy stems from it, in one way or another. In it he provided something of a reconciliation between his rationalist and empiricist predecessors, but in a way that really undermined them both. Nevertheless, the idealist aspect of the transcendental philosophy was in some ways a product of the kind of thought that he had inherited. Many subsequent philosophers have tried to expound the Kantian philosophy without that idealism, with varying degrees of success. Since the starting-point of the system is the individual's own experience, even if not quite in the same way as it was for Descartes, it is questionable whether there is any hope of erecting on that basis a system of thought which will, with any validity, reveal the conditions of objective knowledge. That would mean moving, as Kant sometimes puts it, from what is valid for me to what is valid for all men. But if I start solely from what is valid for me, how can I move to what is valid for all men, unless I presume that finding something valid for me *presupposes* an agreement with others of a kind which provides a basis for publicity, intersubjectivity and objectivity? That sort of reaction was not to come until this century, particularly through Wittgenstein. The immediate reaction was of a different kind – one that took the idealism seriously but found unsatisfactory those aspects of Kant's transcendental idealism which had to do with things-in-themselves, and the limits that he put on understanding and reason.

Post-Kantian German Philosophy

Fichte and Schelling

The first reaction to Kant is to be found in the writings of Johann Gottlieb Fichte (1762–1814). Fichte studied theology and philosophy at Jena, but eventually came under the influence of Kant. He was appointed to a chair at Jena, but had in due course to resign, because certain articles of his on the nature of religious belief led to charges of atheism. Kant more or less disowned his disciple. In 1804 Fichte was appointed to a chair at Erlangen, and then moved to the new university at Berlin. He was a somewhat aggressive man who was not one to pour oil on troubled waters. His main works, including *The Science of Knowledge*, were written in his thirties, but he also tried to write more popular expositions of his philosophy. He is not an easy writer to understand, but he clearly thought of himself initially as carrying on and developing further the Kantian philosophy.

Fichte started from the idea that the ego or self is active and self-legislating. It can know itself as subject, however, only by positing not only itself, but also a non-self opposed to it, through which it can by contrast know itself. That self has two interacting drives – a practical drive towards activity without end, and by contrast with this a theoretical one which makes the self reflect back upon itself and thus put a check upon absolute activity. The results from this are a self-conscious self and a non-self which includes all that Kant put into the world of appearances together with its conditions. But the non-self is a creation of the self posited so that self-consciousness may be possible.

In positing a non-self, the self posits something as independent of itself, and this might be taken as a thing-in-itself. However, because such a thing is by definition unknowable, Fichte claims that a true critical idealism must exclude the idea of a thing-in-itself and accept that nature as non-self is created by the self as a condition of self-knowledge. In one place (1.281 of the collected works) Fichte says that a finite spirit must necessarily posit something absolute outside itself (a thing-in-itself) but must also recognize that the latter can exist only *for it*. Kant was mistaken in not recognizing that. So Fichte maintains that his view is the true critical idealism, as opposed to dogmatic idealism, which ignores the circle that he has made evident, and to transcendent realist dogmatism, which thinks that it can escape it.

It might be objected that this idealism, critical or not, amounts to the thesis that there is really nothing other than me, whatever I as self or ego may posit. How is objectivity possible under such conditions? Fichte's answer is obscure, but in effect he goes back to what Kant said about the self-legislating will and a kingdom of ends. Kant said that the will is both a legislator and subject to the law thus imposed. Fichte appeals similarly to the notion of conscience. In a work entitled *The Vocation of Man* (one of his more popular works) he says that conscience alone is the root of all truth. In the second introduction to *The Science of Knowledge* he appeals to consciousness of the moral law in a similar way. It is that which stands opposed to my action. Consciousness of the moral law forms the basis for an intuition of self-activity and freedom, but being a finite being I must oppose something to my activity, and that is what the world, including other selves, is for me. Conscience is the supreme recognition of the necessity of setting something against my activity.

All this is most obscure, though not untypical of Fichte's philosophy. There are points of connection between it and the philosophy of Hegel, as we shall see. A further point of connection is that Fichte tends to set out series of antinomies in progressing towards his conclusions – something that is a constituent part of Hegel's 'Dialectic'. It is, however, Fichte's use of the notion of the 'absolute', as in his characterizing of the ego and its activity, that reveals him as the first of the 'absolute idealists', of whom Hegel is the arch-priest. For Fichte, in effect, the absolute ego is the one ultimate reality.

Another philosopher who thought in much the same way was Friedrich Wilhelm Joseph von Schelling (1775–1854). Like Fichte he began as a theologian and moved to philosophy. He became a disciple of Fichte at Jena, and then collaborated with Hegel in editing the *Critical Journal of Philosophy*. He eventually held a chair in Munich before moving to Berlin. Schelling is probably the originator of the term 'absolute idealism', meaning by this to assert the identity of the knower with what is known, something revealed to intellectual intuition. But because the knower is active, he not only gains self-knowledge by his action, as Fichte held; he also confirms his own existence. Schelling also saw human history as a progress towards self-consciousness and therefore towards the Absolute, and he thought of art as an essential stage in the revelation of the Absolute to human beings. There is a good deal of mysticism, particularly nature mysticism, in Schelling's philosophy. Hegel was referring to Schelling when in the Preface to the *Phenomenology of Spirit* he spoke of an Absolute which is the night when every cow is black. The implication is that in the end Schelling had nothing to say about the nature of the Absolute, except the complete identity of knower and known. What one is and knows in full self-consciousness is no more than one's self-identity.

Hegel

Georg Wilhelm Friedrich Hegel is the dominant figure of post-Kantian thought. Hegel (1770–1831) was born in Stuttgart, and was a student at the University of Tübingen, where he was a friend of Schelling and of the poet Hölderlin. In 1801 he took up a position at Jena. There he wrote the *Phenomenology of Spirit*, which he described as a 'voyage of discovery'; he completed it on the eve of the battle of Jena, which led to the closure of the university. For a while he was rector of the Academy at Nuremberg, and then in 1816 held the Chair at Heidelberg. After two years he moved to the Chair at Berlin, where he remained until his death from cholera in 1831. Apart from the *Phenomenology*, he wrote *The Science of Logic* at Nuremberg (1812–16), and at Heidelberg he published his *Encyclopaedia of the Philosophical Sciences*. In 1821 appeared his *Philosophy of Right*, followed by new editions of the *Encyclopaedia* in 1827 and 1830. He also delivered extensive lectures on art, religion and the history of philosophy while at Berlin, and these were published after his death. The range and scope of his thinking are immense, and the style of his writing is difficult and complicated. He is far from easy to understand and just as difficult to expound. Moreover, method sometimes takes over in a way that obscures content. Although he regarded the *Phenomenology* as a kind of preparation for the later work of the *Encyclopaedia*, the former is, despite its difficulty, a fresher work than what followed. I shall for the most part concentrate on the *Phenomenology*, giving less attention to the later and more systematic works.

Hegel is a supreme rationalist, and the aim of the *Encyclopaedia* is to take in the whole of reality, the whole of history, and the whole of actual and possible knowledge in a systematic form. Its ambition and presumption are extraordinary, and it provoked various amazed, often angry and sometimes contemptuous, reactions. Modern commentators, if they can maintain patience and overcome the difficulties of style and thought, are likely to be divided between those who are impressed by the system (which manifests itself *par excellence* in the *Encyclopaedia*) and those who are impressed by the particular and sometimes incidental insights and intuitions.

The system exemplifies the theory of dialectic, with its general (though not quite universal) attempt to arrange concepts in terms of thesis, antithesis and synthesis. In this, Hegel looks back to Kant's own theory of dialectic, but claims that reason can in fact transcend the limits to the understanding that Kant insisted upon. The general idea is that spirit (revealed first in the ordinary human self or ego, but emerging in the end as a cosmic form of thought – the absolute concept or notion – which takes in everything) works in such a way that thought naturally expresses itself in terms of opposing ideas which are then reconciled in some higher form of thought. But there the same thing occurs, with a further thesis and antithesis, a new synthesis, and so on. Hegel thinks, however, that this process must come to an end in some absolute, not merely conditional or provisional, synthesis. This is the so-called absolute concept or notion. Reason can therefore go beyond, and must go beyond, the limits that Kant had imposed upon the understanding.

This aspect of Hegel's thought is both inspired by and a product of a reaction to Kant. But as his lectures on the history of philosophy showed, Hegel had a keen sense of how the past affects the present, and there is much in his philosophy, particularly in the *Encyclopaedia*, which reflects aspects of Greek thought (for instance the emphasis in Aristotle on potentiality and actuality, and the Plotinian system centring on the One). Hegel is not only a supreme rationalist; he is also a supreme romantic, and it is a cardinal aspect of his thinking that the history of thought and of institutions reveals a necessary, if not unique, course, which parallels that which he finds in the order of concepts revealed in his system. Indeed, he thought that the voyage of discovery of the *Phenomenology*, the development of ideas in his own mind, was a reflection of that course of history. The absolute spirit working in history takes a path which was followed by Hegel's own consciousness.

If Hegel had been right, he would have produced in his system the complete philosophy and the complete science of knowledge. A cynic might claim that it is all cooked up, and that the philosophy of history and the account of the history of philosophy are specially contrived to fit the philosophical system. Such a claim would not be entirely without foundation. Schopenhauer thought that Hegel was a charlatan and his system entirely meretricious. There may have been some pique in his criticisms, but there can be no doubt that there is an overweening arrogance in Hegel's claim to have produced a complete map of all possible knowledge and of reality. The same applies to Hegel's view that that reality is revealed to, and indeed constituted by, a self or spirit which is universal and such that individual selves and their thoughts are just individual aspects or 'moments' of it.

The Introduction to the *Phenomenology* is supposed to be a preliminary setting out of the path to be followed; yet it also offers a criticism of Kant without mentioning him by name. It does that by maintaining that there is a contradiction in Kant's supposal that there must be something existing 'in-itself' but for ever beyond the understanding. Hegel distinguishes between 'being for consciousness', which is the status possessed by objects of consciousness, and 'being in itself', which is supposed to be the status possessed by what exists objectively and independently of consciousness. 'Being for consciousness' is opposed to 'being in itself' in that 'being for consciousness' is a form of 'being for another'. Hegel then claims that that is a distinction which can be made only within consciousness, so that the claim that there can be a thing-in-itself totally apart from consciousness is self-refuting. The only source of knowledge of anything and the only grounds for claiming the existence of anything are to be found in consciousness itself.

It is worth noting that, despite Hegel's rationalism, that claim is in a sense empiricist. We start from what is evident to our consciousness, and there is no hope of getting to anything that transcends that consciousness; hence, even the very conception of something that exists in itself derives from consciousness. Hegel takes it to follow from this that there is nothing apart from consciousness itself that is 'in itself'; and in the end that must be in and for itself. Strictly speaking, however, it does not follow from the fact that the distinction between 'in itself' and 'for another' exists only for consciousness that there cannot *be* anything which exists in itself independent of consciousness. That it does follow is the belief that lies at the foundation of Hegel's idealism, but the supposition that the notion of an 'in itself' is to be analysed in terms of 'being for consciousness' is no more firmly established than Berkeley's claim that the notion of existence is to be analysed in terms of the having of ideas. In this respect, but in this respect alone, the foundations of Hegel's philosophy are similar to those of Berkeley's – and empiricist in that sense.

Section A of the main fabric of the *Phenomenology* is concerned with consciousness, and Hegel starts from what he calls 'sense-certainty'. The thought is that the senses provide us with immediate consciousness of something. The normal empiricist conception is that the senses provide us with sensations, construed as forms of immediate awareness of objects; but this immediate consciousness comes already divided up into discrete elements – this sensation or sense-datum, and this, and this, and so on. Hegel's argument is that this conception is fallacious, because such a division of consciousness must be mediated by concepts, in order that we may have a datum of red, of square, and so on. To be aware of something as red, square, etc., presupposes the relevant concepts. One cannot escape this conclusion, Hegel maintains, by supposing that the individuation of elements of the 'given' can be carried out by means of demonstratives such as 'this'; for the identification of something as 'this' presupposes a contrast with 'that'. (As F. H. Bradley puts it in a parallel argument to be found in Chapter 2 of his *Principles of Logic*, expressions such as 'this' indicate position in a series.) Indeed, Hegel claims, less securely, that words such as 'this', 'here', 'now' and 'I' all constitute universals, in spite of their apparent demonstrative or indexical character. Hence they cannot determine immediate objects of consciousness, independent of the mediating role of universals. The only immediate thing is consciousness itself.

Even when consciousness is mediated through concepts, which Hegel supposes the mind brings to what is given, and so both modifies and constructs whatever reality that consciousness makes possible, there are further problems. The most immediate problem is how in bringing to bear a number of concepts in this way the mind provides any identification of *things*. In perception we take ourselves to be made aware of objects possessing properties. But, Hegel asks, how do any number of properties (corresponding to the concepts that the mind brings to bear) determine the unique identity of a thing. The problem, he says, is that of the one and the many as set out by Plato when trying to specify the relation between sensible individuals and Forms. How can one property or concept apply to many things and how can one thing, such as a lump of salt, have a unique identity when it is made up of a collection of properties or concepts, all of them universal? This problem is to be solved only by moving to a higher set of concepts, and this is spelled out in the third chapter of the *Phenomenology*, entitled 'Force and Understanding: Appearance and the Supersensible World'.

Hegel's answer to what provides the principle of unity of a thing is in effect *law*. It is lawlike forces which unite the properties of a thing, so making it a unity; these forces constitute its real nature and they interact with other objects and ourselves. In seeking to grasp the unified nature of a thing, the understanding has to move beyond the apparent properties with which it is concerned in straightforward perception to an underlying nature. The latter idea is similar to Locke's 'real essence', except that Hegel supposes that we can have some grasp of it, because the understanding can take us beyond what is given to the senses. It is the move to this idea of force that takes the understanding beyond mere appearance and therefore into the realm of the supersensible.

Hegel goes into some detail about how all this works, and what is achieved by it. But the next move he makes is to use these ideas in order to show that consciousness must thereby become self-consciousness. For, Hegel says, when the understanding comes to see objects in this way, we ourselves come to see that 'not only is consciousness of a thing possible only for a self-consciousness' (which Kant would have said), but that 'self-consciousness alone is the truth of those shapes'.[1] In other words, the supersensible is a reflection of consciousness itself, and consciousness comes to be conscious of that. The move to that conclusion involves a very considerable leap of thought.

Section B is explicitly concerned with self-consciousness. Its first chapter, entitled 'The Truth of Self Certainty', contains a discussion which has acquired some fame and reputation. Hegel argues that self-consciousness properly speaking involves another self-consciousness, the recognition of that other ego and recognition in turn by it. In the *Encyclopaedia* he calls it 'self-consciousness recognitive'. He associates this with practical consciousness or desire, suggesting that consciousness seeks the mastering and destruction of its object. Hence in consciousness of the other there is an impetus towards mastery and destruction of the other with some form of response. The very fact of self-consciousness on the part of an individual implies a relation of this kind with other consciousnesses, and this is supposed to lead to the recognition of a kind of universal consciousness and self-consciousness.

None of that is easy to understand, but part of it involves by way of exemplification an account of the relation between master and slave, or lordship and bondage. It is a passage of exceptional brilliance, in which many have seen a form of political wisdom. That, strictly speaking, is not Hegel's intention at this point. What he claims is that the recognition that the slave gives to the master is a condition of the latter's proper self-consciousness as a master; the complete suppression of the consciousness of the slave could only diminish that self-consciousness. As a result the master sees himself in the slave, and the slave's own individuality is thereby enhanced. All this has of course political overtones, and Hegel recognizes that, but the purpose of the discussion is to show how the notion of an individual consciousness must inevitably take us to that of a social and thereby universal consciousness. That transition is made obvious in the discussion, briefer though it is, of the same topics in the *Encyclopaedia*.

The final stage of this part of the *Phenomenology* discusses the pathological forms of an ideal of universal self-consciousness in which, in effect, the roles of master and slave are combined. The relation between master and slave is an uneasy relation, but it is one on which the very being of lordship and bondage depends, and which reflection shows to be other than appears at first sight. It is a feature of life, which conditions what is possible for us as individuals. The attempts to get beyond it result in movements which echo at the level of spirit certain aspects only of the relationship between master and slave. There is first, Hegel, says, Sto-

---

[1] Quotations are taken from the translation by A. V. Miller of Hegel's *The Phenomenology of Spirit* (Oxford: Clarendon Press, 1977).

icism, which he construes as an attempt to insist upon freedom of thought, although this is really only a formal freedom, in abstraction from the conditions of existence. Opposed to this is Scepticism, which stands to Stoicism as the slave to the master; it recognizes the claim for freedom of thought on the part of the Stoic, but itself sees freedom as possible only as a form of negation. But just as the slave depends upon the master, so scepticism really depends upon something positive in order to maintain the freedom of negativity. Hence the next stage to be detected by Hegel is what he calls the Unhappy Consciousness, which is a kind of uneasy synthesis of the previous two forms of consciousness and their claims for freedom. It is in effect a form of self-deception which Hegel sees as endemic in the human condition. It involves a split of consciousness, and there is vacillation between its parts.

Hegel viewed the Greeks as a happy people, and the Jews as an unhappy people, in that the Greeks affirmed life, whereas the Jews denied it in thought and practice. No doubt these are stereotypes, but Hegel also saw in Christianity an uneasy compromise between the two, and Christianity is for him the prime exemplification of the unhappy consciousness; it is a consciousness of self as dual-natured and contradictory. Judaism emphasizes the separation between man and God; Christianity, through the doctrine of the Incarnation, implies a union, but still emphasizes the gap between the changing nature of the world and the unchanging nature of the divine. The unhappy consciousness involves in general an attempt both to deny and to affirm the gulf between our concreteness and some form of universality. The real synthesis of these two elements lives, Hegel thinks, in reason, which is a form of unity of consciousness and self-consciousness in what he calls 'self-certainty'. With reason we move into the next main part of the *Phenomenology*, C, which is subdivided into four sections: AA, BB, CC and DD.

The transitions in Hegel's thought are not clear, and to represent those transitions as logical would be a travesty of the truth. It cannot be denied, however, that Hegel provides considerable incidental insights and illuminating ways of regarding things. The general trend of Hegel's philosophy may now be evident. I shall be briefer in dealing with what remains. The section on reason (AA) is an attempt to display reasonableness as it manifests itself in various forms. This is identified with self-certainty in that it is construed as the attempt of the mind to find its own principles in its apparent objects – a view which Hegel refers to as idealism and expounds as such. The section has three parts, in the first of which Hegel surveys the various forms of lawlikeness that observation of nature tends to find in it. It is a survey of the findings of science and pseudo-science, in which Hegel notes, first the details of the inorganic and organic world, second the processes of psychology, and lastly attempts at psycho-physical science including physiognomy and phrenology. In the second part Hegel discusses what he calls 'the actualization of self-consciousness through its own activity'. There is another three-fold division, and he deals first with hedonism and its paradoxes, second with the romantic way of the heart, and third with the self-conscious play at virtue in opposition to the 'way of the world'. In the final, third part of AA, he critically considers first those claims to be concerned with a disinterested and single-minded pursuit of goals which are really forms of seeking the recognition of others. Second, there is 'reason the lawgiver', the issuing of general prescriptions such as 'Tell the truth' – prescriptions which are seen to lack universal validity when given detailed application. Finally, there is reason as testing laws, by which Hegel has in mind the Kantian test of universalizability as a criterion of a moral law. This too, Hegel thinks, lacks genuine universality as well as substance.

Reason is too subjective in Hegel's view, and in section BB of the *Phenomenology* he moves to what purports to be its objectification, which he calls 'Spirit' (*Geist*). Here he first discusses the ethical order, which he sees as conformity to social custom and law; he illustrates the conflicts that it produces by reference to examples drawn from Greek tragedy, such as Sophocles' *Antigone*. Next he considers what he calls 'self-alienated spirit' or culture, and in particular the clash between enlightenment and faith, which he sees as something of a mock conflict. Enlightenment tends to consider everything in terms of human ends or in terms of what Hegel calls 'utility', and in the end issues in what he calls 'absolute freedom and terror' as in the French Revolution. The final part of this section has to do with morality – the 'spirit that is certain of itself' – and leads to a discussion of conscience. In the end conscience, which is purely individual and to be respected by others as such, passes over into religion, which is the subject of the next section. I have not at all done justice to the details of the discussions of this section; there is a great deal of percipient comment on a variety of social phenomena and human actions. It is also to be noted that the implications of the section are that the individual conscience and conscientiousness are to be seen as in some sense higher forms of 'spirit' than the social. The implications of the *Philosophy of Right* are the reverse.

Section CC, on religion, traces the movement from natural religion, where God is seen in terms of natural objects, through religion in the form of art, which Hegel sees in the religion of the Greeks and their use of sculpture, to revealed religion which has its epitome in Christianity. But the forms of consciousness involved in all this are finally transcended by that of philosophy itself, which is the subject matter of the last section,

DD, entitled 'Absolute Knowing'. Here self-consciousness becomes aware of itself as self-consciousness, with the recognition that all its objects are in some way part of itself. It involves the ability to see the voyage of discovery that the *Phenomenology* has been supposed to involve as one that leads to Hegel's philosophy itself – or so we are told. Hence that philosophy is not just a record of Hegel's own spiritual development, and not just a record of the path of history itself (although it is, Hegel claims, all that), but also an account of the stages necessary in the explanation of the truth of everything. In it the self and being are supposed to be revealed as identical, and any distinction between objective truth and subjective certitude abolished. But what has been passed through is, in a sense, merely a critique of inadequate ways of thought. If we, perhaps improbably, follow Hegel to the point at which it is claimed that philosophy itself is the only adequate way of thought, we have not yet been told what the true content of that philosophy is. The closing pages of the *Phenomenology* suggest that after all this we are only now at the point of beginning philosophy. This will have three parts: Logic, the Philosophy of Nature and the Philosophy of Mind.

Logic, expounded in the *Science of Logic* and in the so-called 'lesser Logic' which forms the first part of the *Encyclopaedia*, is a systematization of the most general ideas or categories necessary for an account of anything. It is not logic in a sense that has anything to do with a theory of valid argument, or anything of that kind. It is arguably more concerned with metaphysics, although metaphysics of a very special kind. Once again the material is organized throughout in triads: the unsatisfactoriness of the first item provokes a transition to its opposite, where a further unsatisfactoriness leads to an attempt at some kind of synthesis – whereupon the process simply repeats itself. No finally satisfactory explanation of things in terms of categories is possible until one reaches what Hegel calls the 'Absolute Notion'. As with the process of thought of the *Phenomenology*, however, this does not mean that the lower and earlier stages are condemned as mere appearance or illusion. They are somehow taken up into the Absolute Notion and a final and absolute account of reality in its identity with mind must explain why its less adequate aspects exist and lead to the more adequate aspects. The voyage of discovery of the *Phenomenology*, which is supposed to be identical in sequence with the course of history, also has its parallel in reality and thought. These too must be seen as sequential in structure. It is this fact, difficult though it is, that is perhaps the central characteristic of Hegelianism.

Nearly half of the 'lesser Logic' is given over to a survey of previous accounts of philosophy, and of metaphysics in particular, leading up to Hegel's. Logic, as Hegel calls it, is then divided into three doctrines: those of Being, Essence and the Notion. The relation between these doctrines is that the first deals with the immediate and superficial aspects of things, the second with their underlying and inner natures, and the third with their total being. In the first section Hegel opposes the categories of being and nothingness, which are supposedly unified in that of becoming. That notion too is seen as having an inherent contradiction and is replaced by 'being determinate', that is to say, being in possession of qualities. But qualities succeed each other in alteration, and there is an unending reference to something else. This infinite sequence, which is opposed to determinate being, Hegel calls the 'bad' or 'negative' infinite. The true infinite, which comprises the synthesis of the previous two ideas, is being-for-self, which is infinite in the sense that it has limitless application. I shall not go further into the details of this section. The categories so far considered are said to fall under that of quality. Hegel now considers the category of quantity similarly, and finally as the synthesis of the two, that of measure.

The treatment of the doctrine of essence begins with the notion of identity, which is opposed to difference, and the synthesis lies in the very Hegelian notion of an identity in difference, which is identified with that of a 'ground' or rationale. Hegel here brings in the principle of sufficient reason or ground. This leads in turn to a discussion of the categories of existence and thinghood. The relation of a thing to its properties raises again the problem of the one and the many. All this is opposed to the category of appearance, and the synthesis is found in the category of actuality, in terms of which Hegel discusses necessity and possibility, substance, causality and their interrelationship. It is in this context that Hegel asserts the identity of the actual or real and the rational, another view which is central to Hegelian philosophy. The outcome is supposed to be the identification of necessity and freedom, in that the necessary interrelationship of substances is revealed as the free expression of their nature. As Hegel says, the passage from necessity to freedom is 'the very hardest'. It gives rise to the final stage: that of the Notion.

Translations of Hegel tend to capitalize this word (which of course German does automatically). In a way it means simply concept or thought, but that fact has to be seen in the context of the Hegelian identification of thought and reality, and in that context the term gains a somewhat special sense. A notion has a completeness for thought in that it includes within it all the 'earlier categories of thought'; hence it involves a summing-up of the most general categories in terms of which reality is to be construed. Hegel considers first what he specifies as the subjective side of the doctrine of the Notion. Under this heading he considers universality, particularity and individuality. In this part Hegel puts forward what has become known as the doctrine of the concrete universal – the claim that individuals cannot be considered other than as collections of universals and that merely abstract universals are empty and gain content only in a concretized form. The link between individual and universal leads Hegel to consider judgement, its forms and their interrelations in syllogisms. In this part one gets as near as Hegel allows to a treatment of formal logic, something that was taken up in more detail by F. H. Bradley in his *Principles of Logic*.

Opposed to all this is the category of object, and under this heading Hegel considers the ways that objects are made up and the principles involved, including those of teleology. Finally, he invokes the category of the idea, which, he says, is 'truth in itself and for itself'; it is the union of concept or notion and objectivity. Hegel surveys the various ways in which it is manifested: life, cognition, and finally the so-called Absolute Idea. This is the conception of things when there is total conformity between the mind and its object, the possibility of which, Hegel says, Fichte did not see. What one grasps in the Absolute Idea, however, is simply the whole system of categories and its development to this point.

What is one to make of all this? Many have seen in the attempts at system and comprehensiveness a form of paranoia – certainly a form of arrogance of thought. It is not surprising that it produced heated reactions, to which I shall come later. I can be brief with the other two parts of the *Encyclopaedia*. The *Philosophy of Nature* has not been generally well received. It is an attempt to systematize knowledge of nature from the standpoint of the science of Hegel's own day. The *Philosophy of Mind* covers in its earlier parts much the same ground as that covered in the earlier parts of the *Phenomenology*, although in a more detailed and systematic way. The part on Objective Mind is given more detail in the *Philosophy of Right*.

Free will is seen as manifested in personhood, and the liberty of property-ownership that this is said to entail. Hence Hegel considers the law of property, of contract, and of civil and criminal wrongs. Punishment Hegel sees as a negation of the negation of right created by the criminal. Morality proper comes into existence, however, only when the judge and criminal are one, so that the next section has as its concern the morality of conscience. It will be remembered that in the *Phenomenology* conscience was represented as the final stage in this particular process. Here it is made subordinate to social ethics (*Sittlichkeit*) on the grounds that it lacks a basis which is universal; it needs a ground. In considering social ethics Hegel moves through a consideration of the family, of civil society, to the state. He sees the latter in the form of the Prussian state of his time, and he has been seen, probably wrongly, as the originating source of the later Nazism.

Hegel sees the state as a kind of super-person, with the reason, will and standpoint of a person. It is necessary in order to protect and maintain civil society. Ordinary persons achieve their moral status only in relation to the state, and are thus parts of an organic unity which the state comprises. Hegel's view of the state and of its necessity can be viewed as having a continuity with Rousseau's conception of the general will and arising, as with Rousseau, from a dissatisfaction with the idea that the social obligations of individuals are based on a form of contract. That is the foundation of civil society, but the obligation to obey the contract itself requires a higher basis, in something with a superior authority. Rousseau's failure to relate the general will to the will of all in effect implied that that general will could be manifested only in a superior will – a superior person. Hence, to Hegel's mind, the state.

Anyone unsympathetic to this whole idea needs another conception of morality and its basis. If one finds the Kantian notion of a legislating will in a kingdom of ends unsatisfactory, but retains the idea of a legislating will all the same, one needs a superior law-giver. Failing appeal to God, what possibility remains, apart from a human yet superhuman institution? Liberalism tends to revert to the idea of some individual good, such as happiness, the production of which at a maximum is the only moral goal; hence utilitarianism. Others have thought that, given suitable conditions, a conflict between individual human wills could be obviated. Marx, for example, thought that after a dictatorship of the proletariat the state would eventually wither away, because no prop for social justice would be required. Morality would then stand on its own feet. Would it? The problem is still with us.

The final part of the *Philosophy of Mind* deals with Absolute Mind, where self-consciousness implies awareness of its identity with everything. It again takes three forms – art, religion and philosophy – with philosophy its final consummation. In art that which is sensuously given is transformed by free spirit into something that is wholly its expression; it is thus what the mind brings to the aesthetic object that matters. It is nevertheless limited by the form of immediacy in which the beautiful object presents itself. (Hegel had more to say about aesthetics in his lectures on that subject.) In religion, God as self-consciousness is revealed, but in the form of representations or mental pictures. It is philosophy alone that presents the complete vision, and does so in the form of self-conscious thought. The *Encyclopaedia* closes with a quotation in Greek of Aristotle's words from his *Metaphysics* concerning God as mind thinking itself.

The influence that Hegel had on subsequent thought should not be underestimated, although outside Germany Hegelianism became a dominant movement in philosophy only much later in the century, and even then in a modified form. No philosopher since, however, has laid claim to the same kind of comprehensiveness and universality of thought. Whatever one thinks of its achievements, the existence of Hegelianism as a phenomenon, whether to be hated or admired, is a fact of great historical importance. But hatred or admiration seem the only possible reactions to it.

Schopenhauer

Arthur Schopenhauer (1788–1860) thought that Hegel's philosophy was meretricious, and referred to Hegel, always abusively, as a charlatan as well as a 'pedantic scribbler'. It is not entirely clear what is cause and what is effect in Schopenhauer's arrival at that judgement. One element in it is certainly the belief that Hegel had deserted the insights provided by Kant, even if Schopenhauer thought that Kant's insights did not go far enough and that much of his architectonic was unnecessary. He believed that German philosophy had gone wrong and that what he thought about Hegel applied equally to Fichte and Schelling. Whatever one may think about that, one thing is clear, and that is that by contrast with their difficult and opaque style Schopenhauer's writing is elegant and crystal clear. The clarity and beauty of the writing are apparent even in translation.

Schopenhauer also had striking and forceful opinions on a number of subjects, which he put forward in essays collected together in his *Parerga and Paralipomena* (1851). Many who have found Schopenhauer interesting have come to him through those essays. His main work, however, is *The World as Will and Representation* (first published in 1819, although revised editions with additional supplemental essays appeared in 1844 and 1859). That work was, however, preceded by his doctoral dissertation *The Fourfold Root of the Principle of Sufficient Reason* (1813, but revised and enlarged in 1847). Schopenhauer thought that this work should be read as an introduction to his main work, and even contemplated having it printed along with the main work on its revision. Apart from that, his other main works are two essays, *On the Freedom of the Will* and *On the Basis of Morality*, written as prize essays and published together as *The Two Fundamental Problems of Ethics* in 1841.

Schopenhauer was the son of a businessman in Danzig, who intended him to follow the same career; his mother was a novelist of some reputation, a fact to which he reacted competitively and eventually with hostility. Schopenhauer initially determined on an academic career and held a brief appointment at the University of Berlin where he chose to lecture at the same time as Hegel – and nobody came! For the rest of his life he lived on a private income, a rather solitary and sour man, who gained recognition only at the end of his life. He was contemptuous of most of what he saw around him, and of his philosophical contemporaries in particular. He held disparaging views about women, for example, only some of which follow from his central philosophical views. Various stories about him contribute to the picture of him as a rather nasty as well as sour man. He was, however, a man of vast erudition and intellectual insight. He was admired, rather one-sidedly, by Wagner; he had considerable influence on Nietzsche; and Freud claimed that he had derived from Schopenhauer his views about the unconscious, and the so-called primary process of primitive instinctual thought. By and large, however, it is non-philosophers who have acknowledged debts to him, rather than philosophers.

He claims in his main work that his philosophy is the unfolding of a single thought; and so it is, although the thought is rather complex. He acknowledged a great debt to Kant, and in the main work wrote a critical appreciation of Kant as an appendix; but he rejected much of Kant's architectonic, and disagreed with him on many points, particularly on the unknowability of the thing-in-itself. In *The Fourfold Root* he argues that all representations for a knowing consciousness or subject must stand to each other in a lawlike way according to four, and only four, principles of connection which can be determined *a priori*. These are the four forms of the principle of sufficient reason: those of becoming, being, knowing and acting. Perhaps the main source for this last way of putting things is Christian Wolff, who had distinguished three forms of reason or principle, corresponding to Schopenhauer's first three forms of the principle of sufficient reason. Schopenhauer also thought that Wolff had said something which suggested his fourth form of principle, that of acting.

For Schopenhauer, the principle of being had to do with the arrangement of representations in space and time, which he thought, following Kant, were *a priori* intuitions. The principle of becoming had to do with causality, which Schopenhauer thought the only one of Kant's categories it was necessary to presume. He thought that he could show the *a priori* necessity of the principle that every change has a cause, not by reference to Kant's own argument, which he thought defective, but by reference to what he believed to be the workings of the understanding in perception itself. The argument, which is in fact unsatisfactory, is that one cannot perceive anything without presupposing the truth of the principle.

The principle of knowing has to do with reason and truth, because Schopenhauer thought that truth was the reference of a judgement to its ground. Judgement involves relations between concepts (which are in turn abstracted from perceptual representations by reason, not the understanding); but no judgement can express knowledge unless related to a ground or reason *a priori*. In that context Schopenhauer makes interesting distinctions between judgements according to how they relate to a ground. The final principle, that of acting, claims that its one object – the subject who wills – is always determined by motives, which are causes seen from within. The precise significance of this last point will appear later. In the main work he goes over some of the material that falls under the first three principles, although in a less systematic way, and attempts to spell out the different kinds of representation that are the objects of a knowing consciousness. Schopenhauer thinks of himself as a transcendental idealist, and he believes that the world, considered as representations, is transcendentally ideal although empirically real. So far, much of what Schopenhauer has had to say is modified Kant, without a great deal of the latter's apparatus.

In the second book of the main work appears what Schopenhauer thought of as his great contribution to philosophy, and something that Kant had missed: the world as will. Schopenhauer accepts that there must be the kind of basis for phenomena provided in Kant's philosophy by things-in-themselves, but thinks that something provides the clue for a positive identification of that basis. That clue is provided by the nature of action (not the freedom that Kant eventually came to see as the condition of the existence of noumena). Schopenhauer thinks that if we consider action we shall see, directly and immediately, the source of our agency in what he calls 'will'. The will manifests itself only in successive bodily actions, and those actions conform to the principle that they are always subject to motives which determine the will. Nevertheless, agency is such that in acting we are aware, directly and immediately (that is to say, without recourse to inference), of the exercise of will.

Schopenhauer then argues that we are thereby aware of something which is unconditioned, and not conditioned as representations must be according to the reasoning of *The Fourfold Root*. It must therefore be something which falls outside the realm of representations; and he concludes that it must be the thing-in-itself. The argument is unfortunately invalid; even if we were to accept that it shows that knowledge of agency is not simply knowledge of representations, it need not follow that it amounts to knowledge of a thing-in-itself. That identification would be plausible only if we had independent reason to think there were things-in-themselves, and the only reason that Schopenhauer had for that was that Kant said so. Nevertheless, although the argument does not take Schopenhauer as far as he wants, it is of interest in drawing attention to the peculiarities of the notion of agency, and to the way in which that is manifested or realized in bodily action. In that respect some commentators have seen him as anticipating the views of the later Wittgenstein.

If the will falls outside the realm of representations and is thus non-phenomenal, it is not subject to the conditions of space and time to which representations are subject, according to the principle of sufficient reason of being. Schopenhauer concludes that it lies for that reason 'outside the possibility of plurality', and that there is therefore only one thing-in-itself. What we are each of us aware of in willing is that one thing, the will. That is our inner nature, and the difference between us is merely phenomenal. The will is, indeed, the one reality that lies behind all phenomena, which Schopenhauer describes in terms of the Hindu notion of the veil of Mâyâ. Once having discovered, as he thinks, the clue to the identification of the thing-in-itself from what we are aware of in ourselves, Schopenhauer considers a number of phenomena in nature, particularly those that show evidence of teleology, which can be seen in the same way. Indeed a work entitled *The Will in Nature* (1836) is entirely devoted to that end. It is important, however, that what Schopenhauer thinks of as the will in nature is the very same thing we detect in ourselves, not merely something like it. It is for that reason, too, that what we are aware of as motives in ourselves are the very same things as are seen as causes in other phenomena.

In the third part of *The World as Will and Representation* Schopenhauer considers art. Artistic appreciation involves contemplation of what he construes as Platonic Ideas, which reveal themselves in works of art. Such Ideas, he says, constitute grades of the will's objectification. That is a very difficult notion. A Platonic Idea is an ideal exemplar; for Schopenhauer these are representations to which we are directed in contemplating works of art. They are representations of prototypes of varying degrees or grades of perfection, in which the will realizes itself. Schopenhauer argues for them on other grounds too, including the necessity for a bridge between the one will and the world of changing phenomena. As far as art is concerned the most important thing is that in contemplating the Ideas as manifested in works of art there is a temporary stilling of the will.

This is the first of two examples of this kind which involve the paradox that the will somehow stills itself, for the will is responsible for representations, even if their course is determined in accordance with the principle of sufficient reason. The second occurs at the end of the work, where Schopenhauer sees a kind of salvation in the will denying itself. In art there is a temporary occurrence of the same thing. Schopenhauer goes through the various arts accordingly. He recognizes, however, that music does not fit the pattern of the other arts and maintains that it must be treated differently. Music is not a copy of the Ideas, but a copy of the will itself. It is, he says, parodying Leibniz, 'an unconscious exercise in metaphysics in which the mind does not know that it is philosophizing'. Different aspects of music reflect different aspects of the will.

The final book of the main work presents Schopenhauer's ethics and his account of possible salvation from the suffering to which life is necessarily subject because of the will's blind activity. He denies, first, the existence of free will in an absolute sense – what he calls *liberum arbitrium indifferentiae* (literally, free choice of indifference). He allows that I can do what I will, but insists that what I will is not up to me. The only freedom of the will is transcendental – the fact that the will itself is not subject to causes as everything else is. Second, he rejects approaches to ethics of the Kantian kind. He insists that the chief motivation in man and animals is egoism, although there is also malice and compassion. It is the last that is the only true moral motivation. It involves a kind of identification with others, and the metaphysical basis of this is that we realize incipiently, when we are compassionate, that at a level that goes beyond phenomena we are all the same; we are all will.

He goes into considerable detail about the suffering that egoism produces, just as in nature the will in its blindness 'buries its teeth in its own flesh'. Suffering is the order of events, and pessimism the only right attitude. Schopenhauer has sometimes been called the philosopher of pessimism, and perhaps he was a pessimist anyway; but his claim that pessimism is the only right attitude is very much of a piece with his philosophy and his conception of the will. The will is blind because the intellect which could make it otherwise is a function of the brain, and this is one of the phenomena realized by the will. Suffering is thus inevitable.

Goodness lies in compassion for others, and the good man lives 'in the world of friendly phenomena'. Nevertheless suffering cannot be avoided. Suicide is no way out, because it does not provide an escape from the will. The suicide, he says, 'wills life, and is dissatisfied merely with the conditions under which it has come about for him'. The only escape from the will lies in that insight into the real unity of things that underlies virtue. If this is combined with asceticism so that the demands of the body are denied, the will is quietened, and if death comes in this way, 'for him who so ends the world has ended at the same time'. Indeed, as a second best, suffering itself may have the same effect. This is the second example of the will paradoxically denying itself. Schopenhauer makes clear that we cannot ensure that this will happen; it is, he says, like an effect of grace.

Apart, however, from the paradox involved in the will denying itself, there is also the problem of how ascetic death can involve an escape from the will which is not available in the case of ordinary death. In ordinary death it is just phenomena that cease (although 'cease' is the wrong word to use, since Schopenhauer thinks, with Kant, that time is merely ideal, and when we die there is no 'after' for us). Yet the will exists eternally. How then can ascetic death make any difference? Schopenhauer's answer is obscure, although he insists in the closing words of his book that for those in whom the will has turned and denied itself, 'this so very real world of ours with all its suns and galaxies is – nothing'.

Whatever one may think of that, it is possible to see why Schopenhauer says that his work is the unfolding of a single thought. His determination to work out the consequences of his supposed insight is impressive in its consistency. It cannot be denied, however, that the argument is invalid at the point to which he attaches so much importance: the identification of the thing-in-itself with the will. (Perhaps that is just as well!) Nevertheless, Schopenhauer's presentation of his system is fascinating. He also has much that is interesting to say on matters, incidental to his main argument, such as sex, birth and death. The contrast between his approach to philosophical matters and that of Hegel is, however, striking; and, whether or not his views are acceptable, to turn to Schopenhauer from Hegel is to turn from a heady draught of over-rich liquor to something nearer pure water.

Nietzsche

The one philosopher who claimed to be influenced by Schopenhauer was Friedrich Nietzsche (1844–1900), although Nietzsche's philosophical views are very different from Schopenhauer's, despite a superficial resemblance at certain points. In particular, the notion of the will to power, which is important for Nietzsche, is quite unlike Schopenhauer's conception of the will. Nietzsche was born at Röcken in Germany, although he later repudiated his German origins. He studied classical philology at Bonn and Leipzig, where he made an impression on one of the professors, Friedrich Ritschl, through whom he obtained a post at Basle, to lecture on classics and Greek philosophy. He eventually took Swiss citizenship, and then became a full professor at Basle. While there he became friendly with Wagner, who was living at Tribschen, near Lucerne. He wrote various works during this period, but eventually became disillusioned with Wagner, as he made quite clear in *Human, All-too-Human*, published in 1878. In that same year he resigned his post at Basle because of ill health, thereafter leading a more or less solitary life, while painfully producing a number of other works. In 1889 he became insane and lived the rest of his life in the care of his sister, who set herself up as his real interpreter and high priestess of the Nietzsche cult. The madness infects some of the later works, such as *Ecce Homo*. Not all the earlier ones are straightforward either, and Nietzsche's style is as much that of the poet as that of the philosopher. Indeed, *Thus Spake Zarathustra*, which many have seen as the quintessential Nietzsche, is very much a poetic work, parts of which have been adopted as texts by several composers.

His earliest work is the *Birth of Tragedy*, in which Nietzsche distinguishes between the Apollonian and Dionysiac approaches and outlines the tension between them. The work consists of a reappraisal of Greek culture and of the position of art in it. The Dionysiac urge is associated with drunkenness or intoxication, the Apollonian with dreams and visions. The full title of the work is *The Birth of Tragedy out of the Spirit of Music*. Music is at bottom Dionysiac in nature, especially in its connection with the dance. The emphasis of Apollonian art is on depiction of things. Tragedy was born out of an attempt to impose this kind of approach on the Dionysiac urge. It was killed in effect by Euripides, in whom Nietzsche sees the Apollonian aspects taking over; they do this under the influence of Socraticism, for Nietzsche sees in Socrates an undue emphasis on reason as a means to man's salvation. Nietzsche was later to express dissatisfaction with his first work, but there are themes in it which were to become dominant in later works, many of which take the form of collections of aphorisms in which Nietzsche pours out a message for mankind. Perhaps the most dominant theme is the emphasis on life and the role of art-forms in dealing with the problems to which life may give rise, as tragedy bears witness.

There are some who see Nietzsche as a moralist more than a philosopher; he urges men to take up certain attitudes to life, if they can. Those last words need emphasis because of Nietzsche's belief that most of mankind, the herd, are incapable of it, and he speaks in glowing terms, particularly in *Zarathustra*, of the emergence of the *Übermensch*, the Superman, who will transcend the guilt-laden inhibitions of ordinary men, in a joyous, guiltless affirmation of life, yet in mastery of himself and his instinctive drives. This is a form of goodness which is, in the words of the title of another of his books, beyond good and evil in the ordinary sense. For in that ordinary sense good and evil are opposed to each other and presuppose each other. The life of the Superman, however, is seen as something entirely positive, an exercise of complete power without any negativity. Most men are incapable of this; they are human, all-too-human.

It would be wrong, however, to see Nietzsche as concerned throughout just to preach a sermon, even if an anti-Christian and anti-religious sermon. He takes over from Schopenhauer the notion of the will, although, unlike Schopenhauer, he interprets it as the will to power. He also values what Schopenhauer had to say about the forces governing life. But he will have nothing of the idea of the will as thing-in-itself; indeed he rejects all conceptions of that sort, all attempts at that kind of metaphysics, emphasizing a radical subjectivity. It is a subjectivity which repudiates the idea of truth as a form of objectivity (something that might be seen, for example, in correspondence with facts). According to Nietzsche there is no access to facts independent of human points of view; truth lies in the superiority of a point of view in securing dominance. Truth is, then, power.

This involves a radical restructuring of the concept of truth, in a way that has something in common with the relativism of Protagoras' claim that man is the measure of all things, except that, according to Nietzsche, ordinary men are afraid to exercise the will to power in order to achieve a point of view which transcends ordinary ones. The anti-objectivity and, to a point, anti-rationality of all this has made some commentators characterize Nietzsche as an existentialist, emphasizing existence above reason, in opposition to Hegel. To the extent that this is true, Nietzsche can be set alongside Kierkegaard, whom I shall consider in the next chapter, as providing a reaction to Hegel. It is not clear, however, that Nietzsche saw himself in that way.

Furthermore, the kind of subjectivity and relativism that Nietzsche preaches is by no means a form of individualism. Indeed, interestingly from the point of view of contemporary philosophy, Nietzsche laid great weight upon language as a dominant force in forming our view of things, and language is very much a social phenomenon. Hence the subjectivity that Nietzsche espouses is not one that finds its inspiration either in the individualism that Descartes' thought presupposed or in the relationship that Christianity supposes to exist between the individual and God. Nietzsche's relativism and anti-objectivism are social rather than individual. Like Protagoras, Nietzsche thinks that some perspectives are better than others; but for him the better is the stronger (not merely should be). The ordinary emphasis on truth and knowledge is, he thinks, an emphasis on forms of falsification and distortion which are carried out in the interests of the continuance of life. But consciousness and the forms that it takes are essentially social phenomena and depend upon social relationships for their furtherance.

All the same, the Superman has to transcend ordinary social beliefs and attitudes, and in going beyond good and evil he goes beyond ordinary socially determined attitudes. Nietzsche sees ordinary morality as what he calls slave morality, as opposed to the views and attitudes of the master. Ordinary morality and conscience are just the attitudes internalized in the individual through social determination by the influences of the 'herd'. The master embraces power and uses it willingly; the slaves, by contrast, fear it. A morality is in general just a set of rules or customs imposed by society, and as such it is antithetical to what is natural and opposed to life.

In the *Genealogy of Morals* (1887) Nietzsche offers his view of how that comes about. The key notion in that account is one for the expression of which Nietzsche has recourse to the French word *ressentiment* on the ground that no adequate German word is available. There is no reason why we should not speak of *resentment*. The slaves – that is to say, those who are inferior because of their inability to use power – not only fear the master, who has that power, but also resent him. 'Historically', Nietzsche believes, that resentment has been worked out by the slaves getting the masters to adopt their own evaluation of the relationship. Thus power is seen as bad, and the master is made to adopt the slaves' view of what is good. In doing so, he is unable to exercise his will, and he turns this upon himself in the form of self-aggression. From this derive the forms of repression and bad conscience that Nietzsche sees in ordinary society. It is, he believes, brought about by the institution of religion. Nietzsche's declaration that God is dead is well-known; it emphasizes his view of the role of religion in general, and of Christianity in particular, in reinforcing the slave morality.

Hence morality, as it exists at present, is really the imposition of a slave morality on those who should know better. A really noble morality would arise from self-affirmation. None of this is really supposed to be history; it has the kind of status that has most often been attached to the idea of a state of nature. It is an attempt to explain the complexities of men's general attitudes, and to point to a way out of the inhibitions on life which those attitudes produce in us. A master morality would be quite different. In this context Nietzsche invokes the idea of the 'blond beast', as a mark of superior races. It is a notion that has rightly been found abhorrent when used in connection with the Aryan policies of the Nazis, although Nietzsche probably did not intend it in anything like that sense. The 'blond beast' (probably the lion) represents merely a characteristic that superior races may reveal.

The Superman is a free spirit for whom anything is possible, and for whom truth and science are as nothing. Nietzsche has often been described as a nihilist, and in a way he is, at this point. But he himself might not have regarded himself entirely in that way. The freedom and joyousness of the Superman are for him positive things, although the only ones. The freedom that comes with the will to power and the ability to use it is not only the supreme value, it is the only reality, in Nietzsche's view. This represents the height of German romanticism, or of one strand of it; it is not the romanticism combined with rationalism which Hegel manifests, but a romanticism combined with a certain sort of irrationalism, whether or not Nietzsche would have accepted that description.

The joyousness of the Superman is not happiness. The concern for that is the mark of what Nietzsche calls, in opposition to the Superman, the 'last man' – a kind of lowest common denominator of humanity conceived as the herd. Nietzsche thoroughly despised that. His ideal was a totally free spirit whose joy is in that freedom. It might well be said to be a romantic ideal which has nothing to do with the reality that we know about. Nevertheless, Nietzsche was prepared to present it as an ideal. Is it, however, one that he expected to be achieved? He certainly did not think that there was a goal to which things in the world are tending. Indeed, he said that, if there were, it would already have been achieved countless times. For he held a doctrine which in many ways does not seem to fit well with his other views, the doctrine of the eternal recurrence. Exactly the same things (not merely similar things) will happen time after time, and have already happened. It is not entirely clear why Nietzsche held this doctrine, but Zarathustra certainly proclaims it. If there is no final goal, then all is in a sense meaningless, Nietzsche said; but it is a meaninglessness which is eternal. In *Ecce Homo*, written at the end of his life, he said that his criterion for greatness in a human being is the acceptance, and indeed love, of what happens for all eternity. It is a strange ideal, although there may be distorted echoes of Spinoza in it.

Nietzsche suggested that he was perhaps the first tragic philosopher (as distinguished from Schopenhauer's pessimism). Many have been attracted by his views, but in their totality they perhaps reveal too much of a taste for romantic paradox. Certainly philosophy could go no further in this direction.

[15]
Two Reactions to Hegel

It might be suggested that I have already considered reactions to Hegel. But although Schopenhauer was certainly opposed to Hegel, he was more concerned with truths that he thought were to be derived from Kant, but which Kant had failed to see; and although Nietzsche was diametrically opposed to Hegel in his views, it is not clear that he saw himself as reacting to him. The situation is different with the two philosophers to be considered in this chapter, Marx and Kierkegaard, different though they were from each other.

Marx

It has sometimes been denied that Karl Marx (1818–83) was a philosophical figure, or at all events a major philosophical figure. It cannot be denied, however, that his views have been immensely influential, both politically and philosophically, and to leave Marx out of consideration in any history of philosophy would be absurd. On the other hand, many of Marx's works, particularly in his later period – works such as *Capital* (1867 for the first volume, the rest posthumous) and the earlier *Grundrisse* (*Elements of a Critique of Political Economy*, begun in 1857 as a draft from which was abstracted the *Contributions to a Critique of Political Economy* of 1859) – have economics as their main concern. Scholars have argued whether one should distinguish between an early and late Marx with some degree of discontinuity between them. Current opinion seems to emphasize the continuity of his philosophical thought, which, though not Hegelian, was profoundly influenced by Hegel. Nevertheless the greatest amount of philosophical meat is to be found in earlier works such as the *German Ideology*, written with Friedrich Engels (1820–95) in 1846, and the *Economic and Philosophical Manuscripts of 1844*. (Marx and Engels also cooperated on the *Communist Manifesto* of 1848.)

Marx was born in Trier in Germany. He went to the University of Bonn as a law student, but soon moved to Berlin, where he turned to philosophy and became associated with the so-called 'Young Hegelians', a group which included at one time or another Ludwig Feuerbach (1804–72), Max Stirner (1806–56) and Engels, and was led at the time by a lecturer, Bruno Bauer. Marx then moved to Cologne, where he edited the *Rheinische Zeitung*. This was suppressed by the authorities in 1843. He then moved to Paris, where he remained until 1845, much involved with socialist ideas, and began his cooperation and friendship with Engels. He was eventually expelled from Paris and moved to Brussels, where he became a leader of the Communist League. After a brief stay in Germany he moved with his wife and family in 1849 to London, where he remained for the rest of his life, working, as everyone knows, in the British Museum Reading Room.

The Young Hegelians with whom Marx was associated in Berlin were a radical political group, but they were all concerned to reinterpret Hegel in a less mystical spirit. Feuerbach thought that Hegelianism was the rational expression of Christianity, but he interpreted both in an unorthodox way. In *The Essence of Christianity* (1841) he maintained that religion, at any rate in its Christian form, is concerned with the relation of man to his own nature or species, although that nature is viewed as something external. In fact all the attributes of God are attributes of the human nature or species, and knowledge of God is really a form of knowledge of man himself. Man projects his thoughts and feelings about himself on to an external object, which he calls God. The proper study of theology should in fact be anthropology, which involves observation of men, not merely an exercise in reason. What Hegel thought of as God's (or the Absolute Spirit's) consciousness of himself is really man's own self-consciousness, considered as consciousness of his essential nature. This is in effect a materialist interpretation of Hegel.

Something of this survives in Marx's *1844 Manuscripts* in the idea of a species-being or species-life from which man is alienated; but Marx came to criticize Feuerbach, in spite of an enthusiastic first reaction to what he said about religion, on the grounds that the materialism was not dialectical – which is to say that it did not take a proper historical view. In his *Theses on Feuerbach* (1845) Freud criticized Feuerbach for thinking of the essence of man as an abstraction, and not seeing that it is in fact the 'totality of social relations'. Feuerbach was forced as a result 'to abstract from the historical process'. He also insisted that Feuerbach failed to see the sensible world as 'practical, human sense activity'; and he ended with the famous remark that 'Philosophers have only *interpreted* the world in different ways; the point is to change it.'

Marx's reaction to Max Stirner was in some ways similar, but the criticisms were much more sweeping. Stirner objected to the idea of a human essence altogether, along with the idea that it was the goal of man to realize that essence. In *The Ego and its Own* (1845) he put forward a rather Nietzschean idea of a free and independent ego which creates itself and its thoughts. What matters for it, and what alone matters for it, is what it can appropriate. The individual is thus unique: 'I do not develop man, nor as man, but as I, I develop – myself.' Marx criticized this egoism, which he saw as the product of a bourgeois society, and he also attacked Stirner for not recognizing that fact, and for assuming that it is the ego's ideas which determine things, rather than real historical relations. Ideas, Marx said, are determined and altered by life, and that means by the mode of material production and by material intercourse. In all this Marx is claiming that the Young Hegelians do not go far enough in their materialism; the point to be retained from Hegel is the historical or developmental approach, the dialectic, and on this the young Hegelians fall short.

Marx holds that there are 'moments' or phases in the development of self-consciousness, but these are not to be construed in terms of the kind of idealist metaphysics that Hegel proclaimed. Yet the idea that there are such phases is itself essentially Hegelian. It was for this reason that Engels said that Marx meant to 'stand Hegel on his head'. The first phase is that in which man is absorbed in his 'species-life'. By means of his work nature is so to speak constructed, so that it appears as *his* work and *his* reality. The second phase involves alienation from himself and from his 'species-life', and that means that man becomes alienated from other men too, and 'each of the others is likewise alienated from human life'. The 'species-life' of man becomes merely a means of physical existence. The result is private property, which is the expression of man's alienation. Through it, objects attain a value independent of what men have put into them through their labour. There is a process of externalization of consciousness, so that what man *is* is projected on to objects. Hence the notion of alienation; and through man's alienation from himself in this way he becomes alienated from others, and becomes an object for others. It is a negation of the first phase or moment of consciousness.

The third phase – a negation of a negation, in Hegelian terms – is communism. In this there is the abolition of the institution of property. Initially there may be a simple universalization of property in the sense that things are taken to be owned by all. Eventually, however, there has to be complete abolition of property so that there is complete integration between things and human needs. Thereby, Marx thinks, barriers between one man and another break down. As I have described this, there may seem to be a conflation between 'dialectical' phases in consciousness and self-consciousness and historical phases in human existence. It is in fact characteristic of the early Marx that he retains the Hegelian idea of history following the pattern that phenomenology reveals as inherent in the idea of phases of development in forms of consciousness. One aspect of the difference that some commentators have seen between the early and the late Marx is that in the late Marx consciousness and all its forms are seen as aspects of a 'superstructure' that emerge, and can only emerge, from an economic 'base'. I shall return to that idea later, but there is really no contradiction between the two stages of Marx's thought in this respect. For it is not claimed by the earlier theory that economic facts and relations emerge out of prior inter-relationships of consciousness. Rather, there is an identity between the social and economic facts and relations on the one hand and the inter-relationships of consciousness on the other.

This is because Marx does not construe consciousness in the way that Hegel does. For him it is already socialized and material in nature, and to speak of consciousness is to speak of how men treat objects and each other. Moreover, the human species which Feuerbach emphasized is thought of by Marx in terms of the idea of a species-life, which is a form of social existence in which individuals recognize themselves as social beings and as having a socially determined way of existence. Marx's concern with the phases or moments of consciousness is a concern with the forms of social relationship and existence, and he conceives them in materialistic terms. The consciousness which is said to emerge as the superstructure from the economic base, according to, for example, the later *Capital*, is the structure of human institutions and the system of beliefs, values etc., which make up what Marx calls an 'ideology'. The three moments of the more directly Hegelian-orientated thinking of the early Marx correspond roughly to Hegel's 'for self', 'in self', and 'in and for self'.

The first stage is in effect a form of subjectivism; all that matters for human beings is their species-life. This consists in the working-over of inorganic nature or the objective world, in a way that differentiates man from the animals, which produce only what is requisite for their immediate needs. In work and production man duplicates himself, producing a kind of image of himself in what he has created; it is through this that 'nature appears as his work and his reality'. The emphasis in this on work and production is an aspect of the so-called 'labour theory of value' – that the value of a thing is a function of the amount of labour that goes into it, so that any surplus value that is attached to it in the economic process must be a form of exploitation. Marx elaborates this theory in *Capital*, as part of the account of capitalism; but its germs lie in the thinking of the early period, and the view that in the first phase things are in effect what man makes of them by his work. Part of the account of the alienation that follows is that things come to have a status independent of what men make of them by their labour. Making by labour is what corresponds, in Marx's theory, to the active processes of consciousness in making a reality of what is given in Hegel's. It is a socialized and materialized version of idealism, and it is important that this aspect of Marx's thinking should be recognized. It is indeed a sort of premise of his argument, and a dubious one.

The fact that it is merely the first phase or moment does not make it any the less dubious, because the subsequent phases depend on the first. The second phase of alienated labour or self-alienation arises from the externalization or objectification of the objects of man's production. In *Capital* Marx puts this in terms of the idea of the 'fetishism of commodities'. Marx owed the idea of fetishism to Charles de Brosses' *Cult of the Fetish-Gods*, published in 1760, according to which a fetish was an inanimate object given magical powers. The supposition was that these powers were a projection on to an idol of the characteristics of the human beings who set it up. (Feuerbach's conception of religion was in fact fairly close to this.) In Marx's view, commodities gain a corresponding life of their own, and that role is seen *par excellence* in money, whereby use-value (the value given to something because of the role that it has in relation to human beings) becomes exchange value. If this is conceived in terms of the idea that something of the human being is objectified in such objects, the notion of alienation becomes clear; something of what is really human becomes separated from that human being. Marx sees this happening in the most extreme way in the institution of property. Moreover, he thinks that in this form of alienation men become alienated from each other; and they become means for each other, because they too become property to be bought and sold for money. Marx speaks with great feeling of the perverting role of money in this respect: it is the visible god-head but also the universal whore. It is the 'alienated essence of man's work and being' and it dominates man while he adores it.

The final phase must be one in which there is identity between the species-life of man, considered as a social being, and nature. In that case, man's natural existence becomes a human existence, and nature becomes human. It is not easy to understand that, although it is easier to understand, even if not to accept as realistic, Marx's belief that in this state of affairs there will be a genuine community without exploitation of any form. In this case, property will be abolished, and so will the state. Marx came to believe that this was inevitable, because capitalism has an incoherence and so bears the seeds of its own destruction. It will not come about, however, without violent revolution. First there must be the 'dictatorship of the proletariat', but subsequently the state will wither away and true communism will ensue.

But this is part of Marx's later thought, in which there is perhaps greater emphasis upon the historical forces, and upon a supposedly necessary historical development. This came to be called 'dialectical materialism' and has become Marxist orthodoxy. It is supposedly a scientific theory, according to which development along Marxist lines is inevitable, because the capitalist system has inbuilt contradictions which are bound to be resolved by a better system. That much of the Hegelian idea of dialectic remains. It is in the context of this theory also that the distinction between base and superstructure is made. The superstructure of legal and social institutions, and the system of beliefs etc. that make up an ideology, are derived from a base consisting of a system of economic relations and productive forces. This is what makes the theory materialistic.

There has been argument among Marxian scholars about the exact relations between base and superstructure, but this is part of the scholasticism that Marxist thinking has produced. Apart from the official Soviet line concerning Marxism, contemporary Marxists tend to be divided between those, such as Louis Althusser (1918–84), who stress the historical and 'scientific' aspects of dialectical materialism, and those, such as Herbert Marcuse (1898–1979) and other members of the Frankfurt school, who emphasize the more Hegelian aspects of Marx's thought. These Hegelian aspects might be called a sort of materialist idealism, because what is emphasized in them is the way in which human beings construct their world through social practices. The other side of Marx's thought is scarcely that, because it presupposes in the theory of the 'base' a realist account of economic and productive forces.

In fact, however, there is an inevitable tension in Marxist thought, just because what I have described as the idealism is a materialist one. If it is to be that, it must be presumed that the material and social practices which determine consciousness have a reality independent of that consciousness, and are not created by it, as idealism would suggest. That this is so is implied already in *The German Ideology*, where Marx says 'Men are the producers of their conceptions, ideas, etc. – real, active men, as they are conditioned by a definite development of their productive forces and of the intercourse corresponding to these, up to its furthest forms.' The later Marx puts emphasis on the productive forces etc. as the base on which the superstructure is built, but the thought is already there in the early Marx. The Marxist philosophy constitutes one reaction to Hegelianism in that, initially at least, it tries to put Hegel in a materialist dress. In doing so it makes that way of thought incoherent in a way that it was not before – although Hegelianism itself has, one might think, enough incoherences already.

Kierkegaard

The second reaction to Hegel to be considered is that provided by Søren Kierkegaard (1813–55), who is generally regarded as the founder of Existentialism. Kierkegaard was born in Copenhagen and spent almost his whole life there. He was a theology student at the university, but because he was concerned to follow certain literary and philosophical pursuits he did not take his examinations until 1840. In that year he was engaged to Regine Olsen, only to break off the engagement on becoming convinced that marriage and what it entailed was incompatible with his calling. His efforts to explain and justify his conduct have about them a mixture of the comic and the pompous, but his concern over the event stayed with him throughout his life. He was an intensely religious man, overbearingly so to some minds, and he spent a great deal of time in controversy with the Danish state church, which he regarded as perverting the original message of Christ. His views obtained recognition only many years after his early death.

Kierkegaard found Hegel's views anathema, largely because Hegel did not, in his eyes, take account of personal existence and did not recognize the personal nature of God. Man's relation to God is, indeed, the dominant theme in Kierkegaard's works. The first of these, *Either/Or*, published in 1843, presents ostensibly a choice between two ways of life, which he calls the aesthetic and the ethical; but the final outcome is the suggestion that both of these should be rejected in favour of a third way of life, the religious. It is a curious work, beginning with a discourse on the part of 'A', concerning the aesthetic way of life, with a great deal to do with Mozart's *Don Giovanni*. This is followed by the 'Diary of a Seducer', which purports to be something found among A's papers, and is the record of the relations between Johannes, the seducer, and Cordelia, the object of his seduction. It describes the methods adopted by Johannes, who, having in the last two pages got his way, lets her go without any further interest, having, as he says, introduced her to a higher sphere of consciousness! Part Two of the work consists first of two letters, on 'The aesthetic validity of marriage' and 'The equilibrium between the aesthetical and the ethical in the composition of personality', and second of a sermon by an unnamed priest. The letters are written by 'B' as a criticism of 'A', but they reveal that they are in fact written by a Judge Wilhelm who has visited A frequently. Judge Wilhelm stands for the ethical against the aesthetic way of life of A. The priest speaks for religion.

By 'aesthetic' Kierkegaard means a concern for the senses and for what is immediate, including pleasure and eroticism. 'A' advocates the 'rotation method', involving withdrawal from one pleasure in order to sample another, only to return to the first later. Judge Wilhelm, on the other hand, advocates the pursuit of duty from free choice, and a life which has that as its end. By contrast with the temporality of A's life, he advocates the point of view of the eternal, and it is he who presents the choice of 'either/or'. The priest, however, presents the thought that 'as against God we are always in the wrong'. Judge Wilhelm advocates free choice and self-mastery, but these are in effect idols, though ones that by their collapse may take him to God. Another aspect of this is to be found in Kierkegaard's *Fear and Trembling* (also 1843), ostensibly written by Johannes de Silentio (another of Kierkegaard's pseudonyms), in which there is a remarkable discussion of God's command to Abraham to sacrifice his son Isaac. Abraham's duty to his son is set against what he has to do for God, with all the paradox that that involves. In *Purity of Heart is to Will One Thing* – one of the *Edifying Discourses* written in 1846 and published in 1847, ostensibly a 'spiritual preparation for the office of confession' – Kierkegaard sets out as the supreme human failing what he calls 'double-mindedness', a form of self-deception. To will the good, he says, is to will one thing.

The Christianity that Kierkegaard preaches is a very Protestant one, and a great deal of what he wrote can be classified as a very curious form of theology of that kind. One of the key notions for which he is well known is that of dread (*Angst*), which is the call of the eternal in the world of the senses. It is spelled out in *The Concept of Dread* (1844). Obstinate persistence with a life given over to the senses is bound to produce despair, as described in *Sickness unto Death* (1849). *Philosophical Fragments* (1844) discusses how God and the eternal can manifest themselves in time and history, but his main philosophical work is *Concluding Unscientific Postscript* (1846). In it he argues that a philosophical system such as Hegel's is in fact an impossibility, because it cannot take account of actual existence. Truth, he says, is constituted by subjectivity, by which Johannes Climacus (Kierkegaard's pseudonym on this occasion) does not mean to advocate a thesis of the relativity of truth, despite the similarity to Nietzsche's claim. The point is rather that attempts at objectivity on the pattern of Hegel's system cannot deal with the individual and his existence. In its place Kierkegaard advocates 'subjective thinking' and inwardness. 'Only the truth that edifies,' he says, 'is the truth for you.' The human being is caught between time and eternity, and his decisions and choices determine what is so for him. In the end it is between him and God, and the search for what truth there is must be personal.

How much of this is real philosophy is a matter for argument. But the antithesis to and rejection of Hegel is real enough. Kierkegaard's profound but quirky religiosity and his consequent conception of man are phenomena that have to be reckoned with, even if some may find them too much to accept. His thought affords, nevertheless, a proper sense of the religious, and in that way it offers a very definite contrast with the philosophized religion of Hegel, and even more perhaps of Feuerbach. As far as philosophy is concerned, it is the emphasis on individual choice that had most influence, finding its echo, for example, in the philosophy of Jean-Paul Sartre, from which the religion is completely absent.

Nineteenth-Century Empiricism
and Some Reactions to It

Comte

During the time in which Hegel and his influences were dominant in Germany, things were otherwise in France and Britain. After Maine de Biran and until the appearance of Henri Bergson towards the end of the century, the only French philosopher worthy of note was Auguste Comte (1798–1857). In some ways Comte carried on the tradition of the *philosophes*, claiming that all knowledge was based on phenomena and their relations. However, his main concern was methodology, and Comte is known as the founder of positivism, the doctrine that all knowledge proper must be subject to canons of verification in terms of experience. Indeed, he argued that positivism, the positive appeal to phenomena, was the last stage of a three-stage course of historical development, the first two stages involving attempts to provide explanations of things in theological and metaphysical terms respectively. He thought of himself as providing for the first time a positive, scientific account of society, the development of the other sciences being a prelude to this. For this reason, Comte is also sometimes seen as the founder of sociology. By contrast, he rejected both economics and psychology as unscientific, the first on the grounds that it is concerned with only one aspect of a social process, the second because introspection must necessarily alter the phenomena which are the subject matter of psychology. Comte's views were spelled out in his *Cours de philosophie positive* (1830–42; English version, *The Positive Philosophy of Auguste Comte*, by Harriet Martineau, 1853) and *Système de politique positiviste* (1851–4; translated as *The System of Positive Polity*, 1875–7). In the latter he set out what he conceived to be the principles of a scientifically ordered society, complete with a 'religion of humanity'. J. S. Mill welcomed the former, but saw the latter as a system of 'spiritual despotism'.

J. S. Mill

John Stuart Mill (1806–73) was the most famous philosopher in Britain in the nineteenth century. He was the son of James Mill, who wrote *The Analysis of the Phenomena of the Human Mind* (1829) as a handbook of the principles of the association of ideas. Those principles were, of course, invoked by Hume, but they were turned into the general principles of psychology by David Hartley in his *Observations on Man* (1749). In the thinking of both the Mills, associationism went with sensationalism, the doctrine that all mental phenomena can be derived from certain atomic sensations. This view owes much to Hume's view of the dependence of ideas on impressions, and the dependence of all complex impressions upon simple ones.

J. S. Mill was subjected by his father to a very rigorous education; he was profoundly influenced not only by his father's philosophical ideas but also by his father's enthusiasms, one of which was for the views of Jeremy Bentham (1748–1832). Bentham took psychological hedonism as the governing principle of human conduct; pain and pleasure are the 'sovereign masters' of mankind. From this he 'derived' the moral theory known as utilitarianism, that the only end of human conduct is the greatest happiness of the greatest number (a theory which had been put forward by Hutcheson). Bentham is not entirely clear on how utilitarianism is to be derived from the principles of moral psychology that he espoused. His *Introduction to the Principles of Morals and Legislation* (1789), however, indicates that a primary aim was to provide a criterion of acceptable legislation in general and of the use of punishment in particular. A degree of punishment was justifiable only if it had general utility. J. S. Mill's own *Utilitarianism* (1863) is an attempt to elaborate on that theory, with a more general moral aim.

J. S. Mill was employed from 1823 until 1858 in the Examiner's Office of the East India Company. He spent the later years of his life for the most part in Avignon, although he was a Member of Parliament from 1865 to 1868. His employment from 1823 onwards evidently gave him plenty of time for other pursuits, and he published his *System of Logic* in 1843 and his *Principles of Political Economy* in 1848. After his retirement, *On Liberty* was published in 1859, and *An Examination of Sir William Hamilton's Philosophy* in 1865, apart from other works. The *System of Logic* has sometimes been seen as an attack on traditional logic, and there is no doubt that the part of the work that has attracted most interest is the part on inductive logic. Nevertheless, Mill was not an opponent of formal logic; he wished merely to put it on what he saw as a correct empiricist basis.

The work begins with a consideration of language, in the course of which Mill produces a theory of meaning involving a distinction between the denotation and the connotation of expressions. A connotative term is one which 'denotes a subject and implies an attribute'; proper names are non-connotative in that their only function is to denote – a view which, in one dress or another, has been much discussed in recent times. On the basis of this view Mill maintains that necessary propositions are merely verbal, in that they simply make explicit the connotation of a word. Mathematical propositions, on the other hand, are not merely verbal; but they are not necessary either, simply very highly confirmed generalizations from experience. Mill's views in this respect are perhaps the most radically empiricist that there have ever been, and in general they have to be mentioned only to be rejected.

In this respect and in others too, Mill was opposed to William Whewell (1794–1870), who thought that necessary truths were those the denial of which is inconceivable. Mill claimed that Whewell was confused on this point, saying that Whewell supposed himself to be talking of logical inconceivability when he was really talking of what was psychologically impossible. It is probable that the view espoused by Whewell has the greater currency today, although the debt to him is rarely acknowledged. The same is true, as we shall see, over induction.

Mill took inference to involve a move from what is known to what was previously unknown; it must, therefore, provide new knowledge. On that score most deductions are taken by Mill to fail. Some, like the processes of immediate inference (from 'Some *A*s are *B*' to 'Some *B*s are *A*', for example), are mere verbal transpositions. Syllogisms, he thinks, involve circularity, because what I know in the first premise of 'All men are mortal, Socrates is a man, so Socrates is mortal' includes and is dependent on what I know in the conclusion. In other words, having explained inference in epistemological terms, Mill insists that the only grounds for assuming knowledge of the premises of a deductive inference are ones that presuppose knowledge of the conclusion. The only genuine inference must be one that uses the known facts of experience to arrive at general propositions; so-called deductive arguments thus depend upon inductive arguments from particular cases. Hence the importance that Mill attaches to induction. (A defender of deduction must separate the question of the relation between premises and conclusion in a valid deductive argument from the question of what is known in each case, and thus not explain deduction as an epistemological move, as Mill does.)

The only interesting arguments of inductive form are, according to Mill, those concerned with arguing from particular cases within experience to general truths that in a qualified sense hold necessarily. They do this because the phenomena with which we are concerned are subject to causes, and our object in employing induction is to discover those causes. Mill defines 'cause' by means of a refinement on Hume's account, saying that the cause of a phenomenon is the antecedent 'on which it is invariably and *unconditionally* consequent' (and he explains 'unconditional' by saying that B is an unconditional consequent of A if B always follows A subject only to negative conditions, that is to say, B must follow A unless another cause explains why things are otherwise).

Given this, he sets out four methods of experimental inquiry: those of agreement, difference, residues and concomitant variations. These methods have a certain similarity to Bacon's tables of investigation. They differ from them in that Mill is concerned in each case to find a single invariable antecedent of a phenomenon; for that is what a cause is. Thus in the Method of Difference, in trying to discover the cause of Bs, we examine cases in which Bs occur and cases in which they do not occur, in order to find a single difference in the conditions which obtain when Bs occur and do not occur. If As are present whenever Bs occur, but when As are removed Bs do not occur, then A must be the cause of B. Mill regards these as *experimental* methods, not simply appeals to experience, because in them we manipulate events. Nevertheless, he thought of them as sure inductive procedures for discovering causes, despite the possibility, which he admitted, of a plurality of causes, and despite the additional complexities that have to be gone into when we attempt to apply these procedures within the social sciences.

On this too Mill was opposed to Whewell, who proposed something much more like what is now called the hypothetico-deductive method. That is to say that we put forward hypotheses to explain the observed facts, and deduce from them consequences, which can be tested in such a way as to confirm or falsify the hypotheses. These hypotheses are of the form of conjectures which need to be subjected to such a test. This view is close to that of Karl Popper among contemporary philosophers, except that Popper characterizes what he is concerned with as the 'logic of scientific discovery', whereas Whewell thought of the forming of hypotheses as an art of the mind, involving inventiveness and imagination in a way that puts it 'out of the reach of method'. Whewell initiated a number of criticisms of Mill's methods and their preconceptions, pointing out that the conditions that Mill demanded, such as a single difference, are not normally obtainable. Nevertheless, Mill saw what he was concerned with as an essential part of a genuine empiricism.

Mill's epistemological views are similarly empiricist, particularly his account of our knowledge of the so-called external world. This was a genuine problem for Mill, because his psychologism entailed that we are given individual sensations from which we have to construct a world according to the principles of associationism. His solution to the problem was to put forward a radical phenomenalism; things, he said, are merely permanent possibilities of sensation. When we take ourselves to perceive physical objects we are confronted merely with a collection of sensations, but we recognize other connected sensations as possible in such circumstances; this, moreover, is a persistent possibility. Mill set out this view in a chapter of his *Examination of Sir William Hamilton's Philosophy*, entitled 'The Psychological Theory of the Belief in an External World'. Hamilton (1788–1856) was the leading figure in the so-called Scottish school of philosophy; he was philosophically a descendant of Reid, whose works he edited, but he also tried to combine Reid's views with those of Kant at certain points. Mill's demolition of Hamilton was such that the Scottish school never recovered, but his own theory is scarcely acceptable. It is noteworthy that it is put forward as a *psychological* theory; like Hume's, it is an attempt to explain, rather than justify, why we believe in an external world of persistent objects when we are given only sensations.

Mill's moral and political views have perhaps attracted greater interest. In *Utilitarianism*, Mill puts refinements on Bentham's views by distinguishing between qualities of pleasure; happiness is not just a matter of the quantity of pleasure produced – something that would not distinguish human happiness from that of pigs. 'It is better to be a human being dissatisfied,' he says, 'than a pig satisfied; better to be Socrates dissatisfied than a fool satisfied.' It is arguable too that Mill makes a distinction that has obtained wider currency in modern discussions of utilitarianism – that between act and rule utilitarianism. The distinction depends upon whether the calculation about the greater balance of happiness over unhappiness is done on the basis of what will result from the performance of a given act or on the basis of what will result from adherence or non-adherence to a rule, such as the rule that one should keep promises, of which a given act may be an instance. Certainly, when confronting the possible objection that it is not always possible to calculate the results of a given act, and when considering the relation of utility to what may seem the contrary demands of justice, Mill sometimes reverts to a consideration of what would result from a failure to keep the rule. He argues that it is the contribution of certain rules or institutions to general happiness that justifies our adherence to them despite what may seem the counter-utility of the specific act.

Nevertheless, it is the relation of utilitarianism to other apparent moral demands that most concerns Mill when considering possible objections to his theory. He invokes Bentham's dictum 'everyone to count for one, nobody for more than one', saying that it 'might be written under the principle of utility as an explanatory commentary'. Unfortunately, apart from the fact that it seems additional to the principle of utility itself, it does not seem to deal with all cases in which there appears to be a conflict between the demands of justice and the demand to maximize general happiness. However, the main thing that commentators have seen as distinguishing Mill's account of utilitarianism is that he offers what purports to be a proof of it. This is, briefly put, that as the only proof that something is visible is that it is seen, so the only proof that something is desirable is that it is desired. Many commentators have pointed out that 'visible' means 'can be seen', whereas 'desirable' means 'ought to be desired', and they have insisted that, apart from the equivocation which that fact makes clear, one cannot derive an 'ought' from an 'is'. G. E. Moore made particularly scathing comments on Mill on that score in his *Principia Ethica* (1903). Other commentators have sought to find something rather better in Mill's argument than appears at first sight, claiming, for example, that there is some connection between the fact that something is generally desired and its desirability. The argument still goes on and will no doubt continue to do so.

One final point about Mill – his discussion of the idea of political liberty in his short work *On Liberty*. Mill did not think that liberty was absolute, and he tried to set out a proper view of acceptable constraints on it. The answer, as Mill saw it, lies in whether the actions of the individual affect others or not. There should be complete liberty to do those things which are not other-regarding. Restrictions on liberty are acceptable only when harm would otherwise be done to others. Positive freedom consists in the liberty to exercise the desires which are genuinely one's own, and to pursue the development and course of one's own nature. Libertarians have found what Mill has to say here inspiring, although there are certain vaguenesses in it, and we are liable to be confronted with the question when and whether a certain course of action is other-regarding or merely self-regarding. How much of one's own action is really unrelated to others, and what does harm consist in? Should the law prohibit pornography? Are the practices of consenting adults in private totally self-regarding, or does the very example, for instance, affect others? These questions remain with us, however they are to be answered. Mill deserves every credit for trying to establish sure principles of liberty, but argument about them continues.

British absolute idealism

Meanwhile, Hegelianism was beginning to become fashionable in Britain, at a time when it was going out of fashion in Germany and was being replaced by neo-Kantianism, and even by an interest in the kind of epistemology that was typical of British Empiricism. To some extent, therefore, there was an exchange of philosophical roles between the two countries. Hegelianism found its home chiefly in Oxford, but because of local concerns and traditions it was a modified Hegelianism. On the whole, there was acceptance less of Hegelian methods than of its results. F. H. Bradley, for example, spoke of the 'bloodless ballet of the categories', and even denied that he was a Hegelian.

The first of the British Hegelians worthy of note is T. H. Green (1836–82), who was a Hegelian modified by Kant. He attacked the empiricist or sensationalist belief in atomic sensations, stressing that reality must involve relations, which are themselves contributed by the mind. That doctrine is close to that of the early chapters of Hegel's *Phenomenology*. Green also embraced the Hegelian view of the status of the state, as did also Bernard Bosanquet (1848–1923) in his *Philosophical Theory of the State*. Bosanquet also made contributions to logic along Hegelian lines, and was perhaps the most orthodox of the British Hegelians.

The greatest of the British Absolute Idealists was undoubtedly F. H. Bradley (1846–1924). His *Ethical Studies* (1876) is a collection of essays written in frank opposition to utilitarianism. Apart from a notable essay on the notions of free will, responsibility and necessity, he asserts that self-realization is the end of morality, and makes strong criticisms of both utilitarianism and the notion of duty for duty's sake. It is, however, the chapter entitled 'My Station and its Duties' which brings out his basic conception of morals. The self that has to be realized is one that does not stand by itself, but is part of a wider whole, which is the community to which the individual belongs. Each one of us is an organ in a moral organism. The echoes of Hegel here are obvious, although it is not set out in a Hegelian way. Apart from a number of essays on truth, reality and other subjects, Bradley's main works are the *Principles of Logic* (1883) and *Appearance and Reality* (1893). One of the crucial aspects of the former is its recognition of judgement, rather than ideas, as the unit of thought. In this respect Bradley can be set alongside Frege, the early Wittgenstein and others, but the conception really goes back to Kant. Moreover, Bradley came to think that he had not initially emphasized the point sufficiently and had thus allowed for the possibility of what he called 'floating ideas', a possibility from which he was discouraged by Bosanquet.

Bradley thought of judgement as involving the bringing of reality under ideas; the ideas provide the 'what' for which reality, or some part of it, is the 'that'. This means that there is a difference of category between reality and ideas; the latter have merely a predicative role and cannot, properly speaking, figure as subjects. The same point was made in a more logical guise by Frege, at about the same time. It is because ideas have this character that they cannot exist independently of judgement, and cannot be 'floating'. Bradley used this thought in order to criticize Mill and the associationists, for whom ideas are quasi-substantial entities.

Indeed, he set himself against Mill in various ways, arguing, like Green, that reality cannot be made up of discrete sensations, and that association, as he put it in one of his papers, 'marries only universals'. Despite all this, Bradley held that it is the aim of judgement to bring reality completely under ideas and thus to identify the two. But this is impossible because such an identity must always be an 'identity in difference'; the gap between the 'that' and the 'what' cannot really be bridged. For this reason he held that in the end judgement cannot be true to reality.

He argues at length for this conclusion in the *Principles of Logic*, and the argument turns on the point that, as far as judgement is concerned, there is no possibility of an identification of reality or a part of it except by reference to ideas. He presents a classification of judgements, and argues that in the case of none of them, not even those which he calls 'analytic judgements of sense', which purport merely to analyse immediate experience, can a judgement be unconditionally true. That is to say that the best that can be done by means of judgement is to state the conditional truth that if reality is characterized in such and such ways it must also be characterized in such and such other ways. As far as judgement, that is to say the understanding, is concerned, reality can be seen only in terms of interrelated ideas, and the relations in question are 'internal' – more than contingent and not independent of their terms, as external relations are. (The distinction is not dissimilar to that which Hume made between kinds of relation.) For judgement, reality is a system, and truth consists in the coherence of the elements of the system.

In *Appearance and Reality* Bradley goes further, arguing that the concepts that the understanding brings to phenomena involve incoherence and inconsistency. Hence, on the principle that the real is the rational, phenomena cannot comprise reality, and must at best comprise a low degree of reality. He argues for this by considering, first, the relation between things and their attributes, and second, the relation between attributes and relations. The first relation gives rise to the problem of the one and the many that Hegel discussed in the *Phenomenology*, the one difference being that Bradley attaches more importance to the idea that the unity of a thing may be brought about by the relations that relate its attributes. In this respect he uses an infinite regress argument, which has become known as Bradley's paradox of relations – the point being that if relations are merely attributes of their terms, those terms will not be independent of each other, and if they are terms themselves, they will need further relations to relate them to the original terms – and so on with those relations in turn. (It might be argued that Bradley does not take seriously the need for a category of relation, distinct from those of thing and attribute, but he is not entirely blind to that point.) Next he argues that attributes cannot be made sense of independently of relations and *vice versa*, but that they cannot be made sense of together with them either. I shall not go into the complexities of the argument. It has been suggested that the method owes more to the Plato of the *Parmenides* than it does to Hegel. However that may be, at the end of it Bradley concludes that 'our experience, where relational, is not true'. He then applies this conclusion to a number of aspects of phenomena, including space and time.

In the second part of *Appearance and Reality* Bradley argues that reality, by contrast, must be one (for it cannot involve the relations that would be entailed by plurality). We can be sure, however, that it consists of experience, because this was a presupposition of the whole argument. Reality somehow includes appearance, while transcending it. There are indeed degrees of truth and degrees of reality; no judgement is entirely false, but none is entirely true either. It is impossible to go into the complexities of Bradley's account of reality (which is far longer than the account of appearance). Because reality consists of experience Bradley is an idealist; but he is an Absolute Idealist, holding that reality, as experience, is an absolute – indeed *the* Absolute, because one. It is the object of a form of intuition akin to what Russell was to call 'knowledge by acquaintance'. Bertrand Russell began his philosophical life under the influence of idealism, but through G. E. Moore, who produced what purported to be a refutation of idealism, he became converted to realism. Nevertheless, the idea that there is something of which we can have knowledge by a form of direct acquaintance is common to him and Bradley.

Bradley dominated thought at Oxford for some time, but in many ways his theory is the swan song of Hegelian idealism. In Cambridge, J. E. McTaggart (1866–1925) wrote on Hegel, but put forward the thesis of Personal Idealism, according to which reality consists of a community of selves. This entailed a rejection of Bradley's argument against the reality of relations, because a community depends on relations. The selves are spirits who 'prehend' each other, loving what they 'prehend' with a love that is complete. This view is spelled out in his vast two-volume work *The Nature of Existence*. McTaggart was not a monist as Bradley was, and he held that the elements of reality are ordered by what he called the 'C-series', the terms of which arise from and include their predecessors.

The part of McTaggart's philosophy which has attracted most interest, however, is an argument to prove the unreality of time. The argument turns on an analysis of time in terms of A-series and B-series, which McTaggart tries to show are incoherent; they are, as it were, distortions of the C-series. The A-series is the series of events ordered in terms of tense, in terms of past, present and future; the B-series is the series of events ordered in terms of before and after. McTaggart argues that the B-series is temporal only if derived from the A-series, and that every event in the A-series is past, present *and* future. To anyone who objects that in fact an event *is* present, *was* future and *will be* past, or that it can be supposed that every event has all three incompatible characteristics of past, present and future only by ignoring the tense of the verbs used to ascribe them, McTaggart says that this only involves reintroducing the idea of the A-series (for the tenses are past, present or future). We thus invoke the A-series in order to explain it, and we cannot avoid being involved in an infinite regress if we expect otherwise. The argument brings out many of the difficulties involved in understanding tense and time, and has fascinated many later philosophers. Apart from this, however, McTaggart had little influence on others, although in 1933–8 C. D. Broad wrote a long *Examination of McTaggart's Philosophy*.

In Oxford, idealism eventually gave way to a form of Aristotelian realism under J. Cook Wilson (1849–1915). A late example of the influence of idealism is provided by R. G. Collingwood (1889–1943), who began life as something of a Hegelian, but became preoccupied with the philosophy of history and aesthetics, in a way that was parallel to the course taken by the Italian idealist Benedetto Croce (1866–1952). Both philosophers emphasized history in preference to natural science, and argued that it was impossible to ignore the historical context in which a philosophical question arises. Collingwood was an ancient historian and archaeologist as well as a philosopher. He set out his ideas on history most directly in a posthumous work, *The Idea of History*, claiming that the aim of the historian should be to think himself into the situation of the historical characters with whom he is concerned. In *The Idea of Nature*, also published posthumously, he claims that it is impossible to get a clear view of what is involved in theories about nature except historically. The theory behind this is to be found in his *Essay on Metaphysics* (1940), in which he says that every proposition exists only as an answer to a question; and every question rests upon a presupposition, which may be relative to other questions. There must, however, be absolute presuppositions, and it is the task of the metaphysician to discover them even though, as absolute presuppositions, they cannot be demonstrated. Absolute presuppositions may vary according to their historical period; what is absolute is therefore still historically relative. Hence, history is for Collingwood all-pervasive, and in *The Idea of History* he acknowledged Croce's influence upon him in these respects. Like Croce, too, he made contributions to aesthetics, maintaining in *The Principles of Art* (1938) that art, which is to be firmly distinguished from craft, consists in expression.

Pragmatism

In America idealism had as its main proponent Josiah Royce (1855–1916), but in a somewhat individualistic form, which the British idealists thought deviationist. He nevertheless presented a target for attacks by other American philosophers, particularly William James (1842–1910), the main figure in American pragmatism. James acknowledged a great debt to J. S. Mill, but behind him lay also C. S. Peirce (1839–1914). Peirce held a university position for only a short period, and he was relatively unknown during his lifetime. It was only when his papers were collected and published in the 1930s that his stature became evident. His philosophy was a strange mixture of different elements. He was a logician who made important contributions to formal logic, particularly the logic of relations. Many of his views in this area were similar to better-known ones which were put forward elsewhere. This is particularly true of his account of the 'if . . . then' propositional form, which he characterized as the 'illative relation'; he explained it in the same way as Russell explained what *he* called 'material implication', namely that 'If p, then q' merely means that it is not the case that p is true and q is false. He also made contributions to the theory of meaning within a general theory of signs. But, in his later years in particular, he engaged in speculative metaphysics, putting forward a theory which he called 'tychism', according to which in the world as we have it there must be chance events, although the world is evolving towards a 'perfect, rational, and symmetrical system', even if in the 'infinitely distant future'.

The most important aspect of Peirce's thought historically is his account of the criteria to be satisfied for meaningful ideas. In a paper entitled 'How to Make our Ideas Clear', he emphasized the 'practical bearings, we conceive the object of our conception to have'. The meaning of a sign, he later suggested, is to be determined by the rational conduct to which it gives rise. This view, which he called 'pragmatism', attempts to determine meaningfulness in terms of rational usefulness. William James, in his *Pragmatism* (1907), took over the idea but applied it, although none too clearly, to truth itself, so producing the so-called pragmatic theory of truth: that the truth of a proposition is a matter of the useful results that it leads to. This idea was taken further by John Dewey (1859–1952), who interpreted truth in terms of 'warranted assertibility', so assimilating truth to verification. Dewey also took over another Peircean idea, that of 'fallibilism', the idea that one should recognize that one may always be wrong, and that truth is an ideal limit to which one may only tend. Dewey's views have had an immense influence on education in the U.S.A., but comparatively little influence elsewhere.

William James was not only a philosopher but also a psychologist. He held posts at Harvard in both subjects at different times. His *Principles of Psychology* (1890) is a classic attempt to plot the geography of the mind in terms of the various mental functions performed by a human being. In it, James emphasizes the individuality of consciousness, and the idea that there is such a thing as a presentation or *Vorstellung* that could be common to more than one mind is anathema to him. Consciousness is based, he suggests, on 'feelings'. Nevertheless he is opposed to the sensationalist tradition in at least one respect. In the chapter of the *Principles* on the 'stream of thought', he puts forward five principles concerning consciousness, including the statement that consciousness is concerned with objects independent of itself. The most important of these principles, however, are the second and third, in which he insists that within each personal consciousness thought is always changing and yet is 'sensibly continuous'. In this he rejects the idea that consciousness can be 'chopped up into bits', as sensationalists supposed. Consciousness is like a stream or river, although there are pauses amongst the general flux. It is, he says, changing the metaphor, like a bird's life, an 'alternation of flights and perches'. For continuity of this sort to be possible, he maintains, there must be feelings of relation and feelings of tendency, and each state of consciousness stands in a 'fringe' of such relations, which he calls a 'psychic fringe'. The psychic fringe of one state may overlap with that of another, so providing the impression of continuity. The self, James says elsewhere in the *Principles*, is to be identified with the passing thought.

James came to stress this theory even more in his later life, when he concluded that he had not been radical enough in his empiricism in allowing a distinction between thought and its objects. In his *Essays in Radical Empiricism* (published in 1912, after his death) he claimed that we need to posit only pure experience, and that knowledge can be explained in terms of the relation of one part of pure experience to another. In coming to this view he was much influenced by Bergson, whom he took as urging him to 'dive back into the flux'. Within this context, James thought, pluralism was easily sustainable. Bradley's argument against the relations which made that possible was the product of a false intellectualism, which failed to take proper account both of experience and of life. James's empiricism is sensationalism with a difference; it tries to derive everything from experience, but refuses to accept the idea that that experience comes 'chopped up into bits'.

There are other aspects to James's thought, including his early essay on 'The Will to Believe', which stressed the human tendency to go beyond the evidence, and *The Varieties of Religious Experience* (1902), written in something of the same spirit. The most influential aspect of his thought, however, was the pragmatism. Apart from Dewey, C. I. Lewis (1883–1964) shows the great influence of that trend of thought. Lewis made considerable contributions to logic, but philosophically, as is revealed in his most influential work, *Mind and the World Order* (1929), he is concerned to plot the relation between the mind's ordering principles or categories and the 'given', without supposing that the 'given' can be determined independently of those categories. The proper applicability of a category can be decided only by reference to the future course of experiences. Lewis was also a Harvard man, and something of the same philosophical spirit, although with modifications, was handed on, as we shall see later, to W. V. Quine (1908–   ) at Harvard.

Bergson

Although James was influenced by Henri Bergson (1859–1941), they reached their conclusions independently. Bergson's first work, *Les Données immédiates de la conscience* (1889, translated in 1910 as *Time and Free Will*), is an attempt to argue against what he sees as the spatialization of time that takes place in physics, in favour of the continuous flow of time as it appears to consciousness. He therefore distinguishes between *'le temps'* (the spatialized time of physics) and *'la durée'* (the time of consciousness). The latter, as opposed to the former, involves development. The events that make it up are unrepeatable, and there is a continuity between them, looking towards the future. The similarity of this idea to that of James's 'stream of thought' is obvious. Bergson says that the items of consciousness form a continuity through a mutual interpenetration (an idea akin to James's 'psychic fringe').

Bergson came to think of the drive towards the future that consciousness manifests as due to a vital spirit (*élan vital*). In *Matter and Memory* (1896) he emphasized the idea that what we discriminate in the world around us is a function of our bodily needs; consciousness is inversely proportional to the tendency of the body to react automatically to a stimulus. In perception we tend to project on to objects an image of them which is a function of the possible movements of our body in relation to them. Hence there is in Bergson a general tendency to see human beings and their relation to the world in terms appropriate to the fact that they are organisms, and thus in terms which emphasize life.

Like James, Bergson wished to oppose those who emphasize intellectualism instead of life. In *Creative Evolution* (1907) he tried to view the whole universe in developmental terms parallel to those which he had invoked to account for consciousness. The whole universe is to be seen in historical terms, and every stage of it is a development of what has gone before. Every cosmic event, like every conscious event, is unique in that it brings its total history with it. It cannot be repeated, because no other event can have the same history. The situation over the universe is similar to what holds good over the life of an individual. Hence, the emphasis on life appears here too.

Appendix – Mach

The philosophers with whom I have been concerned in this chapter do not form a neat whole. They belong together, apart from the fact that they occupied a single period of history, in that behind them all lies the sensationalism of the Mills and of other philosophers in the nineteenth-century empiricist tradition. They form part of a series of reactions and counter-reactions to that. I mentioned earlier that there tended to be in this period an interchange of philosophical roles between Britain and Germany. This is typified by Ernst Mach (1838–1916), whose *Analysis of Sensations* (1886) tried to analyse everything in terms of sensations or elements belonging to an ego. But Mach belongs chiefly to the history of positivism; he criticized Newton's views on space and time for their lack of empirical content, and the so-called 'logical positivists' of the 1930s looked back to him because of this. Einstein also admired Mach, but in that respect he belongs to another important strand of twentieth-century philosophy, the philosophy of science. I shall make some references to that in the next chapter, but simply as part of one of the two philosophical movements which seem dominant in our century: analytical philosophy, and phenomenology.

[17]
Analytical Philosophy

The title of this chapter is misleading, in that I intend to consider a series of philosophers, only some of whom would have thought of their aims as mainly analytical. In any case, we can with hindsight see that even those who explicitly set out their conception of philosophy as one concerned with analysis were not just concerned with that, any more than Hume, for example, was. A few years ago it was often said that in the early years of this century there occurred a philosophical revolution; such claims have worn a little thin, although the later Wittgenstein's opposition, explicit or not, to Descartes involves a new way of thinking, one which is as important in our time as Descartes' was in his. Both in this chapter and in the next I shall begin with nineteenth-century philosophers who probably would not have seen themselves as part of the movements which I shall discuss as deriving from them. It will also be necessary to make one or two digressions.

Frege
Gottlob Frege (1848–1925) is another philosopher who had comparatively little recognition in his lifetime, although he was respected and admired by Bertrand Russell and Ludwig Wittgenstein. In one way he belongs to a group of people who were concerned with the development of formal logic and the philosophy of mathematics. Attempts to breathe new life into formal logic had begun earlier with George Boole (1815–64), and mathematicians such as Georg Cantor (1845–1918) were interested in the foundations of mathematics. Frege's first work, *Begriffschrift* (*Concept-Writing*, 1879) was an attempt to put forward a new notation for logic which would give it a much wider basis than Aristotelian logic and could be used to deal with issues in the philosophy of mathematics. As a notation it was not a success, but it signalled a complete break from traditional logic. *Die Grundlagen der Arithmetik* (*The Foundations of Arithmetic*, 1884) attempted to show that arithmetic could be derived from the laws or axioms of a system of formal logic; this involves the so-called logistic thesis that arithmetic, and thereby mathematics in general, could be derived from logic.

This programme was carried further in his *Fundamental Laws of Arith-*

metic (*Die Grundgesetze der Arithmetik*, 1893–1903). (Bertrand Russell attempted a similar programme in *The Principles of Mathematics* (1903), and carried it through more comprehensively and formally in *Principia Mathematica* (1910–13), written together with A. N. Whitehead.) In 1902 Russell wrote to Frege pointing out a contradiction in Frege's theory, which he himself tried to deal with by reference to ancillary principles, to the detriment of the elegance of the theory. In any case, in 1931 Kurt Gödel proved that mathematics is incomplete and that there are arithmetical truths which are unprovable within any consistent logical system. This put an end to the logicist programme. However, the philosophical insights that came with the attempts to develop that programme remain.

There is, first, the definition of number. Frege's insight is that numbers belong to concepts (Russell said they belonged to classes). It is not that numbers are properties of concepts, although numerical predicates apply to things only in so far as those things are ordered under a concept (something that Plato appears to have seen). Frege holds that numbers are objects, and the number that belongs to the concept *F* is, on his definition, the extension (range of application) of the concept *equal to the concept* F. The point is as follows. Two sets or classes of objects ordered by the concepts *F* and *G* can be said to be equinumerous if their members can be brought into one–one correspondence – something that, as Frege shows, does not itself presuppose the concept of number. Frege asks what it is to say that the number which belongs to the concept *F* is the same as that which belongs to the concept *G*, and answers along the same lines; it is to say that the extension of the concept *equal to the concept* F is the same as that of *equal to the concept* G, that is, the classes that form their extension have the same number of members. (Analogously, Russell said that five was the class of all quintets, and a number the class of all classes similar to a given class.) Frege then defines zero as the number which belongs to the concept 'not identical with itself' (there being, of course, nothing which is not identical with itself). Having defined zero, then given the notion of succession, which is definable in logical terms, it is possible to determine all subsequent numbers.

The account which I have given is not easy to follow. Russell's version may be easier to follow than Frege's, but it is Frege who has the precedence. It is a remarkable achievement. The flaw that Russell discovered in it lay in the fact that it was possible to produce a paradox over the notion of the class of all classes by asking whether the class of all classes which are not members of themselves is a member of itself or not; if it is then it is not, and if it is not then it is. The possibility of producing that paradox seemed to cast doubt upon the very notion of a class of all classes. Frege tried to deal with the problem by restricting his theory; Russell introduced a theory of types, which is similar to a theory of categories in forbidding us to put things from different types on the same level. Russell's paradox and his 'solution' generated interest in a whole range of paradoxes of analogous kinds, and in the question how they are to be resolved.

Frege was opposed to what he called 'psychologism' – the interpretation of logic in psychological terms. Logic is concerned with propositions, and it is therefore important to be clear what propositions are and what is the status of the terms that make them up. In *Foundations of Arithmetic* he laid down that one should ask for the meaning of a word only in the context or nexus of a proposition. It is propositions that constitute the fundamental units of meaning. He was later to say that the sense of a proposition is a thought, so that it is thoughts, in the form of judgements, which are the starting point for any theory of meaning.

To give an account of propositions Frege had recourse to the mathematical notion of a function. In the expression of a function such as $2x^2+x$ the function is whatever is picked out by the part of the expression that remains when we take away the argument letters, the xs. By comparison with the argument of a function the function itself is incomplete, and the argument place has to be filled in to achieve completeness. Frege put this in his paper 'Function and Concept'[1] by saying that functions are 'unsaturated'. Functions have different values for different arguments. Propositions can be construed as functions which have the values True or False, and so can be termed truth-functions.

The argument of a propositional function corresponds to an object; the expressions that have to be substituted for variables in order to get the value True or False have to be taken as referring to objects. By contrast the function part of a proposition does not refer to an object, but to a concept, which is logically quite different. Frege expounds this distinction in his paper 'On Concept and Object'. He also points out that if we use the expression 'the concept *horse*' we shall have referred, because of the nature of the expression, to an object, with the paradoxical result that the concept *horse* is an object, not a concept. However one thinks the paradox is to be resolved, it is clear that it arises from treating the *terms* 'object' and 'concept' as terms like any other, whereas they have the special role of picking out the different categories of things presupposed in giving sense to a proposition.

In his paper 'On Sense and Reference' Frege goes further into questions concerning meaning. He starts from the observation that 'The morning star is the evening star' and 'The morning star is the morning star' are

[1] Included with other papers in *Frege: Translations* by P. Geach and M. Black (Oxford: Blackwell, 1952).

both true identity statements; the terms in each refer to the same thing, but the first proposition is informative whereas the second is not. Frege suggests that one can explain this only by distinguishing between the sense and the reference of expressions. The sense of a complete proposition is a thought; its reference must be the True or the False, that is its truth-value. The sense of the whole proposition, the thought, is given by the senses of the parts and their method of combination. In order to proceed from sense to reference, that is, to determine the truth or falsity of the proposition, we need to know the reference of the parts.

Frege goes into considerable detail about how this works in various cases, particularly when there is what he calls indirect reference, as in 'Copernicus believed that the planetary orbits are circles', for in that case the reference of what follows the 'that' is determined by the references of 'Copernicus', 'planetary orbits' and 'circles', whereas the reference of the whole proposition is not so determined. Copernicus could have had that belief whether or not it was true. In such cases, Frege says that the reference of the sub-clause is a thought, that is, its sense. Whether or not this account is satisfactory, there can be no doubt that the problems with which Frege is trying to grapple are important.

We have seen in certain previous chapters that some philosophers have taken the subjects and predicates of propositions to stand for objects of one kind or another, which are their meaning. I have not so far referred to subjects and predicates in connection with Frege, but they correspond in fact to arguments and functions. Given this, it is clear that for Frege predicates go with concepts, so that it is a complete mistake to look for objects to which they refer. The distinction between concept and object is fundamental. Moreover, Frege sometimes speaks of the sense of an expression as the mode of presentation of its reference. Since propositions have the primary role as units of discourse and their reference is the True or the False, this gives truth and falsity an important place in the theory of meaning put forward – an idea of which much has been made by recent philosophers. On the other hand, it might well be thought that Frege relies on a dubious analogy in assimilating propositions to functions, and that the theory of meaning espoused is still over-simple, in spite of its advantages over the theory that the meaning of expressions is simply their reference. Argument on these points continues, but Frege's reputation stands higher today than it ever did in his lifetime.

One further point – by 'concept' Frege did not mean anything that goes on in anyone's mind; and the same applies to 'thought'. These terms have to do with a realm of public meanings. In some of his later writings he was to speak of the existence of a realm of entities between physical objects and mental entities, and it was to this realm that concepts and thoughts belong. But this is merely a picturesque way of putting the point that the meaning that propositions and terms have is something publicly accessible, without their being physical. Frege did not ask how that was possible. His contributions to philosophy, however important, were still limited. He did not doubt the real existence of things outside the mind, but he was not interested in further epistemological or metaphysical questions about that. His most recent commentator, Michael Dummett (1925–), has seized on that as an indication of the primary importance of philosophy of language, but that is a disputable matter.

Russell

Bertrand Russell (1872–1970) had wider interests. Earl Russell, as he became in 1931, was a member of a distinguished aristocratic family. He went to Trinity College, Cambridge, to read mathematics, switched to philosophy and subsequently became Fellow of Trinity for a time, returning to it in 1944. In between he taught at Cambridge for certain periods, and visited other universities, particularly in the U.S.A. He was a pacifist during the First World War, and in 1918 spent six months in prison as a result. He was a man of exceptional brilliance – some might think too much so – and his attention was drawn to many things, both in his personal life and in social and political affairs. His work for the Campaign for Nuclear Disarmament towards the end of his life is well known, and he wrote many books on matters which are not strictly philosophical. It is arguable that the best of his philosophy appeared when he was still young, and he was certainly disappointed about the lack of enthusiasm for his last substantial book, *Human Knowledge* (1948).

Russell's first book, his fellowship dissertation, was on the foundations of geometry, and appeared in 1897. It showed the influences of the idealism that was dominant at the time. Russell turned to realism, partly under the influence of G. E. Moore, whom I shall consider in the next section, and partly because he came to believe that idealism could not explain mathematical truth. *The Principles of Mathematics* (1903), preceded by a book on Leibniz, introduced the programme of logicism which I mentioned in connection with Frege, and held to an extreme form of realism according to which anything that could be the possible reference of a term, even non-existent or logically impossible entities, had being in some sense. Russell associated this with the views of Alexius von Meinong (1853–1920), to whom I shall return in the next chapter. He came to think that the view lacked a sufficiently robust sense of reality, and his subsequent writings in this area – the monumental *Principia Mathematica*

(1910–13), written in collaboration with A. N. Whitehead, and the more popular but far from easy *Introduction to Mathematical Philosophy* (1919), written while in prison in 1918 – moved in the opposite direction, even to the extent of denying the reality of classes.

The crucial step in that move was provided by his theory of descriptions, put forward in a paper entitled 'On Denoting' in *Mind* 1905 (and reprinted many times). It was referred to by F. P. Ramsey (1903–30), himself a distinguished philosopher in this area, as a 'paradigm of philosophy'. It has also been said that this and his theory of types were his great contributions to philosophy. I have mentioned the theory of types in speaking of Frege, and I shall not discuss it further; it has something in common, considered as a philosophical theory and not merely as the solution to a technical problem, with other philosophers' theories of categories.

The problem that led to the theory of descriptions was the apparent possibility of referring to non-existent entities. This was a particular problem for Russell because he took it that the meaning of a term is whatever it refers to, the only qualification being that different sorts of terms refer to different sorts of entity. Russell did not accept, or apparently even understand, Frege's distinction between sense and reference, and tended when discussing Frege to reinterpret the distinction in his own terms. There is in his view a particular problem over so-called denoting phrases such as 'The present King of France'. It does not appear meaningless to say that 'The present King of France is bald'; yet if we say that it is false, we could be taken to imply that the present King of France is not bald, whereas the crucial point is that there is no present King of France.

Russell's solution was to say that the apparent form of such a proposition is not what he called its logical form, and that to understand the proposition we need to analyse it so that its proper logical form is revealed (and with this the idea of logical analysis makes its appearance). That logical form is made clear by saying that 'The present King of France is bald' is equivalent to 'There is an x, such that x is now King of France, and for all y, if y is now King of France, y is identical with x, and x is bald'. This analysis makes explicit the assertion of the existence of a present King of France, of the uniqueness of such an individual, and of his possession of the property baldness. When analysed the proposition can be seen to be false, although not in the way contemplated in its unanalysed form.

In discussing a similar issue in 'On Sense and Reference' Frege said that propositions such as the one which we have been considering *presuppose* the existence of something corresponding to the denoting phrase, and if the presupposition is not justified the question of their truth or falsity does not arise. But he went on to suggest that, as a technical device, one could take such phrases as referring to the null-class. The former suggestion was possible on Frege's view because a proposition could have a sense without having a reference. Because he held a different theory of meaning, that move was not open to Russell. When a view similar to Frege's was put forward in 1950 by P. F. Strawson on the basis of a theory which connected meaning with the possible use of expressions, Russell reacted with incomprehension, claiming that Strawson had missed the point.

In the interval, however, the theory of descriptions had been invoked in connection with other views and given other applications. In particular, Russell insisted that there must be what he called logically proper names, expressions such that their reference is guaranteed, with objects corresponding to them. He believed them necessary because thought, as expressed in language, could not otherwise have any firm grasp on reality. Ordinary names are not like that, and in consequence Russell said that ordinary names are really disguised descriptions. The only logically proper names are words such as 'that', 'here' and 'now' (which are not names at all on their ordinary construal). These are 'egocentric' in their use, in that they presuppose the point of view of the person who uses them. The later Russell put a premium on 'egocentric particulars'; earlier he took sense-data to be primary because of certain epistemological views.

These epistemological views showed the influence of the British Empiricists. In *Our Knowledge of the External World* (1914) he argued that physical objects are, as he put it, logical constructions out of actual and possible sense-data (the latter to be called 'sensibilia'). To say this is to say that propositions concerning physical objects can be analysed into propositions concerning actual and possible sense-data. The motive behind the analysis, as revealed in some of the essays in *Mysticism and Logic* (1917), was his acceptance of a maxim which was his version of Occam's razor – that, wherever possible, logical constructions are to be substituted for inferred entities. In a masterly introduction to philosophy, *The Problems of Philosophy* (1912), Russell had thought of physical objects as entities inferred from sense-data; his empiricism now made that objectionable. Russell retained those empiricist leanings throughout his life, but had doubts whether empiricism was tenable in every area of knowledge. Mathematical truths could not be derived from experience – they were analytic – but that is a view common to most twentieth-century versions of empiricism, unlike that of Mill. Russell had greater doubts about the principles which underlie induction, and at the end of his philosophical life, in *Human Knowledge* (1948), he set these out as indicating the limits of empiricism.

Nevertheless, *The Problems of Philosophy* provides in many ways the essential Russellian epistemology. It does this, in particular, in a chapter concerned with a distinction between knowledge by acquaintance and knowledge by description, both of these being concerned with knowledge of objects, as opposed to propositional knowledge or 'knowledge that'. Russell supposes that we have knowledge by acquaintance, certain and indubitable knowledge, of sense-data, memory-data, ourselves, and universals (the last perhaps a curious relic of his earlier Platonism, and a view that he gave up later). William James had in his *Principles* made a distinction between acquaintance and knowledge about, and had claimed that the first object of acquaintance for the child is the whole universe, even if he knows nothing about it. That view is not as implausible as it might seem at first sight, but it does not in any case presuppose anything about the indubitability of acquaintance that Russell presupposed. In making claims to that, Russell was setting himself up in clear opposition to the views of idealists such as Bradley, who denied that sense-experience provided anything that was immediate.

Russell took the contrary view, and so have most other twentieth-century empiricists, although sometimes with misgiving. More importantly, perhaps, Russell set out as a fundamental axiom that every proposition that we can understand must be composed entirely of constituents with which we are acquainted. By 'proposition' he did not mean anything like a sentence, but what a sentence might describe as a possibly (though not necessarily) existing state of affairs. Such a state of affairs, therefore, must either consist directly of objects of acquaintance or be analysable into ones that do so consist. Since objects of acquaintance include universals, it is relatively easy to see how anything that can be said can be expressed entirely in terms of objects of acquaintance related to each other in some way. Just before the First World War, Russell came into contact with the young Wittgenstein, who had come to see him about problems in the philosophy of mathematics. Wittgenstein was already beginning to think along lines which saw the light of day in the only book published by him in his lifetime, the *Tractatus Logico-Philosophicus* (1921). The influence was mutual, and in 1918 Russell published some articles on 'The Philosophy of Logical Atomism', deriving from this contact, in the journal *The Monist*.[1] In these articles, which were based on lectures, he presented an ontology consisting of particulars, to be identified with sense-data, standing in relations of varying orders of complexity.

These particulars and relations form facts of different kinds, and prop-

[1] These were eventually republished in *Logic and Knowledge*, ed. R. C. Marsh (London: Allen and Unwin, 1956).

ositions – now taken as equivalent to statements – are related to facts by meaning them either in a true way or a false way. Particulars are, he says, terms of relations in atomic facts, and complex facts are built up from atomic facts by logical relations. There are problems over negation, and even greater problems over belief-statements, as Frege saw too. Russell thinks that one has to recognize these as a distinct kind of elementary proposition. He invokes the theory of descriptions and the theory of types to deal with certain problems, and ends with a section entitled 'Excursus into Metaphysics: What There Is', in which he raises the question of the status of the sense-data which are the elements of reality. Like Hume he wants to conceive of minds and bodies as constructions out of sense-data, and so he proposes that sense-data should be conceived of as neutral between the mental and the physical – the doctrine of neutral monism which he attributes to James and Mach. The only doubt concerning the acceptability of that theory arises, in his view, from the recalcitrant case of beliefs. For these seem to be mental, and belief-statements, as we have seen, cannot be analysed into further elementary propositions. Russell wondered whether it was possible to give a behaviourist account of beliefs, which would enable them to be analysed in terms of physical processes, and thereby in terms of sense-data. After the war he went to America, where he was influenced by J. B. Watson, the originator of behaviourism as a psychological theory; and the next book to appear, *The Analysis of Mind* (1921), duly presented a behaviouristic account of belief.

So much for a very thumb-nail sketch of what is in many ways Russell's central work. What he wrote thereafter had nothing like the same coherence and status, even if we take into account *The Analysis of Matter* (1927) and *An Enquiry into Meaning and Truth* (1940). 'The Philosophy of Logical Atomism' is also very readable, with evidences of Russell's puckish, if somewhat donnish, sense of humour. One additional thing should be noted about the work, because of its bearing on the views of the later Wittgenstein. Despite what is said about neutral monism in its last section, sense-data are said in the second section to be such that they constitute different objects of acquaintance for different people. They are in that sense private, and Russell draws the consequence that people must mean different things by what they say, since the meaning of their words, what they refer to, is ultimately these private sense-data. It is, he says, the ambiguity of language (although it is of course no ordinary ambiguity) which makes intercourse by language possible. Wittgenstein was to take this, quite rightly, as a *reductio ad absurdum* of the thesis that a language could get its meaning in this way.

Moore and other realists

It was G. E. Moore (1873–1958) who did the most to promote the move from idealism to realism in this country. He was immensely influential, although it is now becoming a little difficult to see why. There is something almost child-like in Moore's philosophical attitudes. He said towards the end of his life that he thought that the only philosophical problems which had concerned him were those suggested by things that other philosophers had said. He also claimed not to be much affected by sceptical considerations. Indeed, Moore seemed constantly concerned to remind us of things that just seemed to him true. He gave up the view that the objects of beliefs are propositions which happen to be true or false, mainly, he said in *Some Main Problems of Philosophy* (lectures given in 1910–11, but not published until 1953), because 'there do not seem to be propositions at all, in the sense in which the theory demands them'. In 'A Defence of Common-Sense' (in *Contemporary British Philosophy*, 2nd series, 1925) he set out, like Reid, to defend common sense by appeal to what seemed to him its obvious truth. In 'Proof of an External World' (*Proceedings of the British Academy*, 1939) he suggested, in a way that was thought by some to be almost scandalous, that he could prove the existence of the external world by holding up his hands and saying 'Here is one hand' and 'Here is the other'. It was as if obvious truth was enough, without any attempt to answer other philosophical arguments to the contrary.

Moore's central concern was the analysis of what we mean by these things, although he denied that philosophy was just analysis. In his view, it is concepts that require analysis, and the analysis of them consists in producing other concepts which together amount to the concept to be analysed, but which are not explicitly mentioned in the expression of the original concept. But he was never really happy with this account and he said that it gave rise to a paradox of analysis. If, for example, we analyse the concept of a brother in terms of the concept of a male sibling, the two expressions 'brother' and 'male sibling' must mean the same, although the two propositions 'A brother is a male sibling' and 'A male sibling is a male sibling' are not the same. The problem is reminiscent of, but not the same as, Frege's problem about the morning star and evening star. It is not the same because Frege was not concerned with the idea that an analysis was being provided by saying that the morning star is the evening star. If there is a genuine problem here it lies in the notion of analysis itself. The idea of the analysis of concepts implies that concepts can be broken down into other concepts in the way that chemical compounds can be broken down into elements. That is a questionable conception.

The explanation of a concept may be provided in a variety of ways, but there is surely no one way which is its analysis.

Nevertheless, Moore clung to this view of philosophy throughout his life. His early attacks in *Principia Ethica* (1903) on attempts, such as those of Mill, to explain goodness in terms of the production of pleasure or happiness, rested on the view that *good* is unanalysable. Moore also thought that the analysis of what we mean when we speak of perceiving an external world must be in terms of the occurrence of sense-data, although he remained puzzled as to whether sense-data were or were not parts of the surfaces of physical objects. Moore did not embrace the notion of sense-data, as Russell did, because they were indubitable objects of knowledge by acquaintance, although in introducing the notion of sense-data in *Some Main Problems* he speaks of them as what we directly apprehend. He did not invoke them, however, in order to provide the foundations of knowledge; he simply thought that we must invoke them if we are to analyse what we mean in speaking of perception of the world.

Given all this, it may seem surprising that he had the influence that he did. It originated in two ways: in his move to realism, and in his conception of ethics. In the last years of the nineteenth century Moore wrote papers expressing his dissatisfaction with the extent to which Bradley had freed himself from psychologism over the notions of an idea and judgement. He thought that Bradley had not made it sufficiently clear that the issues are not about what goes on in individual minds but about what those ideas and judgements *mean*. What we know and believe, Moore said, are propositions, and these involve concepts – all independent of what anyone in particular thinks. I have noted already that Moore later gave up this idea of propositions, but he did not give up the belief in a reality independent of minds. Moreover, in 'A Refutation of Idealism' (1903; included in his *Philosophical Studies*, 1922) he attacked Berkeleian idealism and the proposition that to be is to be perceived, insisting that there is a distinction to be made between, for example, yellow and a sensation of yellow. Sensations are all forms of consciousness, but one must not confuse this consciousness with their objects, which may be different. To have a sensation of red is to be aware of something red, and the awareness is different from the redness. Much of this refutation of idealism, with which Moore later expressed dissatisfaction, is an appeal to something we are being called upon to recognize as obviously true. It is not a refutation of idealistic *arguments*.

Much the same can be said of *Principia Ethica*. In it, Moore says that the task of ethics is to inquire into the nature of goodness. He holds that 'good' is a simple, unanalysable, non-natural quality, and asserts that philosophers who have tried to analyse it in terms of pleasure or some such natural quality have committed what he calls the 'naturalistic fallacy'. Moore is not altogether clear what he means by 'non-natural', except that a non-natural property is not to be identified with any properties that objects have in the nature of things. He believes that 'good' is simple because there is an analogy between it and 'yellow'; it cannot be broken down into other, simpler, properties into which it is to be analysed. The attempt to define 'good' in natural terms is thus a fallacy, and the same applies to supposed *definitions* of 'good' in any other terms. If you define 'good' as '*x*', it always remains an open question whether *x* is good.

Moore accuses philosophers who try to define 'good' of wanting incompatible things. They want to recommend *x* as good, but also want to say that '*x*' is all that 'good' means. That accusation holds, however, only if Moore's opponents really do want to maintain both that it is synthetic that *x* is good and that it is analytic. (Moore suggests that this was true of Mill, but it is far from clear that this is the case.) Otherwise, as other philosophers have tried to show, the naturalistic fallacy would be simply a case of what has been called the 'definist fallacy'. Moore says that if you define good as pleasure, then in saying that pleasure is good you will be saying only that pleasure is pleasure. But is it the case that if you define a brother as a male sibling, then in saying that a brother is a male sibling you will be saying only that a male sibling is a male sibling? The problems involved in the paradox of analysis arise here.

Other philosophers have presented other diagnoses of why 'good' cannot be defined in naturalistic terms – for example, that this will omit the evaluative element in 'good'. Moore's account of 'good' as a simple unanalysable property leaves it quite obscure why anyone should act on the judgement that something is good. Although this part of Moore's moral philosophy acquired some fame at the time, its reputation has worn a little thin.

Fortunately, he said other things in *Principia Ethica* and in the later, smaller, book *Ethics* (1912). He gave an account of the rightness of actions in terms of the production by them of the greatest balance of good over evil, and he was in that respect an 'ideal utilitarian'. He claimed that the goodness or badness of a whole need not be a function of the goodness or badness of the parts, there being what he called 'organic wholes'. He also claimed that the greatest intrinsic goods of this kind involve aesthetic enjoyment and personal relations. This view was welcomed and taken as a guiding principle by the so-called Bloomsbury Group, who, deriving from a society at Cambridge called 'The Apostles', took Moore as their mentor and high-priest. In *Ethics* he also discussed the problems of free will in terms of the question whether we can do something if we choose. But he expressed uncertainty on whether that was enough for free will or whether one ought to ask as well whether we can choose. Much of this discussion, apart from the final uncertainty, has a parallelism to Schopenhauer's, although it is doubtful whether Moore knew of that.

Moore influenced those with whom he came into contact, including both Russell and Wittgenstein. To some extent that must be because he was ever ready to see problems. Without reference to those influences it is doubtful whether, in the long run, his reputation will persist. The influences, however, are beyond question.

It is convenient at this point to enter upon what is, from the point of view of analytic philosophy, a digression, and to consider two philosophers who attempted to produce systems of metaphysics in a non-idealistic tradition. There was, first, Samuel Alexander (1859–1938), whose *Space, Time and Deity* (1920) had some reputation in its day, but is probably now almost totally unread. Alexander claimed that philosophy must be descriptive and at one point even said that he disliked arguments. Alexander was influenced by biology and experimental psychology, but in attaching importance to the notion of space-time in his book he asserted that he had reached his conclusions about it independently of Einsteinian physics. His philosophy embraces a doctrine of emergent evolution. Space-time is the stuff from which emerge matter and things, then living things and mind, at which stage there is consciousness of objects from a point of view, consciousness itself being something enjoyed, not contemplated. Deity is the next stage in the process, and things tend towards this. Apart from the difficulties of understanding what Alexander has in mind in this, it is not a view which many would find attractive today.

A. N. Whitehead (1861–1947), the second of the two philosophers whom it is pertinent to mention, is not much read in this country either, although in North America 'process philosophy', as it is called, has had something of a vogue in certain places. Whitehead began as a mathematician; he cooperated with Russell on *Principia Mathematica*, but subsequently drew apart from him. He produced a number of books, including *The Principles of Natural Knowledge* (1919) and *The Concept of Nature* (1920), which attempted to set out a new philosophy of nature, from which the theory of relativity was to be derived. He put great emphasis upon the relatedness of things, and was opposed to any form of atomism, even one of the Russellian kind. Human beings are natural organisms related organically to the world in which they live, and perception is what he calls the 'prehension' of a part of the environment to which the perceiver is so related. He was to develop this view further, and he tended to think of other relations between things in the same terms. Hence what he calls the 'philosophy of the organism'. He took it to follow that the exact notions of mathematics, especially notions such as those of a point or instant, have no place in our experience, however much they are needed in science. They are nevertheless to be defined in relation to experience by what he called the method of 'extensive abstraction' – approximately the inverse of the idea of a logical construction.

Perhaps the most important of Whitehead's ideas in this connection is his notion of events. Events have duration, and so do not occur at an instant. Whitehead thought that they were, so to speak, the stuff from which nature is formed. They are particular, and as with Bergson, although perhaps for somewhat different reasons, unique. 'Objects' stand in relation to events in something of the same relation that Platonic Forms stood to the flux of the sensible world. They constitute the permanent features of nature, and the relation between them and events is put by Whitehead by saying that they are 'ingredient into events'. The location of an 'object' extends indefinitely into its neighbourhood, to the extent that the events in question are related to other events. This brings in the idea of a system, and in his later works he explicitly said that his aim was to give a realist basis to some of the doctrines of the Absolute Idealists. Events or processes nevertheless form the stuff of the system. Hence the notion of 'process philosophy'.

Whitehead and Alexander admired each other, and both tended to present their view of things as something which the reader is called upon to accept, or at least to see as a possible description of the world. Whitehead moved to London from Cambridge in 1910, and became Professor of Applied Mathematics at Imperial College, London, in 1914. But in 1924, at the age of sixty-three, he took up the post of Professor of Philosophy at Harvard, where he remained for the rest of his life, retiring formally in 1937. Of the books which he produced there, *Science and the Modern World* (1925) and *Adventures of Ideas* (1933) have achieved some currency and popularity, but his main work of the period, *Process and Reality* (1929), which devotees take as *the* Whitehead work, has seemed to non-devotees utterly impenetrable.

Certainly one needs a considerable readjustment of one's ordinary categories to understand Whitehead. Even what I said earlier about the relation between events and objects requires a considerable shift of thought from traditional ways of thinking. 'Objects' are not to be construed as substances; they are the persistent features which come together in an event, so giving rise to the idea of persistent substantial things, in very much the same way as, according to Plato, the flux of the sensible world gains order and a *quasi*-permanence by being brought under Forms. Whitehead is indeed responsible for the remark that the history of philosophy is a set of footnotes to Plato. That is not really true, but there are ways in which his own philosophy is that.

Despite some recalcitrant idealists, such as H. Joachim (1868–1938) in Britain and Brand Blanshard (1892–) in the U.S.A., realism in one form or another was the dominant philosophy of the period up to the Second World War. There were the so-called 'New Realists', particularly R. B. Perry and E. B. Holt in the U.S.A. There were C. D. Broad in England at Cambridge, and J. Cook Wilson, H. A. Prichard and H. H. Price at Oxford. They had little in common except an opposition to idealism. Prichard (1871–1947) is best remembered for a transposition of Moore's views about 'good' to 'ought' and 'duty', maintaining that we know by intuition the principles which prescribe what we ought to do, and that any view to the contrary was liable to confuse morality with expediency. This view was elaborated in a modified form by W. D. Ross (1877–1971), a distinguished Aristotelian scholar, who argued that moral principles prescribe what he called *prima facie* obligations – ones which hold other things being equal – so that we have to decide between them to arrive at what is right overall.

Looking back to this period from our present position, it is now possible to see that the most important contributions to philosophy of a more or less analytic kind were made by Wittgenstein. To consider his philosophy, it is necessary to distinguish between the early and the late Wittgenstein. Between considerations of these two I shall say a little about the Logical Positivist movement, which took part of its inspiration from his earlier philosophy, whether rightly or not.

The Wittgenstein of the Tractatus

Ludwig Wittgenstein (1889–1951) was an Austrian of a distinguished family who eventually became a naturalized British citizen. He first studied aeronautical engineering, and came to Britain in 1908 in that connection. He was, however, interested in the foundations of mathematics and in 1911 Frege advised him to see Russell, which he did, making contact with Moore also. During the First World War he served in the Austrian army and was taken prisoner in 1918 on the Italian front. From there he sent his *Logisch-Philosophische Abhandlung* to Russell. It was published in a journal in 1921, and was re-published in Britain as *Tractatus Logico-Philosophicus*, with a parallel English translation by C. K. Ogden, in

1922. It was re-translated by D. F. Pears and B. F. H. McGuinness in 1961.

After the war he took up life as a school teacher in an Austrian village, adopting an ascetic way of life, and giving up philosophy. Members of the so-called Vienna Circle of Logical Positivists came to consult him, however, and he eventually decided that there was more philosophy to do, returning to Cambridge in 1929. He taught there to a somewhat exclusive band of followers, becoming Professor of Philosophy in succession to Moore in 1939. He spent most of the Second World War, however, as a medical orderly in a hospital, and when he returned to Cambridge he decided that he disliked the life and resigned from his Chair in 1947. He spent some time in Ireland, then discovered that he had cancer and died in Cambridge in 1951. During most of his life he wrote down remarks and sometimes more discursive pieces, much of which has been published since his death. But apart from the *Tractatus*, the only book that he contemplated as publishable was the *Philosophical Investigations*, the first part of which, at any rate, was more or less complete when he died. The whole of it was published in 1953 in German, with a parallel English translation by G. E. M. Anscombe.

There has been much argument concerning the background of Wittgenstein's philosophical views. The influences of Russell and Moore are evident; he knew Frege and other German thinkers, but he did not acknowledge that he had much other knowledge of traditional philosophy. The internal evidence of his notebooks reveals that he had read Schopenhauer and some William James; he may well have known more. The *Tractatus* has something in common with Russell's logical atomist thinking, but does not have the same epistemological interests. It is a fascinating but cryptic work, written in the form of numbered propositions. There are seven propositions prefixed by whole numbers, the others being prefixed by numbers with added decimal places, the number of decimal places supposedly giving some idea of the importance of the proposition in relation to those in the same numbered grouping.

Some idea of the content of the work can be given by reference to the propositions prefixed by whole numbers. The first says that the world is all that is the case, the second that what is the case, that is, a fact, is the existence of states of affairs. The third, which is preceded by remarks about the picturing of facts, says that a logical picture of facts is a thought. The fourth says that a thought is a proposition with sense, and the fifth says that propositions are truth-functions of elementary propositions, which are truth-functions of themselves. The sixth proposition gives what purports to be the general form of a proposition *via* the formulation of a general operation which will produce truth-functions of other propositions. Finally, the seventh, after some remarks about the impossibility of their being propositions of ethics and aesthetics, and some remarks about death, life and mysticism, says, 'What we cannot speak about we must consign to silence.' The previous remark acknowledges that by his own criteria all earlier propositions are nonsensical, and are to be used merely as steps to climb beyond them.

It is impossible to go into all the complexities of the *Tractatus*. The last proposition implies, and preceding remarks make clear, that what can be thought can be said. Hence, if metaphysics is the attempt to set out the nature of reality as it reveals itself to thought, the key to that, in Wittgenstein's view, lies in language. Hence the emphasis on that in the earlier parts of the work. The primary function of language is to state what is the case, so that it is the latter that makes up the world or reality. What is the case comprises, at bottom, a number of simple states of affairs, which are made up of simple objects; and these are represented by elementary propositions. The way that this is done (and Wittgenstein thought of this as his discovery) is by the propositions being in some sense pictures of states of affairs. The constituents of the propositions are names which refer to objects, and the way in which the names are put together in a proposition is in some way a reflection of the way in which the objects go together in a state of affairs. This is the so-called picture theory of meaning. Propositions, construed in this way as representing possible states of affairs, are true if they represent the actual facts, and false otherwise. But because there is the *possibility* of their representing states of affairs, they have a sense which is independent of the facts as they actually are.

In all this, Wittgenstein is in effect saying that names, the constituents of propositions, have a reference in the Fregean way, but they do not have sense; propositions have sense, but do not have reference in the way that Frege supposed. Nevertheless, it is a condition of propositions', and thus language's, having sense at all that there must be simple objects for there to be names of. There must in turn be elementary propositions, which consist simply of names in concatenation, and which do not stand in any logical relation to any other elementary propositions. Complex propositions, on the other hand, are built up from elementary propositions by means of a single logical operation, and it is evident that, if this is so, all complex propositions must be truth-functions of elementary propositions. That is to say that their truth or falsity must be a function of the truth or falsity of the propositions from which they are derived, and of that alone. Extreme cases of this are provided by tautologies and contradictions which are, respectively, true and false no matter what the truth-values of the sub-propositions. Such propositions say nothing, because they do not picture any distinctive state of affairs; they are thus without a sense, although they are not nonsensical.

In an introduction to the *Tractatus* Russell said that Wittgenstein was trying to set out the conditions for an ideal language. This is not true. Wittgenstein thought that language must actually be like this in its analysed form; it had to be, or it would not have sense. That language is like this is not apparent from ordinary language, because the complexity of the latter serves to disguise the fact. The object of philosophy is to clarify our thought by means of the clarification of propositions. That clarification, Wittgenstein thinks, reveals that the propositions of logic and mathematics are all tautologies, that solipsism is in a sense true, although it is coincident with realism, and that metaphysics, including all the propositions of the *Tractatus* itself, together with ethics and aesthetics, are, strictly speaking, nonsensical. That this is so, Wittgenstein thought, does not undermine their importance. We have, as the last few propositions of the work indicate, to use them to see the world aright, in recognizing the unsayable.

There is far more to the *Tractatus* than I have indicated, and I have not attempted to make clear exactly why Wittgenstein says many of the things that he does say. It is an extraordinarily compressed work, and if the reader is to understand it at all he must read and reread it with the help of the commentaries that are now available. Wittgenstein became dissatisfied with it himself during the 1920s. He became unhappy with the conception of language as something like a logical calculus, and with the idea that there are names which get their meaning by direct correlation with simple objects. It is a matter of argument how much of the *Tractatus* remained in his later thought. It used to be believed that he gave it all up, but that is now often disputed. Certainly many of the problems that produced the *Tractatus* remained with him.

Logical positivism

I have already indicated that while he was a schoolmaster Wittgenstein was visited by a group of philosophers who called themselves the Vienna Circle. They were led by Moritz Schlick (1882–1936), who possesses what one hopes is the very rare distinction of being assassinated by a student. Other members of the group were Otto Neurath (1882–1945), Friedrich Waismann (1896–1959) and Rudolf Carnap (1891–1970), but there were originally fourteen in all. These published a manifesto on their aims, and there were others elsewhere, including Hans Reichenbach (1891–1953) and Carl Hempel (1905–   ), who were sympathizers. In Britain, A. J. Ayer (1910–   ) was later the representative of the movement. The Circle split up when Austria was invaded in 1938, and many of the philosophers and distinguished mathematicians and scientists attached to the Circle sought refuge elsewhere. Many of them emigrated to the U.S.A. and undoubtedly affected the course of philosophy there; this was particularly true of Carnap.

Many of the members of the Circle had originally been scientists, and much of their inspiration went back to Mach. They were generally anti-metaphysical. *Tractatus* 4.024 says that to understand a proposition means to know what is the case if it is true. This does not actually say that to understand a proposition is to know what would verify it, but it is close to it. The Vienna Circle asserted that the meaning of a proposition was its method of verification. At least, that is what Schlick claimed and it is implicit in the assertions of others. The history of the logical positivist movement is largely a history of arguments about what it means. But they were agreed that all meaningful propositions must be either logically necessary (that is, analytic) or verifiable in some way by reference to experience. Propositions which fail that test are to be put down as meaningless – and with that goes the whole of metaphysics. Science, on the other hand, had to be preserved, and much of the debate, or certainly that arising from Ayer's *Language, Truth and Logic* (1936), was concerned with finding a version of the verifiability principle which excluded metaphysics but did not exclude science or anything else that they wanted to save. Argument over this has shown that it is difficult to achieve this aim, if not impossible. In any case, a rather simple objection is that one has to understand a proposition before one can go about deciding how it is to be verified. That would affect the original positivist slogan, but it might be held that it bears only indirectly on the claim that only logically true or empirically verifiable propositions are meaningful. What, however, is the status of the principle of verifiability itself?

Questions such as this were discussed almost *ad nauseam* during the heyday of logical positivism. It is clear, however, that if empirical propositions are to be verified by reference to experience, some account must be given of experience itself and of the claim that it can directly provide the verification of statements describing it. Are there any propositions that are directly verifiable by reference to experience and without reference to anything else? That raises all the traditional questions about immediacy. In the positivist movement the issue was generally raised in the form of whether there are any basic or protocol propositions on which all other propositions might be based, and if so what was their nature. In Ayer's early philosophy this amounts to the question whether there are propositions about immediate experience, about sense-data, which are incorrigible because they are verifiable by direct reference to experience alone. Ayer himself has vacillated on this point, and indeed on other issues involved in positivism.

There were other problems. Schlick thought that one had in the end to compare propositions directly with experience, but that what was being ascertained in that comparison could not be put into words. Neurath rejected that idea, asserting that one could compare statements only with statements. Hence the acceptability of any empirical proposition, basic or not, is a matter of whether it fits into the system of propositions. Neurath thus accepted a coherence theory of truth and a notion of system which is more like that of the idealists. This did not please all members of the group, although Carnap too was eventually driven in that direction.

Carnap's first main philosophical work, *Der Logische Aufbau der Welt* (*The Logical Construction of the World*, 1928), was an attempt to show how all the apparatus needed to describe the world could be built up in logical fashion from the series of experiences comprising a person's experiences at a given moment. The basis was thus in a sense solipsistic, and Carnap referred to it as 'methodological solipsism', on the grounds that this point of departure was the one chosen as epistemologically basic for the exercise. He later abandoned this in favour of physicalism. In a later work, *Logische Syntax der Sprache* (*The Logical Syntax of Language*, 1934; English translation, 1937), an immensely difficult and technical work, he set out to show that what can be said by a language, including the language of science, can be said in a way *within* that language. A language is completely specifiable in terms of its formation rules and transformation rules. The first set of rules prescribes what counts as a proper sentence of the language, the second prescribes how one sentence can be derived from another. There is no need for semantic rules in addition to these; so semantics is reduced to syntax (a matter on which Carnap later changed his mind). There can be alternative language systems, and the choice between them is a matter of what he calls the principle of tolerance. Clearly coherence is one criterion for distinguishing between systems; beyond that it is a matter of what scientists happen to accept.

Carnap changed his mind on this because of Tarski's work on the definition of truth. Alfred Tarski (1902–) was a distinguished member of a group of Polish logicians; his paper, translated as 'The Concept of Truth in Formalized Languages', was written in 1933 and became known in the late 1930s. It has had immense influence on philosophers concerned with logic and philosophy of language. It is impossible to go into details about it here. Suffice it to say that it necessitated a distinction between an object-language and a meta-language in which statements about the object-language can be made, including statements to the effect that what is said in the object-language is true.

Tarski actually spoke of sentences, rather than statements, but the most important part of his theory, which he asserted was a version of the correspondence theory of truth, was what is called 'Convention *T*'. This set up the conditions for adequacy of a definition of truth – to the effect that it must have as consequences all equivalences of the form '*X* is true if and only if *p*', where *X* is a sentence in the object-language and *p* is its translation in the meta-language. Tarski thought that it was possible to satisfy these conditions only in a formalized language. More recently, Donald Davidson (1917–) has argued that it is possible to use Convention *T* in relation to ordinary languages in order to produce a theory of meaning for them. At the moment the claim is programmatic only, and there is considerable doubt as to whether the programme can be carried out.

Tarski's theory of truth has been called a semantic theory because it relates truth to the meaning relations that exist between sentences in the meta-language and sentences in the object-language. Carnap seized upon this idea, and his later work is concerned with the formalization of semantics. The theoretical apparatus for this, for example in *Meaning and Necessity* (1947), involved something of a return to Frege and the distinction between sense and reference. At the end of his life Carnap also approached the theory of probability in the same spirit. He always maintained, however, a distinction between logical and factual truth, and this came under attack from W. V. Quine (1908–), whom I mentioned at the end of the last chapter. Quine's attack on the analytic/synthetic distinction in a paper entitled 'Two Dogmas of Empiricism' (included in his *From a Logical Point of View*, 1953), which was in part influenced by pragmatism, has been immensely influential in the U.S.A., but has had much less acceptance in Britain. I shall return to Quine briefly later.

Another philosopher who has been associated with logical positivism, although he has always hotly repudiated the categorization, is Karl Popper (1902–). Popper never embraced a theory of meaning of the positivist sort. He did wish, however, to distinguish science from metaphysics, without necessarily writing off the latter. In his *Logik der Forschung* (1934; translated as *The Logic of Scientific Discovery*, 1959), he emphasizes the notion of falsifiability, claiming that it is liability to falsification that marks off the scientific. Scientific procedure is not inductive, but involves putting forward the boldest hypotheses and attempting to falsify them. If a hypothesis survives falsification it is thereby confirmed, although confirmation is always a matter of degree, and absolute certainty is unobtainable. In this latter respect Popper's views are close to

Peirce's fallibilism, and the resistance to inductivism is reminiscent of Whewell. Many have been attracted by his picture of science and scientific discovery, although there are problems about the details. Whether it constitutes a 'logic' is another matter. That is an issue which has generated some heat.

Popper has attacked 'historicism' in the same spirit, and in *The Open Society and its Enemies* (1945) he produced a polemical criticism of Plato, Hegel and Marx, because in his view they attempted to lay down laws of historical development and advocated a 'closed society', the principles of which are supposed to be utopian and beyond criticism. More recently Popper has put forward an evolutionary account of the growth of knowledge, considered as something objective and independent of 'knowing subjects'. He has also (with J. C. Eccles) produced an elaborate defence of mind–body dualism. It is, however, in his contributions to the philosophy of science that Popper's claim to fame probably lies, and there can be no doubt that his is one of the great names in that area.

The later Wittgenstein

I mentioned earlier that towards the end of the 1920s Wittgenstein became dissatisfied with his earlier views. Since his death it has become clear that he made attempts at several books which would set out his revised views on a number of philosophical issues. Little of this was known during his lifetime, but his views and thoughts permeated the consciousness of other philosophers, partly through the writings of philosophers at Cambridge, particularly John Wisdom (1904–), and through the circulation of typescript copies of some lectures at Cambridge, known as the *Blue and Brown Books*. These, together with the text of other lectures and manuscripts, have been published since his death. The consequence of this was that during the 1930s, 40s and early 50s his views were known in detail to only a few. Philosophers such as Wisdom put out their version of them. Others showed, to one degree or another, the influence of a general Wittgensteinianism, without being direct followers. This is true, for example, of Gilbert Ryle (1900–76).

The *Philosophical Investigations*, the one work which by the time of his death he thought approaching readiness for publication, was eventually published in German, with a parallel translation by G. E. M. Anscombe, in 1953. It is not an easy book to expound. It consists of a series of remarks, some of which involve responses to a hypothetical opponent. The first part starts with considerations about names, language and alternative primitive languages, which Wittgenstein calls 'language-games'. It then deals with 'knowing how to go on', in connection with rules for the development of series, such as that of numbers. There is then a long section concerned with the naming of sensations, and what has become known as the 'private language argument'. After that there are a large number of remarks concerned for the most part with various concepts in the philosophy of mind, and a general preoccupation with what Wittgenstein calls 'the myth of the mental process'.

Part 2 is divided into a number of sections concerned with very much the same things, but there is one long section which has interesting things to say about 'seeing-as', such as our ability to see a puzzle-picture in alternative ways, and the implications of that for a number of other issues. The work concludes with critical remarks about psychology.

Other posthumous works have to do with things of similar kinds, with the foundations of mathematics, with the idea of the foundations of knowledge or understanding, with art and religion, and so on. Even if one restricts one's attention to the *Philosophical Investigations*, however, it is not easy to see its overall aim. Initially it clearly exhibits a revolt against the kind of view of language and meaning presupposed in the *Tractatus*. In a famous though disputed remark at section 43, Wittgenstein says that 'for a *large* class of cases – though not for all – in which we employ the word "meaning" it can be defined thus: the meaning of a word is its use in language'. Some of the language-games mentioned concentrate on the practical contexts of the use of language and raise questions about the conditions under which practical uses of signs really constitute the use of *language*. Wittgenstein emphasizes, indeed, the ways in which language figures in our lives. No doubt similar things are true of the section concerned with knowing how to continue a series. Some have seen that as presenting a certain scepticism about rules and rule-following, but Wittgenstein may simply be emphasizing the extent to which knowledge of how to follow a rule is embedded in behavioural and practical contexts and situations. Our understanding of the use of expressions in language presupposes such knowledge.

It is the section on the naming of sensations that has received the most attention, and there has been seen in it a revolt against, and a complete reversal of, the Cartesian framework. Wittgenstein contemplates someone keeping a diary in which he refers to the particular sensations that he has by name. This leads to a *reductio ad absurdum* of this practice, in a way that is meant to cast light upon the suggestion that we might come to an understanding of those sensations simply through consideration of our own case. It is plausible that what Wittgenstein has in mind is the sort of supposition that I noted in connection with Russell, who maintained that the meaning of the words we use is derived from the private sensations with which each of us is acquainted. Russell, it will be remembered, suggested that this made words ambiguous, but that it was only because of that ambiguity that we manage to communicate. Wittgenstein treats this as a *reductio ad absurdum* of the view that our understanding of the meaning of the words we use is derived ultimately from terms being directly related to private experiences, through a process of what is called 'ostensive definition' (a supposed definition by a direct correlation of words with objects).

He points to the fact that there are natural expressions of sensations such as pain, and that our verbal expressions of these sensations can be assimilated to these natural behavioural expressions. At times, indeed, he seems to be saying that what purport to be descriptions of our sensations are not to be taken as such, but as expressions of sensation akin to saying 'Ouch'. Whether or not that is so, he is certainly opposed to the suggestion that we can understand sensation-words, as he puts it in a famous passage at section 293, in terms of the 'model of "object and name" '. In that passage he supposes that people each have a box in which there is something to be called a 'beetle'; everyone knows what a beetle is only by looking into his own box. He suggests that the word 'beetle' would have a use in the people's language, on these assumptions, even if there were nothing in the box. That would equally be how it would be if we all understood what pain is only from our own case.

The moral to be drawn is that the understanding of sensation-language is not to be construed in this way – not, that is, in terms of the idea that the words for sensations get their meaning simply by referring to sensations as private objects. This is not to deny that there are such sensations; it is to comment on our ways of understanding how we speak of them. A condition of understanding sensation-language is that we should know the behavioural expressions of sensations, and this is something public, not private. It follows that we cannot build up our knowledge of the world from such sensations as its basis. The rejection of that idea entails the rejection of a long line of empiricist thought. That line of thought does not seem to be particularly evident in the *Tractatus*, which is not much concerned with epistemological considerations. It is evident, however, in Russell, and it is clear from other Wittgensteinian writings that Wittgenstein felt its pull. At I.580 he says, in another famous remark, 'An "inner" process stands in need of outward criteria.' What he meant by 'criteria' (a term that appears often in his writings) has been much debated, but the remark certainly emphasizes the necessity for a public context if the idea of an inner process is to be intelligible. That in turn casts doubt upon the whole Cartesian tradition in terms of which one has to start, in one's account of the world, from one's own case and one's own inner processes. The importance of that must not be underestimated.

There has been much discussion concerning all this, construed as a general argument about the possibility of a private language – the so-called private language argument. Some of Wittgenstein's remarks on the necessity for a public check upon the uses of language (something that would not be possible in the case of an intrinsically private language) verge on verificationism (although it is argued that that is not what he intends). At I.242 he says, 'If language is to be a means of communication there must be agreement not only in definitions but also (queer as this may sound) in judgements'; and the previous remark speaks of agreement in a form of life. Elsewhere in Part 2 (p. 226) he says, 'What has to be accepted, the given, is – so one could say – *forms of life.*'

Some have seen such remarks about forms of life, which are repeated elsewhere in his works, as somewhat mystical. But the point is really the same as the one which I have emphasized – human beings are biological entities embedded in a public world, and it is only relative to such a framework that questions of what is and what is not intelligible can be raised. Such questions cannot be answered by reference to such things as data provided by the senses or 'inner processes'. It is arguable that *On Certainty*, a late unfinished manuscript, is concerned to insist, within this framework, that certain things have to be accepted as true if other things are to be even intelligible. There seems to be a reference to 'limits' in this – limits to the understanding – which some have seen as Kantian (a notion which Wittgenstein could have derived through Schopenhauer). Others have insisted that Wittgenstein does not argue for limits which are absolute. He sometimes says that what he is doing is merely providing some remarks on the natural history of man.

There can be no doubt that the most important thing in all this is the insistence on the public context, and on interpersonal agreement, although one at the level of natural, biological, reactions and forms of behaviour. As we shall see in the next chapter, other philosophers in this century have emphasized the role of the body and of being in the world. It is arguable that Wittgenstein's philosophical position is more fundamental than theirs, because he points not just to the importance of these things, but to their *necessity* if we are to make sense of anything else. The underlying argument is, one might say, transcendental in roughly the Kantian sense. The trouble is that Wittgenstein did not think that it was the task of the philosopher to provide such arguments. 'What is your aim in philosophy?' he asks at I.309, and answers, 'To shew the fly the way out of the fly-bottle.' John Wisdom saw his aim as close to that of psycho-analysis, and his philosophy as therapeutic in that sense. Wittgenstein might well have repudiated that particular suggestion, but his aim is nevertheless to come to a correct understanding of things, removing mental cramp, obsession with certain particular cases and conceptual puzzlement in general.

Throughout his life Wittgenstein rejected the idea that philosophy was concerned to produce theories statable in propositions. He did not always say the same thing about what was to be put in its place, but the method that he followed, if there was one, does not make it easy for the commentator to speak with any conviction of 'transcendental arguments'. All the same, if remarks such as the one about forms of life constituting the given are to be taken seriously, his views on meaning and understanding entail a drastic reassessment of the terms of reference for philosophy, particularly epistemology, from those laid down by Descartes and never seriously questioned since. The kind of gestures towards public institutions and practices made by Marx are still within an idealist tradition. If Wittgenstein is right, that whole tradition should be abandoned.

Other recent analytical philosophers

There have been other attacks on the Cartesian tradition in modern times, although not perhaps in quite the same spirit. Gilbert Ryle's *Concept of Mind* (1949) is an attempt to provide a non-Cartesian account of the mind in terms of intelligent behaviour and dispositions towards that. The account is officially built upon a doctrine of categories and category mistakes, which are held to produce various kinds of nonsense. Ryle's thesis is that what Descartes says about the mind involves putting the mental into the wrong category, in that he takes the mind to be a substance functioning as a para-mechanical cause. In fact, Ryle says, to speak of the mind is really to speak of a set of dispositions possessed by intelligent beings. Taken as an interpretation of Descartes this lays emphasis upon only one aspect of Descartes' views. Ryle plays down the idea of inner processes in favour of dispositions to behaviour. Many have seen his views as behaviouristic, although he himself rejected that interpretation, saying that this was evidence of another category mistake. Some of the influences upon Ryle are Aristotelian, others Russellian, but his insistence that we should consider 'what we say' in attempting to elucidate concepts is probably derived from Wittgenstein. Ryle certainly thought that ordinary language had to be taken seriously.

Ordinary language philosophy, as it became known, was taken further by J. L. Austin (1911–60), who in certain rather programmatic papers insisted on the necessity of a close examination of ordinary usage, on the grounds that it contains the inherited wisdom of mankind in thinking about the world. Some critics saw this as a kind of linguistic conservatism, although Austin insisted that ordinary language was the begin-all, not the end-all, of philosophy. In some part, this approach owed its inspiration to Aristotle, who regularly emphasized what is said and how it is said. Ordinary language philosophy was the dominant movement in Oxford for some time. An emphasis upon 'use' and upon the idea that an account of our understanding of the world can be developed from what is implicit in speaker-hearer identification of things, where speakers and hearers are persons, is also to be found in P. F. Strawson (1919–). In his thought, however, there is a return to a metaphysics of a Kantian sort, with the addendum that it is important to recognize the role of the concept of a person, which the concepts of the mind and the body both presuppose. This is spelled out in his *Individuals* (1959), and in what is more overtly a commentary on Kant, *The Bounds of Sense* (1966).

Strawson has also been a critic of formal logic, and in this respect his great opponent has been W. V. Quine, mentioned earlier. Quine began as a formal logician, and has always been influenced in his thinking by logic. I have already referred to his attack upon the analytic/synthetic distinction. It is a two-fold attack. One prong claims that one can make no good sense of the notion of sameness of meaning that the idea of analyticity presupposes; the other claims, historically quite wrongly, that the dogma of the analytic/synthetic distinction goes together with the idea that there are, at the opposite pole to logical truths, basic propositions of the kind postulated by some of the positivists, the meaning of which is given solely by the empirical facts. In place of all this Quine puts forward a view which is due in part to P. Duhem (1861–1916), a notable French philosopher of science, who emphasized the interconnectedness of hypotheses within a theory. Quine represents knowledge as a systematic body of interrelated propositions, such that only those at the periphery are ones that we are willing to give up or modify in the face of apparently falsifying evidence; they are still related to the body of theory, however, and do not have the status attributed by empiricists to basic propositions.

Quine has put forward views on ontology and on language in something of the same spirit. The aim should be to so 'regiment' our language that it becomes clear what ontological presuppositions are involved in it, the hope being that all apparent references to abstract entities can be removed. Quine has gone on to insist that all ontological claims are relative to the language which we speak, and has maintained that the interpretation that we put on what people say must be similarly relative. The most important thesis in this is that of the indeterminacy of translation, first set out in his *Word and Object* (1960) and repeated in several other writings. Quine takes for granted a behaviouristic psychology, and for that reason interprets attempts to understand what other people (and thereby also ourselves) say in terms of attempts to interpret their behaviour. To interpret is to present a theory, and at this point the Duhemian thesis becomes relevant again, in the form of the claim that theories are always underdetermined by data. Quine maintains that there cannot therefore be just one way of translating what someone says, and alternative but conflicting ways of doing so are possible. He combines this with the thesis that reference is 'inscrutable'; there is no fact of the matter about what is being referred to in what someone says. For this reason too there is no fact of the matter about ontology, because the question what there is amounts to the question what can be referred to. Finally, Quine urges us to replace traditional epistemology with what he calls 'naturalized epistemology', the cognitive psychology of the acquisition of knowledge.

Quine has had great influence upon American philosophy, though perhaps less, until recently, on philosophy in Britain. Other important American philosophers are Donald Davidson (1917–), Hilary Putnam (1926–) and Saul Kripke (1940–). Most of these American philosophers have been concerned with logic and philosophy of language, and to some extent with philosophy of mind and action. American philosophy tends to be technical, and the influences on philosophy of science and mathematical logic are greater than they generally are in Britain. No doubt this is in part due to factors that have to do with the American culture and educational system; it may have something also to do with the influence of those philosophers, mostly logical positivists, who went to the U.S.A. as refugees from Europe.

It cannot be said that ethics has exactly prospered during this period. During the heyday of positivism there were attempts to explain ethical propositions in terms of expressions of emotion or emotional excitations. R. M. Hare (1919–) has emphasized the point that ethical statements involve prescriptions and he has attempted to pinpoint their particular ethical content in terms of the idea that the prescriptions in question are universalizable. This apparently Kantian idea has subsequently been taken by him as leading, somewhat surprisingly, to a form of utilitarianism. Most of the debate among recent moral philosophers has indeed been between defenders of some form of utilitarianism and those who wish to embrace a theory closer to that of Kant. In the U.S.A., John Rawls (1921–) has, in his *A Theory of Justice* (1972), attempted to derive a theory which combines liberalism and the idea of justice as fairness from a consideration of what people would choose in what he calls 'the original position'. In this they are under a 'veil of ignorance', so that they do not know of the characteristics they possess or will possess which are relevant to the distribution of goods. The account has received much discussion and some criticism. It has, more recently, been opposed by the somewhat anti-liberalist and certainly anti-egalitarian views of R. Nozick (1938–) in his book *Anarchy, State and Utopia* (1974). And so it goes on.

[18]

Phenomenology and Allied Movements

Brentano and Meinong

The philosophical movement which, in continental Europe, has been parallel to the analytic tradition in Britain and America goes back to Franz Brentano (1838–1917). He was an Austrian priest, trained in scholasticism and well versed in Aristotle. He wrote on a large number of philosophical issues, including ethics, but is now best known for his *Psychology from an Empirical Standpoint* (1874). Apart from his effects upon other German-speaking philosophers, he also had some influence upon the philosopher–psychologist G. F. Stout (1860–1944) in Britain. Brentano advocated a form of descriptive psychology, which is what the term 'empirical' in his title means. He was to some extent influenced by J. S. Mill, but did not accept his views concerning sensations and ideas. Indeed, according to Brentano the nature of the mind is determined by a number of mental acts. By 'act' he meant to bring out the idea that the mind is directed towards certain kinds of objects. He distinguished three kinds of 'act' of this sort – representation, judgement and what he called 'the phenomena of love and hate'; these form a hierarchy in that the later members of the trio presuppose the earlier.

The most important aspect of his views, however, was his attempt to define mentality in terms of the *kind* of object to which these acts 'tend'. For these purposes he resurrected the scholastic notion of an *intentio animi*, the tending of the mind towards an object. Such objects have 'intentional *in*-existence', in that they have an internal relation to the act and do not exist except in that relation. If we judge something, the judgement, as an object of the act, exists, no matter whether there exists any actual state of affairs or situation corresponding to the judgement. The relation that holds between us and the object of our judgement in such a case is not, as Brentano saw it, a real relation, and it is this that he wanted to convey by speaking of the in-existence of the object. Brentano thought it was the characteristic of what was mental, and of nothing else, to have such inexistent objects. In recent times there have been attempts to put all this in a more logical dress, and then to ask whether what is so provided does constitute a necessary and sufficient condition of the mental. It has been suggested that other things, apart from the mental, satisfy the same condition, and that it is not clear, in any case, that all mental events do meet the condition. It is not evident that sensations do so, for example.

Nevertheless, Brentano's ideas turned out to be very influential, although more attention has been paid in the long run to the idea that consciousness involves some form of directedness to an object than to what Brentano said about those objects. Immediately, however, that was not so. The first philosopher to be influenced by him was Alexius von Meinong (1853–1920), whom I mentioned as affecting Russell. Meinong *was* primarily concerned with the objects of mental acts, and he thought that these should be distinguished from the content of those acts, criticizing Brentano for confusing the two. In this he was influenced by a Polish philosopher, K. Twardowski. He accused Brentano, in effect, of 'psychologism' – of confusing ontology with psychology. Brentano in turn hotly rejected the accusation, saying that all that Meinong – and following him, Husserl – were doing was reviving an ultra-realism over universals and the like. Whatever the truth on that, Meinong thought that the content of a mental act must be a feature of the act itself, and so part of psychology. It is different with the object of the act. This can on some occasions be a physical thing, but it does not have to be; it is a mistake, he suggested, to confine objects to the realm of the actual alone. Some objects of thought, like round squares, do not and cannot exist; they are still objects, and so are things such as golden mountains which could exist but do not. Hence objects can either exist or not exist.

Objects of thought which are dependent on other objects, such as relations between objects or things which depend on such relations, *subsist*; they do not exist, but they are none the less real. Subsistence applies also to what Meinong calls 'objectives' – which are, roughly, what sentences and beliefs are about. They correspond to the objectively existing propositions which the early Moore thought were the objects of beliefs. For Meinong, an objective can be the object of a supposal as well, and whether it then amounts to a fact is an additional question. Indeed Meinong seems to have maintained that the factuality of an objective is independent of whether anyone has ever judged it to be a fact, and is a function of the objective's having the quality of 'evidence'. Truth, on the other hand, depends on someone's actually maintaining it. But evidence, or what might perhaps be better called 'evidentiality', the self-intimating character of an objective, if it is to amount to a fact, is quite independent of anyone's recognition of it. This distinction between truth and fact is a rather curious one.

Meinong's objectivism appealed to the early Moore and Russell, and, as I have already indicated, their propositions were not very different from Meinong's objectives. Both philosophers came, however, to reject such ideas, Moore on the grounds that he did not think there were any propositions in this sense, Russell on the grounds that 'Meinong's jungle', as it came to be called, did not reveal a sufficiently robust sense of reality. Most philosophers in English-speaking countries know of Meinong only through Russell (in spite of J. N. Findlay's *Meinong's Theory of Objects* (1933) and, more recently, Reinhardt Grossman's *Meinong* (1974)). Of his main works, *On Supposals* (1902) has recently been translated into English, but most of his works remain untranslated.

Husserl

The situation is different with Edmund Husserl (1859–1938), although his views have received more attention in the U.S.A. than in Britain. His main works are available in English, and it is at least possible for English-speaking philosophers with no knowledge of German to get some idea of Husserl's philosophy, even if it does not enable them to understand why it has come to be the dominant movement in Europe.

Husserl began as a mathematician, but came under the influence of Brentano, and his first work, *The Philosophy of Arithmetic* (1891), was an attempt to derive arithmetic and logic from psychology. This came under considerable criticism from Frege, and thereafter Husserl became an opponent of 'psychologism', although not quite in the same way that Frege was. In the *Logische Untersuchungen* (*Logical Investigations*, 1900–1), which Husserl rewrote in 1913, when he had to some extent changed his point of view, he attacked the empiricist view of logic of the kind that one finds in J. S. Mill, claiming with justification that it is impossible to derive meanings from the purely psychological experiences on which such empiricists rely. But Husserl did not see logic as purely formal either, and other parts of the *Logical Investigations* have to do with such things as the relations between whole and part, relations which are said to inform objects as they reveal themselves to consciousness, and have a necessary character. Husserl claimed that in order to get clear about these matters it is necessary to use what he called the 'phenomeno-logical method'. Originally he regarded phenomenology as a form of descriptive psychology, although not, as against Brentano, an empirical one; but he gradually came to see it as independent of any merely psychological considerations. It is in fact clear that this must be true of it if the objects of phenomenology are to stand in any necessary relations.

In *Ideas* (1913; English translation 1931), he first set out the method of *epochē* (a term derived from the Greek Sceptics, who used it to refer to suspension of belief). Husserl describes what he takes to be involved in this in terms of the notion of 'bracketing off'. It is necessary when considering any phenomenon to bracket off the presuppositions with which we come to it, and thereby to try to see it as it is in itself. What we shall then see is an essence which is an object of intuition for us. Hence the aim of phenomenology is to provide such intuitions of essences – the *noemata* of which consciousness is a *noesis*. Husserl came later to think that this view was incomplete; it did not provide an adequate theory of the relation of these essences to the ordinary world in which we find ourselves. He therefore urged the acceptance of what he called 'transcendental phenomenology'; this was to have the same relation to the sciences as he saw them as Kant's transcendental philosophy had to the science of *his* day. Within this framework bracketing was given a more radical role, and in *Cartesian Meditations* (1931) he used bracketing with a similar end in view to that of Descartes' method of doubt. We have to bracket off the actual world and try to arrive at something which cannot be so bracketed off. In this way we shall see that consciousness itself is the one absolute. Consciousness may presuppose an ego, but it is a transcendental ego, and transcendental phenomenology is an account of the internal objects of the consciousness of such an ego.

All this reveals an increasing tendency towards a form of idealism, following the traditional German pattern. This alienated some followers of his earlier thought, but persistent Husserlians have denied that the developments in Husserl's thinking had this kind of outcome. In some of his later works (for instance, *Formal and Transcendental Logic* (1929), *The Crisis of European Sciences and Transcendental Phenomenology* (his last published work, 1936), and a compilation of writings, edited by Ludwig Landgrebe and published in 1938 after Husserl's death, called *Experience and Judgement*) there is considerable use of the notion of the 'life world'. This might be thought to have some similarity to Wittgenstein's notion of forms of life, and to be used in an analogous way. The similarity is not, however, as close as it may seem at first sight. Certainly Husserl suggests that what he calls the 'pregiven world', the world of sense-perception and science, is derived from the 'original life world', but this in turn is derived in some way from 'subjective operations' – a very unWittgensteinian idea.

There is some similarity between Husserl's thinking and the 'genetic epistemology' of the psychologist Jean Piaget (1896–1980), although Husserl did not understand the processes of derivation which I have mentioned in a temporal sense, so that they could have to do with the development of the individual. The account is meant to be transcendental in a more Kantian sense. It is clear, or relatively clear, from what I have said, however, that Husserl thought of the world as in some sense a construction. This idea has permeated a good deal, though not all, of subsequent European philosophy. It has also had a profound influence on some sociological thinking, particularly through Alfred Schutz (1899–1959), although he, after migrating to the U.S.A., acknowledged also the influence of the social behaviourist G. H. Mead (1863–1931). (Despite the differences between Schutz's background and Mead's, their thought has in common the attempt to argue from the 'I' to the 'we' (the social world), and from that to everything else.[1]) The same Husserlian influences are evident in the 'critical theory' of Jürgen Habermas (1929–) of the Frankfurt school, though in his case a great deal is derived from the 'Hegelian' Marx also, so that there is an emphasis on praxis.

Heidegger

The most immediate influence of Husserl, however, was on Martin Heidegger (1889–1976), a pupil of his, who succeeded him in the Chair of Philosophy at Freiburg in 1928. Heidegger had an association with the Nazi party, and through that influence became Rector of Freiburg University for a while, before resigning in 1934. Disciples of Heidegger have attempted to excuse the association with Nazism and his use of it to obtain authority in the University of Freiburg. It may be that he was appalled by what he considered to be the anti-cultural tendencies in a technological society, and saw the Nazis as concerned to assert the old culture and Germany's mission in that respect. If so, he was profoundly mistaken. Unfortunately, the kinds of attitude that led him to accept Nazism – at least until he saw that it did not quite exemplify the pursuit of the aims he wanted – remained with him even in his later works. Many have seen in his thought profound observations on the position of man in contemporary society; it is just as easy to see it as the continuation of German romanticism, and some of Heidegger's own accounts of the history of philosophy, especially his references to Nietzsche, tend to confirm that impression.

Heidegger's main work, *Sein und Zeit* (*Being and Time*, 1927), was meant to be followed by another volume as its sequel, but the rest of Heidegger's works are in fact in the form of essays and lectures. *Being and Time* is extremely difficult, but so is more or less everything that Heidegger wrote. It and *What is Metaphysics?* (1929) present the essential early Heidegger, and reveal why he is thought of as an existentialist as well as a metaphysician in the German style. The other contemporary

[1] See my 'The Concept of Social Reality', in P. Secord (ed.): *Explaining Human Behavior* (Beverly Hills, London: Sage Publications, 1982).

existentialist was Karl Jaspers (1883–1969), who began as a psycho-pathologist; he laid emphasis upon the idea of an authentic self, in Kierkegaardian style, but the authentic self is set against a transcendent Being, and has to interpret the world for signs of this, even if Being in the end must be beyond a proper conceptual categorization. Like Heidegger, Jaspers was opposed to the increasing scientific and technological views of the world, and what he has to say is said in the name of culture; but he lacks Heidegger's systematic metaphysics, and it is this that has made Heidegger a more 'popular' figure than Jaspers. The 'popularity' is, however, ambiguous. For the Positivists, Heidegger was the epitome of metaphysical nonsense, and Carnap, followed by Ayer, quoted the remark from *What is Metaphysics?*, 'Das Nichts selbst nichtet' ('The nothing negates itself'), as an illustration of this. In other parts of the philosophical scene, on the other hand, Heidegger is treated almost with adulation.

Heidegger says that the fundamental metaphysical question is why there is anything rather than nothing. It is not entirely clear what sort of answer he expects to that question, but his philosophy is in effect an attempt to set out how we are to understand things as they are and as they are to us. So, his starting-point is what he takes to be a fundamental distinction between *Sein* (being) and *Dasein* (being there, being in the world). *Being and Time* is concerned, basically, with *Dasein*; the sequel was meant to deal with being in general, but for this we have to be content with the various essays of the later Heidegger. They are not encouraging. Heidegger has a propensity to go back to the Greeks and engages in extremely dubious etymologizing, with a plethora of neologisms. There may be more substance in the earlier treatment of *Dasein*.

By stressing the idea of being in the world as the fundamental notion, it may seem that Heidegger is trying to abandon the Cartesian framework which was still there in Husserl, and to emphasize the necessity of accepting the idea of a common world as a precondition of all else, in the fashion of the later Wittgenstein. He may be trying to do this, but if so he does not really succeed. For the being in the world that *Dasein* consists in is not the sort of thing that applies to ordinary objects. It is the form of being that applies to *us* as conscious and self-conscious beings. *Dasein*, Heidegger says, is always mine (it has the property of *Jemeinigkeit*). Hence the point of view of *Dasein* is inevitably a personal and individual one; it is, one might say, solipsistic, and if other people and things, together with language as a means of communicating with others, eventually appear on the scene, it is only in a way that is derivative from the solitary individual's initial point of view.

Hence much of what Heidegger has to say about *Dasein* has to do with the problems and standing of the individual in relation to the world. That is what makes his philosophy a brand of existentialism – its concern with the problems of human existence – and is what gives his philosophy the appeal that it has had for many people in troubled times. Heidegger says that what characterizes *Dasein* is *Sorge* (care); it involves a concern for whatever is its object. From this can be derived certain categories of objects – first, the category of things that are ready to hand or of use for *Dasein*, for example tools, and next but secondary to that, things in general. But the crucial thing about *Dasein*, as Heidegger sees it, is that it involves time. Some of what he has to say about that derives from Husserl's *Phenomenology of Internal Time-Consciousness* (1928). Some have found it surprising that for Heidegger time has nothing to do with what clocks measure or keep, and nothing to do with objective facts about temporal relations. It has more to do with what McTaggart called the 'A-series'. This is, however, inevitable, given what *Dasein* is; for *it* time must be the time of consciousness, and in particular the urge towards the future – what some English-speaking philosophers have called 'temporal becoming'. According to Heidegger, the future is a set of open possibilities. But we must equally recognize our finiteness, and the reality of death. Authentic being presupposes that recognition, and the *Angst* (anxiety or dread) that Heidegger, following Kierkegaard, takes to characterize human existence shows us that beyond our existence is simply nothing.

What Heidegger has to say about death as a real possibility, and as something the acceptance of which is characteristic of authentic existence, is an echo of what several other philosophers have said about death. Epicurus said that death is 'nothing to us'; Schopenhauer echoed those words while bringing them into relation with the Kantian view of time as the form of intuition; the Wittgenstein of the *Tractatus* said that death was 'not an event in life'. Epicurus certainly thought of his way of putting it as a form of consolation for the fact of death: there is nothing to be feared in it, because what happens afterwards has nothing to do with us. What perhaps distinguishes Heidegger's account of the same thing is the fact that he brings it to bear on the nature of the self, so that he describes it in one notorious formula (notorious for the difficulty of translating it as well as for what it means) as '*das Seiende, dem es in seinem Sein um dieses selbst geht*' ('a being such that in its being its being is in question'). It is a formula that Sartre has made much of; in a way it brings out the precarious existence of the human self as Heidegger sees it, the reality of *Angst*, and, *as he sees it*, the reality of the nothingness against which existence is to be set. Commentators tend to be divided into those who see all this as a profound insight into human existence and those who see it as the making of a mountain out of a mole-hill, to say the very least.

Sartre

Outside Germany, the philosopher who showed most clearly and most immediately the influence of Heidegger was Jean-Paul Sartre (1905–80). Sartre's philosophical education was in the tradition of Bergson, but he came under the influence of Husserl. His first three philosophical works, two on the imagination and one on the emotions, are works in a phenomenological style and tradition. In 1943 he published *L'Être et le néant* (*Being and Nothingness*), which is very much a translation into French terms of Heideggerian ideas. The idea that consciousness is a nothingness, and the fundamental distinction between the *pour soi* and the *en soi* are both ideas taken from Heidegger, although the categories of the 'for self' and 'in self' also have Hegelian echoes. The 'for self' (*pour soi*), which is what consciousness consists in, is in effect Heidegger's *Dasein*. Consciousness involves consciousness of itself. It is a nothing in the sense that it has no essence. Human beings, as conscious beings, can make themselves by their own free choice, and the existence, as well as the inevitability, of free choice is a cardinal element of Sartre's philosophy. Any attempt to avoid it involves what Sartre calls 'bad faith'.

The emphasis upon absolute freedom and its inevitability is to be found in Sartre's first 'philosophical' novel, *La Nausée*. In it the hero, Roquentin, is constrained to recognize the absolute contingency of things (of the *en soi*) by contrast with his own completely free choice. Things have what Sartre calls 'facticity', and it is concluded from this that their existence is in a certain sense absurd. The absurdity of the world is simply a function of its brute contingency, and that produces nausea, what Heidegger called 'boredom'. It is necessary that one recognizes one's own freedom in the face of this. One has, in a sense, Sartre maintains, to choose one's world.

One problem about this is that each individual has to do the same; choice is individualistic, even if – as he expresses it in his short excursus into ethics, *Existentialism is a Humanism* (1946) – one chooses for all men. This has the inevitable effect that one manifestation of the *pour soi* will come into conflict with another, so that, as it is put in the play *Huis clos*, 'Hell is other people'. Being for self comes into conflict with being for others. As a result Sartre's picture of personal relations is both gloomy and one of inevitable conflict. I must inevitably try to turn the other into what is for me an example of the *en soi*, a thing. The trouble is that the other must do just the same to me. (The thought goes back to Hegel's account of the master–slave relation, and Sartre's use of the example of someone looking through a key-hole, only to be aware of someone else watching him, is a pale echo of Hegel's use of the master–slave relation to show the relationship between self-consciousness and consciousness of others.) The consequences of this are set out in some of the novels.

Whether it is a fraud for him to attempt to confirm his philosophical position by means of the dramatic representations of the plays and novels is a large question. Certainly Sartre's picture of human beings and their relations is not everybody's.

Part 4 of *Being and Nothingness* contains a graphic account of the dangers of allowing the *pour soi* to be taken over by the *en soi*, the dangers of allowing one's freedom to be usurped by a supposedly stable world of things. The world of someone who does this is, he says, viscous or slimy; it is in fact unstable and false. Sartre writes of this in terms of what he calls existential psychoanalysis. He objects to ordinary psychoanalysis on two grounds: first, because the Freudian postulation of an unconscious is the postulation of something incoherent, an unconscious consciousness (a criticism which is valid only if Sartre's terms of reference – that the individual is a consciousness – are accepted); second, because it tries to put into psychological terms, including sexuality, what is really a metaphysical or ontological matter – the individual's necessary loneliness in a world of brute facts, without a god, in relation to which he has to exercise free choice.

Common sense may continually prompt the question whether it is really as bad as all that, and that has been the general reaction of English-speaking philosophers to Sartre. What has perhaps greater recognition is the brilliance of Sartre's account of 'bad faith'. This is perhaps a version of Heidegger's 'inauthenticity' but it is described in more recognizable terms, by reference to examples, undoubtedly drawn from Sartre's café-frequenting world, of the behaviour of such people as a waiter or a girl on the receiving end of a possible seduction. Bad faith is a form of self-deception, and Sartre's emphasis upon it has led to other attempts to deal with the problems inherent in the phenomenon. How can someone really deceive himself without being conscious that this is what is happening, in which case the attempt seems doomed to failure? Or is it? Sartre's rejection of the notion of an unconscious prevents his taking the easy way out by reference to a split self; yet self-deception seems to imply some form of dissociation from oneself. One may not be willing to accept Sartre's analysis of the phenomenon or of its possibility, but his account of it has acquired something of the status of a classic in the literature.

In his later thought, Sartre rather surprisingly turned towards Marxism. The *Critique of Dialectical Reason* (1960), of which only the first volume appeared, was prefaced by the *Question of Method* (1957). According to that latter work, Marxism is the dominant philosophy of the twentieth century, but existentialism can show how the concepts of Marxism have become relevant by 'interiorizing' them, so deriving them somehow from the nature of individual choice. The *Critique* itself in effect abandons this, preferring to consider 'praxis' in completely general and historical terms, not deriving it from individual human action. Moreover, group action is now thought to transcend the difficulties about personal relationships that the earlier writing portrayed so dramatically. The fact is that existential- ism is quite incompatible with Marxism, despite the similarity that may be thought to exist between the notion of bad faith and the notion of alienation as derived from Hegel. Political conviction and political influences seem to have added incoherence to the philosophy. But the same accusation might conceivably be made against a good deal of recent French philosophy.

Merleau-Ponty

It cannot be made, perhaps, against Maurice Merleau-Ponty (1908–61), who is arguably the best of the French philosophers of this century. Mer- leau-Ponty has a closer relation to Husserl than to Sartre, although the two French philosophers were at one time associated with each other. His first book, *La Structure du comportement* (*The Structure of Behaviour*, 1942; English translation, 1965), is an attack upon behaviourism in psychology; it takes very seriously what action is, and how meaning per- meates action through intention. It is in many ways a dry book, but might have been thought of fundamental importance had attention been paid to it at the time. It was twenty years before much the same comments upon psychological behaviourism were made in English-speaking circles. His second book, *La Phénoménologie de la perception (The Phenomen- ology of Perception*, 1945; English translation, 1962), has, despite the implications of its title, more of a claim to be a systematic presentation of his general philosophy; it stands in relation to Merleau-Ponty as *Being and Nothingness* does to Sartre, and it has in part some of the same interests. It too begins with criticism of psychology, on this occasion the empiricist psychology of the sensationalists; it speaks approvingly of Gestalt psychology, but there is more in it than that.

In effect Merleau-Ponty's treatment of perception is an attempt to provide for the concepts of the world, space, time, human agency and freedom what Husserl called their 'fulfilment' in perceptual terms. For Husserl the fulfilment of a concept was what gave it flesh, its realization in concrete terms. According to Merleau-Ponty we need to reject the idea that the world is given to us in sense-perception, as the sensationalists and sense-datum philosophers supposed; we need also to reject the idea that it is all a matter of our judgement, as rationalists and absolute ideal- ists supposed. To understand the concept of a world we need to go beyond the 'prejudice of the objective world' to the pre-objective consciousess, which appears, on investigation, to involve a 'lived-through world' in which the body plays a vital part. In this, experience is constituted by 'phenomenal fields' organized within a 'transcendental field', which is the point of view of the subject or ego.

There is a sense in which the order of thought in this is still self-others-world. (It may be remembered that in connection with Schutz's Husserl-inspired ideas, I referred to the analogous transition from 'I' to 'we' and thereby to everything else.) The importance of Merleau-Ponty is that he adds to this an emphasis on the role of the body in the process. It is tempting to see in this again a similarity to Wittgenstein's emphasis on 'forms of life', and it has been argued that in his later writing that similarity becomes even more evident. Yet the ambiguity of status that we saw to characterize Husserl's notion of the 'life-world' applies here also. For the body is still fundamentally a lived body, owned and lived through by a transcendental ego. It is tempting to call Merleau-Ponty's position solipsism with a body!

Part 1 of *The Phenomenology of Perception* goes into great detail concerning the role of the body and the body-image with considerable reference to empirical findings on such matters. There is a chapter on sexuality and the final chapter deals with bodily expression and, more importantly, speech. In connection with the last, Merleau-Ponty emphasizes the necessity of seeing words as bearers of meaning because of their role in intentional behaviour. Part 2 develops all this into a general theory of perception involving space, things and other people. The role of the body becomes paramount in all this, because it is the body and its movements which provide the 'fulfilment' of our concept of space and thereby of objects within it. It also enables Merleau-Ponty, by intention at least, to bridge the uncrossable gap that Sartre sees between one person and another, because they constitute distinct and opposed consciousnesses. The fact that people have bodies enables the world in which they live to be a common one, and also enables one person to have access to another, at all events through their bodily expressions. Indeed Merleau-Ponty argues that because one is embodied there is no privileged access to oneself, and other people are equally not closed to oneself. There are apparent echoes of Wittgenstein and Ryle here, but it must be remembered once again that the body one is talking about is the 'lived body'.

The last part of *The Phenomenology of Perception* elaborates in similar terms the nature of consciousness, rejecting a bare Cartesian ego, even in the form put forward by Sartre. Merleau-Ponty asserts a conception of human freedom as arising from the fact, as he sees it, that 'no causal relationship is conceivable between the subject and his body, his world or his society'. This view is reminiscent of Schopenhauer or Kant – an attempt to preserve freedom despite involvement in the world through the body. Perhaps the best-known chapter in this third part, however, is that on time. It is certainly derived from Husserl, and is notable for a firm rejection of any conception of objective time. Merleau-Ponty says indeed that 'the very notion of an event has no place in the objective world'; time arises 'from *my* relation to things'. At the end of the chapter he says that the suggestion that the earth may have 'originally issued from a primitive nebula' is in effect unintelligible, and that such a nebula is 'not behind us, at our remote beginnings, but in front of us in the cultural world'. The account is in fact verificationist, tying the meaning of statements about time to the conditions of their verification in perception. We share a common time, he says, only because we share a 'lived present', which, once again, the body makes possible.

All this involves the notions of the primacy of the present and the primacy of perception, which Merleau-Ponty went on to elaborate in later works. These are important notions which it is at least necessary to take account of. Many philosophers, however, especially those of an empiricist turn of mind, would think Merleau-Ponty's account of the essential subjectivity of time enough to reject the whole thing. That would be a pity, for there are important insights in what he has to say. It is, nevertheless, arguable that it is in the account of time that the inability of Merleau-Ponty's theory to explain the possibility of objectivity becomes clear. It is all the same a valiant attempt to deal with the issues from a basically phenomenological point of view, and if it fails it shows the fundamental weakness of that point of view.

Hermeneutics and other recent movements

Another movement which was influenced, at any rate in part, by Heidegger's conception of 'being in the world' is that which has been called 'Hermeneutics' – the study of understanding through interpretation. The idea that there is something special about 'understanding', as set against scientific knowledge, goes back to Wilhelm Dilthey (1833–1911), who maintained that there is an essential difference between the natural sciences and cultural sciences, such as history. The latter depend on an understanding (*Verstehen*) of their subject-matter in terms of the meanings and intentions of individual human beings. The idea has been taken up to some extent by philosophers of history, and by some philosophers concerned with action. Perhaps the main philosopher to adopt these ideas in such a way as to turn them into a general philosophy is Hans-Georg Gadamer (1900–), in his *Truth and Method* (1960). The philosophy is called 'hermeneutics' because importance is attached to the processes involved in understanding a text through interpretation. Gadamer stresses what the individual brings to this through his history. It is easy to see this as involving a relativistic approach to truth. Whatever the case in this respect in connection with Gadamer, it has certainly had this effect in the case of Michel Foucault (1926–84), who has traced the history of a number of conceptions, such as that of madness, in such a way as to stress the temporal and cultural relativity of those conceptions. Foucault's *The Archaeology of Knowledge* (1969) is an attempt to give self-conscious expression to a relativistic conception of knowledge, in such a way as to admit his own relativity of approach. Indeed he sees any other approach to knowledge as simply an attempt to exercise power. Another approach to hermeneutics, which has even more to do with the interpretation of texts, is to be found in the writings of Jacques Derrida (1930–). Derrida's theory, known as 'deconstructionism', turns on the alleged necessity of paying attention to the 'differences' between words and the expectations which they set up, without consideration of their designations. The view has had more appeal to students of language and literature than to philosophers, at any rate to English-speaking philosophers, who have generally found Derrida unintelligible.

Psychoanalysis has had much influence on recent French philosophical thinking, beginning with Gaston Bachelard (1884–1962). The other dominant influence is Marxism. These movements have not had the same effects on English-language philosophy. It has to be said that there has not been much cultural contact between France and Britain in this respect, although there have been some putative bridge-builders, for instance Paul Ricoeur (1913–), who belongs to, if anything, the hermeneutic movement. Much the same is true of Germany and Britain, although there are again one or two bridge-builders. A certain amount of interest in hermeneutics has been taken by the Finnish philosopher Georg Von Wright (1916–), who was once professor at Cambridge and who might otherwise be taken as very much the analytic philosopher. In the eyes of many, however, the leading philosopher in Europe is Jürgen Habermas of the Frankfurt school, to whom I referred earlier. In Britain he has had more influence on sociologists than on philosophers, largely perhaps because of his anti-positivist approach to social theory. His background is mainly Hegelian–Marxist, but he has shown a remarkable talent for bringing this into relation with other, seemingly different philosophical approaches – hermeneutics, philosophy of science, philosophy of language and theory of communicative competence, to mention only some. Nevertheless, the Husserlian idea that men somehow construct their world remains, and to many that will seem a large defect.

It would be wrong for me to close my survey of recent continental philosophy without at least mentioning a philosopher who lies outside nearly everything that I have discussed, Simone Weil (1909–43). During the inter-war years she developed an attitude of almost total commitment, first to the left in the Spanish Civil War, and later during the Second World War to the Resistance. She died of starvation, refusing to eat while others in the war suffered. Her writings are mainly social and religious, showing a profound knowledge of the history of culture. The general atmosphere of commitment that comes over from her writings has seemed attractive to some, but sentimental to others. The main thing about her views, however, is the picture that she presents of human beings and their freedom in an over-socialized and industrialized world. Moreover, both her life and her thought provide considerable material for ethics. She remains an isolated and somewhat puzzling figure.

[19]
The Future

Since I have been highly selective about the present, and there are several notable philosophers at the present time whom I have left out of my discussion, it may seem extremely presumptuous to try to say anything about the future. It must be evident from my account of the history of western philosophy, in any case, that a very great deal depends on individuals who appear from time to time on the philosophical stage – Plato, Descartes, Kant, Wittgenstein, for example. One can never tell when such a person is likely to appear. It has to be admitted that philosophy is a very considerable prey to fashion, and that what is thought obviously right at one period may seem quite wrong even a short time afterwards. Today many philosophers would find it difficult or even impossible to think themselves into the minds of, say, Plotinus or Hegel. But the same sorts of change, even if not quite so dramatic, can take place within the course of a single lifetime. For all these reasons it is impossible to hazard a significant guess as to how philosophy will be even in fifty years' time. Of one thing we can be quite sure, however – there *will* be philosophy.

It has sometimes been suggested that the history of philosophy is the history of human folly. Have not so many thinkers of the past been wrong, however much they thought themselves right at the time? Can one have any confidence in the future? The urge to philosophize remains, however, just as strong as Aristotle said it was. Paradoxical as it may seem, a philosopher can be a great philosopher and still be wrong. The value of his thought lies not merely in its historical influence and relevance, but in the fact that it is a significant attempt to grapple with some of the most difficult problems that exist, to whatever degree of success. In any case, it would be quite wrong to suggest that there are no established philosophical truths. One should not exaggerate the extent to which past philosophers have been wrong. There are many ways in which, as ought to be evident, they have been right.

In that light, what of the future? It is impossible to be sure. One can only present trends. On the whole, American philosophers have become dominant among English-speaking philosophers. American philosophy tends to be technical, formal, science-based and materialistic. There are increasing tendencies to link philosophy with certain branches of science, particularly psychology and cognitive science. The influence of Wittgenstein may be on the wane – to the regret of many philosophers of an earlier persuasion. In Europe the influences of Marx and Husserl are still the main ones, and the different philosophical traditions do not do much to meet, despite some notable exceptions. Elsewhere? The life-blood of philosophy is argument and counter-argument. Plato and Aristotle thought of this occurring in what they called dialectic – discussion. Today, it might be argued that is just the same, except that it operates upon a much wider scale, both historically and geographically. Argument and counter-argument in books and journals is the modern version of dialectic. As a consequence, philosophical changes and developments may be slower to come about, and positions may remain entrenched for longer, at any rate in their fundamentals.

I make that latter qualification because within any given movement philosophers are likely to be conscious of their difference from their neighbours, even if the outsider thinks them both alike. The very number of philosophers who are alive today, the scale of their organization and that of the university system where they are mainly to be found, makes the processes of philosophical change cumbersome. One can be sure only that, given a long enough historical perspective, a seminal mind will appear sooner or later, and such changes will take place. The state of philosophy today *may*, as I have suggested, make that a slower business than it has been in the past; but it is just as possible that it will make it quicker.

It is impossible to judge philosophy by the social advantages it produces, although it has brought advantages of that kind, and it has affected thinking in other fields, sometimes over a relatively long time-scale. That, however, is not the essence of philosophy, if it has one. Aristotle said that philosophy begins in wonder, but it also has to do with the profound problems involved in understanding the world and our place in it. What may be clear to one generation of this may not be clear to another. Attempts to arrive at and formulate that understanding are likely, therefore, to go on. How it will go on is impossible to say. Perhaps we are today in a period of scholasticism; that has certainly been suggested as the case. History will show whether it is so. To repeat, sooner or later the philosophical revolutionary will appear – that is all that one can say.

Suggestions for Further Reading

There are not many comprehensive histories of philosophy. Worthy of mention are:

F. C. Copleston: *A History of Philosophy*, Vols. 1–9 (London: Burns, Oates and Washbourne, 1946–75)
(A monumental work, splendid for facts, less good for philosophical comment.)

B. Russell: *A History of Western Philosophy* (London: Allen and Unwin, 2nd edn 1961)
(Generally thought interesting and amusing, but sometimes idiosyncratic.)

D. J. O'Connor (ed.): *A Critical History of Western Philosophy* (London, Glencoe, Illinois: Collier-Macmillan, 1964; Paperback, Basingstoke: Macmillan, 1985)
(Chapters written by different scholars; contains an extensive bibliography.)

Other works on particular periods:

W. K. C. Guthrie: *A History of Greek Philosophy*, Vols. 1–6 (Cambridge University Press, 1962–81)

E. Gilson: *A History of Christian Philosophy in the Middle Ages* (London: Sheed and Ward, 1953)

A. H. Armstrong (ed.): *The Cambridge History of Later Greek and Early Medieval Philosophy* (Cambridge University Press, 1967)

N. Kretzmann, A. Kenny and J. Pinborg (eds.): *The Cambridge History of Later Medieval Philosophy* (Cambridge University Press, 1982)

J. Passmore: *A Hundred Years of Philosophy* (London: Duckworth, 1957; Penguin, 1968)
(A mine of information about philosophers since the mid nineteenth century, but nothing on ethics or political philosophy.)

J. Passmore: *Recent Philosophers* (London: Duckworth, 1985)
(A sequel to the above.)

A. J. Ayer: *Philosophy in the Twentieth Century* (London: Weidenfeld and Nicolson, 1982)

Also in general:

P. Edwards (ed.): *The Encyclopaedia of Philosophy*, Vols. 1–8 (New York, London: Collier-Macmillan, 1967)
(An invaluable source of information about individual philosophers and movements; includes histories of certain branches of philosophy, e.g. epistemology, logic.)

There is no substitute for reading the works of the philosophers who appear in this history. There are available, however, many books on individual philosophers. Some have been published by Penguin, although only those starred are currently in print: Aquinas (Copleston)*, Hobbes (Peters), Descartes (Williams)*, Spinoza (Hampshire), Leibniz (Saw), Locke (O'Connor), Berkeley (Warnock), Hume (Basson), Kant (Körner)*, Schopenhauer (Gardiner), Mill (Britton), Bradley (Wollheim), Wittgenstein (Kenny)*.

There is also the Arguments of the Philosophers series, published by Routledge and Kegan Paul, which now includes:
The Presocratics (Barnes), Socrates (Santas), Plato (Gosling), Descartes (Wilson), Spinoza (Delahunty), Berkeley (Pitcher), Hume (Stroud), Butler (Penelhum), Kant (Walker), Hegel (Inwood), Schopenhauer (Hamlyn), Nietzsche (Schacht), Marx (Wood), Kierkegaard (Hannay), Bentham (Harrison), Peirce (Hookway), Santayana (Sprigge), Frege (Sluga), Russell (Sainsbury), Wittgenstein (Fogelin), Popper (O'Hear), Meinong (Grossman), Sartre (Caws), Ayer (Foster).

Another series is the Philosophers in Context series published by Harvester Press, which so far includes:
Plato (Rowe), Descartes (Grene), Leibniz (Brown), Locke (Woolhouse), Russell (Kilmister).

Other books of this kind worthy of note are:
G. Kirk, J. Raven and M. Schofield: *The Presocratic Philosophers*, (Cambridge University Press, 2nd edn, 1983)
W. D. Ross: *Aristotle* (London: Methuen, 4th edn, 1945)
M. Schofield, M. Burnyeat and J. Barnes (eds.): *Doubt and Dogmatism* (Oxford: Clarendon Press, 1980)
M. W. Tweedale: *Abailard on Universals* (Amsterdam, New York, London: North Holland Publishing Company, 1976)
J. W. N. Watkins: *Hobbes' System of Ideas* (London: Hutchinson, 1965)
J. Bennett: *Spinoza* (Cambridge University Press, 1985)
N. Rescher: *Leibniz* (Oxford: Blackwell, 1979)
B. Russell: *The Philosophy of Leibniz* (London: Allen and Unwin, 1900)
J. Bennett: *Locke, Berkeley and Hume: Central Themes* (Oxford: Clarendon Press, 1971)
J. L. Mackie: *Problems from Locke* (Oxford: Clarendon Press, 1976)
I. Tipton: *Berkeley* (London: Methuen, 1974)
D. G. C. MacNabb: *David Hume* (London: Hutchinson, 1951)
P. F. Strawson: *The Bounds of Sense* (London: Methuen, 1968)
J. Bennett: *Kant's Analytic* (Cambridge University Press, 1966)
J. Bennett: *Kant's Dialectic* (Cambridge University Press, 1974)
C. Taylor: *Hegel* (Cambridge University Press, 1975)
A. C. Danto: *Nietzsche as Philosopher* (New York: Columbia University Press, 1965)

G. Cohen: *Marx's Theory of History* (Princeton University Press, 1978)

A. R. Manser and G. Stock (eds.): *The Philosophy of F. H. Bradley* (Oxford: Clarendon Press, 1984)

A. J. Ayer: *The Origins of Pragmatism* (London: Macmillan, 1968)

M. Dummett: *Frege* (Oxford: Clarendon Press, 1973)

D. Pears: *Bertrand Russell and the British Tradition in Philosophy* (London: Collins, Fontana, 1967)

A. J. Ayer: *Russell and Moore* (London: Macmillan, 1971)

A. J. Ayer: *Logical Positivism* (Glencoe, Illinois: Free Press, 1959)

A. R. Manser: *Sartre* (London: Athlone Press, 1966)

Index